Tolkien

Tolkien

RAYMOND
EDWARDS

ROBERT HALE · LONDON

© Raymond Edwards 2014
First published in Great Britain 2014

ISBN 978-0-7198-0986-6

Robert Hale Limited
Clerkenwell House
Clerkenwell Green
London EC1R 0HT

www.halebooks.com

The right of Raymond Edwards to be identified as
author of this work has been asserted by him
in accordance with the Copyright, Designs and
Patents Act 1988

A catalogue record for this book is available from the British Library

2 4 6 8 10 9 7 5 3 1

Typeset in Minion Pro
Printed in Great Britain by Berforts Information Press Ltd

To Allison
with love

Contents

Acknowledgements   8

Abbreviations   11

Introduction   13

Part I – The Making of a Philologist

Chapter 1 – Early Years   19

Chapter 2 – University and Edith   50

Chapter 3 – War   76

Chapter 4 – The Young Scholar   104

Part II – Philology in Practice

Chapter 5 – Oxford and Storytelling   133

Chapter 6 – Delays and Frustrations   153

Chapter 7 – A Wilderness of Dragons: *Beowulf* and *The Hobbit*   168

Part III – Achievement

Chapter 8 – In the Background, War   183

Chapter 9 – Peace, Not Rest   211

Chapter 10 – Hyde and Jekyll   221

Chapter 11 – Finished, at Last   227

Chapter 12 – Philology at Bay   238

Chapter 13 – 'My heart, to be shot at'   246

Part IV – Last Years

Chapter 14 – Silmarillion and Scholarship?   259
Chapter 15 – Unfinished Tales   267

Part V – Niggle's Parish

Chapter 16 – Posthumous Publications   281
Chapter 17 – A Cinematic Afterlife   286

Epilogue   289

Appendix – Tolkien the Catholic   291

References   300

Further Reading and Bibliography   321

Index   327

Acknowledgements

In one sense, no one writes a book like this alone; in another, of course, it is an intensely solitary activity, and arguably a selfish one. I am grateful to Stratford Caldecott and to Alexander Stilwell for, in different ways, prompting me to write it, and for their advice and practical help; and to Glynn MacNiven-Johnston for her care and attention to my prose style, and for tireless encouragement. Lucy Lethbridge and Brendan Walsh have indulged my preoccupation with Tolkien and his circle for years; they have my hearty thanks. My parents encouraged and enabled my first interest in Tolkien, after a sensible schoolmaster made me and my ten-year-old classmates read *The Hobbit*. They, and he, have my gratitude.

An early version of some parts of this book appeared in a short introduction to Tolkien published by the Catholic Truth Society; I am grateful for their permission to re-use this material.

I also thank HarperCollins, and the copyright holders listed below, for allowing me to reproduce passages from Tolkien's work.

Letters of J.R.R. Tolkien © The J.R.R. Tolkien Copyright Trust 1981

Beowulf: The Monsters and the Critics © The J.R.R. Tolkien Copyright Trust 1983

Mythopoeia © The J.R.R. Tolkien Copyright Trust 1988

Smith of Wootton Major © The Tolkien Trust 1967

The Adventures of Tom Bombadil © The J.R.R. Tolkien Estate Limited 1961

The Lord of the Rings © Fourth Age Limited 1954, 1955, 1966

The Book of the Lost Tales, Part One © The J.R.R. Tolkien Estate Limited and C.R. Tolkien 1983

The Book of the Lost Tales, Part Two © The J.R.R. Tolkien Estate Limited and C.R. Tolkien 1984

Richard Williamson and Christopher Reuel Tolkien as Executors of the Estate of J.R.R. Tolkien.

Most of all my wife Allison has been unfailingly supportive of my curious obsessions, endless piles of books, and patient of my persistent distraction: this is her book as much as mine.

Abbreviations

ATB	J.R.R. Tolkien, *The Adventures of Tom Bombadil and other verses from The Red Book*. London, George Allen & Unwin, 1962
Carpenter, *Biography*	Humphrey Carpenter, *J.R.R. Tolkien: A Biography*. London, George Allen & Unwin, 1977
Carpenter, *Inklings*	Humphrey Carpenter, *The Inklings*. London, George Allen & Unwin, 1978
Duriez and Porter, *Handbook*	Colin Duriez and David Porter, *The Inklings Handbook*. London, Azure, 2001
EETS	Early English Text Society
Garth	John Garth, *Tolkien and the Great War*. London, HarperCollins, 2003
GCCS	Government Code and Cipher School
H&S	Christina Scull and Wayne G. Hammond, *The J.R.R. Tolkien Companion and Guide*, vol. 1: *Chronology* [H&S 1]; vol. 2, *Reader's Guide* [H&S 2]. London, HarperCollins, 2006
HME	J.R.R. Tolkien and Christopher Tolkien, *The History of Middle Earth*, 12 vols. London, George Allen & Unwin/HarperCollins, 1983–96. References to individual volumes are in the form *HME* 1.123, referring to volume 1, page 123
Interpreters	*Interpreters of Early Medieval Britain*, ed. Michael Lapidge. Oxford, OUP for the British Academy, 2002
Letters	*The Letters of J.R.R. Tolkien*, ed. Humphrey Carpenter and Christopher Tolkien. London, George Allen & Unwin, 1981; frequently reprinted
LOTR	J.R.R. Tolkien, *The Lord of the Rings*

M&C	J.R.R. Tolkien, *The Monsters and the Critics and Other Essays*. London, George Allen & Unwin, 1983; frequently reprinted
OED	*Oxford English Dictionary*
OFS	J.R.R. Tolkien, *Tolkien On Fairy-Stories*, ed. Verlyn Flieger and Douglas A. Anderson. London, HarperCollins, 2008
OHEL	*Oxford History of English Literature*
OTC	Officer Training Corps
OUP	Oxford University Press
Shippey, *Author*	Tom Shippey, *J.R.R. Tolkien: Author of the Century*. London, HarperCollins, 2000
Shippey, *Road*	Tom Shippey, *The Road to Middle-Earth* (3rd edition). London, HarperCollins, 2005
SWM	J.R.R. Tolkien, *Smith of Wootton Major*. London, George Allen & Unwin, 1967
TEnc	*J.R.R. Tolkien Encyclopedia: Scholarship and Critical Assessment*, ed. Michael D.C. Drout. New York and London, Routledge, 2007
TL	J.R.R. Tolkien, *Tree and Leaf*. London, George Allen & Unwin, 1964; frequently reprinted
TLeg	*Tolkien's Legendarium: Essays on The History of Middle-earth*, ed. Verlyn Flieger and Carl F. Hostetter. Westport, CT, Greenwood Press, 2000
TLS	*Times Literary Supplement*
TMed	*Tolkien the Medievalist*, ed. Jane Chance. New York and London, Routledge, 2003
UCL	University College, London
UT	*Unfinished Tales*. London, George Allen & Unwin, 1980

Introduction

It is late in the year; under the vast domed Great Hall of the new university of Birmingham, rows of temporary beds are set up, filled with sick men, most newly back from France. One of them is writing in a small school exercise book.

The year is 1916, and he has been some months with his battalion on the Somme. Already many of his school and university friends have been killed. Compared with them, he is lucky; he has been struck down by a debilitating persistent fever, spread through the trenches by the ubiquitous lice. He is getting better, now, although still weak and exhausted and unfit to return to his unit. Soon, he will be discharged, and able to go to a Staffordshire village to stay with the wife he married only eight months ago, two months before he was sent to France. Meanwhile, he is writing: stories of an age of myth, of elves and dragons and love and despair and hope lost and renewed. His name is Ronald Tolkien.

The stories he wrote at this time were not published for another seventy years; but the themes and characters he described in them gradually found shape and led directly to his famous books, *The Hobbit* and *The Lord of the Rings*. Here, whilst first recovering in hospital, then on a series of home service postings, began his life's work: a corpus of imaginative writing whose overmastering theme, he declared late in life, was Death.

Tolkien is now best known as an author – his published writings run to twenty or so thick volumes – but he was many other things beside: husband, father to four children, professor of ancient language at Oxford, devout Catholic. How did he combine all of these things? How did his writing connect with the rest of his life, and his work? What sort of man was he, who arguably changed forever the sort of books that are written, and read? It is probably impossible to answer all of these questions; but I hope to make some suggestions.

I assume that anyone reading this book has read, or at least seen the film versions of, *The Lord of the Rings* and *The Hobbit*. Accordingly I presume some knowledge of what happens in the books, and have not given extensive discussions of them. There are plenty of good books that already do this; some are listed in the section on 'Further reading'.

My fundamental aim in writing this book is to look at Tolkien's life in the round: to try to understand how his academic interests (which are also to some extent my own) informed his imaginative work, and to give as best I can a clear and full account of the various stages in his life and writing. It is not that the one defines or determines the other; but it may give us a new respect for the man who wrote *The Lord of the Rings* to learn something of the circumstances under which he wrote it, and the real and protracted difficulties against which he constantly fought. He was a remarkable man, and what interested and moved him is likely to be worth looking at, independent of its influence on his fiction; so I make no apology for discussing intellectual interests that some, who have never tried to share them, may suppose are forbiddingly dry or technical. They are not. All that is needed is an open mind, and a readiness to work or think a little harder than usual. It is worth it. If at times, as I suspect, I have fallen into what Tolkien's sometime tutor, Kenneth Sisam, condemned as 'an inclination to follow interest beyond the limits of relevance', I can offer only apology and the hope that, for some readers at least, interest cancels irrelevance.

There are no scandals here, no secrets (at least none that I have found), no obvious interventions in public life; but, amidst an outwardly ordinary life, or as ordinary a life as an Oxford don might have, an imaginative achievement which can hardly be paralleled, and has (I would say) made an incalculable alteration in the nature and scope of literary endeavour. An ordinary life, then: nothing, in fact, like the archetypal 'writer's life' as popularly conceived, all garrets, or villas in the sun. Perhaps there are some men (they would need to be men, I think) who live like this and still manage to write books (Somerset Maugham at one end of the spectrum, or Joseph Roth at another, might be instances), but they cannot be usual. The normal companions of literary achievement would appear to be the bourgeois virtues, and their concomitant worries – houses, children, money, sexual fidelity, 'being settled'. Literary composition usually needs routine, and some measure of peace and quiet; most who live the 'Bohemian' life never manage to publish a word. But hope and exaltation and misery and despair are found as richly and as varied in middle-class life as on the Left Bank (or wherever), although not, maybe, so highly coloured.

In one sense, Tolkien is one of the purest cases of literary vocation that one can imagine: his was a life where, despite a busy job, the responsibility of four children to raise and a difficult wife, plus indifferent health, chronic despondency, and the myriad interruptions of mid-twentieth-century life, he persevered, wrote, and continued to write despite strong (and reasonable) fears that none of it would ever be published, or publishable. Of itself, certainly, persistence is not an index of literary virtue; no one who has ever seen, much less read, the typical contents of a publisher's pile of unsolicited manuscripts could ever be under that illusion. But it is, without doubt, a necessary companion to literary achievement. Another is the courage to risk, and to show what has been written with (it may be) difficulty and stolen effort, knowing it may be rejected, even with derision; and to endure such rejection, and not give up. All of these are moral qualities as much as they are literary; and Tolkien had them.

Incidentally, it might be argued that the very things – marriage, children, domesticity – that according to some pundits (Cyril Connolly, for example) are notorious barriers to literary creativity, were in Tolkien's case the very key that unlocked his imaginative writing to the public.

Tolkien's gift was to recover imaginatively the great literary monuments of the unrecorded heroic past, and create in modern English a world-story that allowed him to share his delight in this recovered legendry: to write tales that when read convey the precise joy and yearning that he, and some few like him, could find in bare word-forms and tables of sound-changes, but for most would remain otherwise opaque, closed, a cipher. He gives us access to a world we might otherwise never know existed, although it is there, in unread volumes by Grimm and Chambers and Ker and dozens of others even less known: the key, in fact, to faërie, at least for a while.

A friend who read a draft of Chapter 2 remarked, 'You make his studies more interesting than his life', and it may well be that some parts of the story as I have told it are duller than they might be: but in one strong sense, his studies were his life: the great adventure of Tolkien's life was in fact an intellectual one, and the humdrum details of school, university, house and home are in some ways incidental, almost irrelevant – backcloth rather than landscape. But these humdrum surroundings are themselves the field of moral action and endeavour as much as, and in one sense decidedly more than, the intellectual canvas is in its fashion; and although we do not and probably cannot know as much about how Tolkien negotiated the empirical problems of the moral life of a husband and father as we do about how he tackled the narrative problems of *The Lord of the Rings*, we may reasonably infer that, in some way, his approach to the two things was not unconnected. But much further than this we cannot go. Without access to his unpublished diaries and letters, much of his inner life must remain unknown to us. We can guess, but only if we admit we are guessing. Life, too, has a way of concealing facts and events that cannot be predicted or inferred from their context; it is entirely likely that surprises of one sort or another would result if we could know all that is there to be known; but not, I suggest, of a quality to falsify the picture we can draw from what we do know. And to this now we should turn.

Part I – The Making of a Philologist

'I'm a philologist,' said Lowdham, 'which means a
misunderstood man.'[1]

Chapter 1 – Early Years

I – Family

It may surprise some to learn that Tolkien, in many ways a quintessentially English writer, was born in South Africa.

Despite his surname, the German in his background was minimal; the family told stories of how their ancestors were originally Saxon nobility, given the soubriquet *tollkühn* or 'foolhardy' after heroism at the 1529 siege of Vienna, and driven to England by one invasion or other. Many middle-class families preserve similar aristocratic origin stories, which may contain smaller or larger elements of truth. Tolkien himself may have believed it, or allowed himself to entertain it on occasion; he repeated it to C.S. Lewis in 1939. Certainly there are Tolkiehns and Tolkiens in Lower Saxony and Hamburg today. It has however been suggested the surname comes, instead, from the village of Tolkynen (now Tołkiny) near Rastenburg in what is now Poland; and that derives not from *tollkühn* but from the extinct Old Prussian language, a (West) Baltic tongue akin to (East Baltic) Latvian and Lithuanian, in which *tolkien* means 'broker' or 'translator'.[2] In later life, Tolkien himself was aware of the suggestion, and scorned it: Slavonic *tolk*, 'interpreter, spokesman', and its cognates were found in Low German dialects and in Dutch, but not in English, he declared; but this is rather to dodge the question, since the claim is presumably that his German surname came from this root, not that it had any sense as an English word.[3]

Whatever the now undiscoverable truth, the Tolkiens' eponymous ancestor had come to England in the mid-eighteenth century, probably from Saxony, but seems to have retained no significant ties to his homeland, or none at least that were passed to his children. They soon became 'intensely English', and whilst keeping their foreign surname, the Tolkiens were solid Birmingham middle class; his mother's family, the Suffields, were originally Worcestershire farming stock. The Tolkiens seem to have dropped their (presumed) ancestral Lutheranism, and are first recorded as Baptists, although (as was not unusual) some of them, particularly those with social position or aspirations, will have worshipped as, and considered themselves, Anglicans. The Suffields, on the other hand, seem to have been Methodist, although John Suffield, Tolkien's maternal grandfather, had at some point become a Unitarian. This type of fluid religious identity, varying between nonconformity and the Established Church, was not unusual in eighteenth- and nineteenth-century England, where the Church of England still considered itself the exclusive religious body for the whole nation. In any case, although the precise details are now beyond recovery, it is clear that Tolkien came of sound Protestant background on both sides.

The Tolkiens had been involved in piano making and dealing in music for generations (legend claimed the original Tolkien immigrant had been, amongst other things, an accomplished harpsichordist). Tolkien's grandfather, John Tolkien, had been a piano maker; his business had failed, and he turned to selling music. He had four children; his wife died, and he then remarried. Arthur, Tolkien's father, was the eldest child of this second marriage. Arthur Tolkien had been working for Lloyds Bank in Birmingham for some years when, in 1888, aged thirty-one, he met Mabel Suffield and they became engaged. She was only eighteen, however, and her father (once a prosperous draper, now, after his business had failed, a commercial traveller for Jeyes Fluid) forbade her to marry for two years.

It has been argued that, in the late nineteenth century, Jeyes Fluid was a new and exciting product (it was given a Royal Warrant in 1896), and this may not have been the down-at-heel recourse we might suppose; although to most ears 'commercial traveller' is not a prestigious calling. At any rate, John Suffield's fortunes seem to have recovered; by 1892, he also owned an iron foundry in Birmingham. He was similarly protective of his youngest daughter, (Emily) Jane. He had at least seven children, five of whom were daughters. Unitarian preacher, deft calligrapher, accomplished doggerel versifier, intrepid traveller and fearsomely bearded patriarch, he may easily stand as the model for the Old Took of The Hobbit, father of 'three remarkable daughters'.

The following year, 1889, Arthur Tolkien sailed for South Africa, where he had got a job with the Bank of Africa in Cape Colony; the year after, he was made manager of their branch in Bloemfontein, capital of the Orange Free State. This gave significantly more responsibility, and better pay, than he could have hoped for at home. This made marriage possible; in March 1891, Mabel, who was now twenty-one, took ship for South Africa. On 16 April, she and Arthur were married in the Anglican cathedral in Cape Town. They lived in Bloemfontein, in a house attached to the bank where Arthur was manager.

The Orange Free State was not a British colony but an independent republic, founded and run by the Boers, settlers of originally Dutch extraction who were fiercely attached to their independence. Together with the neighbouring Transvaal, the Boers of the Orange Free State had defeated a British attempt at annexation a decade before (the First Boer War). Greatly expanded mining operations, however, had since brought many tens of thousands of mainly English-speaking immigrants, like the Tolkiens, into the two Boer republics; these immigrants, known in Afrikaans (the local Dutch-derived dialect) as *uitlanders* ('foreigners'), were allowed no part in the political process or the governance of the country. The Afrikaner population was convinced, not unreasonably, that once in a majority, the *uitlanders* would, if granted civil rights, vote for incorporation alongside the British Cape Colony (which, indeed, had itself begun as a Dutch outpost before the English took over) in a confederation of British South African colonies. The existing Boer states were hidebound, oligarchical and stubbornly opposed to any further British encroachment, and in 1881 had fought a sharp and successful little war to resist it. The authorities in the neighbouring British territories (Cape Colony, Natal, Bechuanaland, the newly established Rhodesia) were understandably concerned at this situation, and made repeated and fruitless efforts to persuade the Boer republics to extend their franchise; there was also much concern at the often brutal and contemptuous attitude of the Boers towards the black population, which (it was claimed) lived in conditions little different from slavery. Arthur Tolkien's wife Mabel was certainly shocked by the treatment of black servants, and was herself at pains to behave in a different and more humane manner. It is likely Arthur would have shared these sentiments. In later life, his son had a profound horror of apartheid and other forms of racial discrimination: this certainly derived from his mother's early example.[4] There was a growing and vocal lobby amongst English speakers across southern Africa for more energetic, which meant military, action. For the moment, however, there was uneasy peace. Matters in the Orange Free State were less tense than in the neighbouring Transvaal, however.

21

Still, although Bloemfontein was the capital of a Boer republic, Arthur Tolkien's business would have been overwhelmingly amongst his fellow *uitlanders*; his bank, the Bank of Africa, was an Anglophone import from Cape Colony operating under special permission from the government, whilst their main competitor, the National Bank, was wholly Afrikaner. The Anglophone population of the Boer republics was both substantial and growing, and there would have been no sense of isolation; rather, the expatriate life, with its usual appurtenances of dinner parties, drinks parties, cricket and (for those so inclined) game shooting, was much as it was in dozens of other places across the Empire.

There, in Bloemfontein, on 3 January 1892, their first child was born, a couple of weeks early. He was christened John Ronald Reuel in the Anglican cathedral in Bloemfontein.

John and Reuel were Tolkien family names;[5] Ronald, Tolkien later declared, because his mother had been convinced she was carrying a girl and had settled on Rosalind as a name, for which Ronald was the first male analogue she could come up with. Compare the character Alboin Errol in Tolkien's unfinished novel *The Lost Road*, whose father tells him 'mother had meant to call you Rosamund, only you turned up a boy';[6] in the Lombardic history of Paul the Deacon, Rosamund is wife to the Lombardic king Alboin. Their subsequent history is a grim one. Alboin Errol is one of several characters in Tolkien's unpublished fiction who stands, or begins at least, as a close historical analogue to its author.

His family called him Ronald; two years later, his brother Hilary was born. Arthur Tolkien enjoyed the African climate; his wife did not, and was moreover concerned that Ronald was suffering from the persistent heat. In April 1895, accordingly, after the end of the summer season (which runs from November until April) she took both boys home to England for an extended leave.

In later life, Tolkien cherished his few memories of South Africa; the first Christmas he remembered, he said, was 'a blazing hot day', the Christmas tree a 'drooping eucalyptus'.[7] Arthur stayed in South Africa; he could not afford to leave his job for any amount of time, but hoped to come and join them before long. That November, he fell ill with rheumatic fever, and could not face the rigours of a voyage and the English winter. Mabel and the boys spent Christmas with her family. In January, after a short recovery, Arthur fell ill again; Mabel decided she must return to South Africa to look after him. Before she could make arrangements, however, Arthur suddenly deteriorated. On 14 February 1896,

Mabel received a telegram saying he had had a haemorrhage and she should expect the worst; the next day, he died. Arthur Tolkien was only thirty-nine. Mabel Tolkien was twenty-six; her sons, four and two.

Ronald had, or spoke of, few memories of his father; he remembered him painting his name on a cabin trunk which accompanied his wife and children on their last voyage to England, and which Ronald kept all his life. For the rest, there are a couple of fugitive hints in his writings, nothing more.

Many years later, he began a poem called *The Fall of Arthur*, his only essay in 'the Matter of Britain'; it is unfinished and has only recently been published. Unfortunately the action of the poem does not extend as far as Arthur's death, so Freudians will need to be more than usually creative to make anything of this. Unfinished works are (as we shall see) not uncommon in Tolkien's life as a writer. Later still, 'John Arthurson' is one of several Tolkien-analogues in his unfinished novel *The Notion Club Papers*.

Had Mabel not returned to England, she and her boys would have likely been caught up in the accelerating political crisis that finally, in 1899, led to the Boer republics declaring war on Britain. As it was, she found herself a young widow, in Birmingham, with a minimal income from her late husband's estate and two small boys to raise.

They lodged in a semi-detached cottage in the small village of Sarehole, then a mile or so outside Birmingham. It is now a suburb of the city, but in 1896 was a real country village with a watermill, a river and strong thickets of trees.

Mabel had always been an active churchgoer; she became involved, now, in a 'high' Anglo-Catholic parish. This led her to Catholicism; in 1900, along with her sister, she became a Catholic, and was summarily disinherited by her family.

Her sister had also just returned from South Africa with two small boys; her husband, like Arthur Tolkien, stayed behind. Unlike Arthur, he survived to make the journey to England, and on his arrival forbade his wife to enter a Catholic church again. She instead took up with spiritualism.

II – Orphaned and educated

Mabel was an intelligent and highly literate woman; rather than send her boys to school, she taught them herself (according to her granddaughter

Priscilla, Mabel Tolkien had been a governess before her marriage). This also helped her financially; she had only a small income from some shares left by Arthur. As well as conventional subjects, she taught them botany, the elements of drawing (both of which were interests that stayed with Ronald throughout his life), and gave them a grounding in languages: French, German and Latin. From the first, it was clear that Ronald had a strong talent in this area.

He and two of his Incledon cousins, like many children, made up a code language, christened 'animalic', in which names of animals stood in for common nouns and verbs; later, when they had their first taste of consciously foreign languages (French and Latin), they (or at least Tolkien and the younger of the two cousins) substituted a grammatically more complex jargon called Nevbosh, the 'new nonsense'.[8] Tolkien himself did not think this making of invented languages an unusual activity; it was his mature opinion that many or most children indulged in something similar, but were educated or corrected out of it. He, for some reason, never quite was.

He was a precocious reader, but mostly, at this stage, of botany and natural history rather than imaginative literature; he was, however, given most or all of Andrew Lang's *Fairy Books* (or those at least that had then been published) and (probably) Dasent's *Popular Tales from the Norse*. The *Red Fairy Book* of 1890 was the most momentous; it concludes with a retelling of the tale of Sigurd the Völsung and the dragon Fáfnir, heavily abridged by Lang from William Morris's translation of the Norse *Völsunga Saga*. Tolkien later declared this was his 'favourite without rival'.[9] We may suppose that at some point, perhaps years later, Tolkien would have read the Morris translation in full. Almost the most striking thing about that is its translator's introduction; Morris confesses himself puzzled no one has previously put it into English:

> For this is the Great Story of the North, which should be to all our race what the Tale of Troy was to the Greeks – to all our race first, and afterwards, when the change of the world has made our race nothing more than a name of what has been – a story too – then should it be to those that come after us no less than the Tale of Troy has been to us.

Tolkien found in Lang's Sigurd a number of resonant themes and images that clearly lodged deep in his imagination: the shards of an ancestral sword, famous in its day, whose reforging opens the way to a hero's fate; lovers ruined by englamoured forgetfulness; cunning avaricious dwarves, steeped in skill and crooked with gold-lust; and the dragon itself, bestial, devious in speech, enwreathed in poison-clouds, greedy of gems. The story was finely illustrated by the artist Lancelot Speed, and Tolkien's own dragon-pictures, when they came to be drawn, are closely reminiscent of Speed's Fáfnir.

As Mark Atherton has noticed, the *Red Fairy Book* also includes a version of a Norwegian story, 'The Master Thief', where a young man falls in with brigands and discovers a remarkable talent for thievery.[10] Both this theme, and a dragon, were to figure large in the first story that Tolkien himself published; but that was decades in the future. To look even further forward, the *Green Fairy Book* of 1892 also contains 'The Enchanted Ring', in which a young man is given a ring that confers both invisibility and supreme power, if only it is not used for ill; overborne by the temptation, he renounces the ring.[11]

In 1900, Ronald was sent to King Edward's School in Birmingham, one of the ancient grammar schools that were the backbone of English education, and probably the best school in the area. It was also where his father had been educated. The fees were paid by a Tolkien uncle. The school was founded in 1552, like many grammar schools from the proceeds of suppressed religious houses; it was at that time based in an impressive neo-Gothic building on New Street, designed by Charles Barry (later the architect of the rebuilt Palace of Westminster).[12] The school's list of alumni is an impressive one; it includes Ronald Knox's brother Edmund, who was a few years senior to Tolkien, and Field Marshal Lord Slim, his exact contemporary in age. There is no record of any notable contact between Tolkien and Slim whilst at school, however.[13] Even if they barely overlapped and did not know each other, it is impressive for one school in a decade to have produced two such disparate but in their own ways striking figures. Nor was this an unusual generation: two decades before Tolkien, Housman had been a pupil; two decades after him, King Edward's also educated Enoch Powell, a man who after a double-starred Classical First (admittedly from Cambridge) was made Professor of Greek at Sydney aged twenty-five (the youngest professor in the Empire, at the time). Earlier still, the school had educated the painter Burne-Jones and a string of Anglican scholar-bishops (Lightfoot, Westcott) as well as Edward White Benson, later Archbishop of Canterbury and father to a remarkable if odd brood of children best known by their initials (E.F., A.C., R.H.). More recent alumni include

Mark Steyn, sturdy polemicist and international music critic.

Now that Ronald was at school, Mabel moved the household from rural Sarehole to a rented house in Moseley in the city centre, near a Catholic church. Ronald was desolate at the move, and was at first unhappy at school, but after a term settled in well enough. After two years, Mabel moved them again, this time to be closer to the Birmingham Oratory, as she had grown to dislike the church they had been attending. One of the Fathers of the Oratory, Fr Francis Xavier Morgan, half Welsh, half Anglo-Spanish (his family were in the wine trade), became a family friend and (we would probably say today) spiritual director to Mabel.

The Oratory also ran a school, St Philip's; Ronald and Hilary were enrolled there in 1902, but after a year, it became clear that although the education was Catholic and the fees were lower than those of King Edward's, the schooling was not of the same quality; and Ronald needed to be stretched. His mother took the boys out of school and taught them at home. With the help of coaching from his mother, and from his aunt Jane (who was a mathematics teacher[14]), Ronald won a scholarship to King Edward's, and returned there in 1903.

At the start of 1904, both Ronald and Hilary were ill with measles and whooping cough; then Hilary contracted pneumonia. Mabel exhausted herself nursing them, and in April was admitted to hospital. She was diagnosed with diabetes. This was before the discovery of insulin, and there was no effective treatment except rest. Ronald and Hilary were sent to stay with relatives; by June, however, Mabel had recovered enough to leave hospital. Fr Francis Morgan arranged for her and the boys to stay in a cottage near the Oratory retreat house at Rednal, in the Worcestershire countryside. They stayed at Rednal for the summer and autumn; it was a welcome return to the country, although when school began Ronald had to walk a mile to catch a train into Birmingham.

At the start of November, after five months of country life, Mabel's illness suddenly and catastrophically returned. She fell into a diabetic coma; six days later, on 14 November 1904, aged only thirty-four, Mabel Tolkien died. Ronald was twelve, Hilary ten.

It is probably fair to say Ronald Tolkien never got over his mother's death. His first biographer noted that, thereafter, his naturally cheerful and outgoing manner was counterbalanced by periods of intense despondency, when he felt 'a deep sense of impending loss. Nothing was safe. Nothing would last. No battle would be won for ever.'[15] Tolkien remembered many years later talking to one of his cousins at this time and 'vainly waving a hand at the sky saying "it is so empty and cold"'.[16] The interests his mother had given him – botany, drawing, the English countryside, and language – were now charged with a strong memory of her; so, too, was the Catholic religion.

Her boys became wards of Fr Francis Morgan. Some of their Tolkien and Suffield relatives wanted to contest Mabel's will, and raise the boys Protestant; Fr Francis arranged for them to live with the one Suffield aunt-by-marriage who was content for them to stay Catholic. He ensured that both brothers' education continued (at King Edward's). He also supplemented the Tolkiens' meagre patrimony from his own private income, and continued to do so for some years. Many years later, Tolkien said his example outweighed that of all the disagreeable or even plain bad priests he had met: 'and he was an upper-class Welsh-Spaniard Tory, and seemed to some just a pottering old snob and gossip. He was – and he was *not*. I first learned charity and forgiveness from him …'[17]

Francis Morgan was born in 1857, the same year in fact as Tolkien's father, in Puerto de Santa Maria in southern Spain, headquarters of the sherry trade. His father, also Francis Morgan, had moved there in the 1840s to represent his family business, wine and spirit import and distribution (although the Morgans were originally from Tredegar, they had lived in London since the eighteenth century). There, Francis Morgan senior married a daughter of the Anglo-Spanish Osborne family, which even today remains one of the great sherry houses. Their four children were all brought up Catholic; the third child, and youngest son, was named Francisco Javier, or Francis Xavier. There had been significant involvement of English Catholics in the sherry trade for generations, but the Osbornes had only become Catholic recently; the Morgans were solidly Protestant. Nevertheless anyone in the wine-shipping business would likely have been more familiar with English Catholicism than was usual.

For many years Francis Morgan senior managed the Osborne business. Like many expatriate children, Francis junior was sent to England for schooling, at the Oratory School in Edgbaston;[18] he then attended Manning's short-lived Catholic University College in Kensington, which folded after systematic mismanagement (and probable embezzlement) by its Rector, one Mgr Capel, a plausible Irish crook and reputed ladies' man who had made a name for himself as a preacher to fashionable invalids in Le Touquet before persuading Manning he was the man to run his Catholic rival to the then dogmatically Anglican ancient Universities. Francis Morgan's time at this patchy institution was supplemented with some terms at Louvain, before, in 1877, he entered the Birmingham Oratory (where Newman, its founder, still lived) as a novice. In 1882, aged twenty-five, he was ordained priest.

There is no doubt these bare facts give little of the man who was, as Tolkien saw it, to be his 'second father'. He was by all accounts loud and ebullient, a pastor rather than one of the Oratory's intellectuals. Children found Francis Morgan embarrassing at first, but soon warmed to him, his incurable fondness for practical jokes, his invariable pipe-smoking; the same is said of Tolkien in later life. Certainly, Tolkien later recalled 'the sudden miraculous experience of Fr Francis's love and care and humour' amidst the desolation after his mother's death.[19]

Orphans are prominent in Tolkien's fiction: Frodo Baggins lost his parents as a child, and was raised by Bilbo, his older cousin; Aragorn's father died when he was two, his mother when he was young, and he was brought up in the household of Elrond, whose hidden house at Rivendell has, not wholly fancifully, been linked to the Oratorian enclave at Rednal; in *The Silmarillion*, orphaned heroes abound: Fëanor, Túrin, Tuor, Beren, Eärendil: all lose their fathers young, many are raised by sometimes strict substitutes. Clearly no single equation between any one of these fictional characters and Tolkien himself, or Francis Morgan, is wholly satisfactory or indeed appropriate: Tolkien is too subtle a writer to be happy with any such simplistic *roman à clef*. But it is not unfair, I suggest, to think that his own experience of being caught in a web of obligation and emotional ties enriched his fiction, and gave him a particular sympathy both for orphaned children and for their wise, well-meaning but humanly (or elvishly) limited guardians.

Moreover, it is not illegitimate, surely, to think that since writers, by the popular adage, write best on what they know, Tolkien's repeated portrayals of orphans and fosterage, although it may owe something to Norse models, where fosterage was usual (conversely, of course, one might cite this as an additional reason for Tolkien's attraction to Norse literature), is related in a strong sense to his own life: this had been his experience of childhood, and it was natural to him to describe it in fiction, and, because it had been his own experience, to do so sympathetically and well.

As we have seen, Ronald and Hilary, after a brief time living in the Oratory itself (which could not be a permanent arrangement as all spare space was taken up by boys from St Philip's), and then some weeks staying with a Tolkien uncle in nearby Kings Norton, went in January 1905 to stay with their aunt (by marriage) Beatrice Suffield, who had married Mabel's younger brother William and lived in Stirling Road, Edgbaston, close by the Oratory. She was recently widowed, and the house was gloomy; like many widows, she took paying lodgers.[20] Ronald discovered one day that she had, without consulting him, burnt the great bulk of his mother's letters and private papers. Beatrice Suffield was not especially fond of children, and the brothers were hardly happy (Tolkien later called it a 'sad and troublous time', and may have found solace in rereading fairy tales[21]), but the monthly stipend Fr Francis gave her for their board and lodging (£4 16s.) was presumably welcome. Even though they could not live there, the Tolkien brothers stayed close to the Oratory. They usually went there, most mornings, to serve Francis Morgan's early Mass, and then eat breakfast in the refectory before going to school; Tolkien said later he had been 'virtually a junior inmate of the Oratory house, which contained many learned fathers (largely "converts")'.[22]

Amongst the other Oratorian Fathers, Tolkien's closest friend seems to have been Fr (Francis) Vincent Reade. One of the younger men (born in 1874, he was eighteen years Tolkien's senior), he was a convert from a family of Cornish gentry: his father was an Anglican clergyman, his brother a Fellow of Keble and expert on Dante and medieval philosophy.[23] He was a connexion of the novelist Charles Reade (now known, if at all, only for *The Cloister and the Hearth*) and of William Winwood Reade, atheist and historian, the Richard Dawkins of late Victorian England, whom readers of Conan Doyle will recognize (from *The Sign of Four*) as author of *The Martyrdom of Man*, an otherwise largely forgotten piece of 'psycho-history' (and, amongst much else, the wholly forgotten *The Veil of Isis, or The Mysteries of the Druids*, one of whose chapters is intriguingly titled 'Vestiges of Druidism: In the Ceremonies of the Church of Rome'). Fr Vincent does not seem to have shared his family's literary bent to any great degree, although he was probably well read beyond the norm for Catholic clergy. He later became Headmaster at St Philip's; he was probably at this time already involved in the school, and may have known the Tolkien brothers from their time there.

Tolkien's piety was of a traditional cast, and was (in later life, at any rate) heavily focussed on the Blessed Sacrament; but his theology is typically expansive and generous, hidebound neither by Thomist categorizing nor by Ultramontane triumphalism. We may look to Francis Morgan, and the humane atmosphere of the Oratory, for this formation.

Each summer, Fr Francis took the boys to Lyme Regis in Dorset for a seaside holiday; he also quietly supplemented their tiny income. They were involved to some extent in the life of the Oratory parish: in May 1909, the parish organized three troops of scouts, under the charge of 'the Brothers Tolkien', who by that time were seventeen and fifteen, and so presumably supervising younger boys rather than scouting themselves.

Tolkien's life was now almost wholly urban. There were occasional trips to the Oratory house in still-rural Rednal (Tolkien remembered this as the only place where Fr Francis would smoke a pipe, and attributed his own later habitual pipe-smoking to this example), and, we should remember, the city of Birmingham was then smaller than it is now; but for the most part Tolkien's schooldays and early youth were spent in the vaunting, grimy surroundings of this busy commercial and Imperial city (Joseph Chamberlain, expansionist Colonial Secretary and advocate of the protectionist 'imperial preference' tariff reform, was a local magnate who had been Mayor of Birmingham before he was returned to Parliament).

All this, of course, only made his memories of rural living, and occasional exposure to it, all the more precious: he could no longer take the countryside for granted. It also, or so some have thought, cast a glamour over the rare eccentricities of the urban landscape: prominent on the skyline were the chimney-tower of the Edgbaston Waterworks, and an odd building called Perrott's Folly, a tower built by a local landowner in the mid-eighteenth century for an uncertain purpose but subsequently used as an observatory. These 'two towers' were a daily part of the young Tolkien's horizon, and have been claimed as the seeds of later imaginings. Tolkien himself never mentioned them, but we may think the connexion suggestive. The great clock-tower of nearby Birmingham University (a memorial, in fact, to Joseph Chamberlain) was then recently built; it too may have made an impression.

III – Schooldays

School now assumed a large part in Tolkien's life. Greek and Latin were the backbone of the curriculum, but he was also taught a good deal of English literature, including Chaucer in the original. He was academically strong, and was soon placed regularly at the top of his class. He was also, although slightly built, a keen rugby player. In 1907, the Headmaster, Cary Gilson, established an army cadet force for the boys;[24] at first, this was an *ad hoc* body of volunteers such as had been common since the

1860s. Tolkien was amongst the 130 boys who became cadets, in what later became the school's Officer Training Corps (OTC).[25]

Tolkien's first close friend at school was Christopher Wiseman, son of a Methodist minister. Tolkien and Wiseman were together in the same class from 1905; Tolkien was placed first, Wiseman (who was a year younger) second. They were academic rivals as well as friends, and vied for these places for the rest of their school careers. Both played rugby energetically and well; they took to calling themselves 'the Great Twin Brethren', a phrase borrowed from Macaulay's 'Battle of Lake Regillus'. Wiseman was a mathematician, and an amateur musician and composer. Both he and Tolkien took their religion seriously, and were convinced of the necessity of a moral framework for artistic and social endeavour; this, although surrounded by a variety of shared interests, remained at the core of their friendship.

Doubtless it helped that their respective father-figures were both ministers of religion; it is likely Francis Morgan and Christopher Wiseman's father, Frederick Luke Wiseman, knew each other, although we have no record of it. When Wiseman senior was appointed President of the Wesleyan Methodist Conference, Fr Francis used to refer to him as 'the Pope of Wesley'.[26] Tolkien in later life spoke highly of Wiseman senior – 'one of the most delightful Christian men I have met';[27] it is probably not fanciful to see in this early contact a seed of Tolkien's later sympathy for ecumenical initiatives between Christians.

Tolkien at this time began dabbling in what was to become an abiding interest: making up his own languages, what he called 'private lang'. We saw above how, as a boy, he and two of his cousins had made up code languages. Now he was armed with a formidable battery of actual languages: as well as Latin, Greek, French (which he disliked) and German, he also had some Spanish (via Fr Francis), some Welsh, some Old Norse and, thanks as we shall see to one of his schoolmasters, Old and Middle English. He began to devise a properly structured language, somewhat after the phonetic model of Spanish, that he called 'Naffarin'. Wiseman, who was interested in Egyptian hieroglyphs, was an occasional confidant. Later, a schoolfellow and would-be missionary bought, by mistake, *A Primer of the Gothic Language* (by an Oxford professor named Joseph Wright), under the impression it might be useful for his proposed avocation; he passed this on to Tolkien. Gothic is the most ancient Germanic language still preserved; Tolkien was instantly bowled over by it.

Wright's *Gothic Primer* is not simply a bare grammar of Gothic; Wright prefixed his formal grammar with a brief but comprehensive history of Indo-European and Germanic sound-changes, which may have been Tolkien's first real initiation into technical philology; it is followed by a substantial appendix of texts in Gothic, specifically extracts from the Gothic Bible, which is the only surviving evidence for the language. The character of these texts, incidentally, makes Tolkien's schoolfellow's mistake in buying it an understandable one: a grammar with an appendix of scripture was a familiar format for language primers for missionaries. The Bodleian Library in Oxford today holds Tolkien's copy of *Chambers' Etymological Dictionary* (bought, it seems, at some point during his schooldays, and kept throughout his life[28]), whose introduction had a philological section that became so worn by repeated reading that it fell out. This probably preceded Tolkien's discovery of Wright's *Primer*, and he described it (in a note pasted into the book) as the start of his interest in philology. Whilst this abbreviated discussion may have fired Tolkien's interest, it seems reasonable, however, to see Wright's *Primer* as his first real exposure to philology in the round. As well as the usual etymologies for each word, the *Dictionary* also contains an appendix of the etymology of place-names (which became a lifelong interest) and a brief stemma of the 'divisions of the Aryan languages'.[29]

Tolkien's other close friend from this time was a boy called Vincent Trought. Trought was a poet with a keen aesthetic sense and, by all accounts, a fondness for bizarre and extravagant rhetoric in debate. He was also a competent full-back on the rugby field, although his health had been much compromised by Birmingham's polluted air. He and Wiseman became the heart of a small group whose friendship and collective influence defined much of Tolkien's remaining time at school and for some years afterwards.

The bulk of Tolkien's schooling was, as was customary, in the Greek and Latin classics and in history, mostly Greek and Roman although including some English (of, presumably, a Whiggish cast); two of Tolkien's schoolmasters, however, were keen to introduce their pupils to English literature. One was George Brewerton, who had been Tolkien's form-master in the Sixth Class, which, after a couple of terms in the Lower Remove, he was placed in when he went back to King Edward's in 1903. Brewerton introduced his class to Shakespeare (whom Tolkien mostly disliked, especially *Macbeth* – he reckoned the device of the coming of Great Birnam Wood to Dunsinane 'shabby' and remembered 'bitter disappointment and disgust' at it[30]) and Chaucer; he read Chaucer to them in the original, and Tolkien was spellbound. Brewerton encouraged his bent to historical linguistics, and some time later lent him an Old English primer (probably Sweet's *Anglo-Saxon Primer*, which alongside an elementary grammar and phonology had an appendix of prose texts for translation[31]).

The other was R.W. 'Dickie' Reynolds, who after Balliol had been a literary critic for the *National Observer* in the 1890s, before returning to King Edward's, his old school, as a master. Reynolds was Tolkien's formmaster when he entered the Fourth Class, in 1906. Reynolds was not, Tolkien observed later, an especially good teacher, but he did make the boys read Milton, Keats and more contemporary poets (Kipling, Walter de la Mare) and carried with him something of the excitement and glamour of the literary life, which made him 'immensely interesting as a person'.[32] Reynolds moved easily in the world of publishers and poets, and may have had some part in prompting Tolkien's interest in writing. He was also in charge of the school's Literary and Debating Societies; the latter at any rate became one of Tolkien's diversions.

As much as anything, though, Tolkien was excited by language – by the forms of words, in addition to (and to an extent separable from) their meaning. In each language he knew, he found a unique element of aesthetic pleasure that, somehow, chimed with his own innate preferences. In later years, he proposed the theory that we each of us have a 'native language' (whether an actually existing language or one 'invented' or 'recovered') which satisfies all our particular linguistic predilections, and that this language is not our 'first-learned language' or mother-tongue.[33] Much of Tolkien's life can be seen, from one angle, as a search for, and an attempt to recover, this 'native language'.

Tolkien made steady progress up the school, usually being placed first or second in the form; by his sixteenth birthday, he entered the First Class, which was under the direct supervision of the headmaster ('Chief Master' in King Edward's School parlance).

In the First Class (which, by a curious inversion, was what King Edward's then called its Sixth Form; it now has the more usual name) Tolkien was given permission by Francis Morgan to attend the headmaster's classes in New Testament Greek; this was a significant concession from Fr Francis.

These were the early years of Pius X's Pontifical Biblical Commission, whose pronouncements (including blanket, and frankly bizarre, prohibitions of modern critical scholarship) embarrassed Catholic scriptural scholarship for a generation; it was also in the immediate aftermath of Pius X's decrees against 'Modernism' (a synthetic catch-all heresy, cooked up by a diligent Vatican official from a conspectus of heterodox views drawn indiscriminately from a range of contemporary historians and theologians), and Rome had encouraged Catholic clergy to denounce it wherever they plausibly detected it. This is not to dispute that some trends in and dogmas of contemporary critical scholarship, when applied indiscriminately, were potentially corrosive of Christianity as traditionally understood; but to compound from these things a catch-all heresy and encourage its delation was in another way just as unhelpful.[34]

To an anti-Modernist zealot, having Catholic boys taught scripture by a Protestant would have been unthinkable. Fortunately there were few of these amongst English Catholics. The exception was the diocese of Southwark, whose bishop, the Gibraltarian Peter Amigo, was privately convinced his episcopal colleagues (especially his arch-enemy, Archbishop Bourne of Westminster) were all closet Modernist sympathizers. None of this had penetrated into the diocese of Birmingham, however, and Oratorians, as non-diocesan priests, had in any case a degree more leeway than would most clergy. Tolkien later commented, 'I certainly took no "harm", and was better equipped ultimately to make my way in a non-Catholic professional society.'[35]

Tolkien was to stay at King Edward's for another three years, until he was almost twenty. This may seem odd to us now, who are used to rigid correlations between age and scholastic progression; but it was quite usual at the time. Boys would stay at their school until they found a university place, or their parents tired of paying fees and found them a job or a trade instead. Tolkien was clearly clever enough to go to Oxford, but was too poor to do so without financial help; and this meant studying hard for a scholarship examination (these, we should remember, were the days before nationally recognized public qualifications: all university entrance was achieved not by a comparison of grades but by the private decision of the university).

IV – First love

Our next topic requires a small step back in time. In 1907, on their annual summer holiday to Lyme Regis, Fr Francis finally discovered from Tolkien and Hilary quite how miserable they were living with their aunt.

He arranged for them to move, although he quietly continued paying a stipend to Aunt Beatrice.

At the start of 1908, Tolkien, now sixteen, and his brother Hilary moved from Beatrice Suffield's house to live as lodgers with the Faulkners, a wine merchant and his wife, in Duchess Road also in Edgbaston, one block away from the Oratory. The Faulkners were active in the Oratory parish, and hosted musical evenings which some of the Fathers attended. The Tolkiens found they had as a fellow lodger a nineteen-year-old girl, Edith Bratt. She and Tolkien became friends, and allies against Mrs Faulkner's constricting household regime (Edith persuaded the housemaid to smuggle extra food from the kitchen to the boys). By the following summer, they decided they were in love. They began to meet in secret.

Like Tolkien, Edith was an orphan; her mother had died when she was fourteen. Unlike him, she was illegitimate; her mother had been a governess in her father's house, and Edith had never been recognized as his daughter by him or his family. Edith's father has been identified as Alfred Warrilow, a paper dealer in the Birmingham suburb of Handsworth. He was married with a five-year-old daughter, and Frances Bratt, Edith's mother, was her governess. In 1888, Warrilow's wife divorced him; Edith was born in 1889. Alfred Warrilow died in 1891, aged forty-nine.[36] Frances Bratt was named sole executrix of Alfred Warrilow's will. Warrilow's estate was valued at just over £8,700, a fair sum, but we know nothing of the liabilities on it, which may have diminished it considerably, nor indeed how it was disposed. Any money or property left for Edith and her mother will hardly have amounted to the full sum proved.[37]

After her mother died in 1903, Edith had inherited small amounts of property in different parts of Birmingham; these, with careful husbanding by her guardian (a lawyer), generated a tiny income that was just enough to keep her, after sending her to school in Evesham. She was musical, playing the piano well, and was by background at least an Anglican. She had hoped, at one time, for a career as a concert pianist, or at least a music teacher; but although Mrs Faulkner was 'musical', she disliked the sound of Edith practising, and inevitably her playing (and career prospects) suffered.

Whether this youthful romance would have, under other circumstances, amounted to anything is obviously unknowable and probably irrelevant; as it was, Francis Morgan learnt of the connexion in the autumn of 1909, and, seeing only something to distract Tolkien from his schoolwork (he was supposed to be studying hard for an Oxford scholarship) insisted it stop. Soon afterwards, Tolkien sat and failed the scholarship examination. Without the financial help from an award, he had no chance of attending the University. In the new year, Fr Francis arranged for Tolkien and his brother to move to different lodgings, with a Mrs MacSherry in Highfield Road.

The year 1910 started darkly for Tolkien; his academic future and his happiness with Edith both seemed imperilled. Throughout his life, Tolkien was subject to black moods, gloom, periodic feelings of hopelessness. Outwardly, he kept busy and sociable, but in his private diary he was often near despair.[38]

Tolkien saw Edith again, secretly; they were seen together, and Fr Francis found out. He formally forbade Tolkien to see her until he should come of age on his twenty-first birthday three years later. Edith, meanwhile, had arranged to move to Cheltenham, to live with family friends. Tolkien saw her again, by chance, a couple of times; again he was observed and reported to his guardian, who was furious, and threatened to stop Tolkien from going to university if he did not break with her absolutely. Tolkien was appalled, but submitted. 'I owe all to Fr. F and so must obey', he wrote in his diary. On 2 March, Edith left Birmingham. Tolkien saw her from a distance, but they did not speak.

This business, forbidding an eighteen-year-old young man to see a girl, may seem to cast Fr Francis Morgan in a tyrannical light. We need to see this within the context of its time: long engagements, and marriages postponed for financial reasons or because of reservations on the part of one or the other family, were a normal part of Victorian life, and were not unusual in the Edwardian age; Francis Morgan may have been a touch old-fashioned in his approach, but no one would have supposed him wrong, or necessarily unreasonable, to act in this way, and indeed he might have seemed irresponsible had he not done so. Tolkien was still legally a minor (the age of majority was twenty-one until 1970) and had only a very modest income from his father's estate; he could not possibly afford to get married without a good job, and that, for him, meant getting a degree. His academic gifts were obvious, and Fr Francis was anxious to help him make the most of them. Tolkien could not in any case have got married, or engaged (an engagement was still at this date a legally binding connexion, which could provoke an action for breach of promise if subsequently broken off) without his guardian's permission.

Tolkien's acquiescence in this, which may seem odd to us, can be partly explained by the social expectations of the time; for the rest of it, we should look to Tolkien's attitude to his religion. He was convinced, not unreasonably, that his mother's conversion and in particular her family's reaction to it had led in part to her early death: better medical care, which they could have enabled, might well have brought her through the crisis that caused her death. This made her, in some fashion, 'a martyr for the faith'. Fr Francis Morgan's subsequent role as guardian was by no means a perfunctory one. He was almost the exact age Tolkien's own father would have been; aside from considerable financial generosity, he also (as we saw) took a close interest in the Tolkien brothers. Francis Morgan, Tolkien said, had been his 'second father'.

Whilst he may have been sometimes privately miserable, Tolkien still had the energy and enthusiasm of early youth. He immersed himself in work, both in preparation for another Oxford scholarship examination that December (1910) and for his own private ends. He had by now a good knowledge of Gothic and Old English and could discourse at length on comparative philology; invited to talk on this subject to the sixth form, Tolkien, with the confidence of his age, gave them fully three hours of lecture and would have said more had the master not stopped him. The school had the custom of holding debates in Latin; this, for Tolkien, was all too easy, and he once, in the role of Greek ambassador to the Senate, spoke wholly in Greek; on other occasions, in the character of barbarian envoys, he broke into Gothic or Old English. Tolkien's hobby of 'private languages' developed, too; he devised hypothetical Gothic words to supplement the meagre vocabulary that had survived from the historical language, and also further elaborated his 'Naffarin' language. In June 1910, for instance, he wrote a longish inscription in pastiche Gothic into his copy of *The Fifth Book of Thucydides*, which he had read for a school prize; the volume turned up in a Salisbury second-hand bookshop in 1965. He 'Gothicized' his name as Ruginwaldus Dwalakōneis; habitués of old book shops may want to take note.[39]

Perhaps not all of this was strictly pertinent to an Oxford scholarship exam; but it reveals him as a young man of varied and exuberant intellectual interests. He also kept up his involvement in rugby and theatricals.

He also worked towards taking the Oxford and Cambridge Higher Certificate (the precursor to the School Certificate, itself later replaced by 'A' Levels), which that July he successfully took in five subjects (Latin, Greek, Scripture Knowledge (Greek Text), History and Elementary

Mathematics) as well as an English Essay paper.

On 17 December 1910, he learnt he had been awarded an Exhibition (a minor scholarship) worth £60 a year to Exeter College, Oxford, to read Literae Humaniores (Classics).[40] Added to this was a leaving bursary from King Edward's, and some money from Fr Francis. Tolkien would not be rich, but he could now go to Oxford.

Tolkien himself reckoned, rightly, that he was clever enough to have won a more valuable Scholarship (and his headmaster later confirmed this to him), but he had not been 'industrious or single-minded', instead spending his time 'studying something else: Gothic and what not'.[41] For Tolkien, keeping his intellectual curiosity, and expenditure of intellectual effort, confined to approved channels was to be a constant and not wholly successful struggle for most of his life.

For the moment, however, his future seemed secure; and he had the best part of a calendar year until the University year began the following October. His last two terms at King Edward's were not exactly idle – he was still obliged to take school exams, and had OTC and First XV rugby, and also edited several numbers of the school magazine – but did allow more leisure for debate, both formal and informal, than had the preceding years. They also saw his first venture into print.

Lord Macaulay's *Lays of Ancient Rome* were then, as for many years, staples of schoolboy recitation.[42] Tolkien is unlikely to have been the first to see their potential for pastiche or parody; but at any rate, he wrote around this time a poem – 'The Battle of the Eastern Field' – in the manner of 'The Battle of Lake Regillus', but taking as its subject a school rugby match.

Tolkien's poem, his first publication, appeared in the school magazine in March 1911.'The Battle of Lake Regillus' tells of a Roman victory over the Latins won by the intervention of the gods Castor and Pollux, whom Macaulay calls 'the Great Twin Brethren'; this is clearly the source of Tolkien's and Wiseman's self-description. Tolkien's pastiche is deft and mildly amusing, although a good deal is exact or near-exact quotation of the original in an altered context; it shows a real affection for Macaulay's verse alongside a relish for the mock-heroic.

We should not perhaps make too much of this, but for a modern attracted by the heroic style (and, like Tolkien and most of his contemporaries, exposed to it constantly in the works of Homer) it is very difficult, almost impossible, to shed our inherited sophistication and write it without irony; attempts at the heroic style fall, almost inevitably, into bathos and parody. In some ways, then, it is easiest to learn the heroic style of writing (of which Macaulay was preternaturally capable) by deliberate parody and pastiche: if we begin with the mock-heroic we may, in time, pass from it to the heroic done 'straight', but if we start with the second, we will almost certainly lapse into the first. We might be reminded of Proust's efforts to achieve his own literary style by writing deliberate pastiche of his favourite authors (Balzac, Flaubert, Sainte-Beuve) so as to avoid writing unconscious pastiche for the rest of his life.[43] Or, as I say, we might not want to make too much of this.

V – 'T.C., B.S. &c.'

Perhaps the most important thing to occur during Tolkien's last term at King Edward's was not part either of the formal curriculum nor any of the school's myriad other activities: it was, instead, a purely adventitious connexion between Tolkien and some of his contemporaries.

At King Edward's, it was the custom for the school library to be run by some of the senior boys; Tolkien and Wiseman were two of them. In the summer term of 1911, his last at the school, Tolkien became senior Librarian; Wiseman and Trought were amongst his assistants, as was R.Q. ('Rob') Gilson, son of the school's headmaster, Cary Gilson. To while away the long unoccupied hours of the examination season (for six weeks, senior boys were required to take exams, but had otherwise no obligations) the four of them started to meet for tea (illicitly) in the library. The habit persisted through the following autumn term, and the group together referred to themselves, humorously, as the 'TCBS', which stood for 'Tea Club [and] Barrovian Society'; their meetings now took place both in the library and at Barrow's Stores in the city. Their talk soon took on a serious and literary character – Tolkien and Wiseman, as we have seen, were inclined to look at artistic endeavour in moral terms; they were also much exercised by questions of patriotic and civic duty. In some ways this sort of thing was a natural outgrowth of the habit of schoolboy debating, itself a corollary to the ancient rhetorical training of making an argument in favour of, or against, an arbitrarily assigned position, but taken to a new level of personal interest not normally possible either in the classroom or the debating hall. These sorts of topics, too, probably never again seem so important as they do to clever and well-read boys in their late teens, on the verge of university or profession and ripe with an intellectual self-confidence and apparent clear-sightedness that, in later years, they might reckon callow. They each had artistic talent, or at least ambition; and they were at an age when anything seems possible.

As well as Tolkien, Wiseman, Gilson and Trought, several others were also associated with the TCBS, but the four close friends were its core. The group expanded to include various other senior boys – Sidney Barrowclough, the brothers R.S. Payton and W.H. Payton, T.K. ('Tea-Cake') Barnsley, Geoffrey Bache Smith. For a while, the tone of their discussions was dominated by what Tolkien in particular thought trivial and lightweight witticism; eventually the group was reformed without those responsible. Some have taken at face value later remarks confining the TCBS proper to four only: Tolkien, Wiseman, Gilson, Smith; but the extant records make it clear that Smith was a peripheral figure until after he and the other TCBS-ites had left school.

As we shall see, the majority of these schoolboy friends did not survive early manhood.

The abbreviation TCBS, which began as a slightly arch joke, became convenient shorthand for their collective sense of themselves, and (more importantly) their artistic ambitions (Gilson had a flair for drawing and design, Smith was a talented poet; Smith also had an interest in Welsh language and poetry, which he shared with Tolkien). It is easy to exaggerate the importance of this type of schoolboy connexion, and from the comfortable disillusion of middle age, perhaps, to mock the vaunting idealism of teenage boys; but the fact remains that it was this time, and these friends, which helped Tolkien to discover that he wanted, above all, to write; and to write, in particular, something characteristically English in the way that, say, Greek or Norse myth was characteristic of those languages or cultures, something England had once had but had because of historical accident lost. Tolkien gradually determined to do this as a poet. But what sort of poet did he want to be, and why? To answer this, it is worth glancing at some of the writers Tolkien was reading.

VI – Literary divagations

We have little hard evidence for who of his contemporaries or near-contemporaries Tolkien was reading in these years; but there were a good number of writers working in Edwardian England whose works clearly made an impact on him, and have left traces in Tolkien's later writing, and in some of his earlier material, whether he read them then or later. In all subsequent discussion of literary influence on Tolkien, we should bear this uncertainty in mind.

Diligent source-hunters have nosed out, in Tolkien's mature work, a number of influences from an in some ways unremarkable range of schoolboy favourites, whom he may be allowed to have read at this time – Rider Haggard, Conan Doyle, S.R. Crockett, Buchan – alongside several contemporary exponents of faërie: Andrew Lang, George MacDonald, Lord Dunsany. There was, too, always William Morris, although it may have been slightly later before Tolkien started reading him seriously. The clear and ascertainable model of his earliest writing, however, was above all the Catholic poet Francis Thompson.

Francis Thompson is, perhaps, not much read today, although *The Hound of Heaven*, or extracts from it, is still sometimes found in anthologies. His manner is arch, whimsical and for the most part curiously bloodless. Thompson was a failed medical student who lived as a down-and-out in London for three years, until in 1888, aged twenty-nine, he was discovered by the Catholic converts and magazine publishers Alice and Wilfrid Meynell, who arranged for his poems to be published. He had developed an addiction to opium, and died in 1907, aged only forty-seven.

Thompson is at best an uneven poet; he is given to fantastical imagery (it might be simplistic to see this as legacy of his opium-eating, but the connexion inevitably suggests itself), an eclectic and profuse vocabulary, and wild flights of a sentimentalism that must sometimes have made even his contemporaries gag. But he can write with deft control of complex metres and with a force of language and metaphor that should not be despised. He was also given to introducing theological themes and reflexions into quite disparate subjects; although, from one angle, all of Thompson's verse is about his own conversion, and the history God had made by drawing him out from the mire of his misery, poverty and addiction. One suspects that this as much as anything attracted Tolkien, who was, remember, a very pious young man; taken together with the richness of Thompson's language and the variety of his technique, this must have made him a strongly attractive figure: an unashamedly Catholic writer at the centre of contemporary verse-making. In a talk on Thompson given four years later, Tolkien professed 'perfect harmony with the poet'[44]. So him it was that, above all, the young Tolkien imitated.

For those who may not know much of him, it is worth giving here a taster of Thompson's verse. This is from the Proem to 'Sister Songs':

From its red leash my heart strains tamelessly
For spring leaps in the womb of the young year!

The first line illustrates Thompson's technical weakness (the asso-
nance 'strains tamelessly'), the second his occasional vigour of metaphor;
the whole couplet, his rather over-coloured circumlocution, the uneasy
prurience of his imagery.

Or, from the same Proem, there is this, which (I think) describes the
sky at evening:

The beamy-textured tent transpicuous,
Of webbéd cœrule wrought and woven calms,
Whence has paced forth the lambent-footed sun;

Kind critics called this sort of thing 'Miltonic'; it is certainly striking.
Other parts of the same poem are simply bad: at one point, Thompson
rhymes 'ladies', 'shade is' and 'Hades', something it is probably kind to
call 'Cockney'. He is also sometimes ponderous, or clumsy: 'If ever I did
do thee ease in song' is a line neither musical nor clear. We could multiply
examples without, probably, shedding much more light.[45]

Tolkien's poems laboured, for years, under the burden of imitating
Thompson; we may reckon he only properly shook free from him when
he began writing in alliterative verse, and in other consciously medieval
metres. Reading Thompson, one is often reminded of Wiseman's
comment on reading an early draft of what became Tolkien's poem
'Sea-Chant of an Elder Day', that (to borrow a phrase) it was like a woman
wearing all her jewellery after breakfast.[46]

It is in one sense distressing to discover that this sentimental, technically patchy and lexically incontinent writer was the literary figure
with whom, above all others, the young Tolkien identified; and it is
tempting to see his later literary development as a gradual shedding of
this influence. Certainly Tolkien abandoned, and came heartily to detest,
the apparatus of daffodowndilly fairy whimsy Thompson found so
appealing; and Tolkien claimed to find in Thompson an intellectual and
theological rigour that his readers today, such as they are, would probably
not trouble to detect, although it is arguably there. What strikes us most
about Thompson, probably, is his saccharine and awkwardly verbose
language, his imagery chocolate-box and phantasmagoric by turns, his
doggerel rhyme-schemes; it is almost embarrassing to find Tolkien a fan.

It needs to be said, however, that Tolkien's early poems are, for the most part, unremarkable except inasmuch as they foreshadow themes from his later writing; and that, throughout his life, there was a strain of whimsy in Tolkien's verse which we might trace to Thompson's influence, or (more plausibly perhaps) assume reflects an aspect of Tolkien's character that found in Thompson's florid fantasias a kindred spirit.

One work by Thompson we may claim Tolkien knew closely is his 'Sister Songs', dedicated to two of the Meynells' daughters. It falls clearly in the (to us) odd tradition of the Victorian sentimentalizing of childhood, of Kate Greenaway and late Ruskin, of Lewis Carroll's unread books (*Sylvie and Bruno*, another Tolkien favourite[47]), of advertisements for Pears' Soap. For Tolkien, however, early childhood was a precious time of lost happiness and unstained promise; he was obviously predisposed to find Thompson's presentation of it attractive. This is a biographical or perhaps psychological fact rather than a literary one; but it had an important literary consequence. Thompson, whose botanical descriptions were unusually exact (another point in his favour in Tolkien's eyes), writes of the laburnum:

The long laburnum drips
Its honey of wild flame, its jocund spilth of fire.

This is a telling parallel with Tolkien's later mythology of the Trees;[48] but the immediate link was between a section of the first poem, which offers a vision of woodland sprite and fairies, and a poem, 'Woodsunshine', written by Tolkien in July 1910 and apostrophizing 'ye light fairy things tripping so gay ... dance for me! Sprites of the wood'.[49] Anything less like Tolkien's later account of elves, and more inclined to revolt an adult modern taste, can hardly be imagined; but Tolkien had been led to this in part by Thompson's own enthusiasm, and in part by the strange Edwardian vogue for fairies, exemplified by Barrie's *Peter Pan*, which Tolkien saw in April of 1910 ('shall never forget it as long as I live. Wish E. had been with me' he wrote in his diary[50]), and a few years later in a base empirical fashion by the frauds imposed on Arthur Conan Doyle and the gullible public as the 'Cottingley Fairies'.[51] Edith seems to have been much taken with this fashion for gossamer fairy things.

Two other of Thompson's poems had specific, identifiable impact on Tolkien's writing: 'Daisy', another sentimentalizing ballad of childhood, is alluded to in a poem Tolkien wrote five years later;[52] whilst in the odd, and

43

rather good, 'Mistress of Vision' (which treats of the rootedness of inspiration in suffering) Tolkien found the name Luthany, and kept it for later.

As we have said, we cannot usually say with certainty when Tolkien first read some writers, although we may guess. It is likely, for instance, that he read Lord Dunsany's works soon after they were published, but we do not know for sure.

Dunsany's major collections of fantasy tales were published between 1905 and 1916; in the period of Tolkien's schooldays, the important volumes are *Time and the Gods* (1906), *The Sword of Welleran* (1908) and, in 1910, *A Dreamer's Tales*; there is also the odd, and slightly anomalous, *Gods of Pegāna* of 1905. Several stories which, it has been argued, had a definite influence on Tolkien appeared only in 1912, in the collection *The Book of Wonder*.[53] These early books were all finely illustrated by Sidney Sime, whose strange polychromatic fantasias (reminiscent, in turn, of Rackham, Beardsley, Lord Leighton, Whistler, Klimt) may well have influenced Tolkien's own burgeoning style as an artist in pencil and watercolour, although Tolkien's control of line was comparatively weak. Nevertheless the visual component of Tolkien's imagination was a strong one, and these striking illustrations would only have heightened the impact of the text. The tales themselves are probably the oddest things ever written by a former Guards officer (Dunsany served with the Coldstream Guards in the Boer War). Teasingly written, occasionally satirical, knowing, they are not really much like anything Tolkien himself would write; but in two particulars they are exemplars. First, in point of literary style: Dunsany took the high aureate prose of the 1890s and tempered it with plain discursive, to its benefit; second, in use of unexplained and resonant allusion to names, places, things otherwise unknown or glimpsed at the margins of another picture. This, the unexpected vista, was to become one of the mature Tolkien's favourite narrative techniques, and he probably learnt it first from Dunsany.

Another influence was Lord Macaulay, who for all that he was a noxious Whig as a historian, had also, in his *Lays of Ancient Rome*, tried to recreate in verse the lost early literature of Rome (one of Tolkien's schoolboy poems, as we have seen, was an affectionate parody of Macaulay's verse).

This also suggests Tolkien was familiar, at very least, with the *Liedertheorie* of epic composition (which claimed later epic poems as assemblages of earlier 'lays' or 'ballads'); in the *Lays of Ancient Rome*, Macaulay had feigned to produce what these early poems might have looked like. This effort to reproduce a lost early literature is, perhaps, an archetypally romantic one; it was to find echoes in Tolkien's later literary activity.

Tolkien in years to come was a fan of the novels of John Buchan, most of which were not yet written; but he may well have read Buchan's early short stories. Of particular interest is Buchan's early collection *The Watcher by the Threshold*, published in 1902 when Buchan was twenty-seven, and Tolkien ten. The title story is narrated by a philologist, 'deputy-professor of Northern Antiquities' at Oxford and an expert on Celtic elements in the Norse *Edda*; a background better able to pique Tolkien's interest could hardly be designed. The narrator discovers 'the Folk', a surviving remnant of aboriginal Picts, and hears something of their stories: 'I heard fragments of old religions, primeval names of gods and goddesses, half-understood by the Folk, but to me a key to a hundred puzzles. Tales which survive to us in broken disjointed riddles were intact here in living form.'[54] Something closer to a philologist's holy grail might hardly be described. Buchan's narrator, needless to say, comes to a sticky end before he can make good on what he has found. The collection also includes the remarkable 'The Far Islands', which tells of a man haunted by an ancestral memory of an enchanted island in the far west. All the stories in the book, however, are 'supernatural' in theme, in one way or another, and are saturated with Buchan's fine mixture of classical learning and interest in Scottish folklore, and (what is very like Tolkien's own later interests) the intersections and parallels between the two. Ten years later *The Moon Endureth* appeared; this, like the previous volume, collected shorter pieces Buchan had written and published over the previous decade. There is perhaps less obviously to connect with Tolkien's work in this later book; although the story 'The Grove of Ashtaroth', a powerful narrative of biblical paganism in an African setting, has descriptions of the South African landscape done with a lyrical precision (like the descriptions of Scots landscape elsewhere in the book) that prefigures Tolkien's own later writing. The South African connexion would surely have been attractive to Tolkien. 'Streams of Water in the South', another tale from that volume, again hints at a 'straight road' across water to an ancestral homeland, although, here, one in the Borders. Most pertinent of all, however, is the last tale in the collection, 'The Rime of True Thomas', where a shepherd, a devout man, hears the music of faërie (the 'Song of the Open Road', the 'Song of Lost Battles', the 'Ballad of Grey Weather', 'which makes him who hears it sick all the days of his life for something which he cannot name') and is driven by longing from his settled avocation to wander the ways of the world.[55]

VII – Farewell to Birmingham

That summer, Tolkien's career in the school OTC reached its pinnacle. In June 1911, he was one of eight King Edward's School OTC cadets chosen to attend the coronation of the King-Emperor George V; along with hundreds of other cadets, they lined the route between the Palace of Westminster and the Abbey. Tolkien was later, on 3 July, amongst seventy-six King Edward's School cadets who attended a review of OTCs from across the nation by the King in Windsor Great Park. On that occasion, almost eighteen thousand young men assembled before their King, representing what *The Times* called the 'intellectual reinforcement that the Military Services controlling the Empire will receive five or six years hence'[56]. We might lazily suppose that war awoke Edwardian England from a glib pacifism; but the truth is that military display, and particularly voluntary soldiering, had played an increasing part in middle-class English life for some decades (Victorian England had experienced several French invasion scares, and had accumulated a large number of bodies of amateur soldiers); the reforms of the Army after the Boer War, where (we should remember) volunteer cavalry had played a large part in Britain's eventual victory, had merely formalized and made more efficient an existing movement of significant strength.

Tolkien's time at King Edward's came to a formal close on Speech Day, that 26 July, with the usual business of speeches and prize-giving (he was awarded one of six Leaving Prizes by the headmaster) topped off with musical and dramatic pieces; the last of these was Aristophanes' *Peace*, in Greek, with Tolkien in the part of Hermes. The school then sang the national anthem, also in Greek, and Tolkien's career at King Edward's was over.

He was nineteen, rising twenty. It is unlikely he experienced leaving King Edward's as the expulsion from paradise lamented by any number of Edwardian Etonians, for whom no later university or other experience could ever equal the heady joys of Sixth Form and its challenges, victories, friendships;[57] but Tolkien had risen to the top of his school, and was academically and (as far as we can tell) socially at ease amongst his schoolfellows. He was a Prefect, Captain of his house rugby XV, a regular member of the school's First XV, Secretary of the Debating Society, and chief Librarian, as well as being active in various other societies. For any clever boy, the transplanting from the familiar and compassed environment of school to the broader, more heterogeneous and less structured surroundings of Oxford is likely to be a challenge and to some extent a shock.

But all that was three months away, a lifetime at that age; and Tolkien's summer was not without planned diversions. The most important of these, and the one that made the most enduring mark, was a journey to Switzerland. This came about in crabwise fashion.

Hilary had left school early to work on the land. After a short time in an office job in his Incledon uncle's firm, he had been offered work by the Brookes-Smith family on their farm in Sussex. The Brookes-Smiths seem to have known the Tolkiens through their aunt Jane Neave, who had been in charge of a women students' hostel at St Andrews; the two Brookes-Smith daughters had been educated at a nearby school. That summer, as usual, the Brookes-Smiths organized a walking tour of the Swiss Alps, and put together a party of a dozen (together with two Swiss). Jane Neave arranged for the two Tolkien brothers to join the party; we may also suspect she paid for them to go, although there is no record of it.

Jane Neave was a remarkable woman. She was the first of her family to receive a university education, gaining a University of London B.Sc. through Birmingham's Mason College (later part of Birmingham University), and thereafter worked as a schoolmistress. We last saw her, as Jane Suffield, Mabel's younger sister, teaching Ronald Tolkien geometry for his entrance examination for King Edward's in 1903; soon thereafter, in the summer of 1905, she married an insurance salesman called Edwin Neave (her family disapproved of him, thinking him common), gave up her teaching post and moved to the village of Gedling near Nottingham, whence her husband travelled for work. Edwin Neave had been a lodger in the Suffield household; he and Jane seem to have had an understanding, if they were not formally engaged, since around the time Mabel Tolkien came back from South Africa. He died young in 1909; he was thirty-seven, and the cause of death was given as 'broncho-pneumonia', which some have speculated was code for, or brought on by, drink. Jane did not repine, but took a residential job as warden of a women students' hostel, part of the University of St Andrews. She resigned from the post in June 1911 (there was a squabble with the Principal, and her mother had been ill), with the intention of moving back to Gedling, where she had bought a farm, which she planned to run with her friends the Brookes-Smiths, although she did not actually take up residence until April 1912.[58] At some point in the summer of 1910 or 1911, Tolkien (perhaps in company with his brother) visited St Andrews; this may well have been the occasion for their invitation to join the Alpine tour.[59]

The party, then, included the Tolkien brothers and Jane Neave, the Brookes-Smith parents and their three children (a boy of twelve and two daughters of fourteen and sixteen), with the balance made up of school-mistress friends of Jane Neave and other friends and acquaintances. Another pair joined the party midway through their venture.

They went by train to Innsbruck, and thence crossed into Switzerland; they then walked, in presumably easy stages, from Interlaken to Lauterbrunnen and Mürren, to Grindelwald past the Eiger, then to Meiringen (seeing the Jungfrau and the Silberhorn), and across the Grimsel Pass to Brig. From Brig they walked to Visp, perhaps also Zermatt, with a far vista of the Matterhorn; then over a high pass to Gruben, then the Forcletta Pass to Grimentz, and at last to Sion. There they took the first of numerous trains back to England, arriving in early September. This was Tolkien's first foreign holiday, indeed the first time he had left England since arriving from South Africa sixteen years earlier: 'a remarkable experience … after a poor boy's childhood'.[60]

That summer was an extraordinary one, with sunshine almost continuous between April and October, and the mountains made a strong and enduring impression on Tolkien's imagination; even forty years later, his vision of mountain scenery is clearly drawn from his Alpine memories of this high Edwardian summer.

The valley of Lauterbrunnen inspires Rivendell (at least visually), whilst the three peaks of Eiger, Monch and Jungfrau may well be the three mountains of Moria (even though Celebdil, Silvertine, is Silberhorn, in name anyway). The Matterhorn, seen from Zermatt, is as good a model as any for Erebor, the Lonely Mountain. Any reader of Tolkien's mature prose will recognize in him an almost mystical feeling for mountain scenery, which was constantly fed on these memories of the summer of 1911; even half a century later, his recall of the scenes of his holiday was exact and rich. Three decades later, as we shall see, he used 'the Mountains' as a shorthand for 'heaven'.[61]

Humphrey Carpenter states that, before leaving for England, Tolkien bought a postcard of Josef Madlener's painting *Der Berggeist*. *Der Berggeist* ('the mountain spirit') shows a bearded and cloaked figure, seated on a rock amidst forest trees with a vista of mountains in the background, with a white deer nuzzling his hands. Tolkien later wrote on the envelope containing it 'origin of Gandalf', although some have specu-lated that the wizard's acerbic manner and brisk efficiency might owe something to Jane Neave. According to the artist's daughter, however, *Der Berggeist* was painted in the late 1920s, and so cannot date from this period; so (if Carpenter's information derives from Tolkien's own memory) Tolkien must have confused this with some other occasion, unless (what seems unlikely) Madlener's daughter is mistaken.[62] Nevertheless, since Tolkien's attraction to mountains was so intense, and there seems to be some link between Tolkien's 1911 trip and his attraction for Madlener's painting, it seemed easiest to notice it here, especially as we have no other clear event to which to tie it. The picture is not perhaps an especially remarkable one, in a minor if attractive vein of illustrations to German folklore (Madlener painted companion pieces of, apparently, a fairy woman of the woods and the mountain spirit Rübezahl); but for some reason it lodged in Tolkien's memory and imagination.

On his return to England, Tolkien wrote a poem, 'The New Lemminkäinen', a pastiche of the manner of Kirby's translation of the Finnish *Kalevala*; we may suspect, as with his earlier Macaulay pastiche, that he was making an oblique approach to themes and styles of writing that, with the self-consciousness of youth, he did not yet feel able to tackle 'straight'.

Chapter 2 – University and Edith

I – Oxford

In October 1911, Tolkien matriculated at the University. He and another Old Edwardian were driven up to Oxford by his sometime form-master, 'Dickie' Reynolds, whose fashionableness ran to keeping a motor-car, then a comparative rarity.

The first four terms of the Literae Humaniores course are devoted to subjects to be examined in the preliminary examination, Classical Moderations ('Mods'). The great bulk of the course was close study of classical authors, most of whom he will have read at school, and the general literary history of Greece and Rome; with, of course, the uncounselled horrors of unseen translations, of 'gobbets' drawn from no set or predetermined text, and the elaborate parlour games of Greek and Latin verse and prose composition. Homer and Demosthenes, Virgil and Cicero were read *in extenso*; whilst close study was made of four Greek plays (Aeschylus's *Agamemnon*, *King Oedipus* and *Electra* by Sophocles, Euripides' *Bacchae*), two of Plato's dialogues, and the first four books of Tacitus's *Annals*. This was all familiar, or mostly familiar, ground, although not without interest or intellectual challenges; but his heart was not in it. He was much more excited by Gothic, or Old English, or Welsh, or (as we shall see) Finnish, after finding a Finnish grammar in his college library a month into his first term. The one exception to Tolkien's uninterest in his official course of study was the optional paper he took; from a list of possible choices, he settled on Comparative Philology of Greek and Latin. We shall look at this in more detail below; but the choice both saved Tolkien's university career and further influenced, if it did not quite determine (his intellectual bent was already to a good degree settled), the future course of his life. We shall come to all this, however, in its proper place.

II – 'Settling in'

The first year at university is for most undergraduates a time of discovery and of adjustment: discovery of one's own interests and limitations, both of which are probably wider than was apparent in the narrow space of school; and adjustment to these facts, and to the freedom of managing one's own timetable and budget. All this is tricky enough, but must be further balanced with the need to follow a determined course of study. This imperative is stronger in some than in others: many Oxford under-graduates in Tolkien's day, as indeed later, had no especial need or desire for academic distinction, and were happy to read for a Pass degree, or for lesser Honours, whilst diverting themselves in the numerous heady ways open to youth gathered for the first time without parental or in-loco-parental supervision (dons, emphatically, are not schoolmasters) and with money or at least credit to hand. Many a promising academic career has come to shipwreck when a young scholar has been drawn onto the rocks of distraction by the siren's song of society, drink and old money. Oxford is curiously prone to giving an exposure to these things to those who may have the taste for them without the permanent means to satisfy it. For a man like Tolkien, however, whose whole bent was evidently to scholarship, and who was moreover financially dependent on an award, his Exhibition, which might be withdrawn by the College if his work fell below par, much of what was on offer was pure distraction; for him, the imperative to balance fun with work, and a good deal of it, was much stronger. Nevertheless it was one that Tolkien sat light to for his first few terms at Oxford. Apart from anything else, without the discipline of compelled early rising (he had, remember, been in the habit of serving or hearing Fr Francis's Mass before school), he found sleep stole away an altogether disproportionate part of his day. Tolkien, like many others before and since, blamed the Oxford climate for his lethargy, but we may suspect late nights, beer and wine, and lack of compulsion to be the more likely culprits.

Some of his activities were continuations of those he had enjoyed at school; he founded a dining-and-debate society, the Apolausticks ('those given to self-indulgence') in that first term, together with other freshmen; and trialled for the College rugby XV (he was not quite good, or heavy, enough for a regular place, but seems to have turned out for them occasionally). Other activities were comparative new departures: town-and-gown scuffles, hide and seek with the Proctors (the university police, who had the unending and thankless task of keeping the undergraduates out of Oxford's pubs) and that Oxford perennial, roof-climbing. This was not exactly usual behaviour for a poor man on an Exhibition who hoped to make his life in scholarship.

But Tolkien was unusual for a scholar in at least one other visible way: he was careful of his clothes and enjoyed good pictures. He bought hand-made suits and some Japanese prints for his rooms, and was pleased by the effect. Tolkien was never an aesthete in the dressy, late Victorian sense, nor in its Edwardian iteration, of a prurient, sexually ambivalent litterateur; but he was certainly aesthetically sensitive to a degree, and liked good clothes and pictures. He would never be Des Esseintes, or Aubrey Beardsley; but there was something in him of the delicate humour and attention of Max Beerbohm, say. He could hardly afford to be a full-blown dandy, but was and remained throughout his life notably well dressed in an understated way.

After the OTC at school, Tolkien clearly wanted to retain some connexion with military matters; at the end of his first term, he enlisted in King Edward's Horse, a yeomanry (volunteer cavalry) regiment open to those born in the colonies. He was Trooper no. 1624. Choosing this regiment must have been a conscious decision; they were based in London, not Oxford. They had originally been raised – as the King's Colonials (4th County of London Imperial Yeomanry) – in 1901, from men originally from the colonies now living in London, as part of the great expansion of yeomanry (mounted volunteers) for the South African War, although they were too late to see action. After the death of Edward VII, they took the name King Edward's Horse (the King's Oversea Dominions Regiment).

He did not lose touch with his schoolfriends; if anything, his closeness to some of them increased. Rob Gilson, as secretary of the King Edward's School Musical and Dramatic Society, organized a production of *The Rivals*; Tolkien was prevailed upon to come down from Oxford that December to take the part of Mrs Malaprop. Several other parts were played by members of the TCBS – Wiseman, Gilson, T.K. Barnsley and G.B. Smith. This seems to have been Smith's first real entry into the TCBS 'inner circle'. Most of Tolkien's TCBS friends were a year or two below him at school; they did not go to university until that autumn, or the one after.[1] For a while, then, Tolkien's social life was as much directed to Birmingham as to Oxford.

Vincent Trought had been ill for some months, and had gone to

Cornwall for his health; on 20 January 1912, he died. Tolkien learnt too late to travel down for the funeral.

In the new year, as his second term opened, Tolkien started to attend tutorials in his Special Paper, Comparative Philology; for this, he was taught by the Professor of Comparative Philology, Joseph Wright, who took a Germanic delight in teaching undergraduates at odds with the usual Oxford approach (where tutoring is done by fellows of the Colleges, and professors reserve themselves for lecturing and research students). Wright was also, as we may remember, author of the Gothic primer Tolkien had owned since he was a schoolboy.

We have little other evidence for what Tolkien did this year; the Apolausticks met regularly, to discuss literary subjects and, from time to time, to eat elaborate dinners. He also seems to have taken part in the Stapeldon Society, the established College debating body. There were probably other activities that have left no record; and he did play, occasionally, for the College XV. He did some work, but spent most of his intellectual energy on extraneous linguistic matters – Welsh, Finnish, Old English and Gothic. College libraries, and the library of the Taylorian, then as now contain enough to distract the intellectual magpie from regular, and apparently tedious, courses of study. During Trinity (summer) Term, he was warned he might lose his Exhibition if his academic performance did not improve. He made some effort to this end, but his heart was not in it. He later blamed 'Old Norse, festivity, and classical philology' for his neglect of his course.[2]

As a schoolboy, and ward of an Oratorian Father, Tolkien had been diligent to the point of rigour in performing his religious duties. Day had as often as not begun with Mass. At Oxford, away from this framework, he had begun to slacken. Again, we do not have detail, and may be looking at little more than occasional oversleeping leading to his once or twice missing Sunday Mass; but it was indicative, or Tolkien felt it to be so, of a general lethargy and dissipation of energy and purpose, enough to generate guilt without provoking reformation.

At some point, probably during the Easter vacation, he again visited his aunt Jane in St Andrews, and wrote there a poem, 'The Grimness of the Sea'.[3]

In the summer of 1912, Tolkien began a poem, a 'fragment of an epic', titled 'Before Jerusalem Richard Makes an End of Speech'; this was an uncharacteristic subject for Tolkien, who seems to have had no more than an ordinary English schoolboy's interest in the Crusades (presumably drawn, like so much else, from *Ivanhoe* and Henty), and was very probably meant as an entry for the Newdigate Prize that year, whose set subject was 'Richard before Jerusalem'.[4] He also went on a walking tour of Berkshire at the end of August, staying around Lambourn, painting and drawing.

III – Edith

Edith, meanwhile, had made a life for herself in Cheltenham. The family friends she lived with, the Jessops, had a large house and a comfortable life. Edith was socially active, in particular in the local Anglican church. She had always been an accomplished pianist, and now took great pleasure playing the organ at her parish church. During this time she injured her back whilst playing the organ; she never fully recovered.

Tolkien had not forgotten her; whilst staying with his Incledon cousins for Christmas 1912, he wrote a play for them all to perform, a light-hearted piece turning on the trials of an heiress living in hiding in a lodging house, who has fallen in love with a penniless undergraduate whom she can marry when she turns twenty-one, two days after the action on the play opens, if her father does not discover her first. Tolkien took the part of the consulting detective hired to find her and prevent the marriage.[5] That the Edith-character was presented as an heiress may be of mild interest; we have seen how, by the terms of her father's will, she had inherited property around Birmingham. It may be that this, to her, was a detail that set her apart from her otherwise unremarkable background; it might, in fact, be thought of as her version of Tolkien's 'Saxon nobility' ancestor-myth. Whilst she might, outwardly, be an orphan of uncertain parentage living in a lodging-house, in reality she was an heiress to a fortune. Many people in adolescence and early youth nurture, I suspect, such comforting illusions, which serve to make the disagreeable aspects of their lives mere temporary and unfortunate disguise, cloaking their real nature. If pressed, they would not insist on them, or indeed volunteer them unprompted, and, at some level, these things are known to be fiction; but they are comforting fictions, and so are privately kept up, and shared only with intimates, and then as great secrets.

At midnight on 3 January 1913, Tolkien turned twenty-one. He at once sat down and wrote to Edith, asking her when they might be reunited. She told him by return that she had got engaged to the brother of a schoolfriend; she had lost hope that Tolkien would still love her. As soon as he could, Tolkien went to Cheltenham to see her; on 8 January, she broke off her engagement and agreed to marry him instead. Her family were unhappy at his apparent lack of prospects, and more so at his Catholicism, particularly as he insisted that a reluctant Edith should herself convert. She resisted, but Tolkien was insistent and she gave in. At this time, the Catholic Church was very discouraging of 'mixed marriages' between a Catholic and a non-Catholic Christian, although they inevitably remained frequent. As well as promising to ensure any children were brought up Catholic, the Catholic party in such marriages was enjoined to work to convert the non-Catholic. Moreover, a 'mixed marriage' might never be celebrated in the context of a full Nuptial Mass, but only in an abbreviated and grudging ceremony of its own. Unity in religious practice within a marriage is surely important; but it is dangerous to think it can be imposed. When Edith told the Jessops that she meant to become a Catholic, she was told to find somewhere else to live. Mr Jessop ('Uncle Jessop' to Edith) wrote to Edith's guardian,

> I have nothing to say against Tolkien, he is a cultured gentm., but his prospects are poor in the extreme, and when he will be in a position to marry I cannot imagine, had he adopted a Profession it would have been different.[6]

We may wonder whether he said anything in addition about Tolkien's religion; but if he did, it has not been recorded. In June, together with an older cousin, Edith moved to Warwick and found lodgings there. Her cousin, Jennie Grove, was at that time forty-nine years old; owing to a childhood accident, she had only ever reached four foot eight in height. She was the closest Edith had to a mother-figure. Edith was to live in Warwick, with Jennie Grove, until 1916; Tolkien frequently visited her there, and their romance shed, for him, an enchantment over the town, which was to assume a prominent role in his early writings.

Tolkien also wrote to Francis Morgan, telling him that he and Edith had renewed their connexion and were engaged. He was very apprehensive of his reaction; but Fr Francis's reply was patiently accepting, if not enthusiastic. Tolkien still relied on him for supplemental funds, but his primary motive in telling him was a sense of duty. Apart from him, however, Tolkien told no one; the engagement was to be a secret, for a while at least. It is tempting to suppose that this was a function of embarrassment or half-heartedness on one side or another, but it is likely to have had a more practical explanation: money. Tolkien was still a poor student, with only a tiny income in his own right; he could certainly not plan marriage until he had a job or at least prospects of one. He promised Edith he would study hard so as to make an academic job a real possibility; there is no evidence he ever thought of any other career.

Resolutions aside, he continued to find his time at Oxford agreeable. In the autumn of 1912, Wiseman and Gilson had both gone up to Cambridge; this would have further weakened Tolkien's social ties to his old school and to Birmingham in general.

As we have seen, he had thrown himself into college social life, but found the work frankly dull. He had trouble maintaining interest in Greek dramas he had read at school and already knew as well as he cared to. He was easily distracted onto intellectual (mostly linguistic) bypaths. The one exception to this was the optional paper he took in Comparative Philology. For this, as we saw, he was taught by the remarkable Joseph Wright.

Wright was a Yorkshireman, and had been a mill-hand, who had gone to work aged six to support his mother and two brothers (his father had gone away). He taught himself to read aged fifteen, then at night-school learnt Latin, French and German; aged twenty-one, he walked to Heidelberg to spend his savings on a term's study at the University. After six weeks, he returned to England and spent six years as a schoolmaster, taking correspondence courses from London University, before returning to Heidelberg. This time, he stayed and took a doctorate in philology. He also studied at Leipzig and Freiberg, and edited and translated German books. He returned to England in 1888 and moved to Oxford. In 1891, aged thirty-six, he was appointed deputy to Max Müller, Professor of Comparative Philology; two years later he succeeded to the chair. Müller had been Professor since 1868, in a chair created for him after he was controversially defeated in the 1860 election to the Chair of Sanskrit; in 1875, in a fit of pique after the University offered an honorary doctorate to his successful rival for the Sanskrit chair, he wanted to resign, but was persuaded to stay on as nominal Professor with a deputy to do the actual work. Wright was the last of these deputies. Müller was notorious for describing mythology as 'a disease of language', a theory Tolkien later criticized;[7] Müller's 1888 Gifford Lectures, on natural religion, were described by the Provost of the Catholic cathedral in Glasgow, Mgr Alexander Munro, as 'a crusade against divine revelation, against Jesus Christ and Christianity'. Müller's alleged religious views (he was in fact a broad church Lutheran) had been a factor in his rejection for the Sanskrit chair in 1860.

IV – Philology

It is unlikely that anyone at a British university today will have heard of philology, let alone studied it, under that name at least. During the late nineteenth century, however, it was one of the most exciting and innovative areas of scholarship. Even today, it is a splendid intellectual adventure.

So, what is philology? It is both a prolegomenon and an essential companion to literary study. It tries to answer some basic questions: how can we discuss what a text says, what an author might have meant, unless we know as much as we can about the meaning and resonance of the words he used? But what can we know of the meaning of languages all of whose speakers are long dead, and which perhaps survive only in fragments? We can know much, philology argues, by using the comparative method. This is widely agreed to have been begun by an English polyglot, Sir William Jones, who in 1786 declared that the similarities between Sanskrit, Greek and Latin were too close and too systematic to be coincidence; they must be related to some common ancestor, from which the Germanic and Celtic languages also stemmed. During the nineteenth century, a series of tremendous (mostly German) pundits explored and systematized this observation, and discovered clear and predictable relations between almost all European languages both extant and extinct, as well as some languages of the Indian subcontinent and of places in between. There were a number of fascinating corollaries to these studies. First, the very regularity of relations between languages, which could be codified as 'laws', meant that words that no longer survived could be hypothesized with a high degree of accuracy; second, language itself became historical evidence.

Hypothetical word-forms, typically earlier and more 'primitive' than those which survive, are when written down by convention prefixed with an asterisk; the resulting language might be called an 'asterisk language'. English *father*, for example, is paralleled by Latin *pater* (Greek πατήρ) and Sanskrit *pitar*, besides the German *vater*, Old Norse *faðir*, Gothic *fadar* and others; this suggests a 'Common Germanic' form *fadēr*, derived from an Indo-European **pətēr*. All the 'Germanic' forms share the same initial change of /p/ to /f/ found, for instance, also in English *fish* besides Latin *piscis*.

Now, a word always refers to something; so if, for instance, all the Germanic languages use related words for 'birch tree', we may reliably conclude that speakers of their hypothetical common ancestor language ('proto-Germanic'), whoever wherever and whenever they were, lived somewhere where birch trees grew. From thousands of similar pieces of evidence, we may construct a picture of the society and culture where an unattested, but historically certain, language was spoken. An asterisk language (what Tolkien once called 'star-spangled grammar') thus leads to what Tom Shippey has christened an asterisk reality. Shippey explains further:

> The thousands of pages of 'dry as dust' theorems about language-change, sound-shifts and ablaut-gradations were, in the minds of most philologists, an essential and natural basis for far more exciting speculations about the wide plains of 'Gothia' and the hidden, secret trade routes across the primitive forests of the North, *Myrkviðr inn ókunni*, the 'pathless Mirkwood' itself.[8]

There was even, famously, a piece of synthetic literature written in Proto-Indo-European, or scholars' then best guess at it. It was a folktale, confected in 1868 by the German philologist August Schleicher, and known as *Schleicher's Fable*. In its earliest form, it ran

Avis akvāsas ka

Avis, jasmin varnā na ā ast, dadarka akvams, tam, vāgham garum vaghantam, tam, bhāram magham, tam, manum āku bharantam. Avis akvabhjams ā vavakat: kard aghnutai mai vidanti manum akvams agantam. Akvāsas ā vavakant: krudhi avai, kard aghnutai vividvant-svas: manus patis varnām avisāms karnauti svabhjam gharmam vastram avibhjams ka varnā na asti. Tat kukruvants avis agram ā bhugat.

But within a few years, Schleicher's professional colleagues and rivals had suggested various emendations and produced various revised versions. A century and a half later, it now looks like this:

H₂óu̯is h₁ék̂u̯ōs-kʷe

[Gʷr̥h̥ₓéi] h₂óu̯is, kʷési̯o u̯lh₂néh₄ ne (h₁é) est, h₁ék̂u̯ons spék̂et, h₁oinom ghe gʷr̥h̥ₓúm u̯óĝhom u̯éĝhontm̥ h₁oinom-kʷe ĝ méĝh̥m bhórom, h₁oinom-kʷe ĝhménm̥ h̥ₓók̂u bhérontm̥. h₂óu̯is tu h₁ék̂u̯oibh(i̯)os u̯euk̇ʷét: 'k̂ếr h̥eghnutór moi h₁ék̂u̯ons h̥éĝontm̥, h̥nérm̥ u̯idn̥téi. h₁ék̂u̯ōs tu u̯euk̇ʷónt: 'k̂ludhí, h₂óu̯ei, k̂ếr ghe h̥eghnutór n̥sméi u̯idn̥tbh(i̯)ós. h̥nér, pótis, h₂éu̯i̯om r̥ u̯lh₂néh̥m sebhi kʷr̥néuti nu gʷhérmom u̯éstrom néĝhi h₂éu̯i̯om u̯l̥h₂néh̥ h₁ésti.' Tód k̂ek̂luu̯ốs h₂óu̯is h̥éĝrom bhugét.⁹

Each of these means, more or less,

The sheep and the horses

[On a hill,] a sheep that had no wool saw horses, one of them pulling a heavy wagon, one carrying a big load, and one carrying a man quickly. The sheep said to the horses: 'My heart pains me, seeing a man driving horses.' The horses said: 'Listen, sheep, our hearts pain us when we see this: a man, the master, makes the wool of the sheep into a warm garment for himself. And the sheep has no wool.' Having heard this, the sheep fled into the plain.

In recent years, Indo-European philology of a technical stamp has become unattractively wedded to diacritics, superscripts and subscripts, and similar typographical horrors.[10]

Returning to Tolkien's day, we might consider the example of Jacob Grimm, who (with his brother Wilhelm) collected and published the *Kinder- und Hausmärchen* (better known as *Grimms' Fairy Tales*). Both Grimm brothers were distinguished academics; Jacob is, in philological circles, equally famous as the author of the monumental *Deutsche Grammatik* and the deviser of 'Grimm's Law', which expresses the regular consonant changes that operate to mark the Germanic languages from their Indo-European cognates. He also wrote a comprehensive *Deutsche Mythologie* analysing the remains of pagan belief across the extant Germanic cultures, making a synthesis from hints and etymologies as much as from surviving legends. He and his brother not only collaborated on the *Hausmärchen*, but also began the great *Deutsches Wörterbuch*, a historical dictionary of the German language on so vast a scale that it was not finished until 1961. This combination of austere philological expertise with an interest in collecting and synthesizing the near-lost fragments of his ancestors' mythology made Grimm, for Tolkien, an emblematic and inspiring figure. He is as close as anyone to a model for the sort of scholar Tolkien was to become.

The late years of the nineteenth century saw a profusion of books and articles claiming to describe the culture and beliefs of the speakers of the languages scholarship had recovered. Some of these early studies seem, now, fanciful or unrealistic; but the attempt itself remains, surely, both valuable and fascinating.[11] Tolkien began to apply exactly this technique to his own invented languages; the search for a context for them was at the heart of his maturing imagined world.

All of this was in the background of Tolkien's mind in these years, and lay behind the teaching of Joseph Wright; but we should not think that Tolkien was wholly studious; in fact, as we have seen, he was for his first four terms at Oxford if anything rather slack. He read widely, but much of what he read was unrelated to his prescribed course of study. Notably, in his first term he found a Finnish grammar in his college library, and was immediately bowled over by the language; he described the experience as like discovering a hidden cellar full of 'amazing wine of a kind and flavour never tasted before'.[12] He had read the *Kalevala* – Elias Lönnrot's nineteenth-century epic-length synthesis of orally transmitted Finnish mythological poems – in his last year at school, in Kirby's English version, done into what will forever be known as 'Hiawatha metre' (after it was used by Longfellow in his poem of that name, although it is in fact the closest English analogue to the metre of the Finnish original);[13] hitherto, he had met Finnish itself only in the *Kalevala*'s proper names. He now lost himself in the language – 'I at once made a wild assault on the stronghold of the original language [of the *Kalevala*] and was repulsed with heavy losses';[14] although he never achieved more than a slow reading knowledge of Finnish, the language – its sounds and structures – became the touchstone of his developing linguistic aesthetic. He abandoned work on 'Naffarin' (and also, he said years later, on 'an "unrecorded" Germanic language': this is 'Gautisk', which probably aimed at reproducing the language of the Geats of *Beowulf* fame[15]), and began to devise a 'private language' based on Finnish. This was eventually named Qenya. Not that all his distractions were scholarly; he was highly sociable, and took a full and lively part in the various concerts, drinks parties, dining clubs and literary societies at his college. He also spent a fortnight with King Edward's Horse in camp near Folkestone in the summer of 1912; he enjoyed the riding, although it was on a succession of intractable horses, and the weather was foul; oral tradition claims he was a natural horseman, and was given a string of difficult mounts to break them in.[16] He was also less diligent about the practice of his religion than he had been as a schoolboy. He was both living slightly beyond his means and, in fact, apart from philology, doing little more work than was absolutely required. In the Trinity Term of 1912, as we saw, the college authorities told him he must do better, or risk losing his Exhibition. He buckled down to work, eventually, but not until the new year.

In February 1913, after four terms of agreeable and educative coasting, and a month after the excitements of his reunion with Edith, Tolkien sat his first public examination, Honour Moderations, and was placed in the Second Class. This was not disastrous, but as an Exhibitioner of his college he was expected to do better. He did particularly badly in his paper on Tacitus, in Latin verse composition and in translating Virgil; whilst his Latin prose and Greek verse compositions were so scruffily written as to be almost unreadable. This suggests that, perhaps surprisingly, it was the rigorously linguistic papers (composition in and translation from the classical languages) that were his weakest point, whilst his essays on literary subjects were acceptable.[17] His tutors, fortunately, were not fools; they noted he had obtained a pure alpha in his Comparative Philology paper (a combination of natural aptitude and the teaching of Joseph Wright), which in fact saved him from being placed in the Third Class (which would probably have meant the loss of his Exhibition, and thus the end of his Oxford career), and suggested he transfer to the English School (that is, begin a wholly new course of study) the following term. The college authorities generously allowed him to transfer his Exhibition, which was strictly for the study of Classics, to this new School. He resigned from King Edward's Horse at the end of the month.[18]

V – English at Oxford

The Oxford English School had been founded only twenty years previously, and was still the object of disdain from the more old-fashioned proponents of more serious subjects (such as Classics). English literature, surely, was something that gentlemen read in their spare time, rather than a proper academic exercise. It was one of the strengths of the philological approach to English that it countered such critics, showing that English might involve proper rigour and discipline, rather than being an excuse for undirected chatter about novel-reading (Tolkien, indeed, never really thought contemporary writing had much place in an academic curriculum). Nevertheless, there was still an air of the comparatively unfocussed: one near contemporary, who like Tolkien came to English after reading Classics, detected in his fellow English students, in comparison with his previous peers, 'a certain amateurishness'. The demographic of the English School was an unusual one, for Oxford at this date at any rate; the same observer noted his fellows were mostly 'women, Indians, and Americans'.[19] Women were not accepted for most of the undergraduate Schools, and English was one of the few subjects for which dedicated teaching was available; whilst the presence of 'Indians' may be explained in part by the decision, in 1855, made by the Indian Civil Service, the most prestigious of all Imperial careers, to include English literature amongst the subjects required for its famously demanding examinations. At another level, of course, all of these were groups excluded by sex or geography from the intensive study of the classical languages that was the enduring backbone of English schooling. Male Englishmen tended to come to the English School after (at least) Classical Moderations. At this date, the School of English Language and Literature was still only a subordinate division of the School of Modern Languages. Despite this, the School had been home to some remarkable scholars.

Its oldest professorial chair was the Rawlinsonian Chair of Anglo-Saxon, established in 1795; it was originally however held only for a fixed term of five years (much like the Professorship of Poetry, although unlike the latter it was not filled by popular election), until the election of Joseph Bosworth in 1858.

The founder of the chair, Richard Rawlinson, was a Non-Juror (one, that is, who refused to take the oath of allegiance to William of Orange and his successors after James II was deposed in 1688, and was thus barred from public office) and a man of formidable and eclectic learning, and equally formidable prejudices. He left a substantial collection of manuscripts and other materials to the Bodleian Library (the manuscripts alone ran to 5,000 items) and property to endow a chair of Anglo-Saxon, which was however not open to Irishmen or Scotsmen, to inhabitants of the Plantations (by which he meant the American and West Indian colonies) or to Fellows of the Royal Society and the Society of Antiquaries, with both of which learned bodies Rawlinson had had fallings-out. It was not until 1795, forty years after Rawlinson's death, that the chair was first filled; for the next sixty years it was held by a series of amateurs of Anglo-Saxon studies, whose expertise in the field was not always clear and whose publications were generally meagre. Only the last of the series, John Earle, Fellow of Oriel and a prolific if unscientific editor of Old English texts, made any real contribution to Old English studies. Three others – John Josias Conybeare, Thomas Silver and James Ingram – published on the subject, but not to any especial acclaim; Conybeare's posthumous *Illustrations of Anglo-Saxon Poetry*, in particular, was the object of immediate and corrosive criticism.

Bosworth, a rural clergyman of private means (he added to Rawlinson's original endowment, and also gave £10,000 to establish a comparable chair at Cambridge) and an Anglo-Saxonist of considerable achievement (his *Anglo-Saxon Dictionary*, albeit revised, is still a standard text), held the chair until his death in 1876, after which it was held again by John Earle. Earle held the post until his death in 1903, aged almost eighty.

Bosworth and Earle were both old-style Anglo-Saxonists, clergyman dons of varied enthusiasms with no more than amateur linguistic competence. This was very different from the approach taken by Arthur Napier, who in 1885 was the first holder of a newly created Merton Chair in English Language and Literature. Napier's early training was in industrial chemistry (he was heir to a Lancashire cotton-spinning magnate, whose wife came from a family of Staffordshire pottery makers), but after he heard Earle and Max Müller lecture at Oxford, his studies at Göttingen had been diverted into philology under the great Anglo-Saxonist Julius Zupitza, and he soon stood high amongst German-trained English philologists. He exemplified the German approach to the subject: thoroughly professional, strictly limited to philological technicality (excluding, that is, anything perceived as literary or historical, not as lacking interest, but as the proper field of other scholars in whose preserves he did not wish to poach), outwardly dessicate. He was unanimously elected to the new chair, despite the efforts of Henry Sweet to get the job.

Sweet, reputed model for Shaw's Henry Higgins, was embittered by this failure. He was both chronically shy and diffident, and overweeningly confident in his own abilities (which were very considerable), and was on occasion given to impolitic bluntness: a combination designed to prevent advancement at Oxford, even for one of his obvious talent and

European reputation. He developed what Shaw called 'a Satanic contempt for all academic dignitaries'. His achievements might not be denied, however: he had written several pioneering works on phonetics and language teaching, as well as producing primers and editions of texts; his famous *Anglo-Saxon Reader* first appeared in 1876, when Sweet was thirty-one, and, only lightly revised, remains in use as an undergraduate textbook almost a century and a half later. His first major work, an edition of the Alfredian *Cura Pastoralis*, appeared in 1871 when he was a (comparatively elderly) undergraduate: he had won a Balliol scholarship aged twenty-four, after five years working in an office. The edition had at once become standard, and was recognized as fundamental for the study of Old English dialect. Unlike most of his English philological contemporaries, Sweet was keen to retain intellectual independence from German scholarly trends, and sought to establish a peculiarly English school of philology; but in this, his difficult personality proved an unsurmountable barrier.

Sweet was made Reader in Phonetics (another, but more junior, salaried post) in 1901 as a belated and inadequate compensation for his earlier failure. He died in 1912, aged sixty-seven; there is no reason to suppose he and Tolkien ever met, although it is possible. Sweet does however illustrate the vigour and diversity of English philology at Oxford in these years.

It fell to Napier to try to establish a proper School of English, rather than a series of unconnected lectures with no corresponding syllabus, ability to award degrees, or indeed undergraduates to take them. He had strictly limited success; a Final Honour School of Modern Languages was established in 1894, with English as one of its branches, but no preliminary course, meaning that anyone coming up 'to read English' would have to follow another course for Honour Moderations, or read for the less prestigious Pass Moderations, and only thereafter transfer into the School proper.

Napier was in time a pluralist: he was elected to the Anglo-Saxon chair on Earle's death, but mostly so the emoluments attached to the job could pay for another Merton chair, provided for by statute but not funded. This was given to Walter Raleigh, a 'literary' scholar par excellence, who soon brought in his former assistant, David Nichol Smith, as Reader. Napier allowed Raleigh some leeway in designing a syllabus; from the start, then, the School's character as a home of pure philology was compromised. From 1908, at Raleigh's suggestion, the syllabus was divided into literary and linguistic options, with medieval literature largely identified with the second of these. This was in part Napier's fault: he, and his predecessors, treated early texts as documents illustrative of linguistic forms and developments, rather than things written, and designed to be read, for pleasure and instruction. This was to make an effective split in the primary sense of 'philology', which now became shorthand for purely technical study rather than the apprehension of texts as a whole.

Napier was a fiercely diligent and accurate scholar, whose energies were devoted to lecturing, supervising graduate students and (unusually for Oxford at that time) running classes for interested undergraduates; ill-health marked his last years in post, and this, together with his teaching load and an obstinate perfectionism (in which he was encouraged by Henry Bradley of the *Oxford English Dictionary*, or *OED*), prevented him from completing, and certainly from publishing, much of his own research. He was also firmly convinced that his own competence as Anglo-Saxon Professor should be confined to technical matters of philology, establishing the texts of older works, examining their language and explaining their plain meaning; the question of integrating this technical philology with literary studies Napier did not consider any of his business, and would refer his students, if they were curious about such things, to (usually) W.P. Ker.

Ker, a polyglossic Scot of formidable reading and comparatively sparse publication (although he did issue several semi-popularized works of enduring value), was, for most of his working life, Quain Professor at University College London; but he also kept a fellowship at All Souls', and was invariably in Oxford at weekends and on odd days. His books *Epic and Romance* and *The Dark Ages* can still be read with profit after the space of a century; they were almost unique, in English at least, as assuming the primary value of early texts to be unquestionably literary; but it was literary judgement backed by profound knowledge of the texts' numerous languages. Their breadth of sympathetic analysis, and fine and accurate insight into a remarkable range of texts in dozens of languages, are still wondrous, and can stand unashamed even after generations of further scholarship; for their day, they were prodigious.

The Dark Ages, in particular, is almost a primer of some of the themes that Tolkien was to develop in years to come, and a handbook of the sources on which he drew: the 'northern theory of courage', whose classic formulation ('defeat is no refutation') is in this book; the *Letter of Alexander*, which I shall suggest as a hidden source for at least one element of Tolkien's writing; the whale Fastitocolon, on which he was to write a poem; riddles. Of course, Tolkien will in many cases have known, also, the sources on which Ker in his turn had drawn, so we should be wary of naming him as spiritual father to any of Tolkien's enthusiasms; but what made Ker unusual, unique even, amongst writers on his subject in English was the lyrical and evocative character of his prose, which bears a perduring resonance of great matters unspoken, at the edge of sight or knowledge. Consider this passage, for instance:

> Boethius was fortunate in the time of his life and death, and in the choice of his theme. No other writer commands so much of the past and future. Between the worlds of ancient Greece and modern Europe, he understands not merely their points of contact, the immediate and contemporary turmoil of Germany and Rome; he remembers the early thought of Greece, long before the Stoic and Epicurean professors whom he disliked, and he finds the response to his signals not in the near future only but far off in the distant centuries: it is commonplace, no doubt, but of a sort that finds its way into some of the noblest passages of literature. Boethius is remembered and his words are quoted by Dante in the meeting with Francesca, and again in the closing phrase of the *Paradiso* ... Boethius has been traced in English literature from *Beowulf* to *Hamlet* and *Lycidas* ...[20]

We cannot be certain Tolkien read *The Dark Ages* in this period, but it seems very probable.[21] Another likely influence, Ker's *Epic and Romance* (first published in 1896, based on lectures given in the early 1890s), is in great part concerned with the northern heroic temper, especially in its Icelandic exercise; it is a moving and deeply humane effort to synthesize and give context to vastly impressive reading and sympathy. One of Ker's pupils, and later his successor in the London chair, R.W. Chambers, was also to have a great influence on Tolkien.

Arthur Napier was for his last years (from 1905) much supported by a succession of deputies, all former graduate students of his; this was made necessary not just by weak health, but by his simultaneous occupancy of two professorial chairs. This scholarly pluralism, by Ker and Napier both, may seem, to us now, evidence of the dilettantism of Edwardian life, or of a benignly perquisitive view of academic jobs that, today, are fought over by hungry crowds of new-minted doctorands and wild-eyed temporary lecturers, for whom any single tenured post is a prize almost beyond conceiving. But this is to misread the evidence; the truth is that, first, competition for academic jobs was even then fierce, although there were confessedly far fewer people running after them than is now the case; and, second, pluralism most usually happened because one position of itself brought no money, and needed to be backed by the emoluments of another, which however was often not a sinecure. These men worked hard, and often died in harness. We shall see that Tolkien, too, never found his salary adequate to his not extravagant needs.

Lastly, there was Joseph Wright, Professor of Comparative Philology. Wright was the first to come to the job of deputy to Max Müller with an established reputation for scholarship (apart from his extensive doctoral work in Germany, and as a translator of German philological books, he had already begun to publish the series of primers he became best known for – in Middle High German, Old High German and Gothic). Soon after taking the job, he was persuaded to become in addition editor of the proposed *English Dialect Dictionary*, a mammoth work that appeared in six great volumes between 1896 and 1905. The Oxford University Press (OUP) was shy of funding another dictionary, so Wright raised the money himself (by subscription, and from his savings). Until he was fifteen, Wright had himself spoken only in dialect;[22] he was moreover wholly undaunted by a series of financial and administrative obstacles that would have crushed a less robust man. He was without question the perfect man for the job.

This, then, was the School into which Tolkien transferred himself, and which, with some small hiatuses, was to be his professional home for his whole working life. It was utterly unlike what any English School looks like today, even (or especially) at Oxford; indeed, if one of today's undergraduates in English was, by some convenient maguffin, to switch places with his or her equivalent from a century ago, it is unlikely that either would recognize the syllabus as having anything in common with what he or she was used to, to a degree that is not true of history, or Classics, or mathematics even.

Tolkien was set to study a range of Old and Middle English texts: *Beowulf, Finnesburg*, 'Deor', *Exodus, Elene*, some of the shorter poems and all of *Sweet's Anglo-Saxon Reader*. The other source-book, for Middle English, was the two-volume *Specimens of Early English*, edited by Walter Skeat and Richard Morris as early as 1872. This was supplemented by longer poems: *Havelok, Pearl, The Owl and the Nightingale* and the Scots

Tale of Rauf Coilyear. There were also compulsory papers in the history of the language, Gothic and Germanic philology and Chaucer. Tolkien took as his special subject Scandinavian Philology, which meant (mostly) Icelandic texts: the *Prose Edda,* some of the shorter sagas and extracts from *Gylfaginning* and *Völsungasaga.*

What may surprise some who assume in Tolkien both a contempt for and an ignorance of any post-medieval writers, is that he was in addition mandated to take compulsory papers in Shakespeare and the history of English literature. Tom Shippey has on internal evidence made a strong argument for Tolkien having read Shakespeare closely and with occasional sympathy.[23]

Tolkien's tutor was to be Kenneth Sisam, a New Zealander only four years his senior who although only a postgraduate student (a comparatively rare bird in 1913) had already established a formidable reputation as an Anglo-Saxon philologist and who was, besides, a collaborator and protégé of the great liturgical scholar Edmund Bishop. His formal position was assistant to Arthur Napier.

Sisam had come to England aged twenty-three, as New Zealand's sole Rhodes Scholar for the year 1910, and since his first degree was in English, he was assigned to Merton College, where Napier held his professorial fellowship. The following year, Sisam began a B.Litt. thesis supervised by Napier; it was an edition of a Latin Psalter with interlinear Old English glosses, Salisbury MS 150. In this connexion, he wrote with a query to Edmund Bishop, at that time unquestioned head of English (and arguably worldwide) liturgical scholarship. Bishop gave a deprecatory and elliptical answer, to which Sisam, unabashed, replied with care and insight enough to intrigue Bishop and prompt a serious response. They stayed in correspondence, on and off, until Bishop's death aged seventy-one, six years later, by which time Sisam was not just Bishop's disciple-cum-protégé, but was also entrusted with seeing his great collection *Liturgica Historica* through the press. This was a scholarly benediction and (as it were) apostolic succession of rare quality, particularly as Bishop was constitutionally (and irrationally) suspicious of Oxford scholarship.

From the Hilary (spring) Term of 1912, Sisam took on some of the teaching and lecturing responsibilities of Napier's Anglo-Saxon chair. Typically, Sisam would lecture on Sweet's *Anglo-Saxon Reader*, Morris and Skeat's *Specimens*, *Havelok* and historical grammar, with regular forays into other areas of the syllabus. He also, as we have seen, acted as tutor to undergraduates reading for English Final Schools (as the final examinations are known). Tolkien recognized him as an accurate scholar and a diligent tutor; Sisam in turn was impressed enough by his pupil to help him find second-hand books for an embryonic scholar's library, and (as we shall see) several times pointed him towards possible jobs. Their relations began happily at least.

After Sisam finished his B.Litt. in 1915, he worked first for the *Oxford English Dictionary*, then for the University Press. His health was by then very precarious, and prevented both conventional war service and full-time work as Napier's assistant. Instead, from November 1917, he took an office job in London with the Ministry of Food, with eventual respon-sibility for bacon contracts. The vagaries of the scholarly life were as marked then as now.

Tolkien had much to do and to read, and a tutor whose acumen and intolerance of laxity were even then notorious; but he did not turn wholly from frivolity. On the night of 11 May 1913, after an unspecified fracas, he was briefly arrested by the local police, probably for town-and-gown rowdiness rather than anything actually criminal. The following evening, he gave a gleeful account of his adventures to the Stapeldon Society. Later that term he was elected Secretary of the Society for the term following. As at King Edward's, Tolkien combined wide-ranging scholarship with vigorous and high-spirited social activities; but unlike there, he was now responsible for his own budget.

VI – Vacation adventures

In the summer of 1913, woefully short of money, Tolkien found a job acting as tutor to two Mexican boys who were pupils at Stonyhurst, the Catholic public school in Lancashire; his primary duty was to escort them to Paris, where they were to meet two Mexican aunts and spend August there and elsewhere in France on holiday, before term at Stonyhurst began in mid-September. Tolkien's role seems to have been otherwise unde-fined, except (in general terms) as tutor and escort; this sort of job was not unusual in those days. He presumably got the job, which could compe-tently have been done by any undergraduate or even sixth-former, because of his Catholicism; it seems likely that he was put forward by Fr Francis Morgan or another Oratorian connexion. In Paris they were joined by a third, younger, boy, fresh from Mexico, and the brace of aunts, who were (it seems) hard work. Tolkien disliked France and speaking French; he also had to use his uneven Spanish. Philological competence of a high order, we should remember, does not inevitably (or perhaps even often) translate to polyglot fluency in spoken tongues. After a week in Paris, where he was irritated by the constant 'vulgarity and the jabber and the spitting and the indecency',[24]Tolkien went with the boys and the elder of the aunts to Brittany; initially delighted to be going to the home of a Celtic language and a vigorous tradition of folklore (Brittany was largely populated by refugees from late Roman Britain, and the Breton language is closely analogous to Welsh and Cornish), Tolkien was disappointed to find their destination a mere seaside resort. A week into their stay there, the aunt was hit by a motor-car and died. This event naturally blighted the remainder of the month, which Tolkien spent helping to make funeral arrangements and trying, with eventual success, to persuade the surviving aunt not to take the boys back to Mexico at once, but allow them to return to England to complete their schooling. At the end of August, after a frustrating two weeks (his main triumph, aside from making various successful arrangements, seems to have been to introduce the boys to proper schoolboy reading – *King Solomon's Mines, Kim, The White Company*), Tolkien and the boys returned to England, and spent two weeks in Bournemouth. On 15 September, he brought them to London, and the next day put them on the train to Stonyhurst. Never, he wrote to Edith, would he take on such a job again, 'except I am in the direst poverty'.[25]

Tolkien visited Warwick, and Edith, at least twice before term began at Oxford in mid-October. His first full year as an undergraduate in the English School was, also, the last year of old peacetime England.

VII – On the eve

The popular image of these last days of peace is, perhaps, a partial one: long summers, great houses, a monied aristocracy given both to taste and to extravagant display; below them, an infinitesimally graded middle class – from *Howard's End* to *Kipps* and *Mr Polly*, and all stations in between – and, lower yet, a vast and unbeneficed working class, whose lives were governed by poverty, cramp, disease, whose only avenues of (comparative) escape were the Army or domestic service. Not a comprehensive or wholly accurate picture by any means; but its primary inaccuracy is the false impression of stasis. Edwardian England (it is easiest to call it this, even though Edward VII died in May 1910) and contemporary Europe were in a condition of rapid (and, for some, wholly unsettling) change.

British political life had been in turmoil, amounting in some eyes almost to revolution, since the election of a radical Liberal government in 1908; the Prime Minister, H.H. Asquith, and his Chancellor David Lloyd George had introduced a series of social welfare measures and, to pay for them (and for a vastly expensive naval arms race with Germany), a number of taxes on landed property including inheritance taxes. Passed by the Commons but rejected by the Conservative-dominated House of Lords, this 1909 Budget had provoked a constitutional crisis, with threats of the mass creation of peers to overturn the Lords' opposition, and the eventual resignation of the government. Two subsequent General Elections returned Liberal governments (who however relied on Irish Nationalist support), and led to the 1911 Parliament Act, establishing the supremacy of the Commons by allowing it to ignore opposition by the Lords to anything declared to be government business. The price of Nationalist support was Irish Home Rule; passed in 1912, but delayed for two years by the Lords' opposition, it was due to come into effect in 1914. The largely Protestant province of Ulster began to organize for armed resistance to Home Rule; significant elements in the Army signalled they would resign rather than obey orders to suppress an Ulster rebellion.

Other European polities were not so inclined to change: all the great autocracies (Germany, Russia, Austria-Hungary) had some-thing approximating to parliaments, which their respective emperors were however prone, at a pinch, to suspend and instead rule by decree. Prussian-led Germany had been united since 1871, born out of the defeat and humiliation of Second Empire France, and was strongly marked both by militarism and by technologically advanced and efficient industry. German scholarship, not just in philology, was justly renowned and emulated; political opposition from Marxist social democrats was neutered by a comprehensive system of social welfare. Meanwhile Austria, Prussia's defeated rival for supremacy in the Germanies, was a patchwork of ethnic and cultural diversity uncertainly bound together by the venerable figure of Franz Josef, but hamstrung by a fractious and insistent Hungarian minority who had engineered a constitution that established in law both their own particularism and their ability to suppress the rights of other ethnicities, and by a recently and unwisely acquired province of volatile Bosnians with ambitions to join neigh-bouring Serbia. Whilst Germany and Austria-Hungary were industrially and culturally highly advanced, and life there was by and large good,

Russia, on the other hand, still had a vast population of peasant farmers tied to an inefficient medieval system of strip farming, and a seething urban proletariat rife with revolutionary activity and prolific of bomb plots and assassination attempts. Defeat in the 1905 war against Japan had spurred a bloody revolution. Thereafter, the Tsar's first minister, Pyotr Stolypin, had tried to implement land reform to create a class of smallholders who would form a barrier to revolution; but in 1911 he was shot and killed whilst at the opera, and the reforms stalled. Nevertheless Russia was beginning to emerge from its habitual backwardness, and there, too, high culture flourished.

At the other end of the spectrum France was, still, mired in the furious and historically bloody rivalries of its nineteenth century: monarchical absolutism and militaristic reaction had, for the moment, lost out to militant anticlericalism and socialist experimentalism, but its defeat was not supposed permanent; over all, the shadow of the Franco-Prussian War – Sedan, national humiliation, the Commune – was deep.

This time was the high-water mark of colonial Europe and especially of the British Empire: across the world, a century of (relative) peace policed by the Royal Navy, and scattered garrisons of regular soldiers; at home, despite the encroachments of income tax and death duties, the great and middling estates of the nobility and gentry still gave a frame-work to rural life in particular, and enabled, for their owners, a leisured existence that, in retrospect, seems both idyllic and difficult to credit. It is (for instance) constantly in the background of most of Buchan's stories, those at least that are not set in an exclusively Scottish context; yet amidst the country house visiting and the taking of shooting and fishing, there is also (for Buchan's characters, at least, and Buchan was an excellent mimic of his adopted class) an expectation of soldiering, or colonial administration, or politics, often hand-in-hand with the Bar. Leisure did not mean inactivity, or irresponsibility.

Yet there had been disquiet abroad for decades. A series of sharp and bloody Balkan wars had been fought between the new states of southern Europe – Serbia, Greece, Bulgaria, Montenegro – and the decaying Ottoman Empire, now shedding the last of its European possessions; the victors soon fell to fighting amongst themselves. In the background, uneasy about spheres of influence and national minorities, was the other old polyglot Empire, Austria-Hungary, also gradually whittled down from its previous extent, and its bumptious and expansionist rival, Russia, keen to use Slav nationalism as a vehicle for its own efforts. Russia was aligned with France, and France in turn, since 1904, had an 'understanding' (the famous *entente cordiale*) with Britain, assuming military and especially naval co-operation in the event of general European war. Austria-Hungary was backed by the new and pushful German Empire, which was busily throwing its weight around in colonial spheres calculated to tread on British toes. Arguably the 1899–1902 Boer War, which had finally brought Tolkien's birthplace under British rule at prodigious expense in blood and treasure, was in one sense a proxy war between Germany and Britain: the Kaiser's government had egged the Boers on to defiance, sold them great quantities of modern arms and allowed the passage of numbers of foreign 'volunteers' to the Boer cause through its own African colonies. Critics of British South African policy at this period, incidentally, although they are right to notice the ambition of the Colonial Office under Joseph Chamberlain and the influence wielded by monied businessmen in the Cape Colony, might do well to remember that the German Empire had, as recently as 1884, established its own vast colony in South-West Africa, which could hardly be seen as anything except a direct challenge to British hegemony in the region, and an invitation to the Boer republics to join an eventual pan-Germanic African bloc stretching from coast to coast and permanently isolating British territory in the south from its possessions elsewhere in the continent. Germany, also, had for the previous decade engaged in a gratuitous and wholly provocative programme of naval construction, building a High Seas Fleet of modern battleships whose sole purpose was to challenge British naval hegemony (Germany had a tiny coastline and comparatively negligible amounts of seaborne and colonial trade).

There was no suspicion of imminent catastrophe, however, when Tolkien returned to Oxford in October 1913 and began a busy year of work; he attended lectures and classes by, amongst others, Sisam, Napier and William Craigie, one of the editors of the *OED*, who was his tutor in Old Icelandic. He was also now joined in Oxford by a junior TCBS-ite colleague, G.B. Smith, who had come up to Corpus (as Corpus Christi College was usually known) on an exhibition with the intention of reading English. He and Tolkien were now much thrown together, and became much closer friends than had ever been the case at school. He was probably Tolkien's accomplice in an undergraduate 'rag' which involved hijacking a bus and driving it up Cornmarket followed by a crowd, which Tolkien then addressed. Clearly scholarship was not a wholly consuming activity.[26]

73

Towards the end of the calendar year, Tolkien wrote to tell his TCBS friends (or at least Wiseman and Gilson – he probably told Smith in person) that he was engaged; he did not tell them Edith's name.[27] He also visited Birmingham and his old school: he was due to open a debate on behalf of the Old Boys, but was taken suddenly ill (Gilson stood in for him); the following day, 16 December, however, Tolkien was recovered enough to captain the Old Boys in a match against the school's First XV. Perhaps he was not wholly well; the school won by a narrow margin. What were now his three closest TCBS accomplices, Wiseman, Smith and Gilson, all also played.

In Warwick, after a short and not wholly satisfactory course of instruction from the local Catholic priest, Edith was received into the Church on 8 January 1914, the first anniversary of her reunion with Tolkien. They then celebrated a formal betrothal in the church of St Mary Immaculate in Warwick. Tolkien does not seem to have said anything further to Francis Morgan, however; Fr Francis was perhaps unaware that Edith had been under instruction in the Faith.

The remainder of the year was devoted to work, and to social life; Tolkien was elected President of the Stapeldon Society, and continued to take an active role in its business. There were several other undergraduate societies that also occupied his evenings; he sometimes also turned out for the College XV. His days were busy with lectures: Napier, and his assistant Sisam, gave the bulk of them (on various Old English texts, and on historical grammar), but Tolkien very likely also heard Craigie on Old Norse (both texts and grammar) and, perhaps, Sir John Rhys on the *Mabinogion*. When, that Hilary Term, he was awarded his college's Skeat Prize for English ('the only prize I ever won (there was only one other competitor)'[28]), he spent the £5 on various verse narratives by William Morris and, to the chagrin of the awarding body, on a Welsh grammar.

He did a good deal of painting in watercolour, especially during the vacation of Christmas 1913, both landscapes and more abstract imagistic works; most were gathered in a sketchbook he called 'The Book of Ishness'.[29] He also revised some poems written originally three or four years before. The penultimate year of a man's undergraduate degree (typically the second of his time in Oxford, although in this case the third) was, and perhaps still is, a time often spent in comparative diversion, even for someone like Tolkien who was hoping for an academic career: the efforts of Honour Moderations were past, and the grand push of Final Schools a year away (which, for a man barely twenty, seems a lifetime), and moreover one was now thoroughly comfortable at Oxford, and could expand into its manifold comforts and sociabilities. At the start of the Long (summer) Vacation, Tolkien went to visit Edith in Warwick.

On 28 June 1914, the heir to the Austro-Hungarian throne, Archduke Franz Ferdinand, made a state visit to Sarajevo, capital of the newly acquired imperial province of Bosnia-Herzegovina, which the Austrians had rashly annexed only six years beforehand. It was a hotbed of Serbian nationalism; one especially virulent group, the Black Hand, consisted of Bosnian Serbs vowed to expel the Austrians by violence, and sponsored by Serbian military intelligence. They took the opportunity of Franz Ferdinand's visit to try to kill him. A bomb attack failed, only wounding bystanders; the Archduke and his wife, after he had given his speech at the Town Hall, insisted on visiting the wounded. On their way back from the hospital, their car took a wrong turning, then stalled outside a delicatessen where one of the would-be assassins, a nineteen-year-old named Gavrilo Princip, had stopped for a bun. Princip emerged, saw the car, and shot them both. They died within minutes, and Europe, bound tight with alliances and elaborately programmed mobilizations dictated by railway timetables, was heading fast for war.

Chapter 3 – War

I – A mythology for England

On 4 August 1914, Britain entered the First World War, in defence of Belgian neutrality, which Germany had breached; Britain found herself ranged alongside France and Russia against the German and Austro-Hungarian Empires. It looked fair to become a war on a vast scale; Britain's small wholly professional army was, in this contest between great masses of European conscripts, quite outmatched (in numbers anyway, although decidedly not in ability to fight), and the government, in the person of the Minister for War, Lord Kitchener, called for volunteers to enlist. Tens of thousands did so at once. Many of Tolkien's friends and contemporaries soon joined up to fight. His schoolfriend T.K. Barnsley's father, Sir John Barnsley, held the rank of Lieutenant Colonel in the Territorials, and was tasked by the city of Birmingham to raise a battalion of volunteers;[1] particular appeal was made to old boys of King Edward's. Barnsley got enough men for three battalions, which became the 14th, 15th and 16th battalions of the Royal Warwicks. Amongst the volunteers were T.K. Barnsley, R.S. Payton and Hilary Tolkien.

Ronald however did not join up, but planned to complete the last year of his degree. This was not from a lack of patriotic feeling, or objection to the war or its aims, although Tolkien refused to join in the widespread vilifying of German culture, which he revered as the fountain-head of philology and as bearer of the northern spirit. Nor did he change his German surname, unlike many from King George V (who now adopted the unexampled 'Windsor') and Prince Louis of Battenberg (subsequently 'Mountbatten') downwards. He may have taken his lead from Joseph Wright, who was so far out of sympathy with anti-Germanism that he tried to start a German-language lending library for wounded German prisoners held in Oxford. But Tolkien was a poor man, engaged to be married and without any obvious prospects except what his mind and learning could bring him. For him, his future required getting a good degree; and so he planned to return to Oxford in October. The war could wait. The day after war was declared, he left for a fortnight's walking holiday in Cornwall with Fr Vincent Reade, whose mother lived locally. Tolkien was overwhelmingly impressed by the rugged coast, and made numerous sketches of the cliffs and coves and bays. The trip over, the last week of August saw him in Warwick again, with Edith.

Some time in September, he went to stay with his aunt, Jane Neave, at her farm at Gedling in Nottinghamshire.[2] On 24 September 1914, he wrote a poem, called 'The Voyage of Éarendel the Evening Star'. This was the first real text of what was to become his life's work, the elaboration of a world-mythology in which his invented languages could be at home. For ease of reference, I refer to this whole body of writing as Tolkien's legendarium.[3] Tolkien later located in this time what he considered a fundamental insight, that language and legend were fundamentally correlated: any language 'depends on the legends which it conveys', which supply the semantic resonance essential for poetically concentrated meaning, just as much as a legend, or body of story, presupposes a language in which it is at home, and out of which, in some senses, it has grown; but these two things, language and legend, are organically linked and may not be separated. Their respective aesthetics are in fact interdependent; any mythology in translation is at once impoverished, although one that retains its original names will preserve at least something.[4]

Amongst the Old English poems Tolkien read at Oxford was *Crist*, a ragbag collection of religious verse, much of it dull stuff, found in the Exeter Book manuscript. Its first section is a series of 'Advent lyrics', based on the 'O Antiphons' of that season. Amongst them, glossing the antiphon *O Oriens* ('O Rising Sun, you are the splendour of eternal life and the sun of justice. O come and enlighten those who live in darkness and in the shadow of death'),[5] is this couplet:

Éalá Éarendel engla beorhtast / ofer middangeard monnum sended

Hail, Éarendel, brightest of angels / over middle-earth sent to men

The word or name *éarendel* intrigued Tolkien. According to the glossaries, it was a star or planet, perhaps Venus the morning star, or Rigel in

Orion; here, it perhaps refers to John the Baptist as herald of Christ, the Sun of Justice.[6] But it was the form of the word that fascinated Tolkien: it was, he thought, both like other Old English words and yet, somehow, of a different and nobler style. Tolkien made a private connexion between this and the mysterious figure of Wade, a legendary voyager in his ship Wingelot; the details of his adventures were long lost.

In his poem, he tried to explore what the word might have actually meant: it is the name of a mariner who pilots his ship across the sky from the west to the light of dawn, hearing the joys and sorrows of the men of earth betweentimes. It is an early work, but in its way remarkable for what it tries to do. We might see a hint of it, if no more, in a passage from Ker's *Dark Ages* commenting on the unaffected mixture of Celtic legend with phrases and themes from scripture: 'So one finds the mystery of Celtic stories illustrated with citations from the Bible; as where in the Arthurian legends the mysterious delivery of captives in an unearthly place beyond the Bridge of Dread is celebrated...with the verses of a spiritual song: "Gawain turned and looked back; and behold, across the river, all the streets of the place were filled with men and women, rejoicing and singing in carol-wise: *The people that sat in darkness have beheld a great light.*"'[7] 'Sat' (from the Breviary) for the usual 'walked' may have fed into Tolkien's image of forsaken and imprisoned exiles.

One of Tolkien's great laments was the absence of any specifically English body of myth and legend, comparable to that collected and synthesized for Germany by Jacob Grimm. First the Norman Conquest, then early industrialization had destroyed beyond recovery all but unmeaning fragments of the great body of legend and heroic story once native to England. By the time anyone thought to write any of it down, most of it had been forgotten. All that was left was 'impoverished chap-book stuff'[8]. No English brothers Grimm came in time; and even if they had, their task would have been immeasurably harder than the Grimms' was. The odd *éarendel* couplet in *Crist* was, Tolkien alleged, one of the few surviving fragments, but almost wholly without a context. What Tolkien was doing here, and what he continued to do throughout his life as a writer, was a form of philological enquiry: he examined the surviving evidence (for now-lost English legends, or fragments of lost or 'invented' languages) and tried to reconstruct what might have lain behind them: the story of Eärendil as it eventually developed (the great mariner who carries a Silmaril into the Uttermost West, to plead for the exiled men and elves in their dark oppression, and who is translated to the heavens as a new star, a sign of hope) is, we might say, the 'asterisk reality' that Tolkien thought best explained the name *éarendel* as it appeared in Old English, and in some few other old northern contexts. It is fair to note, however, that at least one later version of the poem recast it in terms of classical mythology, with Earendel replaced by Phosphorus, the Greek name for the morning star. It is perhaps simplistic, then, to see this as the 'start of the legendarium' in any but an adventitious sense; there was no inevitable progression from here as there was, say, from later tales; but the later tales were able retrospectively to incorporate Earendel with an ease that makes it in hindsight seem inevitable.

As the long vacation came to its end, Tolkien visited Birmingham; he stayed with Francis Morgan at the Oratory for the last Sunday before term, 4 October 1914.[9] Then it was time to begin another academic year.

II – Enlistment deferred

On returning to Oxford, Tolkien moved into a rented house with an undergraduate friend, Colin Cullis, whose health had kept him out of the Army. His college was much reduced by enlistment: only seventy-five undergraduates had come up that term. In their place, part of Exeter was now a barrack for the Oxfordshire and Buckinghamshire Light Infantry and some gunners. The University in wartime was a depleted body; various colleges leased out their buildings to one branch or another of the armed forces, and several University buildings (such as the Examination Schools) were taken over for military use. The usual round of lectures resumed, but in a hole-in-the-corner type of way, with much rescheduling and relocation to out-of-the-way rooms. He now had weekly tutorials with Sisam, and went to lectures by Napier, Craigie and Sir Walter Raleigh. Tolkien was, for a while at least, overcome by remorse and guilt at his decision to resume his degree: 'It is awful. I really don't think I shall be able to go on: work seems impossible.'[10]

He was saved from despair when he discovered he could train with the University OTC whilst completing his degree; this would to some extent replace the basic training he would otherwise have to complete on enlisting. It would also make it very probable he would be granted an officer's commission, rather than (like his brother Hilary) enlisting in the ranks. These distinctions are not trivial even today; in 1914, they were of great moment.[11] Tolkien henceforth spent seven hours a week drilling in the University Parks, as well as listening to lectures on military life, and taking classes on map-reading and signalling. This last was to become Tolkien's especial military skill. The expenditure of time may seem a heavy one; but Tolkien found that regular physical activity gave him more energy, and helped him avoid the endemic lethargy he had come to associate with term-time.

The original Éarendel verses were read to the Exeter College Essay Society in November 1914; Tolkien wrote, perhaps for G.B. Smith, a brief context for the poem, describing Éarendel's voyaging through various climes and adventures: it would be fanciful to consider this as a first 'sketch of the mythology', however.[12] Tolkien wrote another Éarendel poem, 'The Bidding of the Minstrel', over that winter.[13] Tolkien took up this poem several times over the following decade, revising and expanding it. It was also, early in 1915, divided into two parts, perhaps at Smith's suggestion; only the first of these parts has been published, and that only in a late and shortened revision. The original, longer text has never been published, nor has 'The Mermaid's Flute', the second half of the later text.[14]

He also, in light of his continuing enthusiasm for Finnish, began a retelling of the story of Kullervo, taken from the *Kalevala*, in a Morris-inspired medley of prose and verse; the original tale is a bleak, tragic amalgam of heroism, mistaken identity, incest and despair ending in suicide. We should not necessarily take this as an index of Tolkien's mood as much as of his literary taste.[15] Over the previous two years, the hitherto rather nebulous TCBS had shed its outlying members, and become a group of four: Tolkien and Wiseman ('the great twin-brethren'), Gilson and G.B. Smith, who since coming up to Oxford (alone of the TCBS, all of the rest of whom were at Cambridge) in Michaelmas 1913 had become close friends with Tolkien. Prompted by Tolkien and Wiseman, who were convinced of the need for a moral basis for artistic endeavour, their discussions, by letter and in person, gradually assumed a new (or renewed) seriousness.

Wiseman was concerned that the friendship was decaying, stymied by distance and inevitably diverging ideas; Tolkien sought to reassure him that they two, at least, remained united in their conviction that life must have a religious motive and character. For the rest, some things might be differed on, but (Tolkien asserted) some were not negotiable: religion, human love, patriotism and (what seems surprising, even faintly shocking, a century later) a belief in nationalism. A fierce love of country – of England – was for Tolkien utterly basic. His enthusiasm for England was mainly a domestic one, however; he was, he said, 'more and more a convinced Home Ruler'. We do not know whether localism, or religious sympathy for Irish Catholics, was a dominant motive, but it seems likely that both contributed to this shift of opinion.[16] Wiseman reminded Tolkien he had yet to tell him the name of his betrothed. Would his engagement drive out or at least compromise existing close friendships? Although he insisted he abominated the idea of a 'compartmented life' in which Edith and the TCBS were discrete, Tolkien, like many men of his time, and indeed before and since, was never quite sure how to reconcile his romantic life with the claims of male friendship.[17] It hardly needs saying that for the vast majority of Tolkien's contemporaries, this sort of quandary was a function of shyness and all-male schooling rather than latent homosexual feeling.

Most of this, taken in the context of its time, seems unremarkable, and is hardly a profound political or moral manifesto; but it does show Tolkien as a man keenly alive to his age, and to his contemporaries' concerns, and one, also, consciously at odds with some, at least, of them.

On 12 December 1914, the four TCBS friends (Smith and Gilson were already in uniform[18]) met up for a reunion, which they dubbed 'The Council of London'; their talk, that day, was of fundamentals: truth, religion, love, art, patriotic duty. Again, we may dismiss this as youthful idealism, but it seems to have unsealed in Tolkien a source of inspiration. Over the next few months, he wrote numerous poems, and elaborated his new neo-Finnish language, now called Qenya. He began keeping notes of it in a small pocketbook, hitherto used for Gothic, and gradually elaborated both a phonology and a lexicon of it.[19] We saw earlier the impression Finnish made on Tolkien; this was now refined into an attempt to create a language that corresponded even more acutely to his developing linguistic taste.

He continued training with the University OTC; he was also elected President of the Exeter Junior Common Room, now a much-reduced body. He seems to have kept up his social and debating interests and prominence, despite a stronger focus on work and drill. Perhaps, also, imminent war gave him both motive and energy to pursue varied interests without too much dissipation of effort.

Some of his new poems, to judge only by their titles ('Outside'; 'Dark'; 'Ferrum et Sanguis: 1914'), probably related more to the contemporary political situation than to his mythological interests; others ('As Two Fair Trees') were about Edith.[20] Others were lyrical or imagistic: 'Kôr: In a City Lost and Dead' is a vision of a deserted city of white marble on a black hill.[21] It, too, was soon caught up into his developing corpus of legend.

It is probable that it was now that Tolkien explicitly formulated his plan to compile, or recover, a 'mythology for England'; likely, too, that he eventually abandoned work on his retelling of the Kullervo story in favour of poeticized fragments of lost legendry such as the various Éarendel poems.

We have seen the approach Tolkien took to what he reckoned were the surviving linguistic fragments of Old English legend; it was also precisely this same method he applied to the words of his 'private languages'. According to strict philology, these words also implied a world in which to place them, and to a great extent described it. Tolkien always insisted that this was the correct order of his inspiration: first language, then story; although most readers, and even more critics, have had trouble believing him. There is good evidence that Tolkien is telling the truth, however.

Qenya, in this earliest form, was made home to several hitherto unexplained philological cruces: as well as Éarendel and his boat Wingilot, we have a Qenya root ulband-'monster', which clearly echoes the Gothic ulbandus 'camel', from some unknown precursor that yielded also 'elephant'; the root OWO, whence Qenya oa 'wool', and is cognate with *owis (Schleicher's *avis) 'sheep'. The opaque name for a slightly mysterious Germanic sacred pole, Irminsûl, is here compounded of two Qenya roots, meaning 'world-pillar'; whilst the hypothesized non-Indo-European loan word underlying the Greek pelekos 'axe' is revealed as the Qenya pelekko; and the British pre-Celtic *ond 'stone' is likewise a Qenya borrowing (Tolkien would have found many of these philological puzzles in Grimm and other standard authorities).[22] More things of this sort can be discovered by the philologically curious. What Tolkien was doing is clear: he was trying to recover, using his own sense of linguistic taste as a guide, the proto-language that had seeded Indo-European mythology and, hand-in-hand with the language, the legends it told. Indeed, as one writer has put it, 'Tolkien meant Qenya to be a language that the illiterate peoples of pre-Christian Europe had heard, and had borrowed from, when they were singing their unrecorded epics.'[23]

This was obviously a vast project, and one that could be completed only piecemeal. For the moment, during the next two years, he wrote a number of poems whose core was some element of his private languages; the poems were an attempt to express something of this linguistic inspiration in a discursive way: to give the same effect in verse as he had received in a word or phrase of his Qenya.

Robert Graves somewhere explains that, as he sees it, poems function as 'stored magic', a unique and (in his terms) 'inspired' verbal formula that, when repeated consciously, revives in the reader exactly the same emotions that the poet had when writing it. For Tolkien, and indeed for any classical philologist of imaginative bent, the very words of a language functioned in exactly this way, reviving from beyond the grave a freight of emotional and cultural resonance otherwise both untransmissible and inexpressible. Perhaps this is in some senses true of all poems, as well: that at their core is a word or phrase in which their burden is concentrated and to which, in effect, the remainder of the verse is mere commentary or exegesis. Time and again in the years to come, we can trace Tolkien's storytelling back to a single impossibly resonant word or phrase (or in a few cases, an image), to which the rest of the tale serves as explication. Some of these words and phrases (hobbit, *mithril*, silmaril) were his own discoveries, others (the Trees of Sun and Moon, *éored*, ents, the Dvergatal) were taken from contexts in northern legend, where they had sat incongruously, sometimes simply misunderstood or even emended by editors into nothingness, sometimes glossed in ways more or less implausible by the original writers or their later editors, in either case sitting at odds, in some fashion, with the tone and affect of their current surroundings. This business of detection and recovery is an intuitive one, much like what Graves describes as the discernment of true poetic inspiration, a matter of smell and taste (or their invisible analogues), rather than rational analysis and argument. But it is surely true that there are some words or phrases that ring the heart like a bell, no matter where we find them; and it was Tolkien's gift to be able to find these, and his achievement to restore to them contexts, or give them explanations, or (if you like) expand their implications, in a manner that seems utterly consonant with the feeling that, isolated, they can evoke. But this is a delicate subject, and one impatient of long analyses; in a strong sense, either you see it or you don't. I very much hope you do. The feeling, when it arises, is perhaps most like what C.S. Lewis called 'joy', 'beyond the walls of the world, poignant as grief'.

The primary fact of this last year before Schools remains Tolkien's growing and developing imaginative activities: poems, painting and a systematic expansion of Qenya. All, moreover, were beginning to coalesce around what we can with hindsight detect as themes and figures from his later mythology: Eärendil, darkness and light, and cosmological musings on the sun and moon (one of his several-times-revised poems was briefly titled 'Copernicus and Ptolemy', whilst the story from the *Kalevala* of the capture by sorcery of the sun and moon lies behind at least one painting of the time). He saw the TCBS 'Council of London' of the previous December as the spur to this creative activity; we may suppose, also, that the imminence of war and his own part in it prompted him to act.

III – An end to Oxford

In June 1915, Tolkien took Final Schools; on 2 July, when the results were published, he was placed in the First Class. He had now done all he could to begin an academic career, and was free to join the Army. He was commissioned into the Lancashire Fusiliers, which was G.B. Smith's regiment. Gilson had joined the Suffolk Regiment, and Wiseman the Navy, where his mathematics were put to use range-finding on the early dreadnought HMS *Superb*. He saw action at Jutland at the end of May 1916. Tolkien hoped to join the same battalion as Smith, the 19th Battalion of the Lancashire Fusiliers, whose Commanding Officer was (Smith told him) happy to have Tolkien; Smith may have joined this battalion partly because it was training in Wales; he was transferred to it along with Henry Wade-Gery, a poet and Classics don (he was elected to a Wadham fellowship on the eve of war) who joined Smith in admiring Tolkien's poems. But in the event, and to Tolkien's acute disappointment, he was assigned to another unit, the 13th Battalion of the same regiment. This was a reserve and training formation supplying replacements to the regiment's 11th Battalion, which was about to join the British Expeditionary Force in France.[24] Tolkien spent the next few months in Bedford and Staffordshire training, before joining his unit; he also wrote and revised poems,[25] and occasionally saw Edith, who was still living in Warwick.

In July 1915, in 'Moseley and Edgbaston … (walking and on bus)', he composed another short lyric, 'The Shores of Faery (Ielfalandes Strand)', which first mentions Taniquetil, Valinor, Eglamar – names from Qenya that were clearly in search of corroborative legends; and also the Two Trees of Sun and Moon (well, of 'Night's silver bloom' and 'the globed fruit of Noon', but the meaning is clear if archly expressed), alongside Eärendel and Wingelot. Tolkien himself later declared it was the 'first poem of my mythology', in the sense of a connected and ramifying narrative: the 1914 Éarendel texts were later co-opted into it, but had begun as an excursus on a reconstructed Old English astronomical myth.[26]

At the same time (mid-July 1915) he also wrote another poem, 'The Happy Mariners', whilst staying with his Incledon cousins at Barnt Green, then a village next to Rednal. It is a lyrical monologue in the voice of a mysterious character later named as 'The Sleeper in the Tower of Pearl' in the Twilit Isles on the approaches to Valinor; Earendel is seen, departing into a west where the speaker may not follow him. Yet another poem, 'The Trumpets of Faerie' (or 'Faery'), dates from the same period.

On 16 July, Tolkien was granted a temporary commission as a Second Lieutenant; three days later he was posted to Bedford to begin military training. He revised 'The Happy Mariners' soon after arriving in Bedford, and again in early September.[27]

Also in September, in camp near Lichfield, he wrote 'A Song of Aryador', a poeticized picture of the Mercian countryside, peopled with 'shadow-folk'. Its most interesting point, however, is probably its title: Aryador (or, in its Old English subtitle, Éargedor) is clearly 'the land of the Arya'. Tolkien is here making his own hypothesis of Indo-European (or, in these pre-Hitlerian days, Aryan) prehistory.

On 25 September, Wiseman, Smith and Gilson visited him for the weekend. It was to be the last time all four of them met.

That November, Tolkien drafted 'Kortirion among the Trees', a lyrical evocation of Warwick amidst the varying seasons, placing it in a legendary history of faërie. This became part of an extensive series of correspondences between actual people and places and their Elvish names. Like all of Tolkien's early poems, it is an uneven performance; at its best, however, it is very fine indeed. Most published poets of the time would have been happy to have written about

> ... Winter, and his blue-tipped spears
> Marching unconquerable upon the sun
> Of bright All-Hallows.[28]

'Goblin Feet' had appeared in the anthology *Oxford Poetry 1915*; there, it had been noticed by Dora Owen, who was compiling an anthology of 'fairy poetry' for Longmans. She asked if she could include Tolkien's poem; he agreed, and sent her some of his other verse. She urged him to submit them to a publisher, and suggested several; Tolkien was encouraged, and put together a collection which he sent, probably late in February, to Sidgwick and Jackson (whom he may have known already via R.W. Reynolds). It was entitled *The Trumpets of Faerie*, after the first poem in the series (Reynolds warned he thought the title 'a little precious', but Tolkien seems to have ignored him[29]). We do not know the exact contents of the collection, but it was probably substantially identical to the poems sent to Dora Owen: 'The Trumpets of Faerie', 'Princess Ní', 'A Song of Aryador', 'Sea-Song of an Elder Day' (also known as 'Sea-Chant of an Elder Day'), 'The Shores of Faery', 'You and Me and the Cottage of Lost Play', 'Outside'. There may have been others, but Tolkien did not include 'Kortirion among the Trees', by general consensus his best work to date, perhaps because he considered it unfinished, or wanted to hold it over for a separate volume.

If the title and subject-matter of Tolkien's collection now seem odd in an infantry subaltern, we may note that Tolkien was not alone. The contemporary vogue for all things fairy is reflected, for instance, in the second volume of poems published by Robert Graves, *Fairies and Fusiliers* of 1917. Graves was a comparatively hardened soldier: although he was three years younger than Tolkien, he had joined up in 1914 straight from school, postponing Oxford, and had been in France since May 1915 with a regular battalion of the Royal Welch Fusiliers, a quite different type of soldiering from that of Kitchener's New Armies. There is a curious parallel, too, between the presence in the same battalion of Graves and Siegfried Sassoon and the original plan that Smith and Tolkien had hatched of soldiering together.

Tolkien had also sent 'Kortirion' to Christopher Wiseman, away with the Grand Fleet. Wiseman wrote to say that he liked it, but ventured some criticisms based (he said) on the differences between Tolkien's taste, which was for starlight and delicate things, and his own, which ran to vast natural phenomena (mountains, winds) and scientific discovery. Tolkien sent him a sharpish answer; Wiseman began to draft a long reply, but it took weeks to be finished and sent. This awkward correspondence probably illustrates rather than having caused a cooling in Tolkien's friendship for Wiseman; Smith, whom he had seen daily in Oxford and with whom he had hoped to soldier, was now probably his nearest friend. Smith, by the by, had been unequivocal in his praise of 'Kortirion', urging Tolkien to publish it.

Tolkien also at this time wrote a short poem in his invented Qenya: 'Narqelion', on falling leaves in autumn.[30] He also made extensive notes in his Qenya lexicon, adding various names that were to remain: Taniquetil, Eldamar, Valinor, Turambar, Tulkas, Valar; and others that were to fall by the wayside: Erinti, goddess of love, music, beauty and purity, who was Edith, Amillo (Hilary Tolkien), Lirillo or Noldorin, the god of song, Tolkien himself. The outlines of a narrative to contain all these names were slowly emerging.[31] There were various flower-fairies and cognate whimsies. Other Qenya words were more topical, and did not persist: *kalimbarië*, 'barbarity', *kalimbo*, 'a barbarian'; *kalimbardi*, 'the Germans'.

Tolkien knew he was likely to be sent to France soon; he and Edith planned to marry as soon as they might. To support them both, Tolkien had his Army pay. They settled on a date in late March, and towards the end of January he wrote to his TCBS friends to tell them. He visited Francis Morgan to arrange to have his small patrimony transferred to his name, and meant to tell him of his forthcoming marriage; but he could not, in the event, screw up his courage to do so. He eventually told him by letter, sometime in February. Fr Francis did not, as Tolkien had feared, disapprove, but wrote in congratulation and offering to solemnize the marriage himself, in the great Oratory Church in Birmingham. Unfortunately, Tolkien had already made other arrangements, which could not now be changed.

Tolkien returned to Oxford on 16 March for his degree ceremony; whilst he was there, he began a poem, 'The Town of Dreams and the City of Present Sorrow', dealing respectively with Warwick and Oxford. It was quickly finished, although revised later in the year.[32] It begins with barely disguised autobiography: 'In unknown days my fathers' sires / Came, and from son to son took root', although now he is a wanderer between towns. Later texts are written in the person of Eriol the Wanderer, and cast Tolkien's ancestry in the mode 'my father was a wandering Anglo-Saxon'. A later draft states baldly 'There fell my father on a field of blood, / And in a hungry siege my mother died'. In the earliest text, however, the bulk of the poem is a lament over Oxford, deserted in wartime: 'thy clustered windows each one burn / With lamps and candles of departed men.' But although 'war untimely takes thy many sons', the city itself still shows a melancholy grandeur, and holds a lien on his affection. It is a poem of farewell, of departure. He wrote the first draft over three days; then it was back to Staffordshire, and the Army.

On 22 March 1916, Tolkien and Edith were married. The wedding was a small affair, in the Catholic church in Warwick; as it was during Lent, the then custom of the Church forbade a full Nuptial Mass. This was certainly not ideal; there is no suggestion, either, that friends and family attended (except, presumably, Jennie Grove). We may attribute some of this, perhaps, to Tolkien's slightly furtive habit of keeping (male) friendship and emotional life (with Edith) separate one from another, and both from his extended family. Hilary was presumably in France, or otherwise busy, with his regiment; his TCBS cohorts were likewise busy in uniform. Mostly, however, we should probably put it down to the times: the spring of 1916 was, like all times during that war, a time of hurried partings and snatched leave, of hasty embarkations and last lyrical glimpses of familiar places whilst running for a crowded train. It is likely that the Tolkiens were not the only young couple marrying against a military timetable, and Fr Murphy's diary may have been full. Easter that year was very late – 23 April, about as late as it can fall – and waiting until then might have seemed rash, given the constant uncertainty of impending orders.

A week after they were married, Tolkien received a publisher's letter rejecting *The Trumpets of Faerie*.

The Tolkiens began their married life in a series of rented houses and lodgings; Edith's cousin Jennie Grove lived with them during all of this time – Tolkien was busy with Army training and Edith was presumably glad of the company. In April, Edith and Jennie moved to Great Haywood in Staffordshire, to be near the camp where Tolkien was training. Edith struck up a friendship with the Catholic priest of the village, Fr Augustine Emery, who was musical (a violinist) and who, one Sunday, voluntarily celebrated a nuptial blessing for the couple to supply for the one omitted from their Lenten wedding (the congregation, Tolkien wryly observed, probably thought they had been living in sin). Fr Emery kept in touch with the Tolkiens over the coming decades.

IV – Into battle

'Those who survive can write all that is necessary'[33]

On 2 June 1916, Tolkien was ordered to France to join his battalion, the 11th Lancashire Fusiliers, in preparation for the Somme offensive. He had trained as a signals officer, which allowed him in some small way to use his aptitude for code and language. After forty-eight hours' embarkation leave (he and Edith went to Birmingham, and spent the night of 3 June at the Plough and Harrow Hotel on the Hagley Road, close by where they first met), he left her and took a train to London, then another to

Folkestone. 'Parting from my wife then ... was like a death.'[34] On 6 June, he crossed to France. This was only Tolkien's third trip abroad since his arrival from South Africa in 1895.

He wrote a poem to England, 'The Lonely Isle', on the occasion of his Channel crossing; it is dated 'Étaples, June 1916', and is in his best sub-Francis Thompson manner.[35] Étaples, a shoreland town in the Pas de Calais amidst sand and pine-trees, was host to a vast British training and transit camp, including the infamous 'Bull Ring', a sandy amphitheatre where troops in their thousands were hastily drilled in bayonet technique and other military maneouvres. Tolkien's kit (camp-bed, sleeping bag, wash-kit), which he had bought at some expense and with care (advised by Smith), was lost in transit; he had to scrounge replacements whilst waiting to be sent up to join his battalion.

Whilst there, Tolkien wrote another poem, 'Habannan beneath the Stars', a vision of a limbo-like twilit region nigh to faërie, where men wait after death, and 'gather into rings / round their red fires while one voice sings'. It was an image of purgatory, or of some pagan otherworld like that, perhaps, in Virgil; and it was explicitly inspired by his time in military camp in Staffordshire, and later in Étaples. Tolkien felt himself to be amongst the dead, waiting to pass beyond.

Tolkien's brother Hilary had enlisted in the Army on the outbreak of war, in the Royal Warwicks. Hilary had left King Edward's in 1910, aged sixteen, probably without the OTC certificate which would have made him eligible for a commission. After a short time in the office of his uncle Walter Incledon, he had gone to work on a farm in Sussex. He was in France from 1915 to the end of the war, serving as a bugler – which meant, amongst other things, acting as a stretcher-bearer under fire. He was several times wounded, although not seriously; each time, the Army authorities sent a telegram to his designated next-of-kin, who was his sister-in-law, Edith. We can only speculate how she felt.

Tolkien himself wrote to Edith frequently; they had devised a system, whereby pinholes or dots made in his letters would by some device (perhaps by marking the letters of a place-name) show her his position, which he was forbidden to tell her explicitly. One suspects the censor, had he detected this subterfuge, would have been less than understanding: the location of named bodies of troops was precisely the sort of information sought by enemy agents. Edith had a large map of France pinned to the wall in Great Haywood, and plotted her husband's movements on it. He also wrote to Fr Vincent Reade, complaining about the Army (years of OTC had presumably stripped any glamour from the routine military life).[36]

On 27 June, Tolkien left Étaples by train, with other reinforcements for his battalion and other units at the front. They went slowly through Abbeville, and arrived at Amiens the following day. Then there was a ten-mile march through the cornlands and orchards of Picardy to the village of Rubempré, where he joined his battalion. The 11th Lancashire Fusiliers, largely recruited from Lancashire miners and weavers, were part of the 74th Brigade, in the 25th Division, II Corps, of the Reserve Army under General Hubert Gough. They were at once set to last-minute training and battle practice. Over half a million men from Kitchener's New Armies had been assembled for a great assault. In the distance, there was the sound of guns: the five-day-long bombardment of the German lines was coming to its climax.

On 1 July, the Battle of the Somme began. British attacks on this first day suffered severe losses; of the 120,000 in the initial attack, 60,000 men became casualties, including almost twenty thousand dead. Amongst them was Rob Gilson, killed at the head of his men in no-man's-land. Gilson had a sister and two younger brothers, aged six and almost four; he had also just got engaged to be married. Both his sister and his fiancée were working as nurses.

Despite the high casualties, there were considerable successes on the southern half of the front; and as the assault continued on subsequent days, stubborn British attacks slowly pushed the Germans out of their prepared and heavily fortified positions. Over the next weeks and months, in a series of deliberate and generally well-planned attacks, the British Army won a significant if costly victory; the German army was exhausted, all but broken, its commanding general sacked (he had also failed in the long and very bloody assault on Verdun), and early in 1917 was forced to withdraw some miles to an improvised new front line. Little of this was clear to the troops at the front, however.

Tolkien and most of his battalion were in reserve during the first two weeks' fighting; two of its four companies, including Tolkien's, were in action from 7 July, but Tolkien was by now attached to battalion headquarters and was not with them. He managed to find time to write two poems ('A Dream of Coming Home', dedicated to Edith, and 'A Memory of July in England'). He also saw Smith, whose battalion was stationed in the same village (Bouzincourt) between 6 and 8 July. As an incidental curiosity, the village of Bouzincourt contains a number of man-made tunnels (*les muches*) used as refuges for men and livestock in cold weather; they were also in frequent use in wartime, especially during the Great War. We might remember the caverns above Helm's Deep in *The Lord of the Rings*. Smith and Tolkien met every day, until Smith was sent back to the front.

On 15 and 16 July, the remainder of Tolkien's battalion were sent into action. They went over the top at 2.00 a.m. on the 15th, across the muddy corpse-strewn shambles of no-man's-land, ruined by a fortnight of fighting, towards the enemy trenches; German machine-gun fire broke up the attack, and they retreated to their start-line with heavy casualties. At 1.30 a.m. the following day, the attack was renewed by another unit from their brigade, this time with more success. It is incidentally noteworthy that these attacks took place at the dead of night; this argues a concern to achieve surprise and avoid casualties wholly at odds with the casually accepted notion of the tactical pig-headedness of British generals at this stage in the Great War. That the first assault failed was a function of bad luck rather than stupidity; the high casualty rates in even successful attacks had been an unsurprising feature of siege warfare throughout the ages: and siege warfare, in essence, is what most of the Western Front was. Tolkien's battalion was in support, and mounted a successful attack later in the day to relieve a battalion that had been surrounded and cut off. As a signals officer, his job was less dangerous than, for instance, leading a platoon into action; but it was by no means a safe post. Casualties amongst all front-line troops were high, and Tolkien was undoubtedly in danger. The day after, 17 July, in the small hours of the morning, the battalion was relieved and marched back to Bouzincourt, which it reached at 6.00 a.m. Only then did Tolkien hear of Gilson's death, in a letter Smith had written to him two days earlier.

On 20 July, Tolkien was made Battalion Signals Officer. For the remainder of July and all of August, the battalion was rotated in and out of the front line (at Beaumont Hamel, Thiepval, Ovillers). Periods of front-line duty were occupied mainly with digging and reinforcing trenches, rather than direct assaults across no man's land; but they were not without danger, and the battalion lost a steady trickle of men to shellfire and snipers.

Tolkien was now responsible for communications between the battalion and its parent brigade, and also with Divisional headquarters, as well as with neighbouring units. This was no sinecure: breakdowns in communication are one of the most common and destructive causes of military failure, a general truth that was especially apparent in the Great War, where successful assaults required the co-ordination of very large numbers of separate bodies of infantry to a timetable dictated by precisely arranged artillery barrages. In these days before wireless telegraphy, this meant organizing a complex of different means, including runners and carrier pigeons and heliographs, but mostly fixed telephone wires laid through the mud and chaos of the trenches, and frequently cut by barrage or circumstance. The work was unrelenting, filthy and mostly thankless.

Tolkien and Smith met several times in August, in between front-line duty. They shared their poems with each other; Smith had a long poem, 'The Burial of Sophocles', presumably first written as an entry for the 1914 Newdigate Prize, which was on that subject (he hadn't won). He had lost the draft of it in transit to France and had rewritten it from scratch.

They disagreed sharply about the significance of the TCBS now that Gilson was dead. Tolkien's original view had been that they had, corporately, a mission 'to rekindle an old light in the world', something of greater importance even than laying down their lives in a war (as Tolkien believed them to be fighting) of good against evil. But after Gilson's death, he felt 'something has gone crack'; he no longer felt part of 'a little complete body'.[37] Smith, in contrast, reckoned the TCBS was 'an influence on the state of being' which 'is not finished and never will be'.[38] Between 19 and 22 August Smith's unit and Tolkien's were again near each other, and the two of them met daily. Their last meeting, for dinner on the 22nd with Wade-Gery, was interrupted by shellfire. Wade-Gery on this occasion gave Tolkien a copy of Morris's *Earthly Paradise*.

Between the 24th and the 26th, Tolkien was back at the front line near Thiepval, where his battalion was digging new trenches. He wrote two poems – 'The Thatch of Poppies' and 'The Forest Walker'; the second was inspired by a patch of undestroyed woodland he had visited a fortnight before, and alluded to Gilson's death.[39] Tolkien wrote it in the headquarters dugout at Thiepval Wood, now (in contrast) a shattered landscape of burnt and blackened stumps. A few weeks later, another young English poet fought here; he shows us a picture of hell:

The tired air groans as the heavies swing over, the river-hollows
     boom;
The shell-fountains leap from the swamps, and with wildfire and
     fume

The shoulder of the chalkdown convulses.
Then the jabbering echoes stampede in the slatting wood,
Ember-black the gibbet trees like bones or thorns protrude
From the poisonous smoke past all impulses.
To them these silvery dews can never again be dear,
Nor the blue javelin-flame of the thunderous noons strike fear.[40]

The battalion was briefly relieved on the 27th, and spent a day in Bouzincourt resting; then it was back to the front line, this time at Ovillers-La-Boiselle, near the Leipzig Salient (an anomalous British bite out of the German line), for more repair and consolidation work. Constant shellfire here had turned part of yet another wood, Authuille Wood, into a ruin. The battalion was again relieved on 1 September.

September was spent behind the lines, first on trench repair and reconstruction, then (after a five day route march) in training at Franqueville with the rest of their brigade; Tolkien wrote a poem ('Consolatrix Afflictorum') to the Virgin Mary. On the 27th, they returned to the line near Thiepval, where Gough's Reserve Army was in the middle of a successful attack (known to military history as the Battle of Thiepval Ridge). Thiepval itself, and much of its defensive complex, had just fallen. The next day, 28–29 September, Tolkien's battalion saw the capture of part of the Schwaben Redoubt (the remaining German strongpoint in the area) and moved up in support to occupy abandoned German positions. They took some prisoners, who turned out to be from a German regiment that had fought beside the Lancashire Fusiliers (then the 20th Foot) in 1759, at their famous feat of arms at Minden (six British battalions and three Hanoverian, in line, drove off repeated attacks by French cavalry), which was celebrated by the regiment every 1 August. Tolkien tried out his German on one of the officers. Carpenter says they were a Saxon regiment,[41] which cannot however be right, since the Saxons at Minden were part of the French-Imperial army against which the British were fighting; there were Hanoverian and Hessian regiments alongside the British infantry, so perhaps one of them might be meant. Certainly the German 7th Division had as one of its regiments the 165th (5th Hanoverian) Infanterie, who probably descended from one of the Hanoverian units present on the British side at Minden. The mistake may of course have been Tolkien's own, or that of the German officer to whom he spoke. If he was a Saxon, then either or both of them had forgot his Seven Years' War history, since the Saxons, unlike the British, were in that war consistent opponents of Prussia and allies of the French. The apparent coincidence with Tolkien's own distant ancestry may of course have been too good to overlook.

On the 30th, the Lancashire Fusiliers were once more relieved. They marched back to Bouzincourt and spent five days training; on 6 October, they returned to the front line to garrison newly captured German positions near Thiepval, opposite the Schwaben Redoubt, parts of which were still in German hands. For the next two weeks, elements of the battalion rotated in and out of the front line, extending and reinforcing the trenches under shellfire. On the 13th, the whole battalion was moved into the front line. The rest of the Schwaben Redoubt was finally taken on the 14th; now command began planning an assault on the last part of the German fortified complex, known variously as Regina Trench or Stuff Trench (a corruption of the German *Staufen Riegel*[42]). On the 16th and 17th, three of the battalion's four companies were withdrawn to make ready for the attack. Tolkien drew up a map of the respective front-line trenches, marking details of the defences (dugouts, machine-gun posts, gaps in the wire) based on the latest intelligence in the days immediately before the attack. This would have been used to guide the actual assault parties, so accuracy was critical. It is preserved amongst the Tolkien Papers in the Bodleian Library, and is (one suspects) unusually finely drawn and lettered for a trench map: one can see why Tolkien's commanding officer was eager to keep his services.[43]

On the 19th, the 11th Lancashire Fusiliers moved up to Hessian Trench, the old German front line, from which they were due to join in the attack. Heavy rain and mist made communications difficult or impossible, and had damaged some of the trenches; so the operation was postponed for forty-eight hours, and the battalion marched back to its staging-post. In the small hours of the 21st, it was again sent forward into Hessian Trench.

At last, at noon on 21 October, the battalion took part in a successful assault on the German trenches (the Battle of the Ancre Heights), rushing across the few hundred yards of no-man's-land into Regina Trench in three waves, the first behind a rolling barrage from British artillery. In a bare three-quarters of an hour, they took all their objectives. The battalion lost about 150 men killed and wounded (most in fact caused by men staying too close to the supporting barrage rather than by German fire); Tolkien was unhurt. He was probably at battalion headquarters for the whole operation; as Battalion Signals Officer, he sent news of the success to

Divisional headquarters by carrier pigeon. The next day, the battalion was moved behind the lines to rest and refit, before a move to the Ypres sector in Flanders. The day after, the 23rd, they paraded and were inspected first by the Brigadier commanding their brigade, then (after a move by bus) by the Major-General commanding their Division. They then marched to Beauval, where on the 25th they were inspected by General Sir Hubert Gough, Commander of what was soon to become the Fifth Army (the Reserve Army was renamed on 30 October). Lastly, on 26 October, they were inspected and complimented by the Commander-in-Chief, General Sir Douglas Haig. But by this time, this ascending panoply of military approbation may have taken on, for Tolkien at least, a surreal quality.

On 25 October 1916, behind the lines in Beauval, Tolkien began to feel ill; two days later, he reported sick with a fever of 103°. He had caught what the troops knew as 'trench fever', and their medical officers as PUO, or 'pyrexia of unknown origin'. After the war it was discovered to be transmitted by lice, which were endemic in the trenches; the German dugouts Tolkien and the rest of battalion headquarters had occupied were overrun by them. Trench fever's formal name is now *Bartonella quintana*. Its symptoms were high fever, headaches, leg pain and subsequent extreme weakness; when severe, it could leave a legacy of depression. Tens of thousands of men fell sick with it during the war (perhaps as many as a third of all British troops had it at one time or another); for many, like Tolkien, it probably saved their lives.

Tolkien was sent to a hospital in Le Touquet, but got no better, and on 8 November was put on a ship for England.[44] On 9 November, he was admitted to a temporary hospital set up in the Edgbaston campus of Birmingham University. He wrote to Smith and Wiseman telling them of his condition; both replied they were happy he had escaped. By mid-December, he was well enough to be discharged from hospital, but too weak to return to duty. He travelled to Great Haywood in Staffordshire, where Edith was living with Jennie Grove.

V – 'Where is the land of Luthany?'[45]

On 29 November 1916, behind the front line, G.B. Smith was wounded by shellfire; the wound was minor, but became infected. He died five days later, on 3 December 1916. Tolkien, when he heard the news (in a letter from Wiseman dated 16 December), was at Great Haywood with Edith; it was just before Christmas.

We have no record of Tolkien's immediate reaction to his friend's death; we know he wrote to Smith's mother, who replied with a longer account of his last days. He wrote an elegy for his friend, called simply 'GBS'. It has never been published.

After the initial shock and grief, Tolkien realized that if the TCBS was to come to anything, he would now have to try also to say what Gilson and Smith had wanted to, but now could not; Smith, indeed, had directly told him to do as much in one of the last letters he wrote.[46]

So, at this time, whilst recovering in hospital and in lodgings, Ronald Tolkien began writing the first stories from what he called his *Book of Lost Tales*, the first efforts at his 'mythology for England'. Edith copied out some of his early tales. This is the only recorded collaboration by her in his imaginative world; for many years afterwards, he shared it, if at all, only with a few male intimates.[47] The first Tale to be written down was *The Fall of Gondolin*, recounting the destruction of an elven city by hordes of goblins and fire-demons equipped with diabolic mechanical siege weapons; although written in Morris-influenced archaic prose, the mark of the war is clear on it. Some have stated that Tolkien wrote these *Tales* whilst in the trenches; he himself pointed out the sheer impracticality of connected literary work under those conditions. 'That's all spoof,' he said to someone who made the suggestion.[48] There is a passage in a later letter claiming that 'lots of the early parts' of the *Tales*, and the languages, were written 'in grimy canteens, at lectures in cold fogs, in huts full of blasphemy and smut, or by candle-light in bell-tents, even some down in dugouts under shell-fire'.[49] I would suggest, again, that this must refer to notes (particularly to those making up the lexicons) rather than to connected prose. He had managed some short poems, but nothing longer. We may reckon he *thought* much about his legendarium, and especially about his private languages, whilst in France, and very probably made extensive notes that were the seed of later narratives (the two earliest lexicons of his languages are suitably tiny notebooks), but for extended narration, he needed comparative uninterruption, such as a convalescent hospital easily supplies.

He may have turned to prose, rather than narrative verse, after the disappointment of having *The Trumpets of Faerie* rejected the previous spring; certainly, his output of poems now slowed dramatically. He did revise his farewell to Oxford, 'The Town of Dreams and the City of Present Sorrow'; eventually, it was wholly reworked as 'The Song of Eriol', and all direct autobiography (Warwick, Oxford, wartime) ruthlessly excised. He had also written 'The Lonely Harebell' whilst in hospital, and, as we saw, an elegy on G.B. Smith.

The *Book of Lost Tales* is Tolkien's first attempt to give form to his 'mythology for England'. We do not know what part, if any, Tolkien had supposed or hoped his allies in the TCBS might play in this mythological reconstruction; but now that Smith and Gilson were dead, the task fell to him alone. Wiseman was, he may have thought, no longer a sympathetic audience. After *The Fall of Gondolin*, he wrote a 'framing narrative' for the collection, 'The Cottage of Lost Play'.

His method, like his prose style, was largely borrowed from William Morris, whose *Earthly Paradise* takes a group of lost mariners cast up on a strange shore, and has them hear and tell a varied body of myth and legend. We may remember Tolkien was given this book by Henry Wade-Gery on the last night he saw G.B. Smith.

Tolkien, at least in the developed texts that survive (his notes and drafts from this time are but sparsely preserved), has a fifth-century Anglo-Saxon, at this point named Eriol, leave the ancestral home of the English in Jutland and end up cast ashore on Tol Eressëa, Elvenhome. At this stage, Tol Eressëa is the island of England, and there, at the Cottage of Lost Play, Eriol hears tales of the Elvish legendry. We might stress this point: in Tolkien's original conception, England – Britain – is the Lonely Isle, once in the Uttermost West but dragged back to the Great Lands for the elves' 'Faring Forth' (a slightly uncertain concept, and one that never reached full achievement, but which seems to have been an (abortive) expedition by the elves of Valinor to rescue their exiled kindred in the Great Lands), and never removed. The *Lost Tales*, indeed, make persistent attempts to calque the legends onto places in England. The places of Tolkien's private joys – Warwick, Great Haywood, Cheltenham – were given Elvish history and names (Kortirion, Tavrobel, Celbaros – Kortirion, or Kôr, is a name transparently borrowed from Rider Haggard's *She*, although the actual city there, not the name, is the model rather for Gondolin).

'Eriol', although in one place defined as 'he who dreams alone', is at another said to be the Elvish equivalent of 'Angol', a name he was given on account of his homeland: 'Eriol', then, means 'the Englishman'. He also takes the by-name *wæfre*, 'restless, wandering', a transparent equivalent to the Old Norse Gangleri, who in the *Prose Edda* is the questioner catechized on Norse mythology; like Gangleri, Eriol Wæfre asks the elves on Tol Eressëa about the gods and their doings. He seems to be a figure of

Tolkien himself. (There are various clues, aside from the direct insertion of Eriol into the autobiographical *Wanderer's Allegiance*: Eriol's original name is said to be Ottor; this is plausibly rendered 'Otter', which seems to have been Tolkien's by-name in his cousins' Animalic jargon.[50] There is also an Otter, a shape-changer, in *The Story of Sigurd*.)

The *Tales* themselves were said to be taken from 'The Golden Book of Heorrenda', or 'The Tales of Tavrobel'. Heorrenda is son to Eriol; but it is a name from, again, Old English verse: the short poem 'Deor' is a lament by its eponymous poet, who, after listing reversals famous in legend, brings forward his own complaint, that he has been replaced at court by a rival *scop*, Heorrenda, *leoðcræftig monn* (a man skilled in song). Tolkien was privately convinced that Heorrenda was an archetypally famous Old English poet; indeed, in the following decades he would sometimes refer to the poet who wrote *Beowulf* as Heorrenda, in part to avoid the constant circumlocution 'the *Beowulf* poet'.[51] He seems, here, to be another equivalent of Tolkien himself. The 'Englishness' of these *Tales* is not simply a reflex of geography, however; Tolkien sought, above all, to capture a certain character, resonant of English air and soil, that he found hints of in what he identified as surviving fragments of 'English legend'. It may be worth reminding ourselves that Tolkien was conscious of being, albeit at several removes, a descendant of a more recent Germanic migration; Eriol/Ælfwine is also a sign of how an originally continental German may be, at the same time, archetypally English as Tolkien felt himself to be.

Eriol and his sons, then (as well as Heorrenda, he was father to the legendary heroes Hengest and Horsa), were the means whereby the English have 'the true tradition of the fairies', rather than the garbled things found in Welsh and Irish sources. This was 'a specifically English fairy-lore',[52] preserved in England, the 'Lonely Isle' or in Old English *seo unwemmede Ieg*, the Isle Unstained (Tolkien, remember, had written a poem to England with this title in June 1916). Eriol's three sons were settled at places of private significance: Horsa at Oxford (Taruktarna or Taruithorn in the early Elvish word-lists), Hengest at Warwick (Kortirion, 'the round tower'), Heorrenda at Great Haywood (Tavrobel). At one point, Tolkien ventured the device that Old English was the only Mannish language elves would willingly speak, owing to their sometime friendship with Eriol's people.[53]

There were elements, too, that were clearly very private to Tolkien and Edith. The Cottage of Lost Play, setting for the tale-telling, appears first in a poem written in April 1915, when Tolkien was still an undergraduate; the Cottage is a place of refuge and delight for lonely and unhappy children, who travel there in dreams. Tolkien's 1915 poem describes a pair of children who meet, first, in this Cottage, and remember it, and their companionship there, in later life. They are obviously meant for Tolkien and Edith. It is probably no accident that the extant manuscript of the opening Tale, recounting this cottage, is in Edith's handwriting and dated February 1917. This is a rare insight into the very early days of the Tolkiens' marriage; it seems impertinent to analyse it further. As Christopher Tolkien has said, one needs little help to see 'the personal and particular emotions in which all was still anchored'.[54]

The style of the *Tales* is a deliberate mixture of archaizing prose in the best William Morris manner, with a faintly precious Edwardian 'fairy' or 'elfin' quality, all flittermice and flower-lanterns and diminutives (partly down to Francis Thompson, partly we may guess to Edith's fondness for such things), with a dash of whimsy (cat-demons, talking hounds) that may owe something to Lord Dunsany. At moments, the effect is most like not Morris or Dunsany but, oddly, the later Randolph Carter stories of H.P. Lovecraft, which are explicit dream-narratives. These were not written until 1925–6, and were not published until after Lovecraft's death, so there can be no question of influence either way, but there is a certain occasional likeness of tone. Lovecraft was two years older than Tolkien, and their backgrounds were not really alike; but there was perhaps something in the air. Both men, as well, had clearly read their Dunsany.

Dunsany may be counted as a major influence, if only because his example had made it possible to write in a mythological mode, with much use of the historic present, and sly whimsical narratives of the gods and their doings; specifically, we may suspect that Tolkien's Ulmo owes something to Dunsany's Slid, although his depiction in Sime's illustrations to Dunsany is as a smoothly youthful god, not the shaggy Neptune figure of Tolkien's counterpart. There is little else that looks like direct borrowing, here at any rate.[55]

VI – Survival

At the end of February 1917, Tolkien was moved from the Southern General Hospital (Birmingham University) to a convalescent hospital in Harrogate; then, in mid-April, he was posted to the Humber Garrison. He was recovering, but was still too weak to return to France. Edith and

Jennie Grove moved to Harrogate in early March. At around this time, Edith discovered she was pregnant.

Tolkien continued to write his *Book of Lost Tales*, and also compiled a lexicon of a second 'private language', to add to his existing Qenya. This second creation was closer to Welsh, and was called Goldogrin or Gnomish.[56] Thereafter, although their names and the supposed details of their interrelations changed often, these two 'elvish' languages were at the heart of Tolkien's inventions. They eventually emerged, much changed, as Quenya and Sindarin. Wiseman evidently encouraged Tolkien by letter to work on his mythology, which he called 'the epic', perhaps under the impression it was to be a long poem. Certainly he was eager for Tolkien to bring out the connexions between the mythological fragments in his existing poems.[57]

One day in May or June of that year, walking in the country near Roos in Yorkshire, Tolkien and Edith came across a hemlock grove. Under the high hemlock-umbels, Edith danced. This gave rise to one of the longest and most heart-felt of Tolkien's *Tales*, the *Tale of Tinúviel*, which became the story of Beren and Lúthien: a mortal man, fled from war and defeat, sees the elven-fair maiden Lúthien dancing amidst the hemlock-umbels of a forest, and falls in love; together, they overcome, for a while, the darkness and sorrow of their time, and pass beyond even death together.

Tolkien wrote little poetry at this time; on 1 August, he attended a regimental dinner to commemorate Minden, and afterwards wrote 'Companions of the Rose' in memory of Smith and Gilson. By tradition, Minden dinners included a toast to the fallen of that day, and by implication all the regimental dead. Smith, we should remember, was also a Lancashire Fusilier; whilst Gilson's regiment, the Suffolks (then the 12th Foot, or Napier's regiment), had also fought at Minden, as one of the six British infantry battalions. All ranks of the Lancashire Fusiliers wore a red rose on 1 August, the Suffolks red and yellow roses.

Soon afterwards, Tolkien fell ill again; repeated bouts of illness prevented his being posted back to France, where his old battalion was now involved in the series of battles called Third Ypres, or Passchendaele.

In the last stages of her pregnancy, probably in September, Edith went to Cheltenham. Tolkien was by now in hospital in Hull, and the journey to see him was difficult and exhausting; there was, moreover, a perceived danger from Zeppelin raids on the coast (there was a raid on the Humber estuary on 22 August; Hull itself was bombed on 25 September). If she was to be apart from her husband, it made more sense to be both safer and more comfortable, and so Cheltenham, where Edith had been happy and still had friends, it was. Their first son was born there in November 1917, after a difficult labour. He was named John Francis, after Fr Francis Morgan, who came down from Birmingham to baptize him. On the day John was born, his father was in Hull, before an Army medical board, who judged he was fit enough to return to garrison duty. He went to Cheltenham as soon as he could; Edith's health was not good, and she needed time in a nursing home. To pay for this, Tolkien sold up his patrimony, the handful of mining shares he had inherited and which had been his only steady source of income (they generated between £20 and £40 a year). He now had only his Army pay, 7s. 6d. a day or about £140 a year, to support Edith and their son. They moved back up to Roos to be near him.

The *Tale of Turambar* (*Turambar and the Foalókë*) was probably first drafted during this period, very likely after *Tinúviel* was written. It later became the story of Túrin and the Dragon, and is clearly inspired in the main by the same story of Kullervo that Tolkien had worked on before the war, although it is now combined with a dragon-slaying theme analogous to the story of Sigurd. Indeed *Turambar* explicitly refers to similar stories still told by men, 'especially in … kingdoms of the North', but whilst these stories have become 'mingled' with those originally about other heroes and events, *Turambar* is 'the true and lamentable tale …'[58] This is to claim a specific 'asterisk reality' for the growing legendarium, which (we have seen) was implicit in Tolkien's method as early as the 1914 Éarendel poems, but is here, unusually, articulated in full.

Tolkien spent the first quarter of 1918 as part of the coastal garrison; then, on 10 April, a medical board declared him fit for general service. The first of the great German spring offensives had opened three weeks previously, and strained the British line almost to breaking; manpower was urgently needed, and every trained man was at a premium. Tolkien was not sent straight to France, however, but to a series of camps in Staffordshire, which he knew from his training three years beforehand. Edith, baby John and Jennie Grove moved down to be nearby, and lodged at a house called Gipsy Green, which entered the Elvish lexicon as Fladweth Amrod.

At the end of May 1918, Tolkien's former battalion, the 11th Lancashire Fusiliers, was all but wiped out on the Aisne during the great German spring offensive; holding the high ground north of Vesle, it resisted to the last man before being overwhelmed. The few survivors of the battalion were disbanded in August.

Tolkien's time in Staffordshire was pleasant after the wet and cold of the Yorkshire coast; but at the end of June he contracted gastritis, and was sent back to hospital in Hull. Edith, who reckoned up that she and Jennie had moved twenty-two times since leaving Warwick in early 1915, now refused to move again. She had still not recovered fully from giving birth. Tolkien was ruled unfit for service; he lost two stone in weight by the end of August. In late July, a War Office order to him to go to Boulogne and thence to his battalion was soon withdrawn: apart from anything else, there was no battalion to go to. In early September, he was sent to another hospital, this time in Blackpool; on 1 October, they declared him fit for sedentary employment, and told him to report to a Ministry of Labour office in a month's time. The office was in Oxford, in University College. The Army, which had taken Tolkien from Oxford, now brought him back there: but not unchanged.

The TCBS was broken by the war. Vincent Trought, as we saw, had died in 1912. As well as Smith and Gilson, other TCBS-ites were killed: Ralph Payton, like Gilson, died on the Somme in July 1916; T.K. Barnsley, who had transferred to the Coldstream Guards, was buried alive by an exploding German shell in August 1916 and sent back to England with a burst ear drum and shell shock, then returned to France to be killed at Ypres on 31 July 1917 (the first day of Passchendaele). The only survivors (apart from Tolkien and Wiseman) were W.H. Payton, who was in the Indian Army, and Sidney Barrowclough, who like Tolkien was invalided back to England and spent the last part of the war on Home Service. From perhaps nine 'members', five were now dead; of the inner circle of Tolkien's friends, only Wiseman was left.

Nor were his Oxford contemporaries spared: of the fifty-seven Exeter College men who matriculated with Tolkien in 1911, twenty-three were killed or died from the effects of war. Even non-combatants, like his sometime room-mate Colin Cullis, were vulnerable: Cullis died in the Spanish 'flu epidemic of 1919, when a disease of unexampled virulence swept across a Europe weakened by wartime deprivations, and killed more than had the fighting. This was not an unusual casualty rate for an Oxford college, most of whose undergraduates would have fought as junior officers, notoriously the most likely of all Great War soldiers to be killed.[59]

Tolkien survived the Great War, but was not unmarked by it. Famously, in the 1966 preface to *The Lord of the Rings*, he noted, 'By 1918, all but one of my close friends were dead.' His long illness arguably affected his health permanently; for the rest of his life, commonplace illnesses frequently laid him low for weeks, and often impeded his ability to work. Physical inertia and emotional despondency were frequent companions.

There were other effects, too: all too clearly, the Somme underlies his evocation of the werelit horrors of the Dead Marshes, the mounds of blasted earth around the approaches of Mordor, its hurrying columns of cursing soldiery.[60] But these are just the superficial links. On one level, the losses of war galvanized his talent, to complete the work his TCBS friends now could not. Tolkien himself sometimes recognized this; at other times, he wondered whether the war had not stifled his development as a writer: 'I was pitched into it all, just when I was full of stuff to write, and of things to learn; and never picked it all up again.'[61] But this was written in a dark day, when his great book was hardly begun and might never be finished; and all these things are, besides, forever unknowable. Tolkien's writing is rooted, certainly, in his vast and intuitive scholarship, but also in an imaginative reaction by an acutely sensitive and educated Catholic to the staggering trauma of the Great War, a collective experience that still informs and qualifies our view of 'civilized' man. Running through his work is a profound and often heartbreaking meditation on the ruinous perversion of goodness and civilization, on the coterminous arising of aching beauty and unblinking malevolence from the same God-given faculty of subcreation. Above all, his theme (as he said in a late interview) was 'death! – inevitable death', that sets a term to all human achievement, that mars and frustrates our plans, and casts to ruin all we strive to build and create; and yet which is not the last word.

The Armistice was signed on 11 November 1918; the guns at last fell silent, and the threads of pre-War life might, in some fashion, be picked up again. Tolkien had been given permission, although still formally a soldier, to move to Oxford. He now needed to try to resume his academic career, laid aside three years before.

Chapter 4 – The Young Scholar

I – Dictionary work

Back in Oxford, with a wife and child to support, Tolkien needed a job. He cast around his old tutors and contemporaries for help.

Arthur Napier had died in 1916, aged only sixty-three; his Chair of Anglo-Saxon (now renamed the Rawlinson and Bosworth Professorship) was given to William Craigie of the *Oxford English Dictionary*, as an additional responsibility; his Merton chair was left vacant. Craigie was a Scot of formidable industry and remarkable linguistic capacity (he could, it is reliably said, compose Icelandic *rímur* as well as a native speaker) with a quiet but fierce intellectual acumen and (it is also said) a gift of mind-reading and the Sight.[1]

Craigie had taught Tolkien Old Icelandic as an undergraduate; now he recruited him to work on the *OED*, although Tolkien actually reported not to Craigie but to his senior colleague Henry Bradley. The *OED* had been started in conscious emulation of the Grimms' *Deutsche Wörterbuch*, and was (and probably remains) the single most prestigious philological project in English.[2] Tolkien had fallen on his feet.

He seems to have begun work in January or possibly February 1919. In later years, Tolkien used to claim, half-seriously, that he had written the *OED*; in fact, he wrote initial entries, and very comprehensive etymologies, for several dozen words beginning W–, and advised on numerous others. For any one person to claim to have written this astonishing book was a joke obvious to anyone who knew even the smallest thing about it; but Tolkien's time at the *OED* should not be dismissed. He himself claimed to have learnt, in those two years, more philology than in any other comparable period of his life.[3]

He and Edith, with Jennie Grove still part of their household, found lodgings at the end of 1918, in St John's Street, a few houses down from where he had lived during his last year as an undergraduate. Tolkien's brother Hilary, meanwhile, after four years in the Army, bought a fruit farm near Evesham in Worcestershire, and for the next half a century grew and sold plums.

Apart from Tolkien, the only one of the original TCBS quartet to survive the war was Christopher Wiseman; but the Great Twin Brethren were now all but estranged. They had continued to write to each other, and Wiseman had late in 1917 visited Tolkien on the Yorkshire coast; but their talk ended in an argument, not (as before) easily glossed over. Still, he and Tolkien collaborated on an edition of G.B. Smith's poems which appeared in June 1918.[4] Two years previously, Wiseman had nurtured plans of reading law at Oxford when the war was done, and lodging with Tolkien;[5] but in the event he went back to Cambridge, and worked for a while with Sir Ernest Rutherford.[6] In 1921, he became a schoolmaster, later a headmaster; he wrote some Methodist hymns, but otherwise published nothing. He and Tolkien stayed in touch, but the old closeness was gone.

Tolkien's pay at the *OED* was modest; he looked about for other work, which might help with finding a more permanent (and better-paid) academic post. In June 1919, his sometime tutor Kenneth Sisam, still for now at the Ministry of Food (in August 1919 he was made Director of Bacon Contracts, of all things[7]) but, with an enduring connexion to the University (and soon to be ensconced at the University Press), realized he didn't have time to compile a glossary for an undergraduate anthology, *Fourteenth Century Verse and Prose*, that he was preparing, and asked Tolkien to produce one for him. Tolkien set to work with a thoroughness that exceeded what Sisam had expected or required.

Work on the glossary took time; in June 1919, he laid aside, incomplete, the *Book of Lost Tales* he had been writing, on and off, since 1916. By this time it comprised fourteen tales in all; three of these (*Tinúviel*, *Turambar*, *The Fall of Gondolin*) were the Great Tales which Tolkien planned to tell at greater length.

These long tales were in fact the earliest to be written, and date from Tolkien's convalescence in hospital and in Yorkshire; this is certainly true of *Gondolin* and *Tinúviel*, which were written by 1917. *Turambar* may well be as early as that, but more probably was written in 1918. *The Nauglafring: The Necklace of the Dwarves*, conceived on a grand scale, most probably dates from 1919 or 1920. Only 'The Cottage of Lost Play' also dates from the very earliest phase of writing (1916–17).[8] The long tales also, as became clear in the course of their composition, came from comparatively late in the narrative cycle of the *Tales*.[9] During his time at the *OED*, Tolkien wrote a series of tales giving the cosmological origin of the world (the music of the Ainur) and its early 'mythological' history. He also rewrote much of the earlier work, usually in ink over a pencil draft that he then erased, so the very earliest versions of the stories are irrecoverable. Sadly, in what was to become a recurring pattern in his writing, he put the *Tales* aside before the narrative was fully achieved. Between the cosmological/mythological 'tales of Valinor' written in 1918–19 and the long heroic tales written earlier, there was a narrative gap that Tolkien aimed to fill with *Gilfanon's Tale: The Travail of the Noldoli and the Coming of Mankind*, which would have told of the return of the Exiled Noldor to the Great Lands, the arising of men and the catastrophic Battle of Unnumbered Tears; this, however, was little more than begun, although outlines of how it was to proceed are extant. There was also a need to bring the cycle of *Tales* to their proper close, and to this end he purposed a *Tale of Éarendel* for which, again, no connected narrative was at this time written. *The Book of Lost Tales*, then, lacks both a middle and an end.

The lack of a connected Éarendel narrative is a particular grief; according to the narrator of the *Nauglafring*, 'thus did all the fates of the fairies weave then to one strand, and that strand is the great tale of Eärendel'.[10] The tale was sketched in seven parts, of which the extant *Nauglafring* was to be the first; it would thus have been the longest of the Lost Tales.

The lack of a true conclusion to the cycle means we do not have a clear notion of how Tolkien's 'historical' framework for the Tales was developing. The *disiecta membra* of his various attempts have been ably collected and epitomized by his son,[11] but the exact shape a continuous narrative might have taken at any time is necessarily speculative. In the earlier conception, Eriol witnesses the premature and disastrous 'Faring Forth', and indeed in one set of notes he actually provokes it; this is not so in the later 'Ælfwine' revisions. In the earlier concept, however, Eriol fights alongside the elves in their defeat by the Men who invade Tol Eressea. There is a curious passage in an epilogue to the (unwritten) story of this defeat, in the Battle of the Heath of Sky-Roof (Dor-na-Dhaideloth, according to a soon abandoned Elvish etymology), when the Elvish 'Faring Forth' to the aid of their exiled and lost kindred utterly failed. It describes the ruined Heath in terms clearly reminiscent of the war-destroyed landscape of northern France:

> Then was my heart bitter to see the bones of the good earth laid bare with winds where the destroying hands of men had torn the heather and the fern and burnt them to make sacrifice to Melko and to lust of ruin; and the thronging places of the bees ... these were now become fosses and mounds of stark red earth, and nought sang there or danced but unwholesome airs and flies of pestilence.[12]

The famed Two Trees of Valinor, which came first into the Tale *The Coming of the Valar and the Building of Valinor*, may derive in part from a chance hint by (of all people) Kenneth Sisam. The Tale was written down, it seems, during Tolkien's time at the *OED*, between 1918 and 1920.

In 1919, Sisam together with Henry Bradley, Tolkien's boss at the *OED*, published a short and technical piece, 'Textual Notes on the Old English *Epistola Alexandri*'.[13] The text on which they commented, a translation of an apocryphal letter from Alexander the Great to his old teacher Aristotle, was a regular source for medieval traditions of the wonders of the East. Amongst the marvels Alexander finds in India are the trees of sun and moon. These are great sacred trees that at particular times of day (sunset and moonrise, respectively) can speak in prophecy; they also exude balsam. As they stand in the text, their likeness to the Trees of Valinor is perhaps slight: they function merely as vehicles for foretelling Alexander's doom; but this may be another instance of Tolkien purporting to recover in his own work a truer tale than late and corrupt sources have preserved.[14] The most evocative element of the story is in fact the Trees' names, and this alone may have been enough to start him thinking.

The question, though, is where Tolkien encountered them. The complete text of the Old English *Epistola Alexandri* (from the *Beowulf* manuscript, MS Cotton Vitellius A XV) was not published (by the Early English Text Society or EETS) until 1924, at Sisam's instance; extracts from another manuscript of it were printed in 1861 by Oswald Cockayne, and the whole text in the German journal *Anglia* for 1881,[15] but Tolkien may well have not met these things by 1919; a short extract appears in Sweet's *Anglo-Saxon Primer*, read by Tolkien at school. None of these extracts feature the Trees, however. Sisam's short piece, though, certainly mentions them in passing;[16] it is a good bet that Tolkien would have seen this piece, or at very least known of Sisam's work on the text, and (we may say) more than probable that he read the text itself before 1919.[17] Certainly, in a lecture twenty years later, Tolkien referred to the Trees of Sun and Moon as to a thing proverbial.[18] He may have drawn additional detail from a contemporary retelling by Robert Steele, a follower of William Morris who was also a fine medievalist (his editions of Roger Bacon have yet to be replaced) where the boles and leaves of the Two Trees 'that bloom for ever' shine like metal, 'and the tree of the sun was like gold, and the tree of the moon was like silver', details not found in the Latin original or the Old English.[19] It may well be the case that Tolkien knew the story as a boy, and Sisam and Bradley merely reminded him.

It is worth noticing this in detail because the image of the Two Trees, and the fate of their light as preserved in the Silmarils, gradually assumed a central importance for Tolkien's legendarium; and their appearance in the *Letter of Alexander* is incongruous enough to have struck Tolkien in exactly the same way as did (say) Éarendel, or any of the other things in the ragbag of philological hints and fragments that nourished his imagination. To trace this to a passing mention in a short and dry technical piece by his former tutor and his then boss merely illustrates the unexpectedness of the imagination, and Tolkien's facility in lighting on the unusual even in the most unlikely places.

In July 1919, he was at last officially discharged from the Army. This meant the end of his Army pay, but he was given temporary retired pay (£35 a year, or around 2s. a day) until that December on account of his continued physical weakness.

Tolkien also at this time found work as an 'extern tutor' for the University, that is, a scholar who holds no tenured or even temporary position but is employed to teach undergraduates a particular subject, usually one outside the competence of their main subject tutor. There were few who could teach English philology, and a growing number of undergraduates in the Oxford English School; many of them were at the women's colleges, and here Tolkien had the additional advantage of being married, which meant a woman student's college did not have to find an additional person to chaperone her during her tutorials with him (although it seems unlikely that Edith was expected to sit in on the tutorials, so we may consider it as much a matter of form as substance; nevertheless this was invaluable). By the end of May 1920, he was getting enough regular teaching work of this sort to be able to leave the *OED* and teach full time, giving classes as well as individual tutorials.

There had been some changes in personnel in the English School since Tolkien graduated; Napier had died in 1916, leaving both his chairs vacant. The Chair of Anglo-Saxon, as we saw, had gone to Craigie; the Merton chair was left empty until 1920, when Henry Wyld, another philologist educated in Germany (Bonn and Heidelberg), previously at Liverpool University, was elected to it (Wyld had also in 1899 done an Oxford B.Litt., supervised and examined by Napier and Joseph Wright[20]). Wyld's especial interest was in poetic diction across the ages. This restoration of the vacant chair took place as part of a general review of salaried posts across the University. Typically, and rather meanly, the authorities decided that Craigie's salary as Rawlinson and Bosworth Professor need not be increased in line with those of other chairs, since he had in addition his pay as Editor of the *OED*. Craigie's formidable wife reckoned it was as if the University had said 'your husband may do two jobs, if he so chooses, but he is only to get one salary'.[21] He was not now a happy professor.

Also, confusingly, a chair of English Literature (created in 1904 for the literary scholar Sir Walter Raleigh) was in 1914 renamed the Merton Professorship of English Literature. Raleigh held it until his death in 1922. This, however, was decidedly part of the 'lit' side of the School, rather than the serious philological business Tolkien was engaged in. A characteristic Raleigh title was *The English Novel* (1894); he also published studies of Milton (1900), Wordsworth (1903), Shakespeare (1907) and Dr Johnson (1910) plus a number of other books. He was prolific, elegant, philologically incurious; 'not a good lecturer', declared Tolkien,[22] although his published light verse has a pleasing Edwardian humour.

By September 1919, Tolkien's income from teaching and the *OED* had grown enough to make it possible for the family to leave their lodgings and rent a house, in what was then Alfred Street (now Pusey Street) off St Giles', around the corner from St John's Street. Edith was able to bring her piano out of storage, and they engaged a cook-cum-housemaid; for the first time in three and a half years of marriage, the Tolkiens had something resembling a conventional family home.

He retained informal connexions with the University as well as his official ones; in the spring of 1920, he read *The Fall of Gondolin* to the Exeter College Essay Club, revising and abridging it for the occasion (he had read the poem '*Éala Éarendel Engla Beorhtast*' to the same club in November 1914). This is one of the few recorded public outings of Tolkien's legendarium before the 1930s, excepting the publication of some short poems; he allowed a few individuals to read some texts, but was perennially shy of public recitation. He wrote some small things at the time: an unpublished poem, 'The Ruined Enchanter: A Fairy Ballad', dates from (probably) November of this year;[23] whilst at some point he composed two connected sentences in Qenya, known from their incipit as 'Sí qente Feanor', 'Thus spake Fëanor';[24] this is worth noting because the quantity of extant connected text in the Elvish tongues is vanishingly small, and will hardly bear the extensive syntactical and grammatical synthesis recent proponents of their use have placed on it; but that is a discussion for another place.

He seems at this time to have contemplated, and even begun, a thorough and wholesale revision of the *Book of Lost Tales*; there are drafts of a tale of Ælfwine, to replace the old Eriol framework, that show in places a distinct stylistic advance over their predecessor. Consider, for instance, this description of the heart's longing felt by Ælfwine and his shipmates when they come within sight of Tol Eressëa:

> Then came the music very gently over the waters and it was laden with unimagined longing, that Ælfwine and his companions leant upon their oars and wept softly each for his heart's half-remembered hurts, and memory of fair things lost, and each for the thirst that is in every child of Men for the flawless loveliness they seek and do not find.[25]

Apart from these drafts of the one text, however, Tolkien took the revision no further.

Early in 1920, Edith again became pregnant. That June, Sisam told Tolkien there was a job coming up at the University of Leeds, as Reader in English Language (it had previously been a full professorship, but on the death by drowning of its incumbent, F.W. Moorman, in the summer of 1919, it was reduced to a readership). Tolkien applied, and was successful. He later professed to believe that he was only considered for the post because Sisam, whom the Leeds authorities had approached, had turned them down and recommended him instead; but he may have been mistaken.[26] The job began that October; it paid a round £600 a year. Tolkien spent a few weeks living in a bedsitter in Leeds and returning to Oxford and Edith only at the weekends. His second son, Michael, was born in October 1920. His godfather was Augustine Emery, sometime priest at Great Haywood, and thereafter 'Uncle Gus' to the Tolkien children. Emery retired to Milford-on-Sea on the Hampshire coast; the Tolkiens had a family holiday there in 1931.

Edith and the children did not move north to join Tolkien until the start of 1921. Edith's cousin, Jennie Grove ('Auntie Ie' to young John Tolkien), at last left their household; she had been living with Edith since 1913. We may wonder what it was like for the Tolkiens, as a young married couple, to spend the first five years of their married life with her as part of their household in a series of modest lodgings and houses; it may seem, to us, as something that would imply a loss of privacy that most of us, perhaps, would find intolerable. But many people then, and some now, lived and live their marriages in similar or comparable circumstances, with one or more members of their extended family as part of their household. Our contemporary fetish for privacy is not a luxury that most ages or societies have been able to indulge; moreover, it was quite usual for even modest middle-class families to have domestic staff living with them, thus further compromising their privacy considered in absolute terms. Eighteen months into their marriage, the Tolkiens had a child; Ronald Tolkien was ill and poor, and a full-time nurse or nanny for baby John was impossible. Edith was much weakened by childbirth; for them, and especially her, to have the help of another adult to hand was (surely) invaluable, and probably saved her health and sanity. We may reckon Edith certainly, and Ronald probably, saw Jennie Grove's companionship as a God-send rather than an imposition; although as anyone who has ever shared a house with another human being will recognize, no arrangement like this is ever wholly straightforward.

II – Leeds

Tolkien now started a busy and diligent time at Leeds, teaching a growing number of students specializing in English philology, and encouraging (with some success) the incorporation of philological elements (history of the language, and the reading of early texts) into the wider English course. His fundamental conviction was that, at bottom, all literary study should be based in hard linguistic knowledge: and this amalgam he called philology. Tom Shippey has, again, neatly summed this up:

> ... philology is not and should not be confined to language study. The texts in which these old forms of the language survive are often literary works of great power and distinctiveness, and (in the philological view) any literary study which ignores them, which refuses to

pay the necessary linguistic toll to be able to read them, is accordingly incomplete and impoverished. Conversely, of course, any study which remains solely linguistic (as was often the case with twentieth century philology) is throwing away its best material and its best argument for existence. In philology, *literary and linguistic study are indissoluble.* They ought to be the same thing.[27]

This definition was not original to Tolkien; but he was unusual in the care with which he sought to emphasize both parts of the pact – linguistic enquiry and literary awareness not opposed but in combination. For many self-styled philologists, as we saw, it was enough to drill pupils in forms and sound-changes, and let the literary stuff look after itself. Tolkien reckoned this both short-sighted and dangerous, and also a cheating of one's pupils of the proper end of their studies.

The English School at Leeds was a young department in a young university. The University of Leeds had been formed in 1904 from the merger of a medical school and a college of science, both nineteenth-century foundations. The founders, however, had from the start instituted an arts faculty to sit alongside these existing bodies; it was planned to include an English Department within this faculty. Its development was slow, however; only in 1913 was a Professor of English Language and Literature appointed. The job was given to George Gordon, a young (he was thirty-two) protégé of Walter Raleigh, great panjandrum of 'literary' English studies and (as we saw) Professor of English Literature at Oxford since 1904. Gordon had hitherto been a research fellow at Raleigh's college, Magdalen (Raleigh, and his professorship, did not move to Merton until 1914).

Gordon was keen to remake the Leeds syllabus along Oxford lines; war service prevented him from making a start before mid-1919. Tolkien's appointment was key to his efforts: the technical side of philology was not Gordon's strong suit (he was a much-admired, if painstaking, writer of short essays and leading articles on a wide range of literary subjects), but its establishment at Leeds was essential to Gordon's aim of giving Leeds an intellectually robust and attractive English School. Tolkien had very considerable freedom to devise an appropriate philological syllabus, and worked closely with Gordon to integrate it with the general plan of the School.

It was not a big department: as well as Gordon and Tolkien, there were a pair of assistant lecturers and a tutor in English composition. Early in

1922, another lecturer was appointed, a Canadian Rhodes Scholar called E.V. (Eric Valentine) Gordon, who when an undergraduate in 1919 had been one of Tolkien's pupils; Tolkien in fact suggested he be approached. Gordon was a competent and industrious philologist, and he and Tolkien were to collaborate closely at Leeds both in teaching and in writing. At the same time as Gordon was appointed, another lecturer's job went to Wilfred Childe, a man two years Tolkien's senior and a published poet. He shared Tolkien's interests in faërie; he was also a Catholic. He had read a paper to the Exeter College Essay Club in June 1919, and Tolkien would have met him then, if they had not, as seems likely, met whilst undergraduates, perhaps at church (Childe had been at Magdalen, and probably knew George Gordon from there). In 1917, Childe had published *Dream English: A Fantastical Romance.* It is a curious Dunsanian piece, a study in resonant prose and high-coloured image of a medieval England unknown to history, flavoured with Byzantine curlicues and a heavy tincture of William Morris, but the Pre-Raphaelite Morris of love-sickness and carven furniture, rather than the reteller of Germanic legend Tolkien loved. Its plot is negligible, and it is really only a highly written (at times overwritten) string of vignettes. Nevertheless, one can see how its author and Tolkien could easily be friends; it shows a poet's gift for the evocative phrase and the sudden revelation of hidden vistas through an unexplained name or allusion. *Dream English* is now one of those books with the uncertain status of a minor 'cult classic', largely forgotten; would this, one wonders, have been the fate of the *Book of Lost Tales,* if it had been finished and published in the 1920s?

Tolkien was happy in his new job; but he was not settled. In his first term, he was approached by the electors to two professorial chairs in English language, and invited to apply. He did, to both: one in Liverpool, for which he was turned down; the other in Cape Town. It is not at this distance clear who put his name forward for these jobs; it may well have been Sisam again, or Joseph Wright. He was offered the latter job at the end of January 1921; but Edith was still recovering from the birth of Michael, and neither she nor the children were fit to travel. Tolkien was strongly tempted to take the job: he felt a keen desire to revisit South Africa, and the opportunity was a good one; but he would not be separated from his children again, and so he turned it down. The odd parallel with his own father's last years might have struck him, perhaps to his discouragement; certainly he regretted the decision over the next year or two ('I have often wondered since if that was not our chance that came then, and we had not the courage to seize it'[28]), but there was much to be done at Leeds, and Tolkien busied himself doing it.

Over the next few years, the Leeds English syllabus gradually evolved to contain a broader range of philological study, much of it taught by Tolkien himself. As well as Old and Middle English (both philology in itself and the study of texts) and fundamental philology of the Germanic tongues, he also taught Gothic, Old Icelandic, and Medieval Welsh. Those undergraduates who, after a year of general study, chose the English School were given a choice between two 'schemes': 'A' and 'B'. Broadly, the 'A' scheme was mainstream 'literary' study; whilst 'B' was a more exclusively historical and philological course. 'B' students were obliged to study the history of the language, Old English prose and verse, Gothic, and various elements of literary history both particular and synoptic; and to take two optional papers chosen from Old Icelandic, Old High German, Old French, and Palaeography, although these optional papers might be replaced by a thesis. There was in addition a requirement to take courses from other faculties: two years of medieval or modern history, two years of a modern language (French or German) followed by a year of the corresponding literary and linguistic history. Before any of this, too, there was a compulsory year of Latin or Greek. This gave all the essentials of an education in solid philology for those prepared to put in the work. This division of the syllabus, modified over time, persisted until 1983, when it was finally abolished by (of all people) Tolkien's remote successor, Professor Tom Shippey.

When Tolkien began at Leeds, of the sixty undergraduates in the second, third and fourth years, only five had chosen the then embryonic 'B' scheme; by 1924, fully a third of the undergraduate body took it. This was a higher proportion than took the equivalent course at Oxford; we may reckon his reforms, and teaching, a success. Whilst the politics of academic life were not absent (presumably they never are), Tolkien and George Gordon had at Leeds the great advantage of starting from a nearly clean slate: their battles needed to be fought to get money for more staff and books and buildings, rather than against the entrenched intellectual habits or teaching and lecturing routines of senior colleagues. In that sense, Tolkien's time at Leeds was an encouraging one, and he relished his success in bringing on what he affectionately described as the 'dull stodges' of the undergraduate body. He did not abandon his imaginative writing, as we shall see; but the press of work cannot have made it easy.

Tolkien also founded a Viking Club for undergraduates, who met to drink beer, read Norse literature and sing comic songs, some in the ancient Germanic languages, composed by Tolkien and Gordon. The only extant poems in Gothic are two pieces by Tolkien from this period.

At some point in the early 1920s, E.V. Gordon collected these songs into a mimeographed booklet, titled 'Leeds Songs': it contained his own and Tolkien's compositions in the old languages, Icelandic students' songs both modern and traditional and several modern English songs of mildly satirical bent, in which Tolkien and Gordon mock the French, or the 'literary' faction (the 'A' scheme) in the English School. These last are in the (to us, now) deeply unfunny vein of Edwardian humour; we might compare G.K. Chesterton's verses mocking the 'Cocoa Press'[29], or any number of the hundreds of such things to be discovered in volumes of *Punch* from the period. The Old English and Gothic verses are, for us now, much more interesting. Two in particular may be mentioned; both involve the birch tree.[30]

Tolkien was in later life given to calling the birch his 'totem tree'; its mention in these two poems (the Gothic '*Bagme Bloma*', and Old English '*Éadig Béo Þu*') is on one level a simple private joke: in the Leeds English School, the birch stood for the 'B' scheme, as against the oak (Old English *ác*), which was the 'A' scheme. Their respective descriptions reflect this partisanship:

Ác sceal feallan on þæt fýr
lustes, léafes, lifes wan!
Beorc sceal ágan langne tír,
bréme glǽme glengan wang![31]

On another level, Tolkien knew of extensive folkloric evidence that the birch tree was associated with the faërie Otherworld in the lost English mythology whose remnants are scattered through some of the northern ballads collected by the American folklorist Francis James Child (notably 'The Wife of Ussher's Well'); it functioned, in some sense, as both a sign of that Otherworld and a passport to it. Under this aspect, the birch was a doubly potent symbol of philology, at least as practised by Tolkien.[32]

Edith liked Leeds better than Oxford; social life amongst the University wives, and the students, was much less formal than at Oxford, and her own position, too, was now less negligible: she was wife to the rising star of the English Faculty, rather than to an underpaid jobbing tutor. Money was still tight, however: they had rented a house near the

University, but it was cramped and the air polluted. Tolkien was eager to buy a house, and that meant both saving money and trying to earn more of it. He took on work marking School Certificate papers, a dull business that had to be fitted into the ends and corners of time left over when his day's work was done.

In May 1922, Tolkien published his first book: *A Middle English Vocabulary*. It had begun as the glossary to accompany Kenneth Sisam's anthology, but Tolkien's delays and corrections to the text were so extensive that the anthology's first printing (in 1921) did not include it. When the anthology was reprinted, in June 1925, Tolkien's glossary was included, and all later editions, to this day, have retained it. The additional time and care he had taken meant that the glossary was a permanently valuable and useful text; but Sisam was irritated by Tolkien's approach, and this made their subsequent relations difficult.

Sisam was notable for asperity and a briskly ruthless approach to philology; he was temperamentally unsympathetic to Tolkien's more expansive and comprehensive approach. There was probably another reason for tension: Sisam was wholly responsible for the text of the anthology apart from the glossary, and his introductions to individual texts have an undercurrent of robust Protestant, or at least anti-Roman, sentiment (the proto-Protestant Wyclif, for instance, was 'the greatest of those who broke the way for the modern world' whose 'moral courage' in challenging the established (clerical) order was wholly admirable) which Tolkien can hardly have relished. Sisam's years of association with Edmund Bishop had not made him sympathetic to Catholicism.

Certainly he and Tolkien never collaborated on anything again, and, whilst Sisam worked at the University Press (which he did from October 1922 until he retired in 1948), Tolkien published nothing with them (and, Sisam might have added, precious little with anyone else). The one exception was an edition of the alliterative poem *Sir Gawain and the Green Knight*, which Tolkien, together with his colleague at Leeds, E.V. Gordon, had begun in February 1922; this was commissioned not by Sisam, but by the eminent lexicographer C.T. Onions. There was another struggle with Sisam, who wanted to cut down the notes and glossary, and was impatient to publish. This was a foreshadowing of the long and unhappy saga of the 'Clarendon Chaucer', which we will come to soon.

The Tolkien–Gordon edition of *Gawain* was an immediate success; to this day, it remains the standard student edition of the text (albeit in a revision made by one of Tolkien's pupils).

In 1922, two years into Tolkien's time at Leeds, George Gordon was elected to one of the Oxford Merton chairs, left empty by Walter Raleigh's death. This left a vacancy at the head of the department at Leeds. Tolkien applied to succeed Gordon in the Chair of English Literature, but was unsuccessful. The post went, instead, to Lascelles Abercrombie, a poet and critic from the 'literary' school, ten years Tolkien's senior, author of books on aesthetics, the Epic, and Thomas Hardy. The electors went with what they knew, although Abercrombie had been a mere lecturer in Liverpool; he was an extensively published poet, and had known Rupert Brooke and Edward Thomas in their youth. Tolkien's candidacy was not as improbable as it might seem, however; he had been Gordon's closest collaborator, and his effective deputy. He was only two years younger than Gordon had been when first elected. The Leeds Vice-Chancellor, eager to retain Tolkien's services, privately assured him a chair of English Language would be created for him (this was from another angle simply restoring the situation as it was before the death of F.W. Moorman in 1919; he had done Tolkien's job with the title and salary of a full professor). This was to be done in October 1924, when Tolkien became Professor of English Language. In the meantime he was given a pay-rise, to £700 per annum, starting in the academic year from October 1923.

On 26 April 1923, the *Times Literary Supplement* published a review, by Tolkien but unsigned (as all *TLS* reviews were until 1974), of the EETS edition of *Hali Meidenhad* (or *Hali Meiðhad*), a text from a manuscript, Bodley 34, which contains a number of texts written during the thirteenth century for women religious in the West Midlands, in a linguistically consistent style; the texts are known as the 'Katherine Group', after the longest of them, a life of St Catherine of Alexandria.[33] Tolkien was not impressed by the edition, which the editor had left incomplete on his death and which, he reckoned, did no especial service to his memory. Nevertheless the material itself was, he asserted, of the greatest interest both linguistic and literary. He later said that he had at once taken to the language of the texts 'as a known language'; they came, after all, from exactly the same region as his Suffield forebears. This was the first public evidence of one of Tolkien's great academic interests, which he was concerned with for all of his subsequent professional life.

Unusually, Tolkien seems to have published very few book reviews, leaving aside some portmanteau articles for the *Year's Work in English Studies*; it is of course possible that some still lurk undiscovered, signed or unsigned, in places obscure or overlooked; and certainly he sometimes speaks of reviewing as something he is familiar with, but this may simply be a rhetorical allusion to his *Year's Work in English Studies* work. The *Hali Meiðhad* piece seems to have been his only contribution to the *TLS*, according to the index of pre-1974 (unsigned) reviews. His connexion to the paper probably came through George Gordon, his boss at Leeds, whose editorials for the *TLS* were so highly regarded they were reputed to have won him his Oxford chair.

III – Mythology revisited

In May 1923, Tolkien contracted pneumonia and became severely ill; his life was in danger. The polluted air of Leeds had clearly done his lungs no favours. His ninety-year-old Suffield grandfather had come to visit; Tolkien remembered him standing at his bedside, 'a tall thin black-clad figure … looking at me and speaking to me in contempt – to the effect that I and my generation were degenerate weaklings'.[34] The old man then left to take a boat trip around the British Isles; he lived until he was ninety-seven. By mid-June, Tolkien had begun to recover; he took Edith and their children to stay with his brother Hilary at his fruit farm near Evesham. They spent their time kite-flying and helping out with the trees; Tolkien also turned again to his writing.

He had not abandoned work on his legendarium, but rather than continuing or revising the *Lost Tales*, he began to retell some of them in verse. Tolkien still thought of himself as primarily a poet, or perhaps (like William Morris) someone who could work in prose and verse with equal facility.

During his time at Leeds, he did publish a few of his shorter poems. Some appeared in the 1923 collection *A Northern Venture* ('The Happy Mariners', 'The Man in the Moon Came Down Too Soon' and 'Enigmata Saxonica Nuper Inventa Duo'), and the following year others were included in *Leeds University Verse 1914–24* ('An Evening in Tavrobel', 'The Lonely Isle', 'The Princess Ní'). Wilfred Childe also had pieces in both, and may have been responsible for introducing Tolkien to the projects. E.V. Gordon and their student A.H. Smith also featured in both collections. Tolkien's poems also appeared in two local journals: *Yorkshire Poetry*, which in its 1923 issue printed 'The Cat and the Fiddle', another 'nursery rhymes explained' poem; and another Leeds periodical, *Microcosm*, which in spring 1923 had 'The City of the Gods', written in 1915. Presumably Childe, again, was his contact for these fugitive publications.

Apart from 'Enigmata Saxonica' (a pair of pastiche Old English riddles) and 'The Cat and the Fiddle', none of Tolkien's pieces was however a new composition; 'An Evening in Tavrobel' was a revision of part of his 1916 poem 'A Dream of Coming Home'. All the rest we have seen written during the war (apart from 'The Man in the Moon', which first began in the pre-war *Book of Ishness*).

Two new things did appear: *Gryphon* (a Leeds University periodical) for January 1923 had 'Iumonna Gold Galdre Bewunden' (later 'The Hoard') – the title is from *Beowulf*, but the story of cursed gold is really that of Mím the Dwarf, Túrin and the dragon Glórund from the *Lost Tales*; whilst in May 1924, he wrote a five-stanza poem, 'The Nameless Land', which describes Tol Eressëa in a verse-form borrowed from the Middle English poem *Pearl*, a vision of the afterlife usually attributed to the poet of *Gawain*. *Pearl* is composed in a complex metre combining alliteration and rhyme, and Tolkien claimed he had written his poem as an exercise to show this is not the impossible feat that most modern editors supposed.[35] Both of these new poems, notably, took their inspiration from a combination of his academic work and the developing legendarium.

His first effort at a long poem, a *Lay of the Fall of Gondolin*, was in a (not very successful) hexameter line, and was early abandoned. He then decided to use the Old English alliterative line, the same verse form used in the great monuments of Old English poetry such as *Beowulf*. For much of his time in Leeds he worked on an alliterative poem on the Children of Húrin; late in 1924, or early in 1925, he put it aside and began two other alliterative poems, 'The Flight of the Noldoli' and a 'Lay of Éarendel'. Both were soon abandoned.

We have little evidence from this time about what, exactly, Tolkien thought his stories were *for*, inasmuch as a story needs to be *for* anything apart from itself; most of the surviving discussion of storytelling, and specifically his own legendarium, in Tolkien's published letters is from a later date, and concerns books as yet unwritten. We may guess, however; a recent scholar puts it like this:

The principal conceit of Tolkien's legendarium is that it stands as a lost prehistoric tradition, of which the many myths and legends we know in our own primary world are meant (fictively, by Tolkien) to be echoes, fragments, and transformations. Tolkien viewed his legendarium as seeding the world's mythologies and their expansive

119

repositories of tales. Eventually, these seeds would have grown (we are still speaking fictively) into the Greek myths, *Beowulf*, the Eddas, Chaucer, Shakespeare, the Finnish *Kalevala*, and all the rest. In this sense, the 'mythology for England' really becomes universal, almost a mythology for the entire world; *certainly* a pan-European one.[36]

Put starkly, like this, it is the manifesto of a lunatic; one may doubt whether Tolkien would have ever made so explicit a statement of intent. But this does, at some level, express pretty exactly what (it seems) Tolkien was aiming at: the recovery of a 'true tradition' of legendry, recreating stories from fugitive hints and corrupted later versions, testing these surviving elements by the paired touchstones of philological coherence and his own aesthetic sense of what was right, of what 'actually happened'. We do not need to suppose Tolkien thought that the Beren legend, for instance, was a matter of historical record, or the geography of Beleriand a guide to proto-European regions (although in its earliest forms it may have been more patently meant as such); rather, what was important was that his versions of these much-patterned tales were, he feigned, truer as stories than any of their 'later' reflexes and analogues. The worm Glórund (Glaurung) is the *ur*-dragon behind Fáfnir and Beowulf's bane; the elves in their varied splendour are the source of the baffling and apparently contradictory scraps and rumours of faërie, perilous and timeless, alluring and fleeting, jealously gathered by folklorists.

This accounts for two curious features of his work: first, his (presumably laborious, or at any rate painstaking) composition of Old English versions of some of his texts, relics (he feigned) of the lost true tradition; and, second, his calling his longer poems 'lays'. This is not simply, or not even, an arch pseudo-archaic equivalent of 'long poem' (in the same way as, today, 'saga' means no more than 'any long(-ish) or episodic story in any medium whatever'), but a precise and deliberate reference to the nineteenth-century *Liedertheorie* of composition, whereby behind extant literary epic, or narrative history, the cunning philologist might discern primitive shorter narrative verse compositions, 'lays', on which the old historians and poets had drawn. Tolkien would have come across this theory, first, in the preface to Macaulay's *Lays of Ancient Rome*, which he had affectionately pastiched as a schoolboy, and which sought to recreate exactly such 'primitive' verse compositions. Those who are still inclined to dismiss Macaulay's poems should read the stirring account of *Horatius* given by Kingsley Amis in his introduction to *The Faber Popular Reciter*,[37] or, better still, reread the poem itself.

We should not forget that, alongside these narrative elements of the legendarium, Tolkien produced very substantial quantities of purely linguistic writing discussing elements of, and interrelations between, his elvish languages; this linguistic material remains in great part unpublished, and (to judge by such fragments as have appeared) is often forbiddingly technical. Nevertheless, this was an enduring and essential part of Tolkien's imaginative writing, and details or apparent anomalies in the linguistic legendarium were very often the immediate spur to some narrative feature that sought to account for or resolve them. This parallel work, of what we might call the open (narrative) and the hidden (linguistic) legendarium, should be borne in mind in all that follows; the extant remains of Tolkien's linguistic writings run to thousands of manuscript pages, and all of it had to be written some time. It was probably at this time that he wrote *A Descriptive Grammar of the Qenya Language*, which collected and systematized the accidence, syntax and phonology of Qenya as it had developed since 1915. The text is unfinished, but extensive.[38] He also wrote a 'Noldorin Dictionary' (which was now the name for Gnomish or Goldogrin) at this time, to supplement a 'Noldorin Grammar' (*Lam i·Ngolthor*, later *Lam na·NGoluith*) he had been working on since 1921.[39]

IV – Check and advance

By June 1923, George Gordon (formerly Tolkien's boss at Leeds, but now Merton Professor of English Literature at Oxford) had managed to establish Tolkien as his co-editor on a school anthology, *Selections from Chaucer's Poetry and Prose*, which would concentrate on works other than the Canterbury Tales, and be published by the OUP. Gordon's and Tolkien's contact at the Press was, inevitably, Kenneth Sisam. Gordon had come up with the idea in 1922, but now realized he needed a collaborator if the project was to make headway amidst his other heavy responsibilities. Tolkien's glossary to Sisam's anthology, and his work on *Sir Gawain* (with the other Gordon, E.V.), made him, it was thought, the ideal person; he was, besides, a friend and sometime colleague, and Gordon was tenacious in patronage.

For this project, dubbed the 'Clarendon Chaucer' (the Clarendon Press was the University printer), they initially proposed to use fresh texts of Chaucer, drawn from the monographs of the Chaucer Society; but Sisam vetoed this, preferring to use the old edition of Walter Skeat, which the OUP published in various formats including a 'Student's Chaucer'. Tolkien thought this an inferior text, but was told that, for the purposes of a school edition (which, to turn a good profit, needed to be as cheap as possible to produce), it was good enough. He and Gordon selected their texts, and they were set up in proof. Further work on the book was impeded by Tolkien's health, which had not fully returned after his pneumonia, and by his teaching load at Leeds.

Proofs of the Clarendon Chaucer arrived late in 1923; Tolkien started to mark them up two days before Christmas, and resumed work on the glossary and the textual notes.

At the same time, Tolkien wondered whether the OUP would be interested in an *Introduction to German Philology* he was contemplating writing (we may wonder whether Tolkien actually proposed an *Introduction to **Germanic** Philology*, which had somehow been thus misleadingly abbreviated);[40] they would, Sisam thought, if it were not too long or complicated. But first, Chaucer needed to be done.

When Tolkien sent his Chaucer text in, Sisam objected to his proposed changes to Skeat's text, some because he was not convinced by Tolkien's reasoning, but mainly on grounds of cost (each emendation, he claimed, would cost 6d.). In March 1924, Sisam decided he wanted Tolkien removed from the Chaucer project, and conveyed this to Gordon. Sisam was also annoyed that Tolkien was (as he saw it) holding up the completion of the *Gawain* edition. Gordon told Tolkien, and he agreed to step down from the Chaucer project; but Sisam could find no competent substitute, so Tolkien continued working on the glossary, notes and preface. Gordon was too busy to do more than advise on this part of the text; such time as he could spare for the book he spent compiling extracts from various critics illustrative of the selection. The project was becoming a decided incubus.

Late in 1923, the Tolkiens' house in Leeds was burgled; their new maid, it turned out, was involved with a criminal gang. Edith's engagement ring was amongst the things taken. Their domestic situation was, clearly, not ideal; we have noted above the heavily polluted air of the city centre, and now (surely) the Tolkiens would have felt unsafe as well.

At the start of 1924, Edith was distressed to find she was again pregnant. She was thirty-five; her two boys were then six and three. She hoped for a daughter, but, in the event, a third boy was born on

21 November. He was named Christopher Reuel, after Christopher Wiseman. Wilfred Childe stood godfather to him.

That same year, however, 1924, saw Tolkien's promotion to a newly created professorial chair; he was now for the first time, as he would remain, Professor Tolkien. He was thirty-two. Although his promotion did not formally take place until October, on the strength of it (and his new salary of £800 a year) he and Edith that March bought a house on the outskirts of the town, larger than their previous rented place and (what was better still) surrounded by open fields. The air too was noticeably cleaner. This was the house where they first lived with their third son, Christopher.

Tolkien had also assumed another academic task of significant weight: he prepared a review article for the annual *Year's Work in English Studies*, covering *Philology: General Works* for 1923. It ran to eighteen printed pages, and represented a great deal of reading and evaluation. It was well enough received that he was asked to repeat the job for the following two years; after that, as we shall see, he simply did not have the time.[41]

That October (1924), George Gordon assured Sisam at the OUP that the Clarendon Chaucer was almost done: he sent in the text, and its accompanying essays; Tolkien, he declared, had finished the glossary and had drafted the textual notes. This was not wholly true; the glossary was not done. In December, Tolkien wrote to Sisam pleading illness (his own and his family's) as reason for delay; Sisam replied asking for the glossary by the end of the year, and the notes by the end of January. Tolkien sent the glossary to Gordon in early December; Gordon forwarded it to Sisam two weeks later. When he received it, two days before Christmas, Sisam at once wrote to Gordon sternly telling him Tolkien would have to pay for the cost of correcting the glossary proofs if he made as many changes to them as he had to those of his glossary for Sisam's anthology.

Two weeks later, on 5 January, he told Gordon the glossary needed to be cut by ten pages; and he suggested to Tolkien that he drop references to the text, and all 'easy' words: the very things, in fact, that made it useful as a tool for a student to *learn Middle English* rather than mug up a text for an examination. Tolkien dutifully cut the glossary, and sent it to Gordon for review; Gordon sent it on to Sisam at the start of March, with a preface of his own in place of Tolkien's one, which he reckoned too cerebral (Sisam agreed).

That April, 1925, the Tolkien–E.V. Gordon edition of *Sir Gawain* was finally published; it remains the standard edition of the text, although it was revised in 1967 by Tolkien's sometime pupil (and eventual professorial successor) Norman Davis. It was the last full-scale edition of a text Tolkien ever published.

Tolkien also contributed an article to the newly founded *Review of English Studies*, called 'Some Contributions to Middle-English Lexicography'; it appeared in April 1925. Much of the piece was drawn from Tolkien's attention to the (in his view highly deficient) glossary to the EETS *Hali Meidenhad*, and marked the next stage of Tolkien's interest in the language of that text. The previous issue of the journal, its first, had included an article on 'Recent Research upon the *Ancren Riwle*' by one of England's more eminent philologists (in Tolkien's sense of the word), R.W. Chambers of University College London[42]; it gives an inspiring account of the text, praising its vigour and purity of speech and affirming its Englishness against those who had tried to argue for it as a rendering of a French or Latin original. Chambers also, characteristically, claimed it for a tradition of English prose-writing 'deliberately created by King Alfred, three centuries before the rise of French prose' and still preserved in the thirteenth century in the face of Norman Conquest and neglect. He ended by expressing a wish 'for a final edition of this extraordinarily interesting and important text'. This, as we shall see, was to become one of Tolkien's aims.[43] Chambers also commends as 'the best and probably the earliest manuscript' the Cambridge manuscript, Corpus 402;[44] Tolkien was to choose this as his base text, and it is still reckoned the definitive text of the work, although now rather as a later authorial revision than the earliest text. Tolkien and Chambers had met at some point, and became friendly. We shall look more at him next.

The next issue of the *Review of English Studies* had another piece by Tolkien, 'The Devil's Coach-horses', analysing a phrase from *Hali Meiðhad*, *þe deofles eaueres*; these, Tolkien argued, were not boars (Old English *eoforas*), drawing the devil's chariot like that of Þórr, but in fact cart-horses, dobbins (Middle English *aver*, or in West Midland dialect *eaver*, from Old English **afor*, **eafor*), rather than horses for riding. 'The devil appears to have ridden his coach-horses like a postillion.'[45]

In May, elements of the Clarendon Chaucer were set in page proof and forwarded to Tolkien. The glossary was now done; but the textual notes were still missing (Tolkien had not got beyond his first draft of them), as were Gordon's introduction and notes. Sisam, who had expected the textual notes by the end of February, cannot have been pleased. But there was soon to be a larger bone of contention between him and Tolkien.

V – Model and mentor

We saw earlier how Jacob Grimm was, for Tolkien as for others, the very type of the *ur*-philologist, the model and gauge of all their endeavours. There was another man, closer to home and nearer in time, who as much as anyone was a model for the young Tolkien. This was Raymond Wilson (R.W.) Chambers.

Chambers was like Joseph Wright a Yorkshireman, although unlike him not working class or ever a mill-hand. He was a pupil of both A.E. Housman and W.P. Ker, the fine flower of University College London's scholarship, and spent almost all of his professional life teaching at UCL. In 1899, aged twenty-five, he was appointed by Ker as Quain Student; four years later, he was made Assistant Professor; and almost two decades later, in 1923, he succeeded Ker as Quain Professor of English on the latter's death. For much of this time he was also the College's Librarian, and built up a large and impressive collection of books. In a lecture given in the mid-1930s, Tolkien described Chambers as 'the greatest of living Anglo-Saxon scholars'.[46] What (as Tom Shippey has pointed out) distinguished Chambers from many of his fellow philologists, but united him with Tolkien, was his unashamedly romantic nostalgia and enthusiasm for the lost poems and legends their rigorous analysis detected.[47]

Chambers's first large-scale work was his great edition of the Old English poem *Widsith*, an apparently unadorned catalogue of the eponymous poet's (Widsith, 'the far-travelled') wanderings amongst the tribes of Germanic Europe and their neighbours, and the courts of kings and rulers. Chambers draws together sources and analogues for all of these tribes and heroes, and for the legends that, to the original audience of the poem, would have sprung up unbidden as the names were heard. He presents *Widsith*, edited with philological rigour, as no less than a compendium of lost Germanic heroic legend, some of which he was able to retrieve by careful and patient work. It is a book at once scholarly (he was schooled by Housman, remember) and deeply romantic, charged with regret for the lost tales and the heroic age that had been so moved by them that a bare mention of their names was enough for memory, now darkened by long years and the indifference of the supposedly civilized:

One such [the fifth-century bishop Sidonius Apollinaris] has told us how his soul was vexed at the barbarous songs of his long-haired Burgundian neighbours, how he had to suppress his disgust, and praise these German lays. How gladly now would we give all his verses [Sidonius is a copious but unexciting poet] for ten lines of the songs in which these 'long-haired, seven foot high, onion-eating barbarians' celebrated, it may be, the open-handedness of Gibica, or perhaps told how, in that last terrible battle, their fathers had fallen fighting around Gundahari.[48]

Chambers published *Widsith: A Study in Old English Heroic Legend* in 1912, when Tolkien was in his first year at Oxford. It was at the forefront of English philology at the very time when Tolkien was first seriously engaging with the subject. As John Garth has said well, 'Chambers's book reads like a message to Tolkien.'[49] As we shall see, it serves as a template for some of Tolkien's own scholarship.

Two years later, Chambers published a revision of A.J. Wyatt's standard English edition of *Beowulf*.[50] He had in hand a long book on the poem, work on which was severely interrupted by his war service as a Red Cross orderly in France (in 1914 he was forty, considerably over military age); it finally appeared in 1921, as *Beowulf: An Introduction*. To this day it has not been bettered as a textbook for a serious student of the poem; one, that is, who wishes to consider not only literary but also historical and archaeological parallels to the text.[51]

Four years later, as a foreword to Sir Archibald Strong's now-forgotten translation of *Beowulf* into rhyming verse, Chambers published an essay, 'Beowulf and the Heroic Age'; Tolkien reckoned this 'the most significant single essay on the poem that I know'.[52]

A shorter article of the same year, 'The Lost Literature of Medieval England',[53] is by comparison a slightly disappointing work, although done with Chambers's characteristic style and learning. Nevertheless, the title itself was surely evocative enough.

We do not know when Chambers and Tolkien first met; Shippey calls him Tolkien's 'patron and supporter',[54] whilst Tolkien himself referred to Chambers as 'an old and kindhearted friend',[55] and gratefully received presents of books from him. However they met, it seems that Tolkien early acquired the friendship and support of this distinguished and humane man.[56]

VI – Return to Oxford

In June 1925, Sir William Craigie, Rawlinson and Bosworth Professor of Anglo-Saxon, tired of wrangling about salaries and workload (and with his wife's complaints on these topics), resigned his chair after nine years in post and moved to America (he went to the University of Chicago to work on a *Dictionary of American English on Historical Principles* and a *Dictionary of the Older Scots Tongue*, whilst remaining on the staff of the *OED*). The electors to the chair approached their favoured candidate, none other than R.W. Chambers, Professor of English at University College London. Chambers was happy where he was, however – he had inherited the Quain chair from his mentor W.P. Ker only two years previously, and was devoted to UCL – and declined to be considered; so the chair was advertised for election. Tolkien applied.

Tolkien had assembled a formidable list of references, from, amongst others, Henry Bradley,[57] George Gordon and Joseph Wright, as well as his senior Leeds colleague Lascelles Abercrombie, and the Baines Professor of English at Liverpool, Allen Mawer.[58] Statements from them accompanied his application, formally printed and bound into a twelve-page pamphlet. Chambers, having declined the chair, was now an elector for it, and so could not act as a referee, although we may suspect he encouraged Tolkien to apply.

George Gordon's reference was fulsome and generous:

> There is no philological (or literary) scholar of his generation from whom I have learned so much, with whom I have worked more happily, or from whom, in my opinion, greater things may be expected.[59]

Gordon, we should remember, was now Merton Professor of English Literature, and thus a weighty voice in the Oxford English School.

Of all those who applied, it soon became clear to the electors that the choice was between Tolkien and his former tutor and current publisher, Kenneth Sisam. Sisam, as we know, was a man of formidable industry and hard-nosed scholarship, who was moreover only four years Tolkien's senior; like Tolkien, he had once been on the staff of the *OED*. Professional relations between them, as we have also seen, had not always been easy; Sisam's job at the University Press included a good deal of nagging authors, amongst them Tolkien, for overdue texts and the abridgement of overlong ones. Sisam's work was close-hauled, bone-dry, and fiercely restricted to the text; Tolkien, on the other hand, although he was in his own way quite as rigorous, was always open to the larger imaginative and conjectural picture the details of the text suggested. If Sisam was in approach the classic, Tolkien was the romantic.

Sisam had been working for the OUP for two years, and before that had spent five years as a civil servant in and immediately after the war, whereas Tolkien had been for the previous five years a full-time teacher and lecturer; on the other hand, Sisam had been for three years personal assistant to (and effective substitute for) Napier during the latter's long final illness, and thus had immediate experience of the day-to-day responsibilities of the Chair of Anglo-Saxon, which Napier had held concurrently with his Merton chair. Sisam's only major publication to date was his undergraduate anthology, with its glossary by Tolkien; Tolkien's edition of *Gawain and the Green Knight* was recently out, and the Clarendon Chaucer was apparently on the slips. Nevertheless Sisam's academic publications, particularly in the field of manuscript studies, were not negligible;[60] he was a very strong candidate.

We may see this as a choice between the Napier approach, strict focus on technical language to the exclusion of literary considerations (Sisam had been Napier's assistant, and his early inclinations were to manuscript studies, shaped by his apprenticeship to Bishop and his strong admiration for Wanley), versus the Chambers–W.P. Ker method of placing technical philology in its literary context. Tolkien exemplified the latter (his letter of application promised 'to advance, to the best of my ability, the growing neighbourliness of linguistic and literary study, which can never be enemies except by misunderstanding or without loss to both'[61]) which may rightly be thought closer to the original Grimm approach to philology.

There were six electors for the chair; they included Chambers, Henry Wyld, the Merton Professor, and Tolkien's old *OED* colleague C.T. Onions, as well as Hermann Fiedler the Professor of German, Charles Plummer of Corpus (the legendary editor of Bede) and Hector Chadwick, Professor of Anglo-Saxon at Cambridge. Three voted for Tolkien, and three for Sisam: the Vice-Chancellor, Joseph Wells of Wadham, gave his casting vote for Tolkien.

We do not know which three voted for Tolkien, but my guess would be Chambers, Onions and (probably) Wyld. Plummer was primarily a historian rather than a philologist (indeed in an obituary Frank

Stenton stated baldly, 'he was not interested in Old English philology'), although he was also an enthusiast for things Celtic (especially Irish) and Icelandic. Chadwick is perhaps fractionally more likely: his synthetic study *The Heroic Age*, which appeared in the same year as Chambers's *Widsith*, sought to relate Old English and other Germanic heroic verse to Homer and other classical exemplars; although we should note that it was by Chadwick's influence that, in 1917, philology became only an optional part of the English course at Cambridge. Wyld, as we have seen, was a German-educated philologist whose interests were probably closest to Tolkien's; he had, too, been taught by Joseph Wright. Certainly, he and Tolkien worked closely together in the following decades. All this, of course, is utterly speculative. As for the casting vote: Wells was a classicist of an older generation (he was born in 1855) who had collaborated on a great (and still not superseded) two-volume edition of and commentary on Herodotus, first published by OUP in 1912. Interestingly, when it reached a second edition, in 1928, it included a brief note apologizing for failing to incorporate any substantive changes in the light of scholarship in the intervening years, but only correction of 'a few obvious errors', 'owing to the high cost of making changes on stereotyped plates'. It may not be fanciful to detect Sisam's hand here, and suppose, presuming negotiations for the second edition were in hand by 1925, that Wells like Tolkien was irritated by his elevating parsimony, or economical publishing, above scholarship, and may thus not have been disposed in his favour. Wells's classicist colleague at Wadham, moreover, was Henry Wade-Gery, who we will remember had served with Tolkien and G.B. Smith during the war, had known both of them well, and was a fellow contributor with them to *Oxford Poetry 1915*. He would (had Wells asked) have been the source of a good personal report. Lastly, and this may be a point of no significance, Wells's 1923 *Studies in Herodotus* was published not by OUP but by Basil Blackwell.

On 21 July 1925, then, Tolkien was elected to the Rawlinson and Bosworth Chair of Anglo-Saxon at Oxford. This was a remarkable achievement for a man of his comparative youth; to gain an Oxford chair, even so comparatively junior and recent a creation as that of Anglo-Saxon, aged only thirty-three argues a very unusual quality in him. He was also unusual in his religion: he joined the few Catholic dons then at Oxford, although the numbers had grown steadily.[62] Sisam, or his advocates at least, thought they had picked the wrong man. The Russian medievalist Eugène Vinaver wrote, in 1971 after Sisam's death (but before

Tolkien's), 'everyone knows what a terrible mistake Oxford made when they by-passed him for the Chair of Anglo-Saxon'.[63]

Tolkien himself was hardly unconscious of this; when, on his retirement in 1959, he gave a valedictory lecture (in belated place of the two inaugurals custom had expected, but he had never given) he first praised his successor, the New Zealander Norman Davis, then remarked:

> If we consider what ... the Oxford English School owes to ... scholars born in Australia and New Zealand, it may well be felt that it is only just that one of them should now ascend an Oxford chair of English. Indeed it may be thought that justice has been delayed since 1925.[64]

The prestige of his new job was high; its pay was not (the stipend was £1,000 a year[65]). To meet the growing expenses of school fees (the Tolkiens now had three children, aged seven, four and eight months; their fourth and last, Priscilla, was born in 1929, when Edith was forty) and doctors' bills – Edith was often unwell – not to mention normal household expenses, Tolkien again took on work as an external examiner for other universities, setting and marking papers.[66] He also continued to mark School Certificate papers. This was drudge's work, but remained a financial necessity for many years; Tolkien devoted large parts of the University vacations to it.

Tolkien did not relinquish his Leeds post until the end of the calendar year, and so was under an obligation to continue teaching there for another term; it was not until January 1926 that he and his family – Edith, John, Michael, Christopher – moved down to Oxford. They found a house in Northmoor Road (no. 22), in the dons' quarter of north Oxford; they spent three years there, until, after the birth of Priscilla, Tolkien finally admitted that, as Edith had always argued, the house was too small for them. Fortunately, their next-door neighbour, the publisher Basil Blackwell, had a larger house he was ready to sell to them. They moved in January 1930 to Blackwell's old house, 20 Northmoor Road; a large house with many small rooms and an extensive garden, it was to be their home for the next seventeen years.

Part II – Philology in Practice

'… by applying his mind industriously to his subject, with a firm conviction of its value and a resolution not to be deceived about it.'[1]

Chapter 5 – Oxford and Storytelling

I – A new professor

Tolkien's day-to-day job was the teaching of English language by lectures, one-to-one tutorials and tireless campaigning to preserve and if possible increase the position of philological studies. He was constantly reading and rereading the great monuments of the English tradition, both pre-Conquest and medieval, and their analogues amongst the literature of the north, notably Norse and Icelandic texts. From this rich mental soil, aside from his purely academic work, grew two sorts of creative writing: improvised stories for his children, and the high legendary matter of his 'elvish' tales, which (we should remember) he insisted with absolute seriousness began as providing the 'necessary background' for his invented languages. It took a decade or more, but eventually these two genera cross-fertilized, and produced a third thing both like and unlike themselves.[2]

Meanwhile, Tolkien now held a senior post in the country's oldest university; he was kept, and kept himself, very busy. For his first term, indeed, he was as we have seen also teaching at Leeds; even after his formal obligation to do so ended, he gave occasional help for another term, until April 1926.

Tolkien was notable for his careful and very extensive preparation for his lecture series; frequently, before lecturing on a particular text, he would prepare a new edition of it reflecting his own views of its nature and the problems it exhibited. This was both time-consuming and unusually diligent. His method in lecturing, as described by a sometime pupil, was 'to translate and, for "criticism", to hop from crux to crux'.[3] He lectured frequently: most professorial chairs required their holders to give a minimum of thirty-six lectures or classes a year; Carpenter notes

133

that during Tolkien's second year in post, he gave fully 136 lectures and classes.[4] This was not wholly voluntary: the Rawlinson and Bosworth chair, unusually, mandated no fewer than six hours a week of lectures or classes, for a minimum of twenty-one weeks in the academic year: 126 in all.[5] This would amount to six classes or lecture courses each term, spread in each case across seven of the weeks of full term. During these years, Tolkien worked hard.

His formal teaching was confined to postgraduate students; unlike tutorial fellows at colleges, or professors at Leeds, Oxford professors do not, typically, have any responsibility for undergraduate tutorials, although their lectures and classes are in the first instance meant for the undergraduate body. The lack of a teaching load is deliberate: its purpose is to allow the professor the freedom to pursue research, and produce and publish scholarly material that will both advance his subject and (incidentally) be a credit to the University. The electors to the Chair of Anglo-Saxon would have expected much from Tolkien in this regard. As we have seen, however, financial necessity led him to devote the majority of the vacations to acting as an external examiner; this was time lost to scholarship.

By the end of 1925, the notes and other apparatus for the Clarendon Chaucer were completed in draft; when they were sent in to Sisam, still at OUP, however, he objected: the glossary was too long, the notes too extensive, and the preface pitched too high for a school audience. George Gordon drafted an alternative preface, but the rest of the work fell to Tolkien. This was galling, as Tolkien considered he had already expended disproportionate time and energy on the book (the selection of texts covered had been changed when the glossary was already far advanced, which had made necessary a very meticulous and time-consuming unpicking and reweaving of it). Tolkien found that the pressures of his new job left no leisure for the work of compressing his notes; Gordon agreed to do it for him, and took the materials in hand.[6] This was the end of the business for the next five years.

One of the most immediate professional concerns for Tolkien was the status of the Oxford English School itself. As we have seen, when it was established in 1894 it was explicitly only a Final Honour School – that is, no undergraduate might read for it unless he had already passed a First Public Examination (which meant, in practice, either Honour Moderations in Literae Humaniores (Classics), which had been Tolkien's route, or the less demanding Pass Moderations) or had already gained Honours in another subject. It was not possible to begin the specific English course immediately on matriculation; the most that could be done was to read for Pass Moderations with a bias towards literary-philological subjects. Soon after Tolkien returned to Oxford, the English Faculty in Michaelmas (autumn) Term 1926 became formally independent of the Faculty of Medieval and Modern Languages and Literature. One of the first acts of the newly constituted Faculty Board (of which Tolkien was an ex officio member) was to propose setting up a separate and specific First Public Examination in English (the so-called 'English Prelim') to replace the required Honour or Pass Moderations. This request was denied.

His next priority was reform of the syllabus; he made a tentative start. We should remember that Tolkien at Leeds had been given a largely free hand to design a syllabus according to his own sense of priorities and value; any vested interests were by-passed or overruled with the strong help of George Gordon and the University Vice-Chancellor. He may have come to his Oxford job with a similar amount of reforming zeal; certainly, his application had hinted as much. He was to find, however, that his freedom of movement at Oxford was, by comparison, significantly restrained.

One important reason for this was his own lack of authority over his colleagues. As a professor, he had some standing in the English Faculty; but whereas in Leeds (say) this had meant real authority over all who taught his subject in the University, and the capacity, funds permitting, to hire and fire staff, at Oxford this was not so. At Oxford, certainly then, the faculties were comparatively insignificant, particularly in their responsibility for personnel other than the handful of professors and readers. Tutorial fellows were hired by, responsible to, and under the authority of, their colleges above all, and colleges were jealous of their autonomy. Tolkien might persuade or cajole, but he could not order or (much less) threaten.

An additional if related difficulty, and one that had a significant effect on Tolkien's scholarly productivity, was a chronic shortage of teaching staff.[7] This too was a direct consequence of Oxford's collegiate structure, which means that the vast majority of tenured staff are hired not by the University (as Tolkien was) but by individual colleges according to an almost infinitely variable, and unpredictable, schedule of their own private priorities. Thus, if a particular college had a fellow who was able and willing to teach undergraduates a particular part of the English course, he might be able (and willing) to do so only for undergraduates from his own college, or for his own and one other; and, should he die or retire or become incapacitated, there was no guarantee or even likelihood that his position would be filled by a man similarly qualified. As a result, undergraduate teaching across the University was both patchy and precarious. For long-established subjects (such as Classics), a temporary shortage in one college or another might easily be made up; for English, this was emphatically not so. One consequence of this was that the few scholars who held, in addition to or prior to their college fellowships, a salaried University teaching position such as a professorship, were in practice obliged to assume a far wider responsibility for undergraduate teaching than the statues defining their jobs envisaged. In the particular practical case of the English Faculty, at this period there were only three scholars available to teach the technical philological side of the course, which all undergraduates were obliged to follow: Tolkien, C.T. Onions (as Reader in English Philology) and the old Merton Professor of English Language, H.C. Wyld. All of these men gave far more lectures than they might have been expected to give, Tolkien and Wyld each two or three times more, often covering the elementary parts of the subject. Tolkien regularly gave six lecture courses a term. This may not seem a great deal, but we should remember that physical time on his feet talking was a small part of the time and effort needed to write and give a course of study. Few if any of the tutorial fellows at individual colleges made any effective contribution to teaching the philological basics of the course; which meant that the burden of teaching the subject fell on to Tolkien and his salaried colleagues, who were obliged to do so by lectures and classes, rather than the more effective individual tutorials that remain the foundation of Oxford undergraduate teaching. One immediate consequence of all this, in turn, was that many candidates did not learn much philology, and the examiners noticed. For the next twenty years, Tolkien and his allies made repeated efforts to persuade the University to hire more people to teach linguistic subjects, but with very limited success. If a subject is both compulsory and, for whatever reason, not very well taught (and it was a frequent complaint that Tolkien did not lecture well, or at least audibly), it is likely to become unpopular, certainly when compared with flashy and less demanding topics; and this, undeniably, is what happened to the philological side of the Oxford course. An exception to this was the women's colleges, which, for historical reasons, were all well provided with English dons: at least one at each women's college would be a philologist, and so they were usually able to give their undergraduates a good foundation in the technical side of the course in the more congenial, and more effective, environment of the college tutorial, allowing them to take from the professorial lectures the broader and more synthetic knowledge they were designed to impart, rather than attending lectures by world authorities so as to mug up the basics of sound-changes.

A solution to this would, of course, have been to co-ordinate college tutorial appointments across the University so as to ensure effective teaching coverage for all aspects of the English course; but this would require the sort of interference with collegiate autonomy that was practically impossible. A tutorial fellow was elected by the other fellows of his college, who as a class were notoriously impermeable to external persuasion, and were as likely to choose (or reject) a man for his personal qualities as for his scholarship. Many colleges, moreover, were only temporarily persuaded that tutorial fellows in English were worth having in the first place, let alone a particular type of tutorial fellow to suit the exigencies of a new-minted faculty rather than the considered and customary discernment of a Senior Common Room who were, after all, the ones who would have to listen to him at dinner each night.

For historical reasons, then, there were too few teachers of philology at Oxford; and this meant the ones, like Tolkien, who were both present and able, were chronically overworked as lecturers and, also, in the setting and marking of examinations. I would not wish to argue that teaching and examining are worthless activities, or that they formed an unexpected part of Tolkien's job; but they surely assumed a disproportionate position, and often consisted of elementary instruction that should have been done by other more junior staff. A professor was expected to teach, certainly, but also to research and to write, and the amount of teaching Tolkien was obliged to do had a real effect on his capacity to undertake the rest of his job.

II – The legendarium continued

Aside from his professional activities, Tolkien did manage to snatch time for what, if pressed, he might have described as his hobby: his invented languages, and the growing corpus of story that surrounded them.

Tolkien had put aside the alliterative *Children of Húrin* before leaving Leeds; he began, now, a retelling of the Beren and Lúthien story in octosyllabic couplets, with the title *The Lay of Leithian*. He worked on this poem, on and off, for the next six years (from the summer of 1925 to September 1931).

Certain concepts from the *Lost Tales* had by now been modified; the most important was the role of England. Where, previously, England – Lúthany, Lúthien, Leithian – was physically identical to the Elvish Tol Eressëa, now it becomes, instead, the place where elves from the Great Lands took refuge after various invasions, and whence they sailed to Tol Eressëa, now in the Uttermost West. The *Tale*-telling, also, was moved: Eriol was now made a man of the eleventh century rather than the fifth, and renamed Ælfwine, 'Elf-friend'. There was also an attempt, which seems never to have been fully articulated, to connect the Ing (Ingwë, Inwë) of the *Lost Tales* with the legendary and eponymous founder of the Ingvaeones, Pliny's name for the Germanic tribes of the North Sea coasts (the Angles, Saxons, Jutes and Frisians), the Old English reflex of whose name was Ingwine, 'friends of Ing' (and who are so mentioned in *Widsith*). Jacob Grimm had connected this Ing with one of the by-names for the Norse God Freyr; indeed, he had noted, *frey* (Old English *frea*) seems to be a title, 'Lord', and Ing or Yngvi (proto-Germanic *Ingwaz) his original name (Ing and Yngvi-frey appear in a lecture Tolkien gave fifteen years later[8]). In drafts of unwritten *Tales* the Ingwine appear as the Ingwaiwar, the ancestral English in their Baltic littoral home. Ing was to meet elves, or perhaps Earendel, and from them, or him, be given a draught of deathlessness (*limpë*) before returning to found the Ingvaeones. This presumably would account for his later elevation to godhood. The surviving fragments are confusing, and the precise narrative sequence and projected historico-legendary connexion not wholly certain; but Tolkien clearly planned a radical grafting of proto-English history into his legendarium. It never seems to have achieved satisfactory form; no subsequent connected narrative takes it up. The surviving tale *Ælfwine of England*, which may have been revised at this time, does not mention Ing or the Ingwine, although they are prominent in Tolkien's notes.[9]

There remained much in the prehistory of the English that was suggestive and enticing; but Tolkien seems never to have been able explicitly to grasp, or if he grasped satisfactorily to formulate, its 'true narrative'. The material itself, or such fragments as are known or conjectured, is tangled and sometimes contradictory, which cannot have helped.

Early in 1926, Tolkien wrote a short prose text, 'A Sketch of the

Mythology', to give a brief background to the long poems *The Lay of Leithian* and *The Children of Húrin* which he sent to his old schoolmaster, R.W. Reynolds, for comment. Originally meant purely as a background synopsis, the 'Sketch' however now became the primary prose vehicle for the development of Tolkien's legendarium; the original *Lost Tales* were put aside, and never revised further. Indeed it seems probable that Tolkien had not done much to the *Tales* whilst in Leeds, and when composing the synopsis incorporated many developments that had not hitherto been written down or had been silently adopted in the composition of the alliterative *Children of Húrin*. It was this text, many years and layers of development later, which became the book we know as *The Silmarillion*. When Tolkien returned to the prose cycles of his mythology (in part because Reynolds was less than enthusiastic about the poems) he took as his basis not the *Book of Lost Tales* but the 'Sketch'; as John Garth put it, 'the précis turned into a replacement'.[10] Garth, amongst others, regrets this; the *Lost Tales*, he argues, have an 'ebullience, earthiness and humour' lacking from the later versions, which miss, also, the 'physical and psychological detail' of the narrative verse.

Nevertheless, the legendarium is still a literal 'mythology for England': Britain, in this version, is the last remnant of Beleriand, broken in the wars of Morgoth's overthrow; the stories are still told to Eriol, who alone had returned from the Lonely Isle. Eventually, however, Tolkien abandoned their original 'Anglo-Saxon' framework of tales told to a traveller, and an identification of the places of the mythology with England, although he tried hard to find some way to keep the first of these, even in its very latest versions. What he lost, arguably, was that 'contact with the earth' he declared was essential to a living mythology. He also needed a framework for the stories that would make them accessible to the reader.

All of these points are debatable, and their resolution was to a large extent many years in the future. But it was to be some time before Tolkien was to find the necessary middle term between the high matter of his mythology and the grounded experience of the English reader. None of this was made easier by the fact that Tolkien showed his writing to very few. Tolkien needed a properly appreciative audience.

III – Heavy Lewis

On 11 May 1926, at an English Faculty meeting, Tolkien met Magdalen's recently elected Tutorial Fellow in English, a Belfast atheist, frustrated philosopher and aspirant poet named C.S. Lewis – 'Jack' to his intimates; to his undergraduate contemporaries, on account of his earnest intensity, 'Heavy Lewis'.[11] Lewis noted in his diary that evening that Tolkien was 'a smooth, pale, fluent little chap … No harm in him: only needs a smack or two.'[12]

Lewis is now a very familiar figure; in 1926, he was wholly obscure, having published only one unsuccessful volume of verse (a second, equally unsuccessful, appeared that September). It was almost a decade before the first of his major works was published. Like Tolkien, he had been an infantry subaltern during the war; he was in France between January and May 1918. After a month at the front, he too had contracted trench fever, but he had made a quick enough recovery to be sent back in time to be wounded in March 1918, and eventually (again like Tolkien) sent back to England to convalesce. His schooling had been patchy (he had hated his three English boarding schools, but had thrived under a private tutor) but his undergraduate career, resumed after the war, had been academically outstanding. He had taken Firsts in Classical Moderations and Greats and then, after only nine months' work, First Class Honours in English (he had been taught, in part, by George Gordon). Despite this, it took him two years to find an academic job; indeed, he only read English at all to give himself a 'second string' – his first ambition had been to teach philosophy as a tutor in Greats.

Lewis had spent the eight years previous to his election to Magdalen living in a series of rented houses in the Oxford suburbs with a woman called Janie Moore, whose son Paddy had been Lewis's room-mate in military training. Paddy Moore was killed in 1918, and Lewis, on the strength of a promise he had made him, had taken it on himself to make a home with his mother. Lewis's own mother had died when he was ten. This is of course obviously parallel to Tolkien's experience, although if either man ever remarked on this, he did so only privately; but it is worth comparing Tolkien's recorded words on his mother's death (pointing at the sky, and saying 'it is so empty and cold') with Lewis's account in *Surprised by Joy*: 'With my mother's death all settled happiness, all that was tranquil and reliable, disappeared from my life.'[13]

To some extent Mrs Moore was an obvious substitute for Lewis's mother (although she was ten years younger than her), but there seems to have been more to it than that. When she first met Lewis, she was forty-five years old, and had been separated from her husband for a decade; Lewis was eighteen, and emotionally starved. Certainty on this point is not possible, but it seems very probable that their relationship was sexual, at least at first and possibly until Lewis became a Christian in 1931. Whatever the truth of this, his private life was in some definite ways irregular, and was never discussed with intimates.

Lewis was at great pains to conceal the real nature of his domestic life from his family and friends, particularly from his father Albert Lewis, a successful police court lawyer for whom he had in early youth developed a fine and enduring contempt (a quarter of a century later, he wrote, 'I treated my own father abominably and no sin in my whole life now seems to be so serious'[14]), but who had uncomplainingly funded Lewis's university career (and, unbeknownst to him, his domestic set-up) until he finally landed his fellowship. Lewis had deliberately lied to his father about his domestic life and the state of his finances; when, eventually, he had been discovered in the lie, or at least the financial part of it (he had told his father he had money in credit, but was seriously overdrawn), there was a bad scene, in which Lewis said 'terrible, insulting, and despising things' to his father. Albert Lewis, who in his clumsy way loved his sons dearly, wrote in his diary that this was 'one of the most miserable periods of my life'. He never seems to have found out the full extent of Lewis's deceit regarding Mrs Moore, although he certainly suspected it: Albert Lewis was a clever and observant man, who however was determined not to believe anything bad about his sons without inescapable evidence being forced on him. In this he probably resembles many fathers.[15]

Lewis's closest friends were his brother Warren ('Warnie'), a professional soldier three years his senior who was heartily bored stationed in Shanghai and relieved his boredom with whisky; Owen Barfield, an undergraduate contemporary who was now perforce a solicitor, like Lewis a frustrated philosopher (although unlike Lewis a very good one); and a boyhood crony, Arthur Greeves, a chronic invalid of independent means, an amateur painter, stolid, unhappy, homosexual. Only Greeves, who still lived in Belfast, was ever given the true story of Lewis's private life: and he never told (he burnt the relevant parts of Lewis's letters to him). Part of this was an innate and creditable discretion (Mrs Moore was a married woman with a husband still living); part was professional prudence (his university career would have been finished had the authorities learnt of it); part, one suspects, sheer embarrassment. Had his father known (for certain, rather than strongly suspecting), he would certainly have fiercely disapproved, and might well (Lewis feared) have docked the allowance he paid until his son was twenty-six. Albert surely suspected the true state of affairs, but decided to accept Lewis's flat and deliberate denials. When, thirty-five years later, Lewis came to write his autobiography, he gave nothing away:

> ... I must warn the reader that one huge and complex episode will be omitted. I have no choice about this reticence. All I can or need say is that my earlier hostility to the emotions was very fully and variously avenged. But even were I free to tell the story, I doubt if it has much to do with the subject of the book.[16]

The last sentence may strike one as at least a little disingenuous, although Lewis may have believed it true. Lewis was, in at least one particular, definitely his father's son: he delighted in argument, fierce, ruthless, at times unscrupulous; but also in poetry and story to a degree unusual even, or perhaps especially, amongst dons. In this he was also his father's son: Albert Lewis was an intensely literary man, whose book-filled house had provided the enduring foundation for his son's remarkable learning. This, at any rate, was the man, at once immensely private and furiously talkative, who now came into Tolkien's professional ambit.

The previous term (Hilary Term 1926), in an effort to win allies for his proposal to admit more Old and Middle English literature into the syllabus (and full texts, rather than a mere list of sound-changes illustrated by 'gobbets') at the expense of nineteenth-century literature, Tolkien had organized a reading club for dons, to work through the major Icelandic sagas. It was called the Coalbiters (from the Norse *kolbítar*, those who sit so close to the fire that they 'bite the coal').[17] They met twice a term or so, with each man attending being assigned, in advance, a passage of one of the sagas to get up ready for translation (without notes or crib) at the actual meeting.

Some were already more than competent scholars of Icelandic. These included three full professors: Gustav Braunholtz, five years Tolkien's senior, who was elected to the Chair of Comparative Philology (in succession to Joseph Wright, on his retirement) the same year Tolkien was elected to his chair; John Fraser, a decade his elder, and Jesus Professor of Celtic since 1921 (and a fellow Catholic); and the formidably eccentric R.M. (Richard) Dawkins,[18] who was older still (he was born in 1871), Professor of Byzantine and Modern Greek, veteran archaeologist and authority on Greek dialect and folklore. Two decades earlier, Dawkins had been a cohort of the odious but talented Frederick Rolfe ('Baron Corvo'), who repaid his generosity with crude lampooning. Dawkins had inherited property in Wales, where his neighbours were the Pirie-Gordons, whose son Harry was Rolfe's then literary collaborator (and bankroll); he met Rolfe whilst visiting them. Dawkins and Rolfe discovered a shared interest in 'artistic' photography of young men in the Greek manner, and Dawkins took Rolfe off to Venice, where, he reckoned, these things could be better pursued. Rolfe was a difficult companion, and Dawkins moreover was alarmed by his directness in approaching potential subjects, so they parted. Dawkins went on to Greece to archaeologize, leaving Rolfe in Venice, where, for the next five years, he sponged, wrote and brooded on his wrongs, supported by donations from the gullible or prurient, until a heart attack did for him in October 1913. Dawkins himself was massively discreet about his predilections, as was not uncommon at the time; they were more understanding about these things abroad, where he often was.[19]

C.T. Onions of the *OED* was another old hand – he was only two years younger than Dawkins, had been Tolkien's senior at the *OED* and was now also a fellow at Magdalen.

Others were interested, and had read sagas in translation, but had only modest knowledge of the language: these included Tolkien's old Leeds boss George Gordon, John Bryson, who taught English at Merton, and Bruce McFarlane, the Magdalen historian (who became a fellow only in 1927, so may not have been amongst the first members).

Another was the English don at Tolkien's old college, Exeter, Nevill Coghill, a pillar of the University dramatic societies. Coghill's father was an Anglo-Irish baronet, from Castle Townshend near Skibbereen. He had gone up to Exeter in 1919, after war service, and thus knew Tolkien only as an old member. He was however Lewis's exact contemporary in the English School. Coghill was a devout Protestant, and (according to A.N. Wilson, anyway) a homosexual. At some stage, someone (perhaps Coghill, or McFarlane) invited Lewis to come along;[20] he soon became a regular attender, but his acquaintance with Tolkien only ripened into friendship late in 1929, when, at last, Lewis realized that Tolkien shared his visceral enthusiasm for Norse mythology and William Morris. They were also both fond of beer and tobacco (which helped), and of country walks, although Tolkien preferred a more leisurely progress with frequent stops to examine trees and flowers to the twenty-mile-a-day route marches Lewis was given to. We should note that it took fully three years for their acquaintance to ripen into friendship; although Tolkien is mentioned in Lewis's diaries and letters from these years, he appears only in passing.

This initial reserve may have been mutual: Tolkien was unusually private, although often superficially expansive and personable, whilst Lewis was suspicious of what Tolkien stood for on at least two counts, professional and religious; but once it had passed, they discovered a rare sympathy of mind and interests. Soon Tolkien lent Lewis the manuscript of his long poem on Beren and Lúthien; Lewis was enthusiastic, with some quibbling over detail. Tolkien read him some of his prose narratives; he was more enthusiastic still. We should not underestimate the risk Tolkien took in thus sharing his imaginative work; few other Oxford dons would have been receptive to the sort of things he wrote and thought, and the danger of mockery or embarrassment was real. Tolkien's need for a friendly but critical ear was however greater yet, and outweighed the risk. Tolkien wrote, many years later, that Lewis 'was for long my only audience. Only from him did I ever get the idea that my "stuff" could be more than a private hobby'; this encouragement, Tolkien said, was 'the unpayable debt that I owe to him'.[21]

The debt was not wholly one-sided, though; on 19 September 1931, Lewis had a long night talk with Tolkien and their friend Hugo Dyson which was instrumental in Lewis beginning to accept the 'myth of Christ' as true. Soon afterwards, Tolkien wrote a poem, 'Mythopoeia', summarizing their talk. It is an important source for his theory of 'sub-creation'.[22] Lewis had come to a form of theism probably a year earlier, soon after his father's death, in fact, but his acceptance of actual dogmatic Christianity was uncertain before Tolkien and Dyson resolved his doubts. Alister McGrath has made a convincing case that Lewis misdated his initial conversion to theism in his autobiography, placing it a good year or so before it actually occurred; this is not insignificant, since during the year in question, amongst other things, Lewis's father Albert died. One need not be a thoroughgoing Freudian to suppose there may be a connexion between his death and Lewis's turning to God, nor preternaturally suspicious to suspect Lewis of wishing, consciously or otherwise, to obscure any such collocation as it might be made by a lazy reader. He may indeed – and this is just as likely, if not more so – have elided the events in his own memory of the time.[23]

Tolkien was disappointed, perhaps at the time and certainly in hindsight, that Lewis simply returned to his historical practice of Anglicanism, rather than becoming a Catholic; but, as Tolkien must have known, anti-Catholic prejudice was deeply rooted in Lewis, as in any Ulster Protestant of his vintage (his nurse, for instance, may during potty training have referred to the young Lewis's stools as 'wee popes'[24]), and in one sense, which Lewis later acknowledged, friendship with Tolkien of itself represented an ecumenical triumph of a high order:

> At my first coming into the world I had been (implicitly) warned never to trust a Papist, and at my first coming into the English Faculty (explicitly) never to trust a philologist. Tolkien was both.[25]

By this time, Lewis's domestic life had if anything become even odder. His father had died, and his brother, aged thirty-six, took early retirement from the Army (questions had been asked about his drinking, and he was asked to resign from the active list). George Sayer, who knew him well, speculates that Warnie's drinking may have become chronic during the war, when in addition to the danger to himself (Warnie was in the Army Service Corps, rather than a front-line job, but was often under shellfire) he was very worried about his brother, who was an infantry subaltern. Worry led Warnie into nightmares, nightmares to insomnia; and insomnia he dosed with whisky. He finally retired from the active list in December 1932, fourteen months after the purchase of The Kilns (of which more next) was finalized. The stagnation of his career may be gauged, in part, by his promotions: he was made Captain in November 1917, after three years of active service, but was not subsequently promoted in the fifteen years before he retired. This might be down to innumerable reasons, but is at any rate suggestive.

Money from the sale of the Lewis family house in Belfast, combined with Warnie's savings and what money Janie Moore could raise, was when taken together enough for them to buy, collectively, a smallish house set in eight acres of woods and lakes at the foot of Shotover Hill in cast Oxford. This house, The Kilns, now became home to Lewis, Janie Moore, Warnie and, intermittently, Janie's adult daughter Maureen, now a music teacher at various secondary schools. Over the years, they collected a varied household of domestic staff and animals, and the house got shabbier and shabbier. Warnie settled into a pattern of quiet reading and writing (he arranged and transcribed great quantities of the family archive, and was a punctilious and observant diarist) punctuated by drinking sprees; but for the most part he was an unobtrusive companion to his brother and his ménage.

IV – Stories told to my children

It was clearly a great help to Tolkien to have a sympathetic adult audience for his stories; but Lewis was not his only audience. Tolkien's children were, alongside his professional life, another and different spur to his imagination. He used to make up stories for them, often incorporating their favourite toys, or unusual places or things they saw whilst on holiday. Most of these were ephemeral, and have not survived; others were written down, and eventually published. It was here, in fact, that the key to the eventual emergence of his mythological writing was to be found.

The earliest children's stories to survive are a series of letters written to the Tolkien children from, it was feigned, Father Christmas. These began in 1920, when John Tolkien was three, and continued each year until 1943, when Priscilla, the youngest child, was fourteen. They were increasingly elaborate, and were copiously illustrated: Tolkien was a very competent amateur artist in pencil, ink, chalk and watercolour. Another story began as an effort to console his son Michael after he lost a toy dog on holiday at Filey on the Yorkshire coast, in September 1925. It was written down by 1927, but not published, as *Roverandom*, until 1998. The next year Tolkien wrote *Mr Bliss*, an illustrated children's story giving the adventures of some of his children's favourite toys (bears and a clockwork car). It was published only in 1982. Around this time he wrote, also, an early version of *Farmer Giles of Ham*; this began as a story explaining Oxfordshire place-names. It was expanded and rewritten several times over the next decade, and changed its nature a little during the process.

All of these are stand-alone tales, with no point of contact with what still lay at the heart of Tolkien's imagination, the evolving linguistic and legendary corpus of the 'Quenta'. This, as we shall see, was not to be true of the next story to be considered.

In about 1930, sitting at his desk marking examination papers, Tolkien had the happy experience of finding the last page of a script left blank. On that blank page, he wrote, 'In a hole in the ground lived a hobbit.'

Much ink has subsequently been spilt debating the origins of this sentence. Tolkien, however, said it had come to him from nowhere, and it is simplest to believe him. Sometimes the creative faculty works like this: when the mind is tired, or bored with routine work, it pulls from the subconscious (or somewhere) a phrase or image that is, as it were, fully formed. The hobbit seems to have been conceived in this way. Tolkien himself thought the Sinclair Lewis novel *Babbitt*, dealing with a smug businessman, may have influenced the form of the word. He also subsequently gave it a cod-etymology as a worn-down form of a hypothetical Old English *hol-bytla*, 'hole-dweller'; it is not impossible this second account may have been at least as accurate as the first, since it would be quite in character for Tolkien to generate this sort of thing without conscious effort.

Soon, a story grew around that first sentence, and parts of it were told to the Tolkien children during the early 1930s. Unusually, perhaps because the story was on a larger scale than previous efforts, Tolkien wrote much of it down, although the end of the tale may have been composed, if at all, only orally. Certainly, by February 1933 there was enough of it on paper for it to be given to Lewis to read. Lewis was impressed, not merely by the narrative fluency, but also by its distinct imaginative air. He wrote to an old friend:

> Reading his fairy tale has been uncanny – it is so exactly like what we wd. both have longed to write (or read) in 1916: so that one feels he is not making it up but merely describing the same world into which all three of us have the entry.[26]

This first impression on reading Tolkien, of recognition (particularly of something hitherto touched if at all only in Norse myth), is (I suspect) not an unusual one; I vividly remember feeling exactly this when I first read the book, some few years after a half-remembered encounter with retold Norse mythology. Perhaps this sense may be taken as a touchstone of a likely taste for Tolkien's imaginative project as a whole?

Tolkien had written *The Hobbit* in bursts, mostly during the University vacations, over several years, and the manuscripts were (as might be expected) a jumble; he prepared a typescript of the bulk of the book, although the last chapters, when they were finally written down, were left in manuscript.[27] The resulting document, known as the 'home manuscript', was both used as a reading copy (it was Tolkien's custom, during part of the year at least, to read to his children in his study after their supper) and as a text to be lent to selected friends and students, who he thought might like it (and the copy, accordingly, became increasingly dog-eared). We may wonder whether, in expending the significant time and effort to make a typescript, Tolkien had a potentially wider audience in mind; for the moment, however, he had no particular impulse to try to get *The Hobbit* published; like the rest of his writing, it remained a wholly private amusement, to be shared, if at all, only with friends and family.[28]

V – The true tradition of English: the AB language

Storytelling for adults and children was intellectually stimulating, even if only a private amusement; but Tolkien's job also gave him a rich field for intellectual endeavour and excitement.

In 1929, he published an article, 'Ancrene Wisse and Hali Meiðhad', in *Essays and Studies*; it had been in gestation since at least 1925 (he mentioned it on his application for the Rawlinson and Bosworth Chair as 'forthcoming'). It analyses the language of the texts contained in the 'Katherine Group' manuscript, which included *Hali Meiðhad*, alongside that of one of the major manuscripts of the *Ancrene Riwle*, an early Middle English guide for solitary women religious ('anchoresses'); this manuscript called it *Ancrene Wisse*. Tolkien demonstrated that not only were these two manuscripts written in an identical form of Middle English, but that this dialect (which he christened the 'AB language', after the conventional sigla for the two manuscripts – the term has since become a standard one) showed philologically accurate distinctions in the forms of certain verbs carried over, and indeed in some respects developed, from Old English. The consistent and pure English of these texts, written by several different hands, shows (Tolkien argued) that, in at least one place in England (he guessed Herefordshire, which later research has confirmed), there was an established school of writers who employed a standardized language that descended from Old English with informed awareness of its grammatical traditions, elsewhere neglected, confused or lost.

> It is not a language long relegated to the 'uplands,' struggling once more for expression in apologetic emulation of its betters ... but rather one that ... has contrived, in troublous times, to maintain the air of a gentleman, if a country gentleman. It has traditions, and some acquaintance with books and the pen, but it is also in close touch with a good living speech – a soil somewhere in England.[29]

Here at least, Tolkien argued, the catastrophic breach in English literary tradition effected by the Norman Conquest had not occurred.

The article was a bravura performance, one that took the smallest philological details and made from them a wholly plausible inference to a larger linguistic and historical picture, one that shed light both on the texts in hand and the conditions under which they were written and read: told us, in fact, something about English history of which we would otherwise be thoroughly ignorant.[30] It was a fine and worthy product of a professor's chair, at what was near the beginning of a potentially long career; Tolkien's colleagues presumed it was the presage of larger and greater things to come. This hope was, as we shall see, not fulfilled exactly as they might have expected.

VI – Syllabus reform

The syllabus Tolkien followed as an undergraduate had comprised four papers (*Beowulf* and Old English, *Gawain* and Middle English, Chaucer and Shakespeare) compulsory for all taking the School, plus five papers chosen exclusively from a 'Language' or 'Literature' selection. The former excluded almost all 'literary' considerations, but included a compulsory History of Literature paper; the latter in contradistinction excluded any linguistic or philological matter, apart from a compulsory history of the language. The result was that those who had a philological bent were largely deprived of anything other than 'gobbets' to exercise it on, whilst 'literary' students were in large part technically unequipped for close analysis of pre-modern writers. By the time serious consideration was being given to revising the syllabus, fully nine-tenths of those reading English chose the 'literary' option. For Tolkien, whose application for his professorial chair had been founded on promoting philological study at Oxford with as much success as he had had at Leeds, this was an intolerable state of affairs.

As we saw above, the proposal to introduce a pure 'English Prelim' for first-year undergraduates failed; in 1930, however, Tolkien and his allies managed to have added to the available options for Pass Moderations two additional papers, one in Old English and another in seventeenth-century literature. This was hardly enough, but it was something. Nevertheless, the real business of reform needed to happen in the syllabus for Final Schools; and it was on this that Tolkien focussed his efforts.

His initial move, after making some suggestions to the Faculty Board in February 1930, was to publish, in the quasi-official *Oxford Magazine* for 29 May that year, a manifesto for reform of the syllabus. This essay, titled 'The Oxford English School', suggested, in effect, that Oxford adopt exactly the same pattern (of 'A' and 'B' schemes) as he had devised and implemented at Leeds (which was itself, ironically, a modification of the Oxford syllabus he had known as an undergraduate).

The Leeds syllabus was divided into the 'A' (broadly, 'lit.') scheme and the 'B' (philology); Tolkien's Oxford proposal, however, assigned 'A' to the philologists and 'B' to literature. Those studying 'A' would be relieved of the obligation to study the later history of the language (1400–1900), since they were not required to study any books from the corresponding period, and instead encouraged to take cognate languages (Gothic, Old Norse) and study their surviving literature; whilst 'B' students were to be relieved of compulsory nineteenth-century literature (it might still be taken as an optional paper) and instead required to take a paper on Old and Middle English texts with the appropriate philological preparation, and examination on unseen passages. Whilst an observer might think these changes are decidedly, and unfairly, weighted in favour of 'philo-logical' study over literary, Tolkien argued that the philological element in serious English studies was so fundamental (and, although he did not say it, the intellectual effort needed to understand nineteenth-century texts so negligible) that this was a necessary bias; and, moreover, what he proposed was at every point to bind philology close to the study of actual texts, of literary merit and power which might be unlocked only with some linguistic effort, an effort that would however yield corollary benefit to all other parts of the course. Despite Tolkien's fluent advocacy, his proposal was not adopted in this form.

Instead, after long and involved negotiation, Tolkien and his allies (Lewis prominent amongst them) secured the adoption of a syllabus that gave the undergraduate reading for English Final Schools three options, Course I, Course II and Course III.

Course I was hard-core philology: there were seven compulsory papers (Old English Philology; Middle English Philology; Old English Texts; Old English Literature; Middle English Texts; Middle English Literature; Chaucer, Langland and Gower), two papers chosen from a list of subsidiary languages and an optional tenth paper drawn either from the language papers or from a formidable list of special subjects.

Course II was philology with a more 'modern' bent: the compul-sory papers were the same as those of Course I, omitting only the two Literature papers but adding, instead, three others: Modern English Philology (1400–1800), English Literature 1400–1550 and Shakespeare and Contemporary Dramatists. One further paper was taken from a list of five options, all broadly philological apart from Spenser and Milton, and an optional tenth from a more limited selection of the Course I special subjects.

Course III was 'literature'. Here the compulsory papers were wholly different: Modern English (language), Old English, Middle English (each with different set texts from the other two Courses), Chaucer and his Contemporaries, Shakespeare and Contemporary Dramatists, Spenser and Milton, and three papers on literature from 1400 to 1830. An optional tenth paper might be added; here, and only here, was it possible to add a paper on Victorian literature.

I have described this new syllabus in some detail in part because of its intrinsic interest, but also to give some idea of the scale of Tolkien's victory in the negotiations. The Oxford English Course was now rigorously philological in bias, with its core elements designed to give a close and humane education in English philology as classically understood, directed primarily at texts from early and medieval periods. Those whose interests were in later literature, or who were linguistically disinclined, were badly served, and that by design. Oxford was now set up to train a new generation of serious philologists; what Tolkien and his allies had not considered, or chose to ignore, was on the one hand the growing trend in literary study elsewhere (which preferred theory-heavy discussion of recent literature to close study of early texts) and on the other the prevailing inclinations of many, perhaps most, scholars and students, which was not, in the main, towards philology. How much of this we attribute to natural human laziness (it is harder to read *Beowulf* than Jane Austen, if not less rewarding) will depend in part on how highly we rate nineteenth-century and later literature, and in part on whether we think university courses should be intellectually challenging and require hard rote work as well as discursive fluency. But these are larger issues than we have space for here.

We should note, also, that the shortage of qualified teachers of philology remained acute, and this did nothing to ease the transition to the new syllabus, nor to make it popular once it was established. The new syllabus was adopted in 1931, and first examined two years later. For the next twenty years, this was the shape of the English syllabus at Oxford.[31]

The cabal of English dons who had engineered these changes continued to meet up; they took to calling themselves 'The Cave' (of Adullam, where David plotted against Saul): the leading lights were

Tolkien, Lewis, Nevill Coghill, Dyson of Reading and others (amongst them Brett-Smith, Rice-Oxley, Wrenn, Dorothy Everett, M.R. Ridley). Their primary object was to maintain their changes against the 'old guard' of literary scholars personified by David Nichol Smith, Merton Professor of English Literature since 1929. Smith was a Scot, seventeen years Tolkien's senior, and an expert on eighteenth-century writing; he had been elected to the Merton chair when George Gordon resigned on becoming President of Magdalen. He had been Goldsmith's Reader since 1908, when he was brought in by Walter Raleigh, whose deputy he had been at Glasgow, but had missed out on the chair when Raleigh died.

There was, we should note, absolutely no inevitability about this change in the syllabus; indeed, at Cambridge, under the influence of Tolkien's professorial counterpart Hector Chadwick, Elrington and Bosworth Professor of Anglo-Saxon there, the study of Old English was hived off from the English School proper and aggregated to Archaeology and Anthropology, where it was combined with the study of Norse and the Celtic languages and their respective archaeologies and histories (cultural rather than linguistic), forming Chadwick's famous 'Section B', in which philology was optional, and although a wide range of linguistic facility was expected, little actual instruction was provided (many of Chadwick's undergraduates spent their vacations in Kerry or North Wales picking up languages from the locals). This type of study, synthetic, wide-ranging and exciting, but often inevitably superficial, may well have seemed the obvious direction for the English School to have taken at Oxford also; but, in some part thanks to Tolkien, it remained a place where philology was taught in its fullness and as a matter of course.

Increasingly, Tolkien was the directing hand amongst Oxford philologists, especially as the old masters retired or died. In February 1930, for instance, Joseph Wright died, aged seventy-five (his wife recorded that his last word was 'Dictionary'); Tolkien was named executor of his estate.

Chapter 6 – Delays and Frustrations

I – Chaucer, again

In the midst of all this, the business of the Clarendon Chaucer stirred once more. Sisam, still at the OUP, asked Tolkien for a progress report. He replied that George Gordon had had his notes since 1925[1] but had done little with them apart from make some annotations. He had not, as he had agreed to do, reduced them to the limits Sisam wanted. Tolkien was by now impatient of the whole project, and clearly mildly frustrated by George Gordon as a collaborator; unlike his namesake E.V., he seemed content to leave all the philological heavy lifting to Tolkien. Gordon's excuse, that he had in 1928 been elected as President of Magdalen and now discharged the considerable duties of a Head of House in addition to any tutorial and lecturing responsibilities, was perhaps a good one, but did not make his dereliction any easier to bear. Tolkien retrieved his notes, and over the next eighteen months made some concerted efforts to shorten and simplify the notes and settle the text and glossary; but it was not enough to satisfy Sisam, and the book languished unfinished.[2]

Nevertheless, Sisam had not wholly dismissed Tolkien; in November 1930, he proposed he and Tolkien should collaborate on an edition of the *Ancrene Riwle,* preferably a simple edition of one of the better manuscripts (ideally Chambers's favourite, Corpus 402) rather than a full-scale critical text. Tolkien replied that he would rather undertake the latter, especially as (under his new syllabus) the language of the text was to be one of the topics of the undergraduate course; but in any event, he could do nothing until Chaucer was put to bed. Sisam agreed on the last point, at any rate. It may be cynical to see this proposal as a carrot to encourage Tolkien to finish Chaucer, but Sisam was a wily man, and his usual tools, persuasion and cajolery, had obviously failed him, so he may have thought to use bribery. Alas, it did not work either. Tolkien was simply too busy.

Tolkien's lectures on *Beowulf* were by now an invariable part of the English syllabus; from the late 1920s, he supplemented them with additional series examining the Finnesburg episode, the longest of the intercalated narrative interruptions to the main Beowulf story, which is uniquely attested also by a short fragment of another Old English heroic poem on the same subject. The story is an archetypically 'northern' one, involving crossed loyalties, violent death of close kin, vengeance delayed and awoken amidst the cold waters of the Baltic; one of the main actors, Hengest, was (Tolkien reckoned) the same man who figures in legends (fossilized in the *Chronicle*) of Anglo-Saxon origins. His theory explaining the episode is ingenious and fascinating, but so elliptically expressed as to be obscure even to the informed. Tom Shippey has pointed out, however, that Jill Paton Walsh's 1966 children's story *Hengest's Tale* reproduces Tolkien's theoretical reconstruction exactly. Tolkien lectured on this rich and heady subject first in 1928, and again more fully in 1930, 1932, 1934, 1935 and 1937.[3] His explanatory theory became complex and subtle, and required him, as a preliminary, to produce an edition of the text with a comprehensive preliminary glossary of names. From these names, his theory – the tale behind the surviving fragments – grew up. The plan and model of this treatment was clearly Chambers's *Widsith*.

In correspondence with the University Press about the still-unfinished Clarendon Chaucer, he mentioned both his Finnesburg material and a mass of other writing about *Beowulf* (the metre and diction of Old English verse in general, and examination of several particular cruces in the text) that he proposed could be prefixed to his (now practically complete) prose translation of the poem, perhaps as part of a cheap student's edition. He also proposed to produce editions of two other Old English poems, *Exodus* and *Elene*, both set books on which he had frequently lectured: 'they both need editing. I have commentaries to both'; he suggested, in the first instance, an edition of *Exodus* as a follow-up to his *Beowulf* translation. Tolkien's practice in his lectures was to provide an edition of the text he was lecturing on, particularly when, as in these cases, he judged existing editions to be wholly inadequate (of the available texts of *Exodus*, one was 'thoroughly bad, and virtually negligible for our students', another 'merely laughable'). Then he would work systematically through the text, commenting on disputed or obscure points, and explaining the emendations, often (by modern standards) very radical, he had felt it necessary to make. Tolkien, like Sisam, did not have a reflexively high opinion of the accuracy of the surviving manuscripts of Old English verse, and was ready to emend and suppose interpolation and omission in a fashion that strikes his more timid successors as cavalier (the most recent editor of *Exodus* described Tolkien, frankly unfairly, as 'an inveterate meddler'[4]). Unlike Sisam, however, Tolkien did not remark, or if he did remark did not trouble to pursue, the obvious implication of this for philology: if manuscript readings were unreliable in substantial matters of vocabulary and syntax (very often, the unemended texts are simple gibberish), how could they be used as sure sources for the incidental philological minutiae of dialect and sound-change? But these are deep waters, and we need not enter them now.[5]

Tolkien had this material at his fingertips throughout the decade, and we may fairly ask why none of it was then published. In fact, Tolkien was conscious of this, but felt paralysed by 'the Chaucerian incubus', the still-unfinished Clarendon Chaucer. Until his 'mind and conscience' were free of Chaucer, he felt unable to undertake the (he reckoned) small amount of polishing the *Beowulf* material would need, let alone setting the other material in order. And Chaucer showed no sign of being finished soon, despite help offered by David Nichol Smith. What should have been Tolkien's years of greatest academic productivity were becoming dangerously full of incomplete, and probably uncompletable, projects; and, always, there was the chore of marking examinations to make ends meet. In 1935, when the scheme for a new *Oxford History of English Literature* was drawn up, he was approached about writing the volume on Old English, but turned it down owing to lack of time. Lewis, who was surely as busy as Tolkien but significantly better organized, was asked to do the sixteenth century; he agreed with pleasure, although in time the project became burdensome to him.

II – A don's life

It was however almost impossible for someone in Tolkien's position not to accumulate some at least of the subsidiary projects and responsibilities that invest the higher reaches of the scholar's profession. During the 1930s, for instance, Tolkien became first general editor and then chief editor of a series of 'Oxford English Monographs' published by OUP; these were selected B.Litt. theses passed by the English School and considered interesting or important enough for publication. Tolkien did not do this work alone, however; he was assisted first by Nichol Smith and C.S. Lewis, later by F.P. Wilson and Helen Gardner.

The parade of graduate students to be supervised was continuous. Tolkien took pains over his supervision, and remained friendly with many of his students. One such was Simonne d'Ardenne, a thirty-three-year-old Belgian of aristocratic antecedents, who began her B.Litt. in 1932 with Tolkien as her supervisor. She was a member of the Society of Oxford Home-Students (the women's house of study that later became St Anne's College), and lived at the hostel at Cherwell Edge, run by the nuns of the Society of the Holy Child Jesus to accommodate Catholic women.[6] She soon became a family friend and 'unofficial aunt', and lived in the Tolkien household from October 1932 until her degree course finished the following summer. She was awarded the B.Litt. in 1933, for an edition of the Katherine Group text Þe Liflade ant te Passiun of Seinte Iuliene, on the basis of which she later gained a Liège doctorate. Published in 1936, the edition bears her name alone, although Norman Davis declared many years later that it 'presents more of Tolkien's views on early Middle English than anything he himself published' and would, in any context other than that of an academic degree, have appeared as a joint publication.[7] E.V. Gordon was, in a private letter to Tolkien, even more forcible: he professed himself 'grieved that your name is not attached to it, because ... practically all that is especially valuable in it is recognisably yours. There is really no other piece of Middle English editing to touch it.'[8] Tolkien seems to have been given a share of the royalties by Simonne d'Ardenne, but Gordon was unconvinced that was enough. He did not actually talk of messes of pottage, but the implication – that Tolkien was being rashly lavish with help and losing kudos that, rightly and undoubtedly to his benefit, should have been his – is clear. Publicly, Gordon reviewed the edition in generous terms without disclosing Tolkien's contribution.[9] We may speculate that Tolkien felt still so paralysed by the Chaucerian incubus that he had lost hope of ever, or soon, bringing any of his own work on this topic to light over his own name, and decided it was better to publish thus covertly than not at all.

There was a greater aim in view, too: one of the great textual desiderata for the study of early Middle English, in Tolkien's view, was a proper edition of the whole corpus of the Katherine Group; he seems to have realized that, on his own, he simply could not find the time to do this, and may well have decided at this point that Simonne d'Ardenne was an excellent potential collaborator in this project, and should thus be helped in this generous manner. Their joint efforts to this end were, inevitably, delayed and impeded by the usual besetting hosts of rival calls on Tolkien's time and attention. Increasingly, influence on others was to become the primary way Tolkien's academic efforts found expression.

During these years, Tolkien was undoubtedly prodigal with help and advice to other scholars, as a glance at the prefaces to most works of scholarship in his field published during this time shows. Throughout his academic career, his influence was much wider than the list of his own scholarly publications would suggest.

He did however publish a comprehensive two-part article, 'Sigelwara Land', analysing the curious name used in Old English as a synonym for 'Ethiopian', and concluding that, in an original form *sigelhearwan, it referred to the soot-blackened fire-giants of northern legend. This, he reckoned, was another fragment of what England had lost.[10] A different area of interest was explored in another 1934 piece, 'Chaucer as Philologist', which argued that *The Reeve's Tale* preserved accurate northern dialect forms in the speech of some of its characters, whom Chaucer wished to present as 'speaking funny'. The article is fine and illuminating as far as it goes, but it does assume a high degree of scribal accuracy in attributing these forms to Chaucer rather than to a copyist or copyists of northern speech-patterns. Philologists of Tolkien's vintage were briskly confident of their ability to nose out authorial from scribal forms in a way that, to their pallid followers, seems overbold. But he, and they, certainly knew more Middle and Old English than we do, so his nose may well have been better. Much of the business of distinguishing the original readings of a medieval text works by an intuitive sense more akin to smell or taste than anything more rationally accountable (or by extension teachable). Those of my readers, presumably a majority, who have never edited an early manuscript will have to take this on trust; the rest may disagree if they like. This article, incidentally, was the only concrete result of Tolkien's long and involved work on the Clarendon Chaucer.

There was another more ephemeral result. One of Nevill Coghill's great interests was the oral performance of medieval poetry, and to this end, in the 1930s, he organized annual 'Summer Diversions' with John Masefield, the Poet Laureate; at the 1938 'Diversions', Tolkien, in costume, recited the *Nun's Priest's Tale*, and the following year, the *Reeve's Tale*, in both cases possibly from memory (although he seems to have worked from abridgements of Skeat's text, which may suggest he used a crib, or perhaps his own abortive edition); certainly, after almost two decades working intermittently on the Clarendon Chaucer, he will have known these texts very well.[11]

III – Analecta and excurses

At some point in the summer of 1932, probably to while away the long hours invigilating Final Schools, Tolkien wrote a verse account of *viva voce* exams (usually administered only to candidates who would otherwise fail outright) in the style of *Piers Plowman*, the prolix four-teenth-century vision-satire; he called it *Visio Petri Aratoris de Doworst*, and cunningly worked in actual 'howlers' that he had been told by desperate or unteachably stupid candidates. The title refers to the plot of *Piers Plowman*, which includes the figures of Dowel, Dobet and Dobest. One would hope Tolkien's verse is a better read than the original, which is fiercely dull and preachy by turns. His fellow examiners that year were C.S. Lewis, Charles Wrenn and H.F.B. Brett-Smith; the four of them feature as Plato, Grim, Britoner and Regulus, who is probably Tolkien himself (these identifications are perforce partly conjectural). Tolkien made an elaborate and decorated manuscript copy of it, had it bound in vellum, and gave it as a Christmas present in 1933 to his friend R.W. Chambers, an authority on *Piers Plowman*. Only a few lines of it have ever been published.[12]

In 1932, an article by Tolkien appeared as an appendix to the archaeo-logical report on the excavations at the site of a Romano-British temple at Lydney Park in Gloucestershire. After some years of unregulated pilfering, the site's owner had, in 1805, commissioned a comprehen-sive excavation (the report of which took three-quarters of a century to appear, a not unparalleled delay even amongst later archaeological liter-ature); in 1928, the Society of Antiquaries was invited to dig it again and supplement the earlier finds with the application of modern archaeolog-ical science. The 1928–9 excavations were directed by Mortimer Wheeler, the great name in forensic archaeology, and his then wife Tessa; as part of their brief they reviewed the results of the previous excavation, and this included the dedication of the temple that formed the heart of the site. This, as evidenced by several inscriptions, was to one Nodens or Nodons, evidently a god or object of worship. One of the Nodens inscriptions, presumably drawn from the earlier report, was used by Arthur Machen to add colour and texture to his 1890 short story *The Great God Pan*; thence the name 'Nodens' was borrowed by H.P. Lovecraft for a short story (*The Strange High House in the Mist*) published in 1926, and from there it has spread to a thousand Lovecraftian derivatives. None of these, sadly, has much to do with Tolkien.

Tolkien agreed to produce a note analysing the name; typically, he did so with an unforeseen thoroughness that came close to delaying the publication as a whole. The name was otherwise unattested; Tolkien connected it with the Irish Núadu or Núada, Welsh Nudd, an obscure figure with connexions to the underworld (and, Tolkien noted, to Lludd, the Welsh original of King Lear), and with an original meaning of 'snarer' or 'hunter'; although the archaeological record shows clearly that the temple functioned primarily as a centre for healing, with (perhaps) a subsidiary cultus amongst hunters and fishermen, and sailors. Tolkien also added, at a late stage, a more speculative paragraph linking Lludd with the name Lydney; but this was either too late or too venturesome for Wheeler to include it in what was finally printed. The site was dug in 1928–9; Tolkien's note was written some time between 1929 and 1931, and appeared when the report came out in July 1932. Statements that Tolkien was part of the excavation team are without foundation.[13]

It may be worth noticing another small matter arising from this business. One of the curse tablets found on site in the earlier dig was an imprecation directed against a man named Senicianus, who was apparently responsible for the loss of a ring belonging to one Silvianus. Silvianus made an offering to Nodens of half of the ring's value against its return. Wheeler, it seems, was the first to connect this inscription with another artefact found, probably at Silchester (which is eighty miles from Lydney), late in the eighteenth century: a heavy gold ring inscribed with Silvianus's name, bearing an image of Venus and what may be a Christian inscription. This may well be the very ring mentioned, once abstracted by Senicianus. It has been in private hands since its discovery, and is kept at The Vyne, a country house near Basingstoke.

Some time in 2013, an enterprising person made the connexion between all this and the Ring in Tolkien's fiction. Wheeler, it is argued, would have told Tolkien of his 'discovery', and thus the device of a cursed ring was lodged in the leaf-mould of Tolkien's mind, to emerge first in *The Hobbit* and then in *The Lord of the Rings*.

There are unfortunately several problems with this story. First, we have no evidence that Tolkien ever saw the Silvianus ring, or even visited Lydney, let alone The Vyne; it is possible that Wheeler told him the story in the course of sharing the inscriptional evidence with him, but not proven: their relationship seems to have been a purely professional one, conducted by letter, and they may not ever have met. Even if Tolkien had been told the story, it was probably too early to have the sort of influence suggested – in 1930–1, *The Hobbit* was in an early draft, and the ring featured only as a convenient plot device (a burglar's help), not as the more weighty and sinister artefact of *The Lord of the Rings*. Tolkien hardly needed a late Roman find to bring the device of a cursed ring to his notice: the Nibelungs' ring, bearer of the dwarf's curse on his treasure, was ready to hand in *The Red Fairy Book* and all its familiar antecedents. The most we might admit is that this curious and intriguing piece of archaeology may have reminded Tolkien that rings might be lost, and cursed, and their owners try to reclaim them; but all this was a late and unplanned addition to the simple invisibility device of *The Hobbit*, and would not emerge until a decade later. Industrious journalists have made further links between Dwarf's Hill – the local name for the Roman iron mine at Lydney – and Tolkien's dwarves. We may politely regard this as unproven.

None of this, of course, has spoiled a good story, and visitors to The Vyne, now owned by the National Trust, can now see the ring displayed in a special 'Ring Room', with paraphernalia and speculative commentary (and copy of the Ruling Ring inscription) provided by the Tolkien Society, who really should know better. There is also a Middle Earth adventure playground in the grounds of the house.

Those familiar with the literature of interwar Oxford may wonder whether Tolkien knew, or was friendly with, another famous Oxford Catholic, Fr Ronald Knox. Knox, son of an Anglican bishop, had had a glittering career at Eton and Oxford before the war; although only four years older than Tolkien, he was already a Fellow of Trinity by the time Tolkien matriculated. In 1912, he took Anglican orders and became Chaplain of his college. In 1917, however, he converted to Catholicism, resigned from his fellowship, and became a schoolmaster. Nine years later, friends concerned at his stagnation prevailed on the Archbishop of Westminster, Cardinal Bourne, to appoint him Catholic Chaplain to Oxford University. He remained in post for thirteen years until, in 1939, he left to be a country-house chaplain and to complete single-handed a translation of the Latin Vulgate Bible into English (the complete Knox

King Edward's School, Birmingham, as it was when Tolkien was a pupil

The Birmingham Oratory, home to Father Francis Morgan, Tolkien's guardian

The Birmingham Oratory, interior.
As a schoolboy, Tolkien would have
worshipped here almost daily

Perrott's Folly; at left, the top of
the Waterworks tower can be
seen. These landmarks of the
Birmingham skyline have been
claimed as the inspiration for
Tolkien's 'two towers'

The Valley of Lauterbrunnen, which Tolkien visited in 1911, may have inspired Rivendell

The quadrangle at Exeter College, Oxford, where Tolkien was an undergraduate

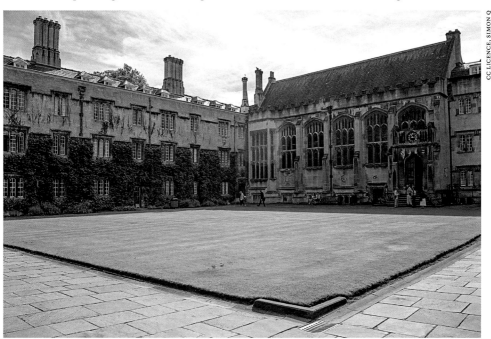

Warwick Castle from across the River Avon. Edith lived in Warwick between 1913 and her marriage; Tolkien often visited her, and the town assumed a role in his earliest stories

Jacob Grimm, pioneering philologist and collector of fairy-tales, and the sort of scholar Tolkien aspired to be

The battlefield at Beaumont Hamel; Tolkien's battalion was in the front line here for some of July and August 1916

The Chancellor's Court of Birmingham University, where the Southern General Hospital was located and Tolkien was sent from France

Pembroke College, Oxford, where Tolkien was a professorial fellow between 1925 and 1945

20 Northmoor Road, where the Tolkiens lived between 1930 and 1947

The Botanical Gardens, where Tolkien often walked

Merton College from the south. Tolkien was a professorial fellow here between 1945 and 1959

The Tolkiens' grave, Wolvercote Cemetery; the inscription names them as 'Beren' and 'Lúthien'

Bust of Tolkien in Exeter College chapel, sculpted by his daughter-in-law

Bible finally appeared in 1950). Knox's ministry was exclusively to the male Catholic undergraduate body; Tolkien habitually went to Mass at the Jesuit-run parish of St Aloysius at the head of the Woodstock Road (now the Oxford Oratory), or at St Gregory and St Augustine in north Oxford, a smaller parish two miles or so to the north-west. He had no immediate reason to visit Knox in the Chaplaincy at the Old Palace on St Aldate's. Nevertheless, it seems improbable that their paths did not cross; Pembroke, Tolkien's college, is close by the Chaplaincy, and Knox was a frequent guest at high tables across the city. There is also a story of Tolkien appearing at a Christmas party for his children and those of Charles Wrenn, held at the Old Palace. He, as often on such occasions, was dressed as a bear.[14] This does not mean, of course, that Tolkien had any dealings with Knox, in or out of costume; but it does make it more likely. There does not, however, seem to be any direct evidence of acquaintance between them; although a chance record of a conversation with the Lewis brothers in the early 1950s might be reckoned as such, the evidence is at best inconclusive.[15]

IV – Poems and prose

At roughly this time, Tolkien wrote two longish poems, the *New Lay of the Völsungs* and the *New Lay of Gudrún* (which he usually called by the Old Norse names *Völsungakviða en nýja* and *Guðrúnakviða en nýja*), to fill up long-debated lacunae in the extant legends; this was a fine intersection between professional philology and his private endeavours.[16] It was utterly characteristic of Tolkien's unconventional approach to his subject that he thought the best way to resolve textual cruces was to write another poetic treatment of the subject; it was also, unfortunately, one that was unlikely to gain wide acceptance amongst his scholarly peers. Work on these poems probably replaced that on *The Lay of Leithian*, which he laid aside in September 1931.

After putting the Völsung–Gudrún poems aside, Tolkien seems to have turned to writing another work in the classical Old English alliterative line, this time on an Arthurian subject. *The Fall of Arthur* was planned in a number of cantos or 'fits', and runs, in its extant fragments, to almost 1,000 lines.[17] In 1934 Tolkien lent the poem, as far as it then went, to R.W. Chambers, who was strongly enthusiastic, and urged him to finish it. Tolkien may have worked on the poem as late as 1937, but, like much else, it was never completed.[18] Nevertheless, apart from the intrinsic value of the fragments (and it is amongst the best alliterative verse Tolkien ever wrote), the exercise was not a wholly fruitless one: Tolkien seems to have been groping towards a synthesis that would incorporate 'the Matter of Britain', too, in some way into his legendarium: Arthur's departure after his mortal wound at Camlann is not to Glastonbury, but oversea, to Avallone, which at this time became another name for Tol Eressëa, the Lonely Isle. This was part of a wholesale and wide-ranging attempt that Tolkien seems to have begun at this time to gather and correlate legends, preserved amongst littoral peoples, of an old straight path to the vanished Uttermost West; we will look at this in more detail in a later chapter.

Some may wish to speculate about a personal connexion: was Tolkien, on some level, trying to externalize a lament for his own father, Arthur, who had died across far-sundering seas? Such a thing is not of course impossible, and Tolkien of all men would have been alive to the link that names make; but the poem as it stands gives us too little of Arthur himself, and nothing of the later events of his downfall, and so can hardly stand as evidence of its author's emotional disposition.

Tolkien had not published any short poems since 'The Nameless Land' in 1927[19]; in the 1930s, he placed occasional pieces in *The Oxford Magazine* (the same semi-official journal that had printed his 1930 piece proposing a revised syllabus): in 1933 'Errantry', a metrical *feu-de-joie* exploring trisyllabic assonances; in 1934 'Looney' (later 'The Sea-Bell') and 'The Adventures of Tom Bombadil'; and in 1937 'The Dragon's Visit' and 'Knocking at the Door' (later 'The Mewlips') and a revised text of 'Iumonna Gold'. 'The Dragon's Visit' was one of a sequence of six poems set in an imaginary English seaside resort, and of a primarily satirical or humorous intent; 'The Mewlips' is a Dunsanian mood piece; 'Tom Bombadil' a picaresque series of Oxfordshire landscapes tied together by a character inspired by one of his children's toys. Of the new items, only 'Looney', which expresses the dissociation felt by a returned traveller from faërie, is primarily a serious piece; and even that was not the grim lament it later became. These are for the great part 'occasional verses', professorial diversions rather than efforts of high imagining. If Tolkien retained any ambition as a poet, it was not expressed in these pieces.

Despite all this miscellaneous activity, Tolkien had not abandoned his legendarium: he had been working on an expanded and revised version of the 1926 'sketch of the mythology'; this was completed in 1930, with the title *Quenta Noldorinwa* ('the history of the Noldor'); it was the only version of the 'Silmarillion' narrative tradition ever fully completed.[20] It was deliberately conceived as a compendium or summary of stories that, at least notionally, were told in a fuller form elsewhere. The island of Britain, as in 1926, remains the fragment of shattered Beleriand; the *Quenta* itself is attributed to Eriol, who (Tolkien feigned) made it as an epitome of the *Book of Lost Tales* which he had condensed, in turn, from the *Parma Kuluina*, the Golden Book of Kortirion on Tol Eressëa. Only the last of these was not an existing text; Tolkien clearly at some level desired to preserve, in some form, the earlier *Lost Tales*. This made the *Quenta*, as Charles Noad has noted, 'an epitome of a redaction'.[21] Tolkien also composed fragments of an Old English version of the *Quenta*, as made by Eriol/Ælfwine.

At about this time, he began two further prose works recounting the stories of the legendarium, the *Annals of Beleriand* and the *Annals of Valinor*, in an annalistic format like that of the *Anglo-Saxon Chronicle* (in fact, Tolkien also translated some of these *Annals* into Old English, to reinforce the Old English connexion). He revised them later in the decade. The *Annals of Beleriand* were attributed to Pengolod the Wise of Tol Eressëa, those of Valinor to the Elfsage Rúmil; the Old English texts of both to Eriol/Ælfwine. Tolkien now seems to have thought of the 'Silmarillion' as a three-part text: the *Quenta Noldorinwa*, plus the two sets of *Annals*.[22] He was still careful to locate his legendarium within specifically English history; although a subsidiary text from later in the decade, the *Ambarkanta* or 'Shaping of the World', shows him uncertain how to reconcile the obviously 'unscientific' world-picture of the Tales with something like a Copernican universe.[23] The original creation myth, *The Music of the Ainur*, was now recast and expanded as *Ainulindalë*, explained as a tale recited by Rúmil to Ælfwine.

V – Domestic troubles

Tolkien's professional life, then, was busy, and his imaginative writing varied and prolific (if all, at this stage, exclusively for private consumption); his personal life, though, was not easy. There were difficulties in his marriage; Edith had never settled into the social life of Oxford dons' wives, and had never been part of Tolkien's circle of (male) friends. Tolkien was usually out for much of the day, and often in the evenings also. She was lonely, and felt neglected by her husband. She had had no particular preparation for running the large household she now had (four children, plus domestic help of one sort or another) and tended to cloak uncertainty with authoritarianism. Money was tight, even with Tolkien's constant work as an examiner; Edith's health was often precarious (she suffered from debilitating headaches and chronic back pain), and doctors' bills were another worry. Also there was religion: with time, Edith came to feel that Tolkien had unfairly pressured her into becoming a Catholic, and she resented this, particularly as her experience of Anglicanism in the years they were apart had been a happy and sociable one. At some point in these years, probably towards the end of the 1920s, she stopped practising as a Catholic, and was unhappy that Tolkien took the children to church; occasionally, she let her resentment spill over into anger. Tolkien himself kept the emotional loyalty to the faith of his childhood (as far as we can tell, he kept up his religious practice during these years, although he may have lacked something in fervour), and was grieved by what he saw as Edith's desertion of it. Years later, he remarked on 'the dreadful sufferings of our childhoods, from which we rescued one another, but could not wholly heal the wounds that later often proved disabling'.[24] Carpenter said, baldly, that Tolkien's 'marriage, never easy, had begun [in the late 1920s] to go through a long period of extreme difficulty'.[25]

Nevertheless, amidst the quarrels, there was both forgiveness and enduring affection; although their domestic life was clearly often unhappy. Tolkien wrote in his diary, on 1 October 1933, 'Friendship with Lewis compensates for much'.[26] Lewis himself, in 1939, wrote to his brother that Tolkien's 'trials, beside being frequent and severe, are usually of such a complicated nature as to be impenetrable'.[27] Part of this 'impenetrability' may be the result of Lewis's notorious refusal to interest himself in his friends' home lives (his own, which as we have seen was itself complex and to outsiders inexplicable, was strictly off limits to everyone), part the result of Tolkien's habitually oblique manner of self-expression. We should not doubt, however, that Tolkien suffered mental anguish of a high order from various sources (relations with his wife; her health; guilt for neglecting his religion; worries about his children; doubts about his literary work), or that Lewis's encouragement of him was a great help in bearing it.[28]

Lewis himself was assiduous in keeping up with older friends, and probably relied less on Tolkien than Tolkien did on him; in September 1931, he wrote to his oldest friend, Arthur Greeves, about Hugo Dyson: 'I meet him I suppose about four or five times a year and am beginning to regard him as one of my friends of the 2nd class — i.e. not in the same rank as yourself or Barfield, but on a level with Tolkien or Macfarlane.'[29] Lewis's brother, although he and Tolkien were on friendly terms, sometimes thought he took too much of his brother's time and attention (of which he was decidedly jealous): 'Confound Tolkien! I seem to see less and less of J. [Jack] every day.'[30]

In 1934, Fr Francis Morgan died aged seventy-seven. He had kept in touch with Tolkien, and on occasion joined family holidays to Lyme Regis; all three of Tolkien's sons were sent, as Francis Morgan had been, to the Oratory School near Reading. Fr Francis left Tolkien and his brother £1,000 each in his will (this would not have been far short of Tolkien's annual salary). Hearing the news of his death, Tolkien said to Lewis he felt like 'a lost survivor into a new alien world after the real world has passed away'.[31]

VI – The Inklings

Some time in the mid-1930s,[32] an informal literary and discussion club was started by Lewis, centred on him and his friends. They borrowed the name of a defunct undergraduate literary society, 'The Inklings'.[33] Tolkien was one of the original circle. They met every week or two during term-time, and listened to one or more of their number read from a work-in-progress. This was followed by general talk, often until the small hours. Later, they also met one morning a week to drink beer in, usually, the Eagle and Child pub on St Giles'; in fact, Tolkien and Lewis had since the late 1920s regularly met for morning talk over beer, and this opened it to a wider circle.

A deal of over-solemn analysis of this group has been written, claiming it as a deliberate and organized attempt to change the course of twentieth-century cultural and literary history by the reinsertion into contemporary contexts of older ideas: to replace modernism with a robustly Christian appropriation of mythical forms and methods, and to recast Christian apologetics in an accessible form. Most of this analysis is, to put it no stronger, exaggerated. The Inklings was, above all else, a collection of Lewis's friends; his friends, by and large, were interesting men, educated, curious, with (in some cases great) literary talent, and overwhelmingly Christian. Like most 'writers' groups', their main function was as an audience, to listen and criticize and encourage. For a writer to have a regular and sympathetic but not uncritical audience is an unmeasurable boon. It was part of Lewis's gift for friendship that he could coax quite disparate people, and some like Tolkien who were shy of making their work public, to engage in such an enterprise. If the Inklings did nothing else, its function as partial midwife for *The Lord of the Rings* would mark it as a significant literary phenomenon; but this was part of the normal function of friendship, at least as Lewis understood it. The Inklings are important because of what some of them (Tolkien, Lewis, Charles Williams) individually achieved, and the way the group as a whole encouraged those achievements, not because (like other self-conscious literary groupings before or since) they set out with a manifesto to change the world. In fact, if the Inklings as a whole have any shared traits, suspicion of exactly such movements and manifestos is decidedly one of them. There is surprisingly little information extant about the early years of the group; their activities from the following decade are much better documented. The earliest 'members' (although this was, we should remember, a loose and informal category), aside from Lewis and Tolkien, were Nevill Coghill, Lewis's brother Warnie and Adam Fox, Magdalen's Dean of Divinity (college chaplain) and an amateur of poetry. Lewis's old sparring-partner Owen Barfield was unhappily bound to his solicitor's office in London, and thus was only an occasional attender, as was Hugo Dyson of Reading.

Another early member was Lewis's doctor, Robert Havard, known to history as 'Humphrey' (allegedly because Hugo Dyson couldn't remember his real name). Havard's father was an Anglican clergyman; he himself became a Catholic in 1931, aged thirty. In 1934 he took over an Oxford medical practice, with surgeries in both St Giles' and Headington: he was Lewis's doctor, and friend, before he was Tolkien's. He and Lewis became friendly in 1934 or 1935, and Havard was soon thereafter invited to the Inklings. Havard seems to have become the Tolkien family doctor in the early 1940s; he found Tolkien 'extremely good company' with lightly worn but profound scholarship and a sharp verbal wit, although 'neither was ever paraded or used to inflict pain'. Nevertheless, he wrote later, 'we were, I felt, worlds apart in outlook, apart from our common religion'.[34] He also, sensibly, observed, 'there does seem to be some tendency to take us all more seriously than we took ourselves'.[35] Havard remembers C.L. Wrenn and Lord David Cecil as being at these early meetings.[36] Wrenn however was in 1939 appointed to the Chair of English Language and Literature at King's College, London, and so presumably thereafter came irregularly if at all (indeed, his later reported shock at Tolkien's literary activities can hardly be accounted for if, during his London years, he came much to the Inklings). Cecil had only ever come occasionally. Havard did war service in the Navy, and so was from 1939 only an intermittent member.

As the years passed, other men were drawn into the circle, some only fleetingly, others more permanently. We shall encounter some of them in later chapters.

Chapter 7 – A Wilderness of Dragons: *Beowulf* and *The Hobbit*

I – Reclaiming *Beowulf*

On 25 November 1936, aged forty-four, Tolkien gave a lecture which revolutionized the study of the Old English poem *Beowulf*, and has pretty much defined the trend of subsequent criticism of the poem, and of much Old English verse besides. He had been lecturing on *Beowulf* every year since he was appointed to his Oxford chair, and had taught countless classes and individual students. His sense of what *Beowulf* was, and his sympathy for the temper and manner of its author, had grown and developed enormously. He was given the chance to summarize all of this for a broader academic audience when he was invited to give a prestigious British Academy lecture. Tolkien went to Manchester on 9 December 1936, and repeated the lecture to the Manchester Medieval Society (at the invitation of E.V. Gordon, who had been Professor of English Language and Germanic Philology at Manchester since 1931). His paper was called 'Beowulf: The Monsters and the Critics'; and no one afterwards has been able to read the poem in the same way.[1]

The lecture was in effect a synopsis of a series of lectures, titled 'Beowulf and the Critics', which represent a course with the advertised title 'Beowulf: General Criticism' given three times over the previous four years.[2] The original course went into significantly more detail about the specific critics whose views on *Beowulf* Tolkien considered so corrosive.[3]

We should not think that Tolkien was wholly original in his approach; his overarching *historical* attitude to *Beowulf* might, in fact, be summed up in the words of Chambers, first published a decade and a half previously:

... we are justified in regarding the poem as homogeneous: a production of the Germanic world enlightened by the new faith. Whether through external violence or internal decay, this world was fated to rapid change, and perished with its promise unfulfilled. The great merit of *Beowulf* as a historic document is that it shows us a picture of a period in which the virtues of the heathen 'Heroic Age' were tempered by the gentleness of the new belief: an age warlike, yet Christian: devout, yet tolerant.[4]

Indeed, the very title of the lecture was an oblique homage to Chambers: Chapter 4 of *Widsith* is titled '*Widsith* and the Critics'. Nevertheless, there were important differences in their respective approaches: principally, Tolkien unlike Chambers thought the poem as we have it was a coherent literary artefact.

In insisting on the coherence of the poem as a poem, then, Tolkien was going up against not just the heavyweights of German *Beowulf* scholarship – Müllenhoff, ten Brink, Klaeber – but also the two home-grown champion philologists of University College London, Ker and Chambers, both of whom are cited by name, quoted, and refuted – refuted, it is true, with respect and courtesy, but refuted nonetheless.

Tolkien was insistent about the Englishness of the poem; this he saw as compounded of two elements – language, and existence under 'our northern sky and soil'. The second element was one that Tolkien thought immensely important, in (amongst other ways) a purely physical sense. He once commented to Lewis that

the feeling about home must have been quite different in the days when a family had fed on the produce of the same few miles of country for six generations, and that perhaps this was why they saw nymphs in the fountains and dryads in the woods – they were not mistaken for there was in a sense a *real* (not metaphorical) connection between them and the countryside. What had been earth and air & later corn, and later still bread, really was in them. We of course who live on a standardised international diet (you may have had Canadian flour, English meat, Scottish oatmeal, African oranges, & Australian wine today) are really artificial beings and have no connection (save in sentiment) with any place on earth. We are synthetic men, uprooted. The strength of the hills is not ours.[5]

Tolkien claimed that *Beowulf* illustrated exactly this sort of connexion: it was thus an *English* poem, then, but also an English *poem*. *Beowulf*, he argued, must be read not as a quarry for other things, but (as it was) as a poem, and a poem by a Christian man at that: one who lived, nevertheless, in the shadow of the old paganism, and who felt nostalgia for and a sympathy with those who had died according to its bleak, defiant code. This code, which Tolkien called 'the northern theory of courage', may be crisply summarized as the claim that (in Tom Shippey's words, borrowed ultimately from W.P. Ker[6]) 'defeat is no refutation'; that even if all human endeavour is finally doomed to end in decay and failure, and if (as Norse legend claimed) at the end even the gods would be defeated by the powers of evil, nevertheless it was still right to fight for truth, and loyalty, and honour, even (perhaps especially) without hope of victory or reward. The 'monsters' – the ogres Grendel and his mother, and the dragon that is Beowulf's bane – are proper opponents for a man in this setting.

If this, now, is how the poem is typically understood and approached, this is in large part down to Tolkien. Previously, it had been treated as (at best) a source of antiquarian lore of one sort or another, overlaid with a bizarre and frankly distasteful monster story, clearly unworthy of its author, whose verse, most admitted, showed some skill. Tolkien changed all that. The lecture remains a major contribution to scholarship; but it was the last significant academic publication in his lifetime. Tom Shippey has argued that subsequent critics of *Beowulf* have if anything taken Tolkien too literally in focussing exclusively on the poetic character of the text, to the neglect of its proper and valid use as an historical document; some of Tolkien's own lectures on other aspects of *Beowulf*, posthumously published as *Finn and Hengest*, show him taking its historical claims very seriously indeed; but, unlike 'The Monsters and the Critics', these are forbiddingly technical in tone, and have been virtually ignored even after their publication.[7]

At around the same time, Tolkien was also writing a more unusual piece of critical scholarship, a poem in the English alliterative metre giving a sequel to the events of the Old English poem *The Battle of Maldon*, which is one of the major places where the 'northern theory' is exemplified, in English at least.[8] But it would be almost twenty years before Tolkien's poem was published. He had probably come to write it when asked to help with an edition of the poem by an old friend, his sometime Leeds colleague and 'devoted friend and pal',[9] E.V. Gordon.[10]

After Tolkien left Leeds, Gordon was appointed to his old post as

Professor of English Language; five years later, in 1931, he moved to Manchester as Smith Professor of English Language and Germanic Philology. He and Tolkien had stayed in close touch, and were frequent collaborators as examiners and on works of scholarship. Tolkien had proofread Gordon's celebrated *Introduction to Old Norse* (which appeared in 1927, but was very probably begun whilst Tolkien was still at Leeds), and also, as we have seen, his 1937 edition of *The Battle of Maldon*. In both cases Tolkien's help was very considerably more than simple proof correction: he had made suggestions and provided textual and philological help, in the manner the pair of them had grown used to when preparing their great edition of *Gawain*. Tolkien and Gordon had planned to collaborate on further editions of texts: the Middle English *Pearl*, and the Old English *Wanderer* and *Seafarer*. Work had begun on all of them. The *Wanderer* and *Seafarer* editions, indeed (which had begun as two books, with Tolkien senior partner on the first and Gordon on the second, but had been amalgamated to allow a more extensive glossary), were effectively complete in manuscript by the mid-1930s; but, inevitably, they were overlong and needed reduction, and this had yet to occur. But in 1938, E.V. Gordon died, suddenly, aged only forty-two. A routine operation to remove his gall-bladder discovered a terminal failure in some supra-renal glands; it would, eventually, have led to a slow and painful death. As it was, it carried him off in days. He left a wife and four children.

Gordon's death put an end to all his collaborations, actual or projected. Tolkien offered Gordon's widow, Ida, one of his former Leeds pupils who also now taught at Manchester, help with some outstanding obligations: he took over some of Gordon's work as an external examiner, and undertook to complete his edition of *Pearl*. In the event, it did not appear for a decade and a half, and then done, mostly, by Ida Gordon. She also assumed responsibility for the *Wanderer* and *Seafarer* editions; only the second was ever finished, and that not until 1960. Tolkien made significant contributions to all these texts, but not, as had been planned, as a co-editor. Progress had been slow since he left Leeds; but Gordon had been notably productive ('an industrious little devil', Tolkien had noted early in the friendship[11]), and would perhaps have chivvied Tolkien into doing more than he was later able to manage (although, we might note, he had not managed to bring Tolkien to complete a project in the decade since he had left Leeds). His death was a blow; apart from his personal feelings, Tolkien now knew only too well how far the pressure of administrative business, supervisions, lectures and endless examining both domestic and external impeded his own freedom to work on what, after all, was one of his primary functions: academic research. He clearly needed a collaborator to prompt and cajole and help with the spadework; but he did not find them easily.

II – Time travel, space travel – 'what we really like in stories'

Tolkien recalled years later a conversation with Lewis about speculative fiction in which both lamented the lack of the sort of books they liked to read; Lewis proposed they should make good this lack themselves. Lewis took space travel as his theme, Tolkien time travel. This at least is the story. John Rateliff has argued, plausibly enough, that this conversation, which most probably took place in 1936 (and is sometimes called a wager), happened under the spur of Lewis's recent reading: the science fiction novel *Voyage to Arcturus* by David Lindsay, and *The Place of the Lion*, a 'supernatural thriller' by a prolific author, Charles Williams. Both of these took avowedly popular forms of writing and used them as the vehicle for highly moral, or even 'spiritual', themes. This clearly appealed to the two of them, who were keen to write fiction of high seriousness, but baffled about how to present it. Rateliff also notes that both Lewis and Tolkien looked, at this juncture, rather like unsuccessful writers: Lewis had published nothing apart from two unsuccessful books of verse (the last a decade previously) and, three years before, *The Pilgrim's Regress*, an allegorical account of his return to Christian belief. None had made any great impact; his first major scholarly book, *The Allegory of Love*, was about to be published; but as an imaginative writer, and especially as a poet, he seemed to have failed. Tolkien's case was if anything worse; he had not tried to publish any of his imaginative writing, other than a few short and fugitive poems, since 1916, when *The Trumpets of Faerie* had been rejected. His legendarium remained a 'private amusement'; his only audience was Lewis.[12]

In Lewis's case, the conversation (or, perhaps, wager) led directly to the first of his science fiction novels, *Out of the Silent Planet* (in which Tolkien appears, thinly disguised, as the philologist Elwin Ransom). Tolkien, characteristically, was more elaborate and piecemeal in his efforts. In the years 1936–7 he drafted parts of a story called *The Lost Road*, in which a father-and-son pair are traced backwards through successive ages from the present to a time of myth, where the recurring theme of a 'lost road' to the Uttermost West (which is found in dispa-rate early medieval legends attached to Irish saints, to Lombardic heroes, and the mysterious King Sheave of early English legend) finds its proper exemplar in the downfall of Númenor, Tolkien's Atlantis. This was done, in part, to exorcise a recurrent dream of a great wave drowning a sunlit land that Tolkien had experienced since childhood. Like much else written at this time, however, *The Lost Road* was never completed; Tolkien returned to the theme a decade later.

The form of the novel is an unusual one; it has a close parallel, however, in John Buchan's *The Path of the King*, where a series of chrono-logically separated stories are linked by an (unwitting) genealogy, which turns out to be the tale of the ancestors of George Washington.[13]

The father-son-grandson triad that opens *The Lost Road* (Oswin Errol – Alboin Errol – Audoin Errol) may well present, in analogue, the relations between Francis Morgan, Tolkien and his son Christopher. Oswin is a schoolmaster (Francis Morgan had some involvement in schoolwork), whose name means 'God-friend'; as the story opens, his son Alboin is twelve, the age Tolkien was when Francis Morgan became his guardian, and it is set on the coast in what could easily be Lyme Regis. A later scene has Oswin gently chiding Alboin for neglecting Greek and Latin in favour of invented (here, truly 'discovered') languages, and admitting he is worried Alboin will not get a scholarship: 'Cash is not too abundant'[14]. Oswin Errol dies soon after the novel's beginning; Francis Morgan, we may remember, had died in 1934, perhaps two years before Tolkien started to write. Stories of Númenor's fall in the novel are transmitted through father-and-son pairs by descent and some species of 'race memory' (this sort of idea was common currency for much of the late nineteenth and early twentieth centuries, so we should not be too exercised by it); Tolkien saw an instance of this in the way that one of his sons, Michael, had inherited the same 'Atlantis haunting' dreams he himself experienced.

There are remarkable parallels, too, between Lewis's novel and what survives of Tolkien's: both, Tolkien averred, were to end with 'the discovery of Myth' – in Lewis's case, the rebellion of Lucifer and the Fall; in Tolkien's, the downfall of Atlantis. Their protagonists have, moreover, the same name: Alboin-Ælfwine-Elwin. Lewis undoubtedly borrowed this from Tolkien, as he later did Númenor (misspelt 'Numinor') in *That Hideous Strength*, the names of his primæval human pair in *Perelandra* (Tor and Tinidril, clearly parallel to Tolkien's Tuor and Idril) and, very likely, his 'angelic' beings, the *eldils* (a name too like Eldar for coincidence, although Tolkien's Eldar are not angelic). These things illustrate, more than anything else, how close in accord Tolkien's and Lewis's imaginations were at this time: they borrowed quite naturally from a common fund of name and story. Both books aimed to smuggle myth in under the form of popular fiction since, as Lewis and Tolkien had both discovered, there was no apparent appetite for it in its more expected forms – heroic verse, or William Morris-style prose.

The Lost Road seems to have marked the first appearance of Númenor, a concept integrated from the start, or almost so, into the formed legendarium; indeed, its Downfall provided a useful mechanism for transforming the older 'naïve' flat-world cosmology of *The Lost Tales*, the *Quenta* and the *Ambarkanta* into something like our contemporary world-picture: with the Downfall of Númenor, the old straight road is now bent. Some, however, were still able by chance or favour to sail that old road, and come at least within sight of the Uttermost West; amongst these, Tolkien noted, was 'Ælfwine father of Eadwine', who reached Eressea and was 'told the Lost Tales'. This indicates that even now the original framework for the legendarium survived, if varied in detail; although there are hints that Tolkien contemplated abandoning it[15]. The character Alboin Errol of *The Lost Road* is, of course, merely Ælfwine Eriol of *The Lost Tales* in modern English; his putative Anglo-Saxon cognate, Ælfwine Wídlast ('the far-travelled'), is (again) nominally identical with Eriol Wæfre. If *The Lost Road* was to end in the 'discovery of myth', the myth was to be not, as in Lewis's novel, a neglected piece of Christianity, but a fragment of Tolkien's own formed legendarium, here made deliberately a 'mythology for England'.

At first sight, the poem 'King Sheave' inserted into *The Lost Road* seems incongruous; but Tolkien (here as in much else following R.W. Chambers) associated the figure of Sceaf (as he is called in *Beowulf*) with the Lombards or Langobards ('long-beards'), who although we associate them with northern Italy, where they eventually fetched up, were in origin a tribe of the North Sea coasts, and thus neatly placed to preserve a legend of a mysterious sea-borne foundling who becomes a culture hero, bringing the arts of cultivation and the rule of law. He then becomes a mythical ancestor, whom they then passed to the Anglo-Saxons, their sometime neighbours in the northern coastlands, and thence his appearance in *Beowulf*.[16] Behind these broken fragments of Germanic legendry, Tolkien hinted, was a memory of something coming from out of the

Uttermost West, to the enlightening and strengthening of men before that living in darkness. This, taken with the historically attested Lombard names Audoin and Alboin ('bliss-friend' and 'Elf-friend', parallel to Old English Eadwine and Ælfwine, Edwin and Elwin), led Tolkien to bring the Lombards into the sphere of those who were somehow carriers of the legacy of Númenor, and thus beyond that the Elven West. There was the difficulty, which Tolkien acknowledged, of somehow relating this to the surviving story of the Lombards Alboin and Audoin, which, although Chambers called it 'the greatest of all Germanic tales',[17] is compounded of revenge and considered brutality. We may remember Tolkien's earlier attempts to incorporate the mythical Ing, founder of the littoral Ingvæones and notional ancestor of the English, into his legendarium. Christopher Tolkien argues that his father 'was envisaging a massive and explicit linking of his own legends with those of many other places and times: all concerned with the stories and the dreams of peoples who dwelt by the coasts of the great Western Sea'.[18] We noticed in a previous chapter Tolkien's introduction of this theme in his proposed retelling of the end of King Arthur.

As before, the very considerable effort needed to harmonize these very disparate elements into a coherent story was not one that, at this time, Tolkien was able to make; but we see him here in full philological form, collecting and trying to make sense of materials obviously related but also baffling in their incongruities. The attempt was too ambitious, however; the material Tolkien was trying to marshal was not patient of his purpose. Perhaps, with more time, he might have made something workable of it; but the time he might have given it was spent, instead, on another book. *The Lost Road* was not to make Tolkien's name; this was to come about from a wholly unexpected quarter: one of the stories told to his children.

III – *The Hobbit*: style and sources

We last saw *The Hobbit* as an unfinished story, or one finished only orally, known to Tolkien's children and to a small number of his close friends and sometime pupils, mostly connected with the hostel for Catholic women students at Cherwell Edge, run by the nuns of the Society of the Holy Child Jesus.[19] Some time between 1933 and 1936, Tolkien lent an unfinished typescript of *The Hobbit* to one of his students, Elaine Griffiths;[20] she passed it to a friend, Susan Dagnall, like her a sometime resident at Cherwell Edge, who now worked for the publisher George Allen & Unwin.[21] She in turn strongly suggested the story be finished and submitted for publication; and this Tolkien did in late 1936.

We may wonder why it is that Tolkien was able to complete *The Hobbit* but not at this time any of his myriad other projects; I strongly suspect it is because it was confessedly a children's story and thus not fundamentally, in Tolkien's mind, a serious work, and one that could thus be issued even if imperfect, so evading the inner perfectionist who vetoed or sabotaged his grander schemes.

Unwin's chairman, Stanley Unwin, paid his ten-year-old son Rayner a shilling for a report on the book; Rayner liked it, and Unwin agreed to publish. In some ways Unwin was an unlikely partner for Tolkien; he was a non-smoking, teetotal pacifist and Nonconformist of distinctly left-wing views (he had published both Bertrand Russell, and Arthur Ransome's shameless apology for Bolshevism, *Six Weeks in Russia*): he and Tolkien would have disagreed on pretty much everything. Nevertheless, Unwin was a canny businessman, and recognized a classic when he saw one.

This turn of events ended any immediate chance that *The Lost Road* would be completed; it would, in any case, have been a tricky task, but in the months (up to December 1937) when Lewis was finishing *Out of the Silent Planet*, Tolkien was obliged to set aside *The Lost Road* to complete and revise *The Hobbit*, and be at pains to satisfy Unwin's need for ancillary material – maps, blurbs, illustrations – to make it a publishable book. He obtained 'puff pieces' (or, more formally, testimonials) praising the book from various well-disposed friends and colleagues, including R.W. Chambers; George Gordon promised one, but there is no indication whether he made good on it ('I may warn you that his promises are usually generous,' Tolkien told Unwin[22]). In September 1937, *The Hobbit* was published; Tolkien was forty-five.

He also took some trouble to get Lewis's book published; J.M. Dent, who had published *The Pilgrim's Regress*, rejected *Out of the Silent Planet* as 'bunk'. Tolkien persuaded Unwin to look at it, but to no avail; his reader also rejected it. Tolkien protested, and Unwin was prevailed on to take it to the Bodley Head, another publishing firm of which he was also chairman. They accepted it, and it was published on 23 September 1938.

The Hobbit had started, as we saw, at Tolkien's desk some years earlier during his annual chore of examination marking. As usual with him, a name gave rise to a story; it soon attracted to itself further names from Tolkien's professional life. The names of the dwarves, and the wizard Gandalf, come from the *Elder Edda*, in a list (the *Dvergatal*) usually dismissed as a meaningless rigmarole; Tolkien decided it in fact preserved the roster of a famous quest for lost treasure. Mirkwood, of course, came straight from the asterisk reality of *Gothia; the dragon, Smaug, has elements of the drakes of Beowulf and Sigurðr; the cross-country journey of Bilbo and the dwarves bears some resemblance to William Morris's *Icelandic Journals*. The dwarven 'Longbeards' borrow, of course, the name (and perhaps the grim humour) of the Lombards, whom (as we saw) Tolkien was much exercised by at this time. This cross-fertilization of names brought with it, perhaps inevitably, a similar cross-fertilization of theme: most readers of *The Hobbit* will note how, as the story progresses, it becomes by degrees more serious until, at its end, with the debates before the Lonely Mountain and the Battle of the Five Armies, it approaches the high seriousness and brusque moral complexity of Icelandic saga.

There was another source, too, besides Tolkien's philological day-job; names and characters and settings from his legendarium (Gondolin, Elrond, the Elvenking in his halls) found their way into the story, and gave it another layer of resonance and what Tolkien called 'depth': the sense of untold stories and half-seen vistas at the edge of the tale. This not only had implications for Tolkien's literary technique; it also meant that hobbits were now a tangential part of his legendarium. This was to have tremendous consequences for his writing.

It is fair to claim, however, as Tolkien himself did, that *The Hobbit* in its original form was not intended as part of his legendarium; although the manner in which it developed during its writing makes it not quite accurate to state, as Christopher Tolkien has done, that '*The Hobbit* ... as it stood in 1937 ... was not a part of it.' Nevertheless he is quite correct to declare that 'Its significance for Middle-Earth lies in what it would do, not in what it was.'[23]

IV – *Quenta Silmarillion*

Meanwhile, Tolkien began writing a fine manuscript copy of the *Quenta Silmarillion*, incorporating all the numerous revisions he had made to the tales since the *Quenta Noldorinwa* of 1930.[24] It was probably at this time that he revised the *Annals of Valinor* and the *Annals of Beleriand*, and wrote a short text called the *Lhammas*, or 'account of tongues', which described his invented languages and their interrelations.

We may reasonably ask what, exactly, Tolkien thought of as the relations between the various texts of his legendarium at this juncture; what were its constituent texts, and how were they to be accounted for? Charles Noad, whose research is fundamental here, has attempted a careful reconstruction of the notional scheme for the 1930s Silmarillion.[25]

The Silmarillion seems to have been adopted as a general title for the whole corpus of legendarium writing; it was to consist of (1) the *Quenta* (or *Qenta*) *Noldorinwa* (also called, variously, the *Pennas inGeleidh* ('history of the gnomes'), *I Eldanyárë* ('history of the elves') or, simply, *Quenta Silmarillion*), with, as an appendix, genealogies of the houses of men and elves, a *Tale of Years* and a *Tale of Battles*;[26] (2) *The Annals of Valinor*; (3) *The Annals of Beleriand*; (4) the *Lhammas*. Other longer versions of some tales were to appear as appendices: *Ainulindalë*, *Ambarkanta* and the long poems on the Children of Húrin and Beren and Lúthien.

The notional 'real-world' status of the texts, given in a short preamble, was much as for the 1930 version. Britain is still a fragment of Beleriand; the *Quenta* represents Ælfwine's translation into Old English of a synopsis made by Pengolod of Gondolin (later of Tol Eressea) of various legends – prose and verse alike – written in the Golden Book, some of which were translated directly by Ælfwine; the *Annals of Valinor* were originally by Rúmil, completed by Pengolod, those of Beleriand by Pengolod *ab initio*; the *Lhammas* was Rúmil's.[27]

V – They asked for a sequel

The Hobbit was an immediate success, and Tolkien's publisher was eager for more. He asked Tolkien to write a sequel. Tolkien was not unwilling, but asked Unwin if he would like to consider any of the stories he had already written. Unwin was happy to do so; so, in mid-November 1937, Tolkien met Unwin in London and gave him a large bundle of manuscripts. These included versions of the children's tales *Farmer Giles of Ham* and *Mr Bliss*, and the unfinished *Lost Road*; most importantly for Tolkien, however, he also handed over the unfinished long poem *The Lay of Leithian* and the fine manuscript text of the *Quenta Silmarillion*, comprising the first two-thirds of the text (the remaining third, as yet unrevised, was not included). Most of this was given to a publisher's reader named Edward Crankshaw to be assessed; apart from, it seems,

The Silmarillion itself. Crankshaw (1909–84) was a sometime journalist, reviewer, novelist and historian; he had lived in Vienna for much of the 1930s, and was fluent in German. He later worked for MI6 attached to the wartime Military Mission to Moscow as a SIGINT (Signals Intelligence) specialist, before being assigned to Bletchley Park. After the war he became a prominent authority on Soviet affairs, and a fine amateur of Austrian history. He wrote a large number of books, including some well-regarded biographical and historical studies (on Bismarck, Maria Theresa, *The Fall of the House of Habsburg* and various others).

The Lost Road, however, after being partially (and inaccurately) typed up by the publisher from Tolkien's barely legible manuscript, was given to Susan Dagnall, who had recommended *The Hobbit*; she said it was 'a hopeless proposition'.[28]

Crankshaw, meanwhile, confessed himself puzzled by *The Lay of Leithian* (and according to Carpenter 'he was very rude about the rhyming couplets'[29]), but very impressed by the few pages of the prose version (unidentified, but presumably part of *The Silmarillion* in some form) he had been given to read as background. These few pages were all he saw, however; for some reason, the full text as it had been given to Unwin was withheld, and the only person to see it was Stanley Unwin himself. This was unfortunate; Crankshaw, as far as one can judge from his own books, was a man of wide culture and unusual imaginative sympathy, and could well have been enthusiastic had he read the whole *Silmarillion* as it then existed.

As it was, Crankshaw did not feel able to recommend any of the texts he had seen should be published; Unwin conveyed this to Tolkien on 16 December, with the hope that *The Silmarillion* might be the source for further stories like *The Hobbit*. Tolkien confessed to 'a sense of fear and bereavement, quite ridiculous, since I let this private and beloved nonsense out'. Understandably, he was under the misapprehension that *The Silmarillion* had been read in full before being rejected, but took comfort from what he mistakenly interpreted as the general approval of it: 'if it had seemed to you to be nonsense I should have felt really crushed'[30]. The result was unexpected to both sides: 'They wanted a sequel. But I wanted heroic legends and high romance. The result was *The Lord of the Rings*.'[31]

There is of course no knowing what might have happened if Crankshaw had actually been given the whole *Silmarillion* to read, or if it had even been published; but it is utterly certain that, if it had been accepted in 1937, the sequel to *The Hobbit* would have been very different. The rejection of the 1937 *Silmarillion* was the direct cause of *The Lord of the Rings* in its eventual form; it was also the major reason *The Silmarillion* was never completed.

Part III – Achievement

'It is written in my life-blood, such as that is, thick or thin; and I can no other.'[1]

Chapter 8 – In the Background, War

I – The tale grew in the telling

Tolkien began the 'new *Hobbit*' the same year the original was published, in fact by 19 December 1937. It was not finished until twelve years later, and not published for another six after that. The completion and publication of the book are, in some ways, the central achievement of Tolkien's life, one carried through in the midst of numerous adversities and discouragements; although, ironically, this was neither the great book he meant to write, nor (really) the sequel he had been asked for. Circumstances, or providence if you like, arranged matters otherwise; these chapters try to give some account of the winding paths Tolkien and his magnum opus took.

The development of *The Lord of the Rings* has been traced in absorbing detail by Christopher Tolkien in four magisterial volumes; readers interested in Tolkien's drafting process, and the slow development of the story from a (rather aimless) straight sequel to *The Hobbit* (Bilbo has run out of money, and needs to go adventuring again) to the grand design of the finished work, gradually drawing in (or, better, being attracted towards) the high matter of the legendarium, should consult the relevant volumes of *The History of Middle Earth*. Here I will only give a broad outline.

Tolkien made several unsatisfactory drafts of the first chapters between December 1937 and March 1938; then he laid the book aside until August 1938, when he took it up again and worked solidly between then and December 1938; for much of 1939, although he told his publisher he hoped to finish the story by mid-June, he worked on it only in desultory fashion, not helped by the uncertainties of the political situation, and by a head injury that left him concussed and unwell for some months.

He was also distracted by the need to research and write a lecture to be given at St Andrews in commemoration of Andrew Lang, which was not finished until late February. Slowly and inexorably, though, as had happened increasingly with *The Hobbit* in the last stages of its composition, the sequel was drawn into the ambit of Tolkien's wider legendarium. As a modern writer has noted, 'In Tolkien's fiction, all roads lead to "The Silmarillion".'[2]

But we have run a little ahead of ourselves. In the fallow interval of early 1939, he wrote and gave his lecture 'Fairy Stories' which we will discuss below; and perhaps, also, wrote *Leaf by Niggle*, an allegory of the creative life and its frustrations and hopes.[3]

The lecture was given at St Andrew's on 8 March, as the latest in a series commemorating Andrew Lang. Tolkien had been asked to give it in the previous June; in fact, he was the University authorities' third choice, after the classicist Gilbert Murray and Hugh Macmillan, a Law Lord, but neither of them was available for the academic year 1938–9. March was unusually late in the academic year for the Andrew Lang lecture, which was typically given in November or December; we may suppose pressure of work (particularly examining) meant there was little spare time beforehand. Time to prepare it had to be stolen from the new *Hobbit*; perhaps unsurprisingly, as it was written instead of his own imaginative work, the lecture became an extended meditation on the nature of story-telling, particularly of the sort he himself practised.

In preparation for the lecture, Tolkien (who knew himself an amateur beside the great savants of comparative fairy-tale lore, but also relied on what he – rightly – saw as an imaginative and creative sympathy for, and in a certain sense access to, the material) began a furious programme of reading. He did not draw up a list of works of folklore studies, however; instead, he reread all twelve of Lang's coloured *Fairy Books*, and probably also Grimm and Dasent's *Popular Tales from the Norse* (he is on record as disliking Hans Christian Andersen). One of the few academic texts he drew on directly was Christopher Dawson's *Progress and Religion*, which attracted Tolkien mostly (we may guess) because of its excoriating analysis of the faults of contemporary secular society and culture; this was useful to rebut charges of 'escapism' – if 'reality' was sufficiently horrible (and Tolkien and Dawson both thought it was) then 'escape' from it, as a mental category at least, became not a fault or an immaturity but a duty. Dawson had nothing particular to say about fairy stories per se; but he was, also, a Catholic (he was soon to become editor of the *Dublin Review*, although at this date he did not hold a university job[4]). The main sources for the philo-sophical underpinning of Tolkien's lecture, although it did not become fully explicit until later revision, were however G.K. Chesterton (in partic-ular a collection of his short fiction called *The Coloured Lands*, and most especially the introduction to it by Maisie Ward) and *Poetic Diction* by Lewis's friend Owen Barfield. From Barfield Tolkien took – or assented to – the notion that language and mythology (or folklore) are both coeval and correlate, and from Ward's introduction to Chesterton the bold claim that in storytelling we co-operate with God in the enrichment of creation (although, as I say, this is at this stage only implicit).[5]

Again characteristically, Tolkien seems to have prepared more material than he could use, and had to abridge the lecture in delivering it. No text of the original 1939 lecture survives, although there are very full newspaper accounts of it;[6] but it was clearly an important text for Tolkien's development as a writer, confirming his notions of the high seriousness of his imaginative fiction and, inevitably, reacting on the tone of the 'Hobbit sequel' when eventually he took it up again. The lecture itself was put aside, with a view (presumably) for publication: the Lang lectures were usually issued as pamphlets by the OUP the year after their delivery. Tolkien's, as we shall see, took a while longer to appear; events elsewhere were upsetting all plans.

II – The return of the shadow

As is now notorious, in September 1938, the British government under Chamberlain agreed at Munich, with French complicity, to sanction the German annexation of the Czech Sudetenland. Thereafter, only the most sanguine or muddle-headed thought war with Germany could be long avoided.

In March 1939, the War Office, as part of a general gearing-up for conflict, conducted an assessment of potential cryptographers. Tolkien was amongst those who took a four-day course in London run by the Government Code and Cipher School (GCCS), who ran the now famous operation at Bletchley Park; he was amongst fifty dons from the ancient universities approached by the GCCS either as having previous experi-ence in cryptography (like Ronald Knox's brother Dilwyn, Fellow of King's and an expert in a very obscure Greek fragmentary dramatist, who had worked as a codebreaker during the Great War and retained a connexion with the business) or as having potentially useful expertise.

He was not in the event called on to work in this area (which probably allowed *The Lord of the Rings* to be finished); or, if he was offered a full-time position, he declined it – presumably on financial grounds, since the GCCS was offering £500 per annum, less than half of what Tolkien was struggling to support his family on.[7]

The opening of the Second World War that September took no one, really, by surprise. In September 1939, the staff of the OUP's London office moved to Oxford; amongst them was an editor called Charles Williams. Williams was a prolific writer of 'spiritual thrillers' and an exponent of romantic theology (that is, human love as an authentic route to knowing God) in what he reckoned was the style of Dante. He was also a confirmed dabbler in the occult, mostly in its mistier forms. Between 1917 and 1927, he was a member of the Fellowship of the Rosy Cross, an offshoot, founded by veteran occultist A.E. Waite, of the more famous Order of the Golden Dawn. The Hermetic Order of the Golden Dawn was founded in 1887 by a trio of freemasons – a coroner called Westcott, a retired doctor called Woodman and a sometime clerk, Samuel Liddell 'MacGregor' Mathers – for the study and practice of ceremonial magic based on some enciphered manuscripts and the claimed guidance of 'secret chiefs', both of uncertain provenance. It was a fashionable diversion for various writers, actors and the like for a decade or more, and ran 'temples' in London, Paris, Edinburgh, Bradford and Weston-super-Mare, until it dissolved into squabbling factions early in 1900. Williams was given to claiming membership in the original Order, to overuse of abstract nouns and to prolonged flirtations with impressionable young women. Williams clothed these flirtations, which in a couple of cases were prolonged over years and involved hundreds of letters, with a pseudo-mystical flummery borrowed from Dante, Swinburne and the whole overripe Blavatskian-Hermeticist tradition; but to all but dedicated fans, this stuff reads like transparent special pleading for what has aptly been called 'moral adultery'.

Many, like the writer Arthur Ward ('Sax Rohmer' of Fu Manchu fame), Algernon Blackwood and a string of others, were similarly given to passing off their belonging to one of the myriad Golden Dawn splinter-groups as membership in the original Order; presumably each of these shards considered itself the true inheritor of the Golden Dawn apostolic succession. Williams certainly knew Evelyn Underhill, who had some association with the original Golden Dawn, and may have known Arthur Machen, who was on the fringe of the group. In any event, the interconnexions, feuds, squabbles and alliances that existed at this time amongst the habitués of the whole hermetic-theosophical movement (if this ragbag of muddle-headed borrowings from hither and yon, bolted together into ramshackle systems by a series of magpie minds, can be dignified with that description) were so labyrinthine as to be opaque to anything other than close study, which, for any except would-be adepts, it hardly repays.

C.S. Lewis had read some of Williams's work, Williams had read Lewis's *Allegory of Love* in proof, and they had exchanged admiring letters. Soon Lewis read Williams's poems, of which perhaps the politest thing to say is that they are an acquired taste. Williams was in the process of writing a series of long poems on Arthurian themes, whose involute language, layered with abstractions and polysyllabic Byzantinisms, and allegorical pretensions were wholly outside Tolkien's taste, and formed a strong contrast to his own unfinished Arthurian verse tale, *The Fall of Arthur*. Lewis's loudly expressed enthusiasm for Williams's Arthurian cycle (he wrote a commentary on it, eventually published in *Arthurian Torso* of 1948) would only have confirmed Tolkien's decision to lay his own Arthurian work aside, or (at least) not show it to Lewis, which may almost stand as a precondition for any of his works being completed. There is in fact no evidence that Lewis ever read *The Fall of Arthur*, although it is possible such evidence has merely not survived; nevertheless, Lewis's enthusiasm for Tolkien's alliterative verse in general (the alliterative verse was the only element in the poems of *The Lord of the Rings* that Lewis liked) makes this an odd omission. Perhaps Tolkien reckoned Lewis's own taste in Arthuriana was so far from his own to make the exercise a pointless one; but there is probably little to be gained from further speculation here.

Now that Williams was living in Oxford, Lewis was quick to incorporate him in his circle of friends, and this included meetings of the Inklings. He also got Williams official permission to give lectures at the University; in February 1943, Williams was awarded an honorary MA, in some part arranged by Lewis and Tolkien (although it was a distinction routinely awarded to long-serving employees of the OUP). Very obviously Williams, rather than Tolkien, was now the primary object of Lewis's enthusiasm. Tolkien was a sensitive man, and quickly noticed. Lewis professed to believe that closeness to one friend does not diminish with the arrival of another; but Tolkien, and I suspect most of us, would disagree. It is difficult to have two best friends simultaneously. He, along with Lewis's other friends, was now expected to join in Lewis's admiration for Williams's writing. This Tolkien was temperamentally unable to do; he liked Williams, but found his writing baffling and distasteful by turns. He was also, unsurprisingly, uncomfortable with Williams's 'dabblings in the occult'.[8] In November 1943, or thereabouts, Tolkien wrote a poem on Williams, titled 'A Closed Letter to Andrea Charicoryides Surnamed Polygrapheus, Logothete of the Theme of Geodesia in the Empire, Bard of the Court of Camelot, Malleus Malitiarium, Inclinga Sum Sometimes Known as Charles Williams'.[9] Though it is an affectionate treatment, Tolkien's exasperation with Williams's writing (particularly his occasionally ludicrous mock-cabbalistic identification of his idiosyncratic geography with human anatomy – 'buttocks to Caucasia!') is obvious.

The arrival of Williams in Oxford marks the first stage in the decline of Tolkien's relations with Lewis. Emblematic of this is the change in the central character, Elwin Ransom, between the different books of Lewis's science fiction trilogy. In the first two he is transparently based on Tolkien; in the third, *That Hideous Strength* (published in 1945), he now uses the by-name 'Dr Fisher King' and is emphatically Charles Williams.

There is an interesting paragraph in a letter Lewis wrote to his brother soon after war was declared:

> Here's a funny thing I found out yesterday: that Tolkien is descended from one of the Saxon nobility to whom Frederick the Great gave the alternative of exile or submission when he took Saxony; and the old *graf* chose exile and came over to England and became a clock maker. T. is the very last of my friends whom I shd. have suspected of being *geboren*.[10]

We may detect a hint of amused scepticism here; it suggests that Tolkien was comfortable enough with Lewis thus to share with him a cherished (if mildly implausible) piece of family mythology, and also, perhaps, that he ever so slightly misjudged Lewis's reaction, or (at least) mistook, as it is so easy to do, affection for uncritical acceptance. Lewis's native satirical bent, which he consciously suppressed as a requirement of Christian charity, remained not far below the surface.

III – The exigencies of wartime

Whilst Tolkien was not called up to fight nor formally enlisted in government service, the war made significant changes to his daily life, aside from the common inconvenience of rationing, air raid precautions and general shortage. Soon after war was declared, petrol rationing induced Tolkien to sell his car (he never bought another). The War Office did not require his services as a cryptographer, for now at any rate; he was in fact never called on to help, which was probably a good thing since it would have been financially disastrous. He took on war work as an Air Raid Warden, and spent one night a week with another warden on duty in a post in Park Town, a quarter of a mile from his house in Northmoor Road. Either he or his fellow warden would sit up all night watching, whilst the other slept as he might. At some point, perhaps because of their work with officer cadets, the occupation of Oxford dons was declared 'permanently reserved' and so Tolkien was exempted from other service.[11]

Lewis, who was six years younger, joined the Home Guard and, one night in nine, patrolled 'the most malodorous and depressing parts of Oxford' with an antique rifle.[12] His brother Warnie was recalled to the active list, and promoted Major; from the start of September 1939, he was on duty first in Yorkshire and then with the British Expeditionary Force in France. He seems to have spent much of this stint of active service in hospital with an unspecified illness; Warnie was overweight and out of condition, but the primary culprit is likely, as usual, to have been whisky. Some might reckon the Army Service Corps, Warnie's distinctly unglamorous unit, was not a dangerous posting, when compared with front-line service; but in the chaos of May 1940, when the British Expeditionary Force rushed into Belgium only days before the German armoured attacks in the Ardennes drove deep into France behind them and threw the Allies into catastrophic disorder, even a line-of-service station was not safe. Many British line-of-service troops were caught up in the chaotic fighting of that May. At the very least, Warnie and his unit would have been bundled out of France amidst a disorganized host of troops and refugees, an experience to shake the nerves of a younger and more active man. After his unit was evacuated back to England in May or June 1940,[13] he was, in August, transferred from the active list back to the Reserve of Officers. He joined the Home Guard and used to patrol the rivers in his motorboat. George Sayer notes that 'he never spoke about his experiences in the Second World War', and reckons 'his silence suggests deep shame'.[14] Nevertheless he remained 'the Major' for the rest of his life.

A good proportion of the normal undergraduate body was off in uniform, and most undergraduates now took only one-year courses, which might be converted to 'proper' degrees after the war was over; instead, there were amorphous classes of cadets from the armed services to be taught. Special six-month cadets' courses were devised; from March 1943 until March 1944, Tolkien was responsible for the English course taught to Naval and RAF cadets. He devoted much time and effort to this, and to the frustrating business of devising shortened undergraduate Honours courses, which were the invariable object of criticism from colleagues who had not been so occupied.

More practical impact was made by the University's decision to suspend recruitment and replacement of staff for the duration of the war. As posts fell vacant, proportionately more work devolved onto the remaining dons.

Edith was ill at the end of 1939, and had to go into hospital for an operation. The resulting doctors' bills were a worry, since (owing again to the war) many of Tolkien's usual sources of additional income (examining and external lectures) had dried up. He badgered Stanley Unwin to publish *Farmer Giles of Ham*, in the absence of the promised *Hobbit* sequel (which Tolkien told him he hoped to finish in the spring of 1940). Unwin in reply asked that Tolkien finish the preface he had promised for a revision of the old Clark Hall translation of *Beowulf* (in fact, he had barely started it); Unwin still thought *Farmer Giles* was best kept until after the new *Hobbit* was done, but in the meantime offered Tolkien £100 as advance of royalties due the following April.

At the start of 1940, burst water-pipes meant Tolkien had to spend some weeks in a nearby hotel.[15] Edith and Priscilla seem to have gone to Weston-super-Mare for some at least of the time, so Edith could recover from her operation; Christopher had presumably returned to school. Tolkien sent his Clark Hall preface to Unwin, after being assured that it would be printed despite its unsolicited length, and his extensive metrical appendix too. The book was published in July 1940; Tolkien was paid five guineas.[16] In mid-May, he had to remind Unwin to pay him outstanding royalties for *The Hobbit*: money was again very tight. In the summer and early autumn of 1940, two women evacuees from Ashford in Kent were billeted in the Tolkien household.

The war had a larger effect on Tolkien's children; John, his eldest son, had gone to Rome to begin priestly formation at the English College only in November 1939 (he had been an undergraduate at Tolkien's old college, Exeter, between 1936 and 1939); when, in May 1940, the German attack on France and Belgium opened and it became clear that Italian neutrality was a temporary business, he along with other students at the College were sent back to England, travelling in mufti. They spent five days on trains crossing Italy and France, then took the last boat out of Le Havre. After a brief time in Ambleside in the Lake District, the College settled in Stonyhurst for the duration of the war. John Tolkien, as well as studying, acted as head gardener, helping to supplement the College's rations with home-grown vegetables (he had for some years been his father's chief accomplice in keeping up their large garden in Oxford).

Michael, his second son, was in 1939 still in the Sixth Form at the Oratory School in Caversham; he left and volunteered for the Army, but was told to spend a year at university first. This seems to have been in part an act of late adolescent rebellion.

Michael was at Trinity in Oxford reading history until mid-1940, when he joined the Royal Artillery. During the Battle of Britain, he manned anti-aircraft guns on aerodromes, and was awarded the George Medal. At the end of the year, he was injured in a motor accident whilst on night training; whilst in hospital, he met a nurse four years his senior (he was barely twenty) whom he proposed to marry. His father urged caution and delay, despite or more probably because of his own precipitate wartime marriage, but the marriage took place anyway in November 1941.[17] Tolkien was not present; indeed, the marriage may have happened clandestinely. Michael Tolkien's son, another Michael Tolkien, has said his grandparents disapproved of Michael's marriage on the grounds of its haste and his youth and also, privately, because of Joan's 'apparently uncultured, lower middle class, C.of E. background'; he also claims she was 'one of many nurses he fell in love with when he was being treated for the shell-shock he only superficially got over',[18] which is inaccurate in at least one point: Michael Tolkien senior's 1940 hospitalization was caused by a motor crash; the shell-shock came three or four years later. By the time he was married, after Sandhurst (although it is unclear if he was ever commissioned) and a spell in coastal defence at Sidmouth, he transferred to the RAF, and fought first as a gunner in night fighters, then as a rear-gunner in bombers.[19] After almost three years of this, his nerves were gone, and he was declared medically unfit for further service. He returned to Trinity in 1944, to finish his degree in a year; in 1945, he was placed in the Second Class. His father reasonably blamed Michael's war service, and the truncation of his degree course, for his failure to get a First. By now he had two children, and needed a job. He didn't settle to one until 1946.

Christopher had also been at the Oratory, but a heart condition meant he had spent much of his time at home taught by a private tutor. He returned to school in the autumn of 1940, after three years at home. In 1942, when he was only seventeen, he also started a year at Trinity before entering the RAF the following July. In 1944, he was sent to South Africa for pilot training. Both Michael and Christopher had their fees reduced by Trinity as a favour to Tolkien, whose finances were, as usual, straitened.

Priscilla spent the first three years of the war at home, taught by a governess (the school she had been attending was taken over for war work); from 1942, she attended the Oxford High School for Girls as a day pupil.

IV – *The Lord of the Rings* continued

'The darkness of the present days has had some effect on it.'[20]

Now, having seen how the war affected Tolkien's family, we need to return to the dark days of 1940, with Britain's army, defeated, evacuated to England but mostly without equipment, the Air Force fighting for the country's life in the Battle of Britain, and British cities nightly bombed.

Tolkien took up *The Lord of the Rings* again in August 1940, and wrote steadily until term started in October. He had previously reached Balin's tomb in Moria in the autumn of 1939, and then stopped, baffled. Now he again put the book aside until the Christmas vacation of 1940–1; throughout 1941, he worked intermittently until, by the end of the year, the story had reached Lothlórien. He also rewrote his 1936–7 text *The Fall of Númenor* (prompted, presumably, by the growing connexions he discerned between Aragorn and Elendil). Paper was very short in these years, and Tolkien needed a lot of it. He re-used a large quantity of an American candidate's examination scripts he was sent by the University in August 1940, writing on the blank verso sides of the sheets and the blue covers of the booklets; he also resumed the habit of drafting his texts in pencil, and then subsequently overwriting them in ink as they were revised (and this was aside from the inevitable insertion of pasted-in riders, recast pages from earlier versions and persistent niggling over names and time sequence). The original pencil drafts were sometimes erased, occasionally not. The resulting manuscripts present formidable problems of interpretation now; at the time, his son Christopher was, when he was at home, much employed as an amanuensis, typist and general helper (this, as we shall see, was only a foretaste of a task he took up forty years later).

In October 1940 C.S. Lewis published *The Problem of Pain*, the first of his explicit works of Christian apologetic; it was dedicated to the Inklings, to whom it had been read chapter by chapter. Lewis and Tolkien's doctor, R.E. 'Humphrey' Havard, now often known as 'the Useless Quack' or 'U.Q.', contributed an appendix on the clinical experience of pain. Tolkien was mildly sceptical of Lewis's new-minted status as amateur of theology, but kept his peace.[21]

This book was the seed of Lewis's wartime career as itinerant apologist: he spent much of the next years making a round of dreary RAF bases to talk, night after night, to roomfuls of unreceptive men, at the request of the Air Force chaplaincy; this was interspersed with journeys to London to deliver or record broadcast talks for the BBC that were to form a basic course in Christian apologetics. It was weary, dogged work, on top of Lewis's teaching, his enforced involvement in college administration, and his heavy domestic responsibilities. In light of all this, it is a wonder that he managed anything else; but as we shall see, these were busy years for the Inklings.

Tolkien was also busy, and likewise discouraged. On the night of 7 November 1940, incendiary bombs destroyed the binder's warehouse where stock of the second printing of *The Hobbit* was held, along with most of the Unwin backlist; the entire remaining run of the book was amongst the one and a half million books burnt. Paper was by now severely and increasingly rationed, and it was two years before Unwin managed to schedule a reprint. During this time *The Hobbit* was virtually unobtainable, and sales – and Tolkien's royalties – fell off almost to nothing. A week later, Tolkien was working late when he saw a glow on the horizon; it was the city of Coventry, forty miles away, burning.

Oxford proper was never bombed, although there were sporadic air raid alerts throughout 1940–1, and the Cowley motor works were certainly a target; there is usually said to have been an informal agreement that England's ancient university towns would be spared if, reciprocally, neither Heidelberg nor Göttingen was bombed, although there is little actual evidence for this assertion. Another theory argues that Hitler planned to use Oxford as capital of a conquered Britain, and so wanted it intact.

On 22 March 1941, the Tolkiens celebrated twenty-five years of marriage; they ate dinner with friends, including Lewis and Hugo Dyson; of their children, only Priscilla could be present.

On 4 May 1941, an RAF Whitley bomber crashed in Linton Road, which adjoins Northmoor Road. The crew were killed, and three residents injured. Christopher, aged sixteen, had been watching the plane through his telescope; his father, as an Air Raid Warden, attended the scene of the crash.

Tolkien was increasingly depressed by the progress of the war; he developed a loathing of aeroplanes as weapons of war, and was quietly appalled that two of his sons were in the Air Force. He was also disheartened by the effect of the war on the perception of the Germanic spirit, even more than in 1914:

> I have in this War a burning private grudge – which would probably make me a better soldier at 49 than I was at 22: against that ruddy little ignoramus Adolf Hitler … Ruining, perverting, misapplying, and making for ever accursed, that noble northern spirit, a supreme contribution to Europe, which I have ever loved, and tried to present in its true light.[22]

Tolkien was a strong patriot, but was also (what might seem to some now unusual) avowedly anti-Imperialist – 'I love England (not Great Britain and certainly not the British Commonwealth).'[23] We have little information as to the exact nature of his anti-Imperialism, although one may speculate that reflexion on his time in South Africa might have contributed. Nevertheless, in later years he did look back nostalgically to the apogee of British power, Victoria's Diamond Jubilee, which occurred when he was five.[24] It is difficult to grasp the full sense of gradual and inevitable decline in British power and position that Tolkien must have experienced during his lifetime; when he was born, and during his formative years, the Empire seemed a vast and immutable fact, founded on unassailable supremacy at sea. In 1942, he witnessed the unthinkable – the fall of Singapore, fortress of the East, to an army of the hitherto despised Japanese, after the sinking of a British battle squadron by Japanese aircraft. Whatever one's views of Empire, the moral shock of these events must have been considerable.

The records for the Inklings from this time are unusually full; in the midst of war and its uncertainties and privations, and the manifold extra duties whether academic or military that it brought, the familiar routine of Tuesday morning beer and Thursday evening talk amongst old friends took on, it is reasonable to think, a greater importance than before. Certainly, Charles Williams's advent had galvanized Lewis at least, and (together with Lewis's own peripatetic evangelism) had given the group, or at any rate individual members of it, a higher public profile. These were the years not only of *The Lord of the Rings* but also of Lewis's *The Problem of Pain* (first published in 1940), *The Screwtape Letters* (1942), *Perelandra* (1943) and *The Great Divorce* (1945) and Williams's *Region of the Summer Stars* (1942) and *All Hallows' Eve* (1945), and of the early drafts of Warnie Lewis's first book on Louis XIV and his times, which finally appeared (as *The Splendid Century*) in 1953. It is not likely that all of these books will be equally to the taste of any given reader; but a dispassionate observer must (surely) be impressed by the range and quality of the wartime productions of this small idiosyncratically assembled group, which Tolkien half-seriously called 'the Lewis séance';[25] it may well be that, aside from the stimulating and co-ordinating function of Lewis (and to some extent Williams), the threat of imminent destruction by war had an effect analogous to Dr Johnson's prospect of hanging.

Tolkien may have entertained quiet doubts about Lewis's apologetic writing; but Lewis's admiration for Tolkien's work was undiminished. He wrote to an American correspondent,

> *The Hobbit* is merely the *adaptation to children* of part of a huge private mythology of a most serious kind: the whole cosmic struggle as he sees it but mediated through an imaginary world. The Hobbit's successor, which will soon be finished, will reveal this more clearly. Private worlds have hitherto been mainly the work of decadents or, at least, mere aesthetes. This is the private world of a Christian. He is a very great man. His published works (both imaginative & scholarly) ought to fill a shelf by now; but he's one of those people who is never satisfied with a MS. The mere suggestion of publication provokes the reply, 'Yes, I'll just look through it and give it a few finishing touches' – wh. means that he really begins the whole thing over again.[26]

Lewis dedicated *Screwtape* to Tolkien, who (he later admitted) was mildly puzzled as to why.[27] Many years later, Tolkien discovered that Lewis had not, apparently, much liked *Screwtape*; he was, though, wryly amused rather than offended.

During the Christmas vacation of 1941–2, Tolkien pressed on with

The Lord of the Rings. By the end of January 1942, he had drafted the first four or five chapters of Book III. He then laid the work aside for the rest of the academic year.

He may have written *Leaf by Niggle* during this hiatus, probably in April 1942.[28] Certainly its portrait of the painter Niggle, caught up in an ever-ramifying work he is unable to complete, may serve as an objective correlative (to borrow a term Tolkien would probably have disliked) of Tolkien's state of mind at this time. We might also notice the way Niggle's great unfinished and unfinishable picture is housed in a shed built on his sometime potato patch; potatoes, Tom Shippey has plausibly argued, may stand for Tolkien's professional concerns as a philologist, which were increasingly edged out by his imaginative writing. It was not that Tolkien abandoned philology – if anything, *The Lord of the Rings* is philology sublimated or transformed – but that the simple time occupied by writing it inevitably encroached on other activities. The productive years of middle life are the period when, for scholars as for other men, what has been wrought by the energies and enthusiasms of early youth – such as Tolkien had amply evidenced – is broadened and built upon, the large structures of evidence and argument raised, the solid work done, intuition heightened and buttressed into achievement. Grimm was thirty-four when he published the first edition of his *Deutsche Grammatik,* fifty when *Deutsche Mythologie* first appeared, sixty-three for the *Geschichte der deutschen Sprache;*[29] Chambers was thirty-eight when he published *Widsith,* forty-seven when he published *Beowulf.* There is a particular quality to a work of learning informed also by enthusiasm, where the heart of the writer is engaged as well as his learning and effort; it is this (and, although this is a separate point, literary style) that marks out scholarship that will, or should, endure. Each of us can, probably, think of several books that would fall into this category, membership of which is determined in large part by personal taste. I would name, in no particular order (and with no claim to exhaust even my own predilections), Peter Brown's *Augustine,* Ker's *Dark Ages,* Stenton's *Anglo-Saxon England,* Bishop's *Liturgica Historica.* Tolkien, however, poured his scholarly heart into his legendarium; deprived of any other outlet, it informed and transformed *The Lord of the Rings.* This did not exhaust his capacity for scholarship; but, aside from the bare mechanics of time spent, it did give an outlet for an impulse that would otherwise have been satisfied only by a heavyweight book of philology, written with (we may guess) infinite pains and reworkings, and to this day on the bookshelves of all who care about language, and English, and the northern spirit. What we might call the moral place of this notional book in Tolkien's life was taken up by *The Lord of the Rings*. He could do nothing else.

Leaf by Niggle is in many ways an important work for understanding Tolkien's aesthetic, and his sense of being overwhelmed by his work and responsibilities. It also portrays his conviction that he was naturally lazy and given to procrastination; Niggle is 'sometimes just idle, and [does] nothing at all'.[30] But we should note, primarily, the tension it portrays between the painter's artistic compulsion to complete his picture, which has absorbed all of his other interests and projects, and his moral obligation to his neighbour. The fact that Niggle, finally and grudgingly to be sure, follows the second at the expense of the first leads almost naturally to the final redemption of his unfinished work, and its transformation into a real and living Tree, exactly as Niggle had first envisioned it, as it would have been (in fact) were man unfallen and his sub-creative powers uncompromised by sin and toil. Our artistic efforts – our makings – are, Tolkien claims, taken up in God's providence and made real, not just as objects to be admired, but also as bearing a sacramental function within the economy of grace, set within the context of the apparently humdrum makings of our 'unartistic' neighbours. The Tree becomes not something to be admired in isolation, in some sort of celestial museum or botanical garden, but the heart of Niggle's Parish, a country made with the conscious and essential collaboration of his neighbour, which is (for some) 'the best introduction to the Mountains'. The Mountains are God's country: heaven. Tolkien's memories of his 1911 trip to Switzerland here achieve apotheosis.

This is a great deal more than a simple claim for the social importance of art; our imaginative efforts, our storytelling (Tolkien is saying), contribute directly, under God's mercy, to the redemption of the world and the salvation of our neighbour, even if we can never complete them as we would wish (this obviously raises other questions also that we will look at later).[31]

Idleness, then, and the distraction of the legendarium both got in the way of professional philological research. Another factor, of course, was Tolkien's perfectionism, as described above by Lewis; he would not submit material for publication unless utterly sure it represented his last word on the matter and, in the nature of things, this degree of satisfaction was, for one with so many calls on his time, almost impossible of achievement. Needless to say, this attitude was a particular bugbear of

Kenneth Sisam at the University Press, who throughout his professional life was constantly exasperated by learned authors refusing to let books out of their clutches. As late as 1954, when he was retired, Sisam was still insistent on this; his daughter Celia had taken up his long-delayed edition on the Salisbury Psalter, and he modestly said, 'My part will be to counsel her against perfectionism and other bars to publication.'[32] He was perhaps unduly affected, alarmed even, by the example of his own master, Arthur Napier, neither of whose great projects (a historical grammar of English, and an edition of all the previously unpublished Old English homilies) was completed, in part because of the constant burden of teaching, supervising and examining, in greater part because of an incurable perfectionism. Sisam, who had the highest respect for Napier's powers and learning, saw this as both a grievous loss to scholarship and a cautionary tale for others.[33] This disposition is likely to have made things difficult for Tolkien even if the long shadow of the Clarendon Chaucer had not lain across his relations with the University Press.

His old friends and fellow scholars George Gordon (his old boss at Leeds, latterly President of Magdalen) and R.W. Chambers both died that spring, Chambers on St George's Day. Chambers was only sixty-eight, Gordon sixty-one. Chambers had retired the previous year, but was much dispirited first by ill-health, then by the effects of the war: University College London was moved to Aberystwyth for the duration; bombs destroyed much of the College library Chambers had spent his adult life building up, and also severely damaged Chelsea Old Church, where Thomas More, whose biographer Chambers was, had worshipped. Chambers did not repine, but his resources were depleted by the strain and illness took him off suddenly. He left a mass of unpublished work on *Piers Plowman*.

Gordon had been ill with cancer for much of 1941; he was known to be dying, although not to himself. Tolkien is likely to have known, however, since that year it was Lewis's turn to act as Magdalen's Vice-President, and because of Gordon's illness he was required frequently to stand in for him. Lewis was a very bad administrator, and was prevailed on to step down as Vice-President after only a year; something of his hatred for college business may be detected in the vitriolic scenes of (fictional) college meetings in *That Hideous Strength*, written at this time.

With Gordon's death, the whole burden of the still-pending Clarendon Chaucer fell on Tolkien; although, practically, this had been the case almost since the book's inception.

V – The fruits of scholarship

At some point in these years, Tolkien wrote *Sellic Spell*, a short story reconstructing the mythological or folktale elements in *Beowulf* as they might have been before their combination with the historical matter of the poem (the Freswæl, the Swedish wars); *Sellic Spell* exists in as many as four different versions, besides a text in Old English; it was published for the first time in May 2014. Tolkien's friend Gwyn Jones, Professor of English at Aberystwyth, reckoned it should be required reading for all students of *Beowulf*; it was set to be published in Jones's journal the *Welsh Review*: which, however, folded before the relevant issue could appear.

Sellic Spell may, in fact, stand as a colophon to the influence on Tolkien's academic work of Chambers, who now was dead. The impulse behind it can arguably be traced to a passage in Chambers's *Beowulf: An Introduction* where, after discussing parallels between *Beowulf* and *Grettis Saga*, and positing behind them both a tradition of folk or fairy tale, Chambers concluded:

> to speak of *Beowulf* as a version of the fairy tale is undoubtedly going too far. All we can say is that some early story-teller took, from folk-tale, those elements which suited his purpose, and that a tale, containing many leading features found in the 'Bear's son' story ... came to be told of Beowulf and of Grettir.[34]

Sellic Spell was an imaginative effort to recreate exactly that 'folk-tale', but this was just the latest of Tolkien's debts to Chambers; *Widsith*, as we have seen, lent a title to 'The Monsters and the Critics', and its form and approach to Tolkien's Freswael lectures (*Finn and Hengest*), which also drew on Chambers's *Beowulf*; the latter work contains a careful analysis of the Sceaf legends, which undoubtedly influenced another of Tolkien's imaginative recreations, the poem 'King Sheave' (in *The Lost Road*).

Sellic Spell and 'King Sheave', together with Tolkien's alliterative poem 'The Homecoming of Beorhtnoth' and his versions of the Völsung legends, represent a characteristic use of what we might call 'tertiary composition' of an independent literary text, often a poem, to reconstruct a learned crux. This was not unprecedented amongst scholars – Axel Olrik had reconstructed the Old Norse *Bjarkamál* on the basis of fragments of the original and an epitome in Saxo's Latin, whilst Nicolai Grundtvig and others were convinced *Beowulf* had originally been written in Old Danish and might be reconstructed as such; and, of course, there was *Schleicher's Fable* – and can be seen as a literary reflex of exactly the same motive as underlay all philological endeavour: if we can by intellectual work and imaginative sympathy reconstruct the words our distant ancestors used, why can we not combine those words, or their lineal descendants, into the very patterns (stories) they set them in, where these, too, are recoverable? On one level, this sort of activity – writing pastiche Old English folk tale, in the original language – looks very like donnish whimsy, a diversion of intellectual energy into fruitless bypaths; on another, however, it may be seen as in one sense the culmination of the whole philological project, recreating those very lost tales whose rumour, perhaps, first stirred our hearts to enter the dry world of sound-changes and asterisked grammar: where grammar, in fact, becomes gramarye. It is no chance, or mere bagatelle, that *Sellic Spell* also exists in an Old English version. The sadness, indeed, lies in the fact that this sort of scholarly enterprise is not usually, or these days, admitted into the ranks of 'proper research', since the capacity to do it is precisely what philology was always aiming at creating in its adherents.

VI – Frustrations

The Long Vacation of 1942 gave Tolkien time to return to *The Lord of the Rings* and write the remaining chapters of Book III, bringing the story past the defence of the Hornburg to the fall of Isengard and the quelling of Saruman. He may have written an opening page, no more, for the first chapter of Book IV. Then he stopped, and wrote nothing more (except possibly some notes and outlines) for almost eighteen months.

Basil Blackwell, who had been given Tolkien's translation of the Middle English *Pearl* to read, was so impressed by it that in August 1942 he offered to have it published in return for a sum to be set against Tolkien's substantial outstanding account at Blackwell's bookshop. Tolkien agreed, and began to contemplate writing the introduction for the modern reader that Blackwell thought it needed. He doesn't seem to have made much progress.

That December, Foyles arranged to publish an edition of *The Hobbit* for their Children's Book Club; Unwin were able to schedule a reprint of their own edition as part of the same run. The book finally appeared in July 1943.

Unwin wrote to Tolkien telling him about *The Hobbit* reprint; on 7

December, Tolkien replied, evidently encouraged by the news; he had been meaning to write for a while, he said, to ask whether finishing the *Hobbit* sequel was worth while, 'other than private and family amusement'. He admitted to misgivings: it was long, in places distressing, not really a children's book at all.[35] He already had thirty-one chapters, he told Unwin, and reckoned he needed another six; it could be finished, he thought, 'early next year'. The wartime shortage of paper would, he recognized, be a problem. Meanwhile, he wondered if Unwin was interested in a compilation volume made up of *Farmer Giles*, some other short stories and the Tom Bombadil poems. Unwin, politely, was not.

Despite his expressed hope of finishing *The Lord of the Rings* early in 1943, Tolkien in the event did almost nothing to the book all that year. What, then, did Tolkien do in 1943?

He prepared an edition of the Middle English *Sir Orfeo* for the use of cadets from the armed services studying six-month courses at Oxford; it was reproduced as a mimeograph by the University's Copying Office. Based closely on the text in Sisam's *Fourteenth Century Verse and Prose*, it was clearly meant as a substitute for copies of that book, which was probably then unavailable, as it was reprinted in 1944. Tolkien also, perhaps at this time, prepared a modern English translation of the text.

Tolkien in fact was given the task of organizing the whole of these cadets' courses, as they related to the English School. This took up most of his spare time; he was of course still giving his usual round of lectures and tutorials. Christopher and Priscilla were enlisted as typists of *The Lord of the Rings* as it then existed; Christopher also redrew the maps.

In the first half of the year, Tolkien revised and expanded his lecture 'Fairy Stories'; now entitled *On Fairy-Stories*, it became, in this form, the primary statement of Tolkien's mature aesthetic: what he thought stories did, why we tell them and what, ultimately, their value is. The prompt for this revision may have been a plan for its long-delayed publication; as we saw, the Lang lectures were typically published the year after being given, but Tolkien's had (we may guess) run afoul of general wartime disarrangement and entropy. As well as general revisions and expansions, he seems to have added, at this stage, the specifically theological 'Epilogue' to the lecture, introducing the theme, which we saw in *Leaf by Niggle*, that our imperfect stories may be taken up into the providence of God and both completed and, in his mercy and in keeping with our status as 'makers' in his image, be themselves contributory to the efflorescence of creation itself. This theme certainly appears in *Leaf by Niggle* before it does in the lecture, and may be reckoned to have been introduced into the latter as a consequence of the former. Obviously the two texts were closely related in theme, and probably also in time; the introduction of this theme into the 1943 revision of the lecture is probably another argument for the later dating of *Leaf by Niggle*, to 1942 rather than 1939, and also may explain Tolkien's mistake in dating the story to the earlier year: he clearly remembered the connexion between *Niggle* and the lecture, but mistakenly located it at the time of the original writing of the lecture rather than its later revision. In the event, the lecture was not published at this time, either because it was unfinished or because the OUP postponed it.

By March 1943, Blackwell had made up proofs of Tolkien's translation of *Pearl*; it still needed an introduction 'for the lay reader' and, of course, checking. Neither of these things Tolkien found time to do.

In April, Lewis published *Christian Behaviour*, the third series of apologetic talks given for the BBC; it now forms Book 3 of *Mere Christianity*. Tolkien took the strongest objection to Lewis's chapter on 'Christian Marriage', which argued for a two-tier system of religious and non-religious marriages. He drafted a long letter to Lewis giving his reasons for disagreeing; if it was ever sent, it did not cause Lewis to change his views.[36] There was, years later, to be a curious and unexpected practical sequel to this.

That July, Christopher Tolkien was conscripted into the RAF; his work as his father's typist and map-drawer came to an abrupt end. Basil Blackwell asked Tolkien again about the proofs of *Pearl*; and again, nothing came of this. The Foyles Children's Book Club *Hobbit* was finally published.

Blackwell, with admirable persistence, wrote again in September asking about *Pearl*; something, he said, needed to be put against the large debit balance on Tolkien's bookshop account. Tolkien sent him a cheque and an excuse. Blackwell replied hoping for the proofs before Christmas. Needless to say, they were not forthcoming.

In November, Tolkien seems to have written his satirical 'Closed Letter' to Charles Williams.[37] Williams's lectures continued to be popular amongst the much-diminished undergraduate population; on one occasion that month, his lecture on *Hamlet* clashed with one of Tolkien's Old English lectures, and all of Tolkien's usual audience deserted him, apart from one who was sent to take notes for the rest. Tolkien gave his lecture, then went for a drink with Williams.[38]

At some point this year, Tolkien took up the study of Polish, with the aim of helping a Polish soldier come up with a renewed technical vocabulary. Like so much war work, it seems to have issued in no actual result, other than a deal of wasted time and effort.

At the end of the year, Christopher Tolkien was sent to South Africa to train as a pilot. His father began a series of long letters (numbering at least eighty) sent to him by airmail.

All this time, *The Lord of the Rings* lay if not untouched, then certainly unfinished and (Tolkien began to think) unfinishable. The dam seems to have been breached after a lunch with Lewis and Warnie on 29 March 1944; Lewis had begun a new story (probably *The Great Divorce*) and, Tolkien wrote to Christopher, was 'putting the screw on me' to complete *The Lord of the Rings*. 'I needed some pressure, and shall probably respond.'[39] Tolkien's letters for the next two months mention frequent meetings with Lewis alone, for the sole purpose of reading him the latest chapter or section of the book; Tolkien was also coaxed into reading some to the Inklings, although reluctantly. Lewis clearly saw that Tolkien's book was on the verge of becoming another great project lost to the collateral damage of war, and seems to have exerted himself to coax and encourage and cajole him into taking it up again. This was by no means least amongst Lewis's services to his friend and, if we may be grandiose, to literature. The personal inconvenience to him (he was furiously busy with his usual work, and was still in demand as a lecturer to servicemen and on the radio, although he tried to keep these things outside term-time) was likely considerable.

Tolkien, then, did not tackle Book IV (Frodo and Sam's journey to Mordor) until April 1944, during the last three weeks of the Easter vacation (Trinity Term that year began on St George's Day); by the end of May, after a series of very late nights and much rewriting, it was done. This was perhaps the only part of the book written, rather than revised, during full term; he had that term an unusually light lecture list, and professedly skimped as much other work and responsibility as he could. Nevertheless, bringing the book so far in so short a time took great effort, and was exhausting. Chapters were sent to Christopher in South Africa as they were written. June was occupied by examinations – setting, invigilating, marking – and producing typescripts of the new *Lord of the Rings* chapters (some done by Tolkien, some by a friend of Charles Williams). After the exertions of April and May, Tolkien was written out:

I am absolutely dry of any inspiration for the Ring and am back where

I was in the Spring, with all the inertia to overcome again. What a relief it would be to get it done.[40]

July and August were barren of literary activity: he did some lecturing to cadets, and made further typescripts to send to Christopher, accompanied by long letters to him: these were most of what Tolkien wrote that summer. Christopher was now, he considered, his primary audience.

In September 1944, Basil Blackwell wrote yet again asking what had become of the *Pearl* translation, set up in type but never revised or given a preface; he offered to pay Tolkien a royalty rather than a flat fee for the copyright. Tolkien pleaded pressure of time, which left him no leisure to write a preface. Meanwhile Priscilla was enlisted as *Lord of the Rings* typist, beginning with its earliest chapters.

We come, now, to another much-written-about Inklings tableau. At midday on 3 October 1944, drinking in the Eagle and Child with Charles Williams and the Lewis brothers, Tolkien met Roy Campbell, who was there alone, eavesdropping. Campbell introduced himself, and joined the company.

Campbell was South African, a recent convert to Catholicism, who had been in Spain at the outbreak of the Civil War and had witnessed anti-Catholic atrocities perpetrated by the Republican government and their sympathizers (he had gone to France in the early 1930s to save money, and moved to Spain in 1933 to avoid a law suit). He was – is – a very fine poet, but one whose view of reality was unconventional and whose approach to truth-telling, particularly with regard to his own exploits, was a roundabout one. Lewis had once mocked Campbell in a poem printed in the *Cherwell*, and now quoted it from memory to Campbell's face.[41] Campbell had published 'Flowering Rifle', a long narrative poem praising Franco's fight against the Reds, and had carelessly embroidered his own part in the fighting. In fact, he had made a single trip to the front line as a war correspondent, during which he fell and hurt his hip. But you would not know this from the way he wrote and spoke about it, especially when amplified by beer. He regaled Tolkien and company with war stories, which Tolkien at least took at face value, and with anecdotes of famous progressives (the sculptor Epstein, for example, who was married to his wife's sister) he had known in London between the wars and had insulted.

There was also, so they discovered, an older connexion: Campbell had lived in Oxford in 1919, after coming there from South Africa with the aim of attending the University but failing the entrance examinations. He had fallen into an 'aesthetic' circle including William Walton, the Sitwells and Wyndham Lewis, but also Tolkien's undergraduate contemporary T.W. Earp, poet and critic (one biographer has claimed Earp and Campbell were homosexual lovers, for a while at least), and his later Leeds colleague Wilfred Childe, Christopher Tolkien's godfather. Campbell had been uncomfortable in this Bloomsbury world (not least when he discovered his wife was having a lesbian affair with Vita Sackville-West), and had lampooned it in vigorous heroic couplets before decamping to the continent with his wife and children. Since returning from Spain, he had joined the Army, despite indifferent health and being over-age (he was born in 1901); he ended up as a sergeant in the Intelligence Corps, working as a censor in Nairobi then a coast-watcher in Mombasa. He finally managed to get himself enrolled in training for jungle warfare, with the aim of going to fight the Japanese; but instead he had a motorcycle crash and injured his hip, which had never been right since his Spanish adventure, and in April 1944 was discharged from the Army as unfit. He was sent back to England, and after some time in hospital ended up in Oxford, staying with friends.

Understandably, Campbell himself dwelt only on the creditable aspects of his colourful past, damascened by rhetoric and alcohol. He told a good story, and Tolkien was clearly impressed by him. Writing to Christopher, Tolkien compared Campbell's first appearance to that of Strider (or the character who became him) in *The Lord of the Rings*.[42] After their initial encounter, Campbell may have joined Lewis and Tolkien in the Eagle and Child on other occasions; he does not seem to have become a regular member of their circle, however, although he did come to an evening Inklings later that week. Lewis remained suspicious, which Tolkien put down to residual anti-Catholicism; also Campbell's circumstances took him away from Oxford. There is no suggestion he attended further evening Inklings apart from an isolated occasion two years later (on 28 November 1946) when he read a translation of some 'Spanish poems', perhaps his celebrated versions of John of the Cross, although he was a prolific translator and so it may have been another text altogether.[43]

By the end of 1944, the war began to seem like a business tending towards a conclusion, rather than a permanent state. The Inklings planned a celebration in the (it was hoped) not too distant event of victory: they proposed hiring a country pub for a week, and spending it in talk around the clock. Things were to turn out rather differently.

Tolkien began Book V of *The Lord of the Rings* that October; he quickly discovered anomalies in the parallel timelines for the distinct strands of the story, and expended much effort in fixing them. At this time he and Lewis discussed collaborating on a book on '"Language" (Nature, Origins, Functions). Would there were time for all these projects!'[44] According to Lewis, the book was tentatively titled *Language and Human Nature*; he said to a friend in 1948 that it was to be published the following year, by the Student Christian Movement Press.[45] In a letter dated 12 January 1950, Lewis was more realistic: 'My book with Professor Tolkien – any book in collaboration with that great but dilatory and unmethodical man – is dated, I fear, to appear on the Greek Kalends!'[46] Needless to say, nothing further came of this. This is a tremendous shame; but I suspect most of us, given the choice, would settle for *The Lord of the Rings* over even such a book as this might have been.

During the next two University terms and vacation, Tolkien managed some sporadic work on *The Lord of the Rings*. After March 1945, however, he did nothing more to the book until September of the following year: 'real life' made a violent intervention.

VII – Distractions

On 26 January 1945, the Merton Professor of English Language, H.C.K. Wyld, died. Wyld, remember, was a German-educated philologist, who had also been a pupil of the famously cantankerous Henry Sweet; he had been Merton Professor since 1920, and was one of the electors to the Chair of Anglo-Saxon in 1925. Tolkien mentioned years later 'seeing Henry Cecil Wyld wreck a table in the Cadena Café with the vigour of his representation of Finnish minstrels chanting the *Kalevala*';[47] Wyld was also the prime mover in a spoof rendering of the opening and closing lines of *Beowulf* into cod-eighteenth-century heroic couplets, printed in the *Oxford Magazine* in March 1925 under the title *Gothique*, attributed to one 'Mr Beach'. His accomplice in this prank was H.F.B. Brett-Smith, an authority on eighteenth- and early nineteenth-century verse, and one of Tolkien's fellow examiners in *Doworst*. Four years later, Wyld published a short article, 'Experiments in Translating *Beowulf*' in a *Festschrift* for Frederick Klaeber, rendering passages in the style of Pope, Tennyson and Longfellow's *Hiawatha*. Some may find this type of humour a touch elephantine, but it surely belies the mirthless reputation of philologists.

He was in any case one of a fast-diminishing breed of scholar.

There were, as we saw earlier, two Merton chairs of English at Oxford; at that time, they and Tolkien's Rawlinson and Bosworth Chair were the only professorial chairs in the English Faculty. The Merton chairs were more prestigious and better paid than Tolkien's position, although of more recent foundation (1885 and 1904 respectively, as against 1795 for the Chair of Anglo-Saxon). They also came with a fellowship at Merton, one of the richer and physically more agreeable colleges, certainly compared to Tolkien's then college, Pembroke, which was poor, formal, unfriendly and (Tolkien reckoned) constitutionally suspicious of papists. He was unofficially sounded out whether he wished to be considered for the job. He decided he did. In the meantime, as one of the two surviving professors in the English School, proportionately more administrative work devolved onto Tolkien. This, and the normal business of term-time (lectures, tutorials, supervision of graduate students, interminable meetings of college and faculty), meant no leisure for writing.

Leaf by Niggle appeared in the *Dublin Review* that January. Stanley Unwin saw it in March, and liked it; he thought three or four such things could make a book. Tolkien was willing to try to put them together, but doubted he would have the leisure to do so. Three weeks' uninterrupted work, he declared, should be enough to finish *The Lord of the Rings*; of late, though, he admitted finding work on it difficult, mostly because of the absence abroad of Christopher, 'my real primary audience'. He was desperately worried about Christopher's safety (fatal crashes were common amongst trainee pilots) – 'my heart is gnawed out with anxiety' – and freely admitted to spending such small free time as he had writing not *The Lord of the Rings*, but letters to him.[48] Unwin, whose own son Rayner was now a naval cadet, presumably understood.

Other outstanding responsibilities crowded in on Tolkien: examining both local and external; E.V. Gordon's posthumous *Pearl* edition, which Tolkien had agreed to complete, and which Gordon's widow was chasing; the interminable Clarendon Chaucer; an edition of the Middle English *Seinte Katerine*, being done in collaboration with his former pupil Simonne d'Ardenne and promised to the EETS (they had also projected an edition of the shorter Katherine Group text *Sawles Warde*); his own edition of the *Ancrene Wisse*, likewise promised to the EETS; and, inevitably, Basil Blackwell's *Pearl*, still unproofed and unprefaced. As well as Wyld's Merton chair, various philological jobs at other universities had fallen vacant during the war years, and Tolkien was much in demand as adviser, elector and referee.

Christopher Tolkien now returned from South Africa; he was stationed at an RAF base in Shropshire. Although war in Europe ended on 7 May, fighting against Japan in the Far East was to continue for some months. There was still a strong possibility that Christopher would see combat; he transferred to the Fleet Air Arm, which if anything made it more likely he would see action (a large part in the proposed assault on Japan was to be taken by the Royal Navy's Pacific Fleet, which had a heavy component of aircraft carriers).

On 15 May 1945, Charles Williams died suddenly after a supposedly routine operation. Tolkien and, especially, Lewis were shocked. They contributed to a memorial volume (it came out at the end of 1947); Tolkien offered the revised and expanded version of his 1939 'Fairy Stories' lecture, including the longest expression of his theory of 'sub-creation'.[49] In one way, Williams's early death crystallized his position in Lewis's affections; the damage to his friendship with Tolkien would not, now, be undone.

Lewis persisted in his inability to see that his friendship with Williams had affected his relations with Tolkien; indeed, he all but explicitly made them the illustrative example of exactly the reverse point in his book *The Four Loves*:

> Now that Charles is dead, I shall never again see Ronald's reaction to a specifically Caroline joke. Far from having more of Ronald, having him 'to myself' now that Charles is away, I have less of Ronald. Hence friendship is the least jealous of loves.[50]

The book was published in 1960, based on notes for radio talks given two years earlier. Lewis had brooded on this matter for more than a decade.

During the war, Lewis had discovered with glee and relish the long 'romances' of E.R. Eddison, a retired civil servant with a gift for pastiche seventeenth-century prose and convoluted plots in a heroic pre-modern setting. He had introduced Tolkien to the books, and Eddison had twice been invited to the Inklings (in 1943 and 1944), on the second occasion reading from an unpublished book. Tolkien liked Eddison's writing, although he was unimpressed by his characters and philosophy.[51] On 18 August 1945, Eddison died; he was sixty-two.

At the end of May, the electors to the Merton chair met and agreed to offer it to Tolkien. As well as the Vice-Chancellor and the Warden of Merton, the electors were C.T. Onions of Magdalen and the *OED*, David Nichol Smith (the surviving Merton Professor) and Kenneth Sisam; Tolkien himself would normally have been of their number, but was replaced first by F.M. Powicke, Regius Professor of Modern History, and then (of all people) by C.S. Lewis. A month later, on 23 June, Tolkien was formally elected; his new job began with the academic year, that October. He had now, at the age of fifty-three, reached the highest position open to an English scholar of philology: he was the undisputed head of his profession. In the short term, however, this was more a burden than anything else, as he had to cover, in addition to his new responsibilities, those of his former chair as well. Procedural delays meant that a new professor of Anglo-Saxon (Tolkien's old friend C.L. Wrenn) was not appointed until April 1946, to begin work that October. Tolkien in effect did two jobs for a whole year. From this point on, the focus of Tolkien's academic work (lectures and graduate supervisions) was Middle English, the primary responsibility of his chair, rather than Old English as hitherto.

Tolkien's successor Wrenn was one of several considered by the electors; the others included Dorothy Whitelock of St Hilda's, whom many considered the stronger candidate, and who had support from, amongst others, Kenneth Sisam and Professor Frank Stenton of Reading, whose magisterial *Anglo-Saxon England* had appeared first two years before, in 1943. Tolkien voted for Wrenn, some have claimed from prejudice against women scholars. This is rather belied by his close collaboration with Mary Salu and Simonne d'Ardenne, and his later support of Dorothy Everett for the Readership in English Language (to which she was elected in October 1948); although one might argue that it is one thing to have women as junior colleagues, and another to support one as one's own successor. Tolkien did hold views on women's intellectual predilections of a traditional cast;[52] but there is exactly no evidence this prejudiced him against recommending them for jobs. The very next month, indeed, Tolkien was part of a committee that recommended Whitelock for a University Lectureship. Whatever the truth of all this, it is probably more likely that Tolkien was not biased against Whitelock so much as biased in favour of Wrenn, who was a friend and co-religionist. The Tolkien and Wrenn families had gone on holiday together before the war.

Tolkien's new colleagues at Merton were, on the whole, more agreeable to Tolkien than the 'old gents' at Pembroke;[53] they included Hugo Dyson, elected to a tutorial fellowship at much the same time as Tolkien was to his new chair, and Kenneth Sisam, who since 1942 had been Secretary to the Delegates (that is, operational head of the University Press) and as such had been given a Merton fellowship.

Chapter 9 – Peace, Not Rest

I – A false start?

In December 1945, the *Welsh Review* (edited by Tolkien's friend Gwyn Jones) published Tolkien's poem 'The Lay of Aotrou and Itroun', a pastiche 'Breton lay' treating man's dealings with faërie. As the year drew to an end, Tolkien's friend and former pupil Simonne d'Ardenne came to stay in Oxford, very likely with the Tolkien family, to work closely with him on their joint edition of *Seinte Katerine*. She and Tolkien both were in poor health, however, and this, together perhaps with Tolkien's other activities, meant the edition was not then completed.[1]

The week after full term ended was earmarked for the delayed 'Victory Inklings', a comparatively subdued affair compared to the heady plans of the year before. Tolkien and Warnie Lewis took a morning train that Tuesday to Fairford in Gloucestershire, which the Lewis brothers had visited that autumn, went for a walk in the afternoon, and, as their first choice of pub was full of Polish soldiers, spent a quiet evening reading. The next day, C.S. Lewis arrived by train, and Havard drove down. Barfield was ill and could not join them, and Dyson could not come; the absence of Charles Williams was (we may reckon) acutely felt. Havard drove back to Oxford that afternoon. The remaining three of them spent that day and the next in walk and talk; after lunch on the day after that (the Friday) they took the train back to Oxford. They made the best of it, but there had been a definite change, and it was, in all likelihood, a faintly melancholy affair. Yet their Thursday evening meetings continued; and it was now that they received their most direct literary analogue, in another work by Tolkien.

For many years Tolkien had experienced vivid dreams, which were (he felt) closely connected with his creative life; we earlier noticed the

'Atlantis dream' that underlay the Númenor story in *The Lost Road*. At the end of 1945 and the start of 1946, during the long hiatus in the writing of *The Lord of the Rings*, he began *The Notion Club Papers*.[2] This purports to be the records of a group of dons analogous to (indeed transparently based on) the Inklings, who in the course of discussions of the nature of dream, and its use in time and space travel, are borne in upon by a series of cataleptic dreams involving the 'old straight road' to the west, culminating in a new version of Tolkien's Atlantis myth. It recasts *The Lost Road* of the previous decade, and rather improves on it; but, as so often, it was unfinished. This is a shame, as although the story begins slowly and wordily, it builds to a high pitch of tension, advancing as scraps of unknown languages, texts and legends (all fabricated with care and plausibility) are recovered by various of the dons. In the end, though, the Númenor story outgrew its contemporary frame; as Stratford Caldecott has observed, however, the resulting clarification of the place of Númenor in the legendarium may have been justification enough for the work.[3]

There are several matters of biographical interest in the text as we have it: one of the characters (several of whom are clear Tolkien-figures, despite superficial identifications with others of the group) remarks, of the historical basis for the 'Matter of Britain', 'there was a man called Arthur at the centre of the cycle';[4] another tells of browsing in the second-hand department of what is obviously Blackwell's bookshop, and finding a manuscript, since disappeared, entitled *Quenta Eldalie*, by one John Arthurson: this is obviously the *Silmarillion*, unpublished and forgotten as Tolkien reckoned it might be: Tolkien himself is of course the 'son of Arthur'. He had not forgotten his own father; presumably meditating on the patterned father–son relationships that underlay *The Lost Road* had brought him to mind. 'The link between father and son is not only of the perishable flesh', he had written to his troublesome son Michael, some four years previously, 'it must have something of *aeternitas* about it. There is a place called "heaven" where the good here unfinished is completed; and where the stories unwritten, and the hopes unfulfilled, are continued. We may laugh together yet ...'[5] Caldecott comments:

This link between generations, through which life and hope are transmitted from father to son, is also the way back through memory and language from the present world to a world that can accurately be described only in myth.[6]

Caldecott has also, more speculatively, connected Tolkien's often-expressed sea-longing with his memory of leaving his father, Arthur, at the far end of a long sea-voyage when he was four.[7] Those who collect fortean correlates should note that the action of the story is set in 1987; and that the climax of one of the cataleptic visitations provokes a great and destructive storm (in the story, an analogue and in some way an irruption of the cataclysm that drowned Númenor). The reader will perhaps remember the Great Storm of 1987 that caused astonishing destruction across England, and draw whatever conclusion his metaphysics suggests.

Tolkien wrote drafts of these texts at a furious pace over Christmas 1945, with the presumed intention of completing them before the academic term started, and also (perhaps) to reassure himself that his creative powers had not been permanently affected by his failure (as it seemed) to complete *The Lord of the Rings*. The strain of this, after a term of double workload, was simply too much, and his health gave way.

John Rateliff has argued, plausibly enough, that Tolkien continued work on *The Notion Club Papers* between putting aside *The Lord of the Rings* in October 1944 (when concentrated work finished, although as we have seen he made some desultory progress until March 1945) and August 1946, when Warnie Lewis's diaries record him reading a completed Atlantis story (presumably, the reworked *Drowning of Anadûnê* that concludes *The Notion Club Papers*) to the Inklings. Only at this point did he finally respond to the repeated proddings of his publisher, Unwin, and resume work on *The Lord of the Rings*.[8]

The Notion Club Papers are linked, clearly, with Lewis's unfinished 'Ransom' novel, now known by its editorial title *The Dark Tower* (the manuscript is untitled); Rateliff, again, has made a very good case for dating this to 1944–6, rather than (as was previously supposed) 1938, making it an unfinished fourth in Lewis's science fiction sequence rather than an abortive second. Its theme fits well with what Tolkien described in a December 1944 letter to Christopher Tolkien as Lewis's 'fourth (or fifth?)' novel (after the three published Ransom books, and possibly *The Great Divorce*, written at this time); it also, as Tolkien notes, clashes with his own ideas for *The Notion Club Papers* (which become his 'dimly projected third' novel, after *The Hobbit* and *The Lord of the Rings*, which Tolkien clearly reckoned on finishing and publishing in short order). Both books are explorations of time travel, taking up (in varying degrees) the theories of the Anglo-Irish aeronautical engineer J.W. Dunne's then famous *An Experiment with Time* (Dunne argued from an experience of precognitive dreams to the non-linear nature of time). Tolkien's book is significantly better than Lewis's; indeed, Lewis's fragment is decidedly not his best work, to the degree that it has been claimed as an editorial forgery (something, alas, which manuscript evidence definitively refutes). A combination of this, with the reasonable charge that he was trespassing on what had by their compact been Tolkien's territory (time rather than space), may have led Lewis to turn from it to other things.

II – Picking up the threads

That February, Tolkien's eldest son, John, was ordained priest. Tolkien served his first Mass, in the church of St Aloysius, Oxford, on 11 February 1946.

In the middle of March 1946, Tolkien's doctor ordered him to take a thorough rest for six months to avoid a complete physical collapse; in the event, he spent three weeks at Stonyhurst, where the English College students (John Tolkien amongst them) had been quartered during the war. This was hardly the six months off he had been prescribed; the rest did him some good, though, enough to carry him through the remainder of the academic year. He said later that at this time he came 'near to a real breakdown' and returned 'to a term so troublous that it was all I could do to get through it'.[9]

Unwin reprinted *The Hobbit* again that March. He sent Tolkien advance royalties on the book, which were as ever very welcome. In the event, problems with the bookbinders meant that it did not appear for another eighteen months.

Tolkien returned to Oxford at the start of April; Edith was away, so he went to stay in an inn in Woodstock with his son Christopher, who was on leave from the Fleet Air Arm prior to returning to Oxford to finish his degree. They spent a week and a half in the Oxfordshire countryside. Then Tolkien returned to Northmoor Road, and a fortnight's administrative work before full term started (this included superintending the election of Wrenn to Tolkien's former chair). He also at this time published one of his few book reviews, in (of all places) *The Sunday Times*.[10]

After term ended, he and Edith spent a week at Stonyhurst, their first holiday together without children since the Great War.

At the end of June 1946, the other Merton chair, in English Literature, also fell vacant; its occupant, David Nichol Smith, had reached retirement age. Smith had held his chair for thirty-eight years; between the wars, he had been, for Tolkien and Lewis and their allies, the bad old English School personified – self-consciously 'literary' criticism in the Saintsbury manner, studies of older critics, elegant editions of philologically unchallenging texts. His retirement meant, for the time being, yet more administrative work for Tolkien (he would in effect be running the English School single-handed); it also involved him in selecting a successor. Tolkien's preferred candidate was either of two of his friends and academic allies: Lord David Cecil or C.S. Lewis. Lewis was by now one of the best-known English dons in Oxford, and was a natural choice for the vacancy, and Tolkien argued for him; but he was passed over, in large part (it seems) because some of the electors were suspicious of Lewis's activities as a Christian apologist. According to George Sayer (who probably had this directly from Tolkien), his fellow electors – H.W. Garrod, Helen Darbishire and C.H. Wilkinson – were unanimous in refusing to consider Lewis, who, they collectively reckoned, had not done enough pure scholarship, was opposed to research degrees (as indeed was Tolkien) and was best known for three novels and some books of popular theology: 'They thought his election would lower the status of the professorship and even discredit the English School.'[11] Cecil was also rejected. The job went, instead, to Lewis's former tutor, F.P. Wilson. Wilson, who had like Tolkien attended King Edward's, Birmingham, was three years older than Tolkien, nine years older than Lewis; at the time of his election to the Merton chair, he was fifty-eight. He was an authority on Shakespeare and Elizabethan literature, an editor of texts, co-editor of the *Oxford History of English Literature* series: a worthy but dull scholar, certainly not a radical-reactionary in the Tolkien–Lewis mode. Further reform of the English School was now significantly less likely, at least in the directions Lewis and Tolkien thought necessary. Tolkien pleaded this unhappy business as excuse for not writing during the summer.

It was not until September 1946 that Tolkien again took up the manuscript of *The Lord of the Rings*. He returned to Book V, which was finished by the end of October 1947, and also revised Books I and II. He also, as an exercise, wrote a new fifth chapter for *The Hobbit* (Bilbo's finding of the Ring, and the subsequent riddle contest with Gollum), to make it better fit with the later story. Tolkien had told Unwin in July 1946 he hoped to have the whole *Hobbit* sequel finished perhaps by October, but certainly by the end of the year. In the event, the material of Book V (the siege of

Minas Tirith, the ride of Rohan to its relief and the passage of Aragorn through the Paths of the Dead) was recast and re-ordered numerous times before Tolkien was happy with it.

Christopher Tolkien, again an undergraduate, now accompanied his father to meetings of the Inklings, although he was soon reckoned a member in his own right, 'independent of my presence or otherwise'.[12] He was deputed to read aloud chapters from *The Lord of the Rings*, as his delivery was generally considered better than his father's.

Michael Tolkien spent some months doing photographic research for the Admiralty (perhaps arranged by Robert Havard?), then a year teaching at the Dragon School in Oxford before landing a job at his old school, the Oratory. He was to spend the rest of his life as a schoolmaster.

III – The shifting of friendships

The years immediately after the war saw a change in the personnel usually attending the Thursday evening Inklings: Wrenn was back in Oxford from 1946, but does not seem to have resumed his connexion; and David Cecil, as we noted, was only ever a sporadic feature. The death of Charles Williams made a definite and epochal gap in the company: thereafter, as far as the records tell us, there was a distinct shift in those attending. At least half a dozen men who had, previously, had only tangential contact with the group now started to attend more often. Much of this is an inevitable consequence of the end of the war: as the University lifted its freeze on hiring lecturers, and men returned from war service, the number of dons in Oxford grew and, with it, the pool of potential Inklings. Charles Williams's prominence in the Oxford lecture list had been, we should remember, almost wholly a function of wartime exigency. This later version of the Inklings is the model for Tolkien's *The Notion Club Papers*, written in the first half of 1946.

We have already noticed Christopher Tolkien as a new member; Colin Hardie, Magdalen Classics don and later an authority on Dante, was another. Hardie, a Scotsman from distinguished academic stock, had been at Magdalen since 1936 (he had been first undergraduate then a don at Balliol, before three years at the British School in Rome); his brother Frank had spent a year at Magdalen before moving to Corpus, where he was eventually Head of House. Hardie came to Christianity, indeed to Catholicism, after his marriage in 1940. He was finally received in 1945; he seems to have been involved in the Inklings only thereafter.

There was also, initially at Tolkien's invitation, one of his ex-pupils, a young New Zealand research student, J.A.W. (Jack) Bennett; he attended sporadically from 1946 on. In 1947 he was elected to a tutorial fellowship at Magdalen, and took over the Old and Middle English teaching from Lewis. Another Tolkien invitee was R.B. (Ronald Buchanan) McCallum, the history don at Pembroke (elected in 1925, so exactly contemporary with Tolkien there); he was felt by some to be rather self-imposing than invited. He seems to have been active around 1948.

Another self-invited member was Fr Gervase Mathew. He was younger brother to the remarkable David Mathew: historian, sometime naval officer, would-be Carthusian and yet another of the unsettled intellectual clergymen in which the English Catholic Church has historically specialized (Newman, Adrian Fortescue, Robert Hugh Benson, Ronald Knox; in our own times Fr Ian Ker), David Mathew was first Chaplain to London University, then an auxiliary bishop in Westminster, and eventually apostolic delegate to British colonial Africa and Archbishop of a titular see *in partibus*. His time in Africa was successful, but on his return in 1953 he was passed over for English sees and retired to private life and the writing of history. Unlike his brother, Gervase Mathew found a congenial place in the English Dominican province, and was a habitué of the Oxford Blackfriars for half a century. More learned than his brother, even, but in recondite medieval and Byzantine bypaths, he was also an incurable collector and wielder of 'influence' in the characteristic Oxford string-pulling-through-personal-acquaintance manner (we shall see a not wholly happy effect of this on Tolkien). In this endless quest, he sought and gained access to the Inklings; Warnie Lewis's diaries do not mention him before 1946, although he claimed to have attended meetings as early as 1939. Mathew rather inserted himself into the circle, so we may suppose his early attendances to have been irregular and occasional; he was an enthusiast for the poems of Charles Williams, particularly in their Byzantine afflatus, which Tolkien disliked, and this, together with his efforts on Williams's behalf during the war with the Theology Faculty, may have helped him to get closer to the group.

Mathew, Hardie and Bennett were all Catholics (although Bennett converted only in the early 1950s); there were another three men whom Lewis brought along, two of whom were from other traditions. One was C.E. Stevens, the indefatigable ancient history don at Magdalen, who was active in the Inklings from November 1947; another, a legacy of wartime, was James Dundas-Grant, a retired naval officer (and another Catholic).

In 1944, he was appointed to command the Naval Division of the Oxford cadets in training, and given rooms and dining rights by Magdalen; he became friendly with Lewis, and attended occasional evening Inklings. After the war, he moved to Oxford as warden of a house for Catholic undergraduates, and joined morning pub sessions also. He remembered Tolkien 'jumping up and down, declaiming in Anglo-Saxon'; he also described him as 'tall, sweptback grey hair, restless', which seems inaccurate in one (subjective) particular (Tolkien was, in fact, very slightly below average height), and possibly conflatory in another: photographs of him in the 1940s show his hair still dark, although by the end of the decade it was greying.[13]

Last of the trio was John Wain. One of Lewis's quondam pupils, he was from 1946 to 1949 a Fellow of New College, and (from 1947 to 1955) also held a lectureship at Reading. He was a frequent attender between, probably, 1946 and 1951 or so, years before he found fame as a novelist. He was not, on the whole, sympathetic to the general aesthetic or theological or political tenor of the Inklings, but seems to have enjoyed their talk.[14] Perhaps Wain had, then, the ambitious young man's chameleon quality of disguising from his elders such views as he knew would offend; but it remains true that the inclusion of one so fundamentally out of sympathy with their collective dispositions suggests that the Inklings was, in some degree, running out of steam. Nevertheless it carried on, borne by habit and Lewis's jollying, until the early 1950s.

IV – Dispersed effort, sporadic results

Tolkien was in desultory correspondence with Unwin about publishing *Farmer Giles*; he had no leisure to finish any stories that might, when added to it, make a big enough book to be worth making a fuss over, apart from *Sellic Spell*, which 'might not seem so suitable'. He was convinced, too, that *The Lord of the Rings* was qualitatively so much better than these other things that any time he could spare must be devoted to it. Unwin decided that *Farmer Giles* might be better published on its own, bulked out with illustrations.

The academic year 1946–7 brought some alleviation of Tolkien's workload; Wrenn assumed the Chair of Anglo-Saxon, and Tolkien also relinquished the chairmanship of the English Faculty Board. This did not by any means abolish the perpetual round of committee meetings and other administration, but it did diminish it appreciably. When

Michaelmas Term ended, in early December 1946, Tolkien told Unwin he was 'on the last chapters' of *The Lord of the Rings*, and would finish it by January.[15]

There was another interruption early in 1947. On 14 March, Tolkien, Edith and Priscilla left their big house in Northmoor Road, where the children had grown up but which was now too large and too expensive for only three people (especially with the income tax newly raised again by Major Attlee's socialist government, and the lack of any domestic help), and moved to a small Merton College house in Manor Road. Amongst their neighbours were Austin Farrer, Chaplain of Trinity and a very notable Anglican theologian, and his wife Katharine, who was a fan of *The Hobbit* and became a friend. Later Tolkien lent her texts from *The Silmarillion* to read.

The Farrers had one daughter, who had what would now be called learning difficulties. Katharine suffered from chronic insomnia, and became dependent on drink and barbiturates; still, in the 1950s, she wrote a series of Oxford-set detective novels. Whilst Tolkien certainly met Austin Farrer socially, they do not seem to have become friends; he may, perhaps, have detected something of Farrer's strong anti-Papalism – 'I dare not profess belief in the great Papal error. Christ did not found a Papacy. No such institution appeared for several hundred years. Its infalliblist claim is a blasphemy ... Nor is this an old or faded scandal – the papal fact-factory has been going full blast in our own time, manufacturing history after the event'[16] (this probably refers to the proclamation of the dogma of the Assumption in 1950). This sat, for Farrer, comfortably alongside his general 'Catholicism' in theology and liturgy.

The move to Manor Road was not a success. Uprooting from a house the Tolkiens had occupied for twenty years was physically disruptive, leaving aside the sentimental wrench of leaving a much-loved family home. Inevitably, some of Tolkien's papers were lost during the move. Their new house was soon found to be altogether too small; Tolkien had no room to use as a study, and had to move all his working papers to his college rooms. It was three years before a larger college house became available. The move meant that February and March were lost to writing, and *The Lord of the Rings* remained unfinished.

It may seem tedious to mention these routine physical dislocations, let alone dwell on them; most of us, after all, are obliged by circumstance to move house from time to time. For a writer such as Tolkien, however, the physical context for his work was of great importance; he was not a man like, say, Charles Williams, who wrote his books balancing a notebook on his knee in a train carriage. Tolkien needed to have his copious drafts and working notes to hand; he had by now generated many thousand manuscript pages connected with dozens of different stories or versions of stories, most of which were interlinked and existed in numerous drafts, much overwritten and interleaved; not to mention his very extensive linguistic writings. All of these texts were kept in innumerable box files, not always in the best order. To move all of this material bodily was intensely disruptive to Tolkien's working methods.

Nevertheless, he continued to work on *The Lord of the Rings*, and to bring chapters to be read to the Inklings; Hugo Dyson had however developed an intense dislike of the book (oral tradition has him exclaiming, during the reading of a chapter and the appearance of an unspecified character, 'oh fuck, not another elf'[17]) and was allowed to veto the reading of it; we do not know how often he exercised his veto, but he had been elected to a Merton fellowship in 1945, and so was presumably now a regular attender. Warnie Lewis in his diary records at least one Dyson veto. Confronted with this, Tolkien was disinclined to allow his book to be read out at all.

Faced with these varied obstacles – disrupted working patterns, public discouragement, physical ailments and his private tendency to despondency – the simple fact that Tolkien persevered with *The Lord of the Rings* is remarkable testimony to his strength of will. The temptation to set aside this vast self-imposed burden must have been great.

Farmer Giles was still unpublished; Tolkien suggested one of Priscilla's contacts, Milein Cosman, a young German expatriate who later married the music critic Hans Keller, as illustrator, and on the strength of this he agreed to give Unwin a completed text by the end of June 1947 (although he thought the royalty could be bigger). He sent the corrected typescript in on 5 July.

Later that month, Tolkien finally finished an introduction for E.V. Gordon's posthumous *Pearl* edition, and sent it to Gordon's widow Ida, who was readying the book for publication. He also, on a visit to London, dropped off a typescript of the first Book of *The Lord of the Rings* for Unwin to look at; Unwin passed it to Rayner, who was enthusiastic and asked for more.

Chapter 10 – Hyde and Jekyll

I – Unfinished business

August and early September 1947 were 'devote[d] ... mainly to philology' – 'Hyde (or Jekyll) has had to have his way';[1] Simonne d'Ardenne stayed again with the Tolkiens during those months, and she and Tolkien did more work on *Seinte Katerine*. Tolkien managed to fit in a five-day walking tour in Malvern with the Lewis brothers, who thought he dawdled, distracted by plants, insects and his own talk; they marched ahead ('ruthless walkers', Tolkien declared), whilst Tolkien was left to follow at his own pace in company of one of Lewis's former pupils, who made the fourth in their party. After returning to Oxford, Tolkien took his daughter Priscilla for a week's stay at Stonyhurst; then, in early September, he had a few days with his Incledon cousins in Sussex. Edith does not seem to have come on any of these trips.

On 21 September, he sent Book II of *The Lord of the Rings* to Unwin for Rayner to read and comment on. Rayner was still at Oxford as an undergraduate, and was able subsequently to visit Tolkien to collect text as it became ready. At the same time, after looking at proofs for the reprint of *The Hobbit*, Tolkien sent Unwin a list of corrections for future reprintings, a list he had promised in July; he also included the speculative revised text of the book's fifth chapter (Bilbo's finding of the Ring, and the subsequent riddle contest with Gollum) 'for your amusement'; Unwin misunderstood, and had it inserted into the text against its next appearance.[2] The new chapter meshed much better with the nature and purpose of the Ring in the *Hobbit* sequel. The reprint did not in fact appear until November; it did not of course incorporate any of Tolkien's September revisions.

Soon after sending the new *Hobbit* chapter off, Tolkien spent four days with Merton's Warden (or Head of House, at that time the philosopher G.H.G. Mure) and Bursar visiting the college estates in Cambridgeshire, Leicestershire, and Lincolnshire. Although it was a piece of college duty (one of the fellows was always nominated to accompany these regular visitations), Tolkien found the trip both enjoyable and instructive.

That December, *Essays Presented to Charles Williams*, the now posthumous *Festschrift*, was published. Tolkien's revised 'Fairy Stories' lecture now first appeared, alongside pieces by both Lewis brothers (Warnie, remember, was an amateur of eighteenth-century French history), Owen Barfield, Gervase Mathew and Dorothy Sayers; C.S. Lewis also wrote a preface paying tribute to Williams.

Farmer Giles was still hanging fire; at last, in mid-January 1948, Unwin sent Tolkien a specimen illustration done by Milein Cosman. Tolkien was not enthusiastic, but after meeting Cosman agreed to her doing the job, if Unwin still wanted her. They prevaricated, and asked her for more samples.

Tolkien's health was poor again in February, and he was given three weeks' leave during term-time to recover. He and Christopher spent some of it in Brighton. The remainder of that academic year was again a busy one, filled with committees and negotiations over lectureships and readerships, and lectures and supervisions and associated whatnot. A major distraction was the introduction, at last, of the 'English Prelim', a dedicated First Public Examination that would allow undergraduates to read exclusively for English for the whole of their Oxford career. It was over two decades since it had first been mooted. Tolkien had been a member of the English Faculty committee charged with devising the syllabus for the 'Prelim', and with negotiating its approval by the University; they had managed successfully to avoid the suggested imposition of additional optional subjects (philosophy and modern languages) that would have diluted its critical and philological character. This was a minor triumph, perhaps, but also (and inevitably) a source of extra work, not least in examining.

II – Almost done?

As the long vacation started, Tolkien made plans to split his time between Oxford and his son Michael's house in Woodcote (Michael was now teaching there at the Oratory School, which had moved from Caversham during wartime[3]), where he hoped to write. Unwin sent him more sample illustrations by Cosman for *Farmer Giles*; Tolkien disliked them, and said so at length. He was by now transparently frustrated by what he saw as Unwin's foot-dragging over the book. Unwin started to look for another illustrator.

Tolkien spent some time at Woodcote in late July and early August; in mid-August, when Michael went on holiday, he went there for a full month to try to finish *The Lord of the Rings*. There, at Payables Farm, between 14 August and 14 September, he completed a draft of Book VI. Soon afterwards, the academic year began again. The complete work was revised, and typed up, by October 1949; Tolkien commented:

> this university business of earning one's living by teaching, delivering philological lectures, and daily attendance at 'boards' and other talk-meetings, interferes sadly with serious work.[4]

Because he could not afford a professional typist, he typed the whole book himself, twice; some passages were done and redone multiple times. He mostly worked

> on my bed in the attic of the tiny terrace-house to which war had exiled us from the house in which my family had grown up.[5]

The intervening year did not pass without incident, naturally; Tolkien was still in poor health, and much burdened by administrative tasks. He asked about the possibility of a sabbatical leave, perhaps including the Trinity Term that year; the Registrar seems to have misunderstood an enquiry as a request, and arranged for him to have the term off. There was too much pressing work to hand, Tolkien decided, to allow his original plan (which had been to request both Trinity and the following term off), so instead he proposed (after telling the Registrar of the misunderstanding) to ask for the following two terms, Michaelmas 1949 and Hilary 1950, instead. This was granted.

At the end of January, Christopher was accepted as a probationary B.Litt. student. His supervisor, who was not appointed until December, was his father's former pupil Gabriel Turville-Petre, now Reader in Icelandic. Turville-Petre and Christopher collaborated on an edition of *Heiðreks Saga* (perhaps the most archaic and interesting of the Norse *fornaldarsǫgur*, the 'sagas of ancient times'). At the end of February, Tolkien went to Downside for a rest.

The chances of *The Lord of the Rings* being ever published improved slightly that March, when paper was no longer rationed, although it was not yet abundantly available.

Tolkien spent a fortnight that summer in the Irish Free State, as an external examiner for the National University. This was his first journey abroad since 1917; getting a passport was troublesome, owing to his having been born in South Africa and some of his family papers being lost. The Irish trip became almost an annual event for the next decade, usually supplemented by an additional visit in early autumn.[6] He grew to like Ireland, although he found the Irish language, after several attempts to learn it, wholly intractable. The financial imperatives for this additional examining work had clearly not diminished, even though his two oldest children were no longer a charge on him; medical bills for himself and for Edith only grew with age and debility.

He began gathering material for appendices to *The Lord of the Rings* (which seem to have been a foreseen part of the book even at this stage), and wrote a foreword, dedicating the work to the Inklings (he later added his children also).[7] Calendars, annals, family trees, linguistic essays, accounts of scripts and runes, synoptic chronologies of the narrative: all of these, together with some straight historical narrative, were begun and in some cases highly elaborated to round out the story, which, now, was in almost its familiar form. Work on this ancillary material stretched into 1950.

III – Teeth, and other things

In the meantime, another problem was added to Tolkien's litany of physical woes: his teeth. They had been identified as a problem by his doctors as early as October 1947. In February 1949, the enquiry about a sabbatical mentioned that it would be partly to write, but also to have his teeth, 'which are said to be poisoning me', drawn. In the event, as we have seen, his leave was postponed, and his teeth were left until April of the next year, when in a series of procedures they were all removed. This may seem a mildly shocking procedure to twenty-first-century sensibilities, but we should remember that dental health was until the last half-century chronically bad, and comprehensive tooth-drawing was seen as the cure for any number of conditions even when the teeth in question were not (as they seem to have been here) thoroughly rotten (my own father, for instance, born when Tolkien was thirty-six, had a half-set of false teeth from (I think) his late forties). Tolkien was now fitted with a set of false teeth, which for the next quarter-century he used as an intermittent prop or physical distracter (even if they were prone to come loose during 'the excitements of rhetoric'). They were, for instance, in later decades sometimes passed to inattentive shopkeepers along with money (or so at least Humphrey Carpenter tells us, although I confess to finding the notion a faintly revolting one[8]). He suffered much from throat problems, with frequent bouts of laryngitis making lecturing often difficult; over the next decade he several times had to postpone or cancel lectures, or radio talks, because of the state of his voice. In fact, as Tolkien approached his seventh decade (he was fifty-seven, remember, when *The Lord of the Rings* was finished) his habitual proneness to physical complaints grew; lumbago, arthritis, fibrositis, rheumatism, sciatica: all feature in his letters as reasons for the non-completion of work, or its chronic postponement. Many of these ailments were, in fact, brought on by habitual sitting for long hours at a desk writing. We may in part agree with Rayner Unwin that these excuses were 'a defence against his failure to achieve some rashly-promised goal',[9] but we should remember that, although Tolkien and especially Edith were frequent invalids, and probably made much of their medical affairs, there were for both of them genuine physical complaints that increasingly impeded them as they grew older. We should also remember that Tolkien's long bout of trench fever had, it seems clear, permanently damaged his health, and made him less able to resist other things, and more heavily burdened by them when they came.

There was also, undoubtedly, a psychological and even moral aspect to some at least of Tolkien's illnesses. George Sayer quotes something Tolkien said in commendation of his doctor, 'Humphrey' Havard:

> I told him that I was feeling depressed, so depressed that I hadn't been to Mass for a couple of weeks. I wasn't sleeping well either. He said I didn't need drugs, what I needed was to go to Confession. He was at my house at 7:30 the following morning to take me to Confession and Mass. Of course I was completely cured. Now that's the sort of doctor to have![10]

IV – An end to Chaucer, and to children

Kenneth Sisam retired from the OUP at the end of 1948, aged only sixty-two. He had continued to write scholarly articles in the intervals of his office work, and began now to collect them for republication. An impressive collection, *Studies in the History of Old English Literature*, appeared in 1953, the same year as a seminal British Academy paper on Anglo-Saxon royal genealogies was published.[11] Sisam was elected to the Academy in 1941; Tolkien never was. Sisam's sponsors included R.W. Chambers and Sir William Craigie. Some might have observed that Sisam, a full-time publisher in habitually poor health, had managed to write and publish more on Old English than his successful rival for the Anglo-Saxon chair had in a quarter-century of tenure. A dozen years later, aged seventy-seven, Sisam published *The Structure of Beowulf*, a short but pithy work which included some trenchant criticism of Tolkien's famous lecture. 'As an account of what the poem means to Professor Tolkien, or of the way in which he, as a storyteller, would treat the plot, I have no criticism of it,' he declared, before going on to dissent strongly from pretty much all Tolkien had said about the poem's construction.[12] He also pointedly omits Tolkien's lecture from a preliminary footnote listing the most useful books on the poem.[13] Sisam was not without detractors, however; James Wyllie, sometime editor of the *Oxford Latin Dictionary* and a long-term collaborator on the *OED*, wrote a twelve-book epic poem in which Sisam featured as the Antichrist, plagiarizing his scholarly articles from lecture notes stolen from his old master Napier. Wyllie, to be fair, was at the time quite mad.

The old project of the Clarendon Chaucer was resurrected after Sisam's retirement. Nothing had been done to it since Tolkien had set it aside in 1932; Sisam had suggested it be taken over by a younger or more industrious or less busy scholar, first (before his untimely death) E.V. Gordon, then Tolkien's former student, J.A.W. Bennett; but neither, in the event, had taken it over.[14] Now that Sisam had retired, his successor, D.M. Davin, approached Tolkien; Tolkien said he was happy to give the OUP the extensive materials that he still retained (galley proofs with handwritten revisions), for someone else to complete. He did not do this at once, though, probably because the material was not ready to hand.

By now, Priscilla, the youngest Tolkien child, had gone up to Lady Margaret Hall to read English (she matriculated in October 1948); she moved into college rooms, and thus Tolkien and Edith were alone for the first time since 1917.

Chapter 11 – Finished, at Last

I – 'His Tree, finished'

In some ways, *The Lord of the Rings* underwent something of the same transformation as *The Hobbit*; as Tolkien wrote, the story became increasingly drawn into the web of stories that was the *Silmarillion* material, which became, in fact, the ancient history of the world in which Tolkien's characters moved. *The Lord of the Rings* became the elegiac conclusion to Middle Earth's long history, the final episode in the gradual fading of elvish things from the world. Here, as in *The Hobbit*, allusions throughout the text and appendices give an impression of 'depth', only to a far greater extent.

One critical difference between *The Lord of the Rings* and the earlier *Silmarillion* stories is the presence of hobbits. They function not only as a vehicle for Tolkien to express his love for a vanished (and idealized) rural England (parochial, smug and ignorant of its neighbours, but also rooted in history and good sense, with a slow-burning indomitable courage and, when awoken, a deep sensitivity to the heart-breaking melancholy of the world's beauty and perishability), but also as a 'way in' for the reader unfamiliar with the high literary modes of romance, myth and epic. Tolkien's story values deeply unfashionable qualities (nobility, loyalty, self-sacrifice, ceremoniousness) which an audience accustomed only to 'realistic' novels typically find baffling or repellent; but we see these qualities, mostly, through the eyes of the hobbits, whose initial reactions may mirror our own, but who allow us gradually to enter into these themes, as they do, without cynicism or irony. The hobbits provide a focus for the narrative that mediates between our normal reactions to events and the high style appropriate to an earlier literary age, which Tolkien, boldly, wanted to revive.

As in *The Hobbit*, but on a greater scale, Tolkien drew on his professional interests for *The Lord of the Rings* (the Rohirrim, for instance, are an idealized portrait of early Mercians). However, although it is possible to discern sources for elements in *The Lord of the Rings*, it is not necessarily helpful to itemize them, as if that explained how they work in the finished book; Tolkien integrated elements from a wide variety of sources both literary and personal into a story that functions on its own terms. Thinking that by identifying the source of a particular theme or passage or event, we have thus understood or explained it, is to fall into exactly the same mistake Tolkien complained of in the critics of *Beowulf*. Not that this activity is without interest, or wholly unprofitable: it is intriguing and often illuminating to trace the workings of Tolkien's mind, or at least to note the disparate sources he drew on.[1] But it does not necessarily tell us anything about *The Lord of the Rings*, or somehow reduce Tolkien's achievement in writing it. The art in making a book, especially one of this length, is shown exactly in the sublimation of its component elements into a new thing, a story; and it is only this new thing, this story, that may properly be judged. If it moves, delights, instructs, enthrals, seizes and compels us, it does so as itself, not as an assemblage of component parts, an analogue in words of Dr Frankenstein's monster, more or less competently riveted together from the hacked or discarded limbs of other entities. Rather, a story is (or should be) a new being, with its own life and motive power, not one borrowed or compounded from others.

As with the best of his legendarium, Tolkien felt that he was not engaged in a process of pure literary invention, but 'recording what was already "there", somewhere'.[2]

II – Authorship and its discontents

After some months of crossed purposes and misplaced letters, Tolkien finally went to London to look at samples by potential illustrators for *Farmer Giles*. He settled on an unknown artist, Pauline Baynes, who had been chart-making for the Admiralty and had produced for Unwin some delicate work in the style of medieval manuscript marginalia. Tolkien was delighted by her drawings; her work on *Farmer Giles* led directly to her most famous work, for (of all people) C.S. Lewis.

Lewis had been unstinting in his encouragement and praise of *The Lord of the Rings* as it was read to the Inklings, or passed to him privately; Tolkien however was less enthusiastic about Lewis's own 'big book', the sixteenth-century volume of the *Oxford History of English Literature* (known as *OHEL*, pronounced 'oh, hell'), which was also slowly gestating during these years. It was finally published in 1954, and runs to fully 700 pages. When the series had originally been mooted in 1935, Tolkien (we may remember) had been asked to write the volume on Old English literature, but had turned it down owing to lack of time. Tolkien took strong objection to Lewis's estimation of St Thomas More, and to other aspects of the book which he felt illustrated Lewis's aboriginal anti-Catholicism. Lewis criticized More both as a stylist and, on the basis of his polemical writings, as an example of Christian charity. This must have offended Tolkien not merely on purely denominational grounds, but also as a deliberate contradiction of the high place accorded More on both counts by R.W. Chambers, who, although an Anglican, had in various studies of More's life and works done much to advance his cause for canonization. More and John Fisher were both canonized in 1935; Chambers, in recognition of his work, received from Pope Pius XI a letter and a signed photograph, which he treasured.

Tolkien's opinion of Lewis's *OHEL* seems to have changed over time; a decade or more later, he wrote that it was 'a great book, the only one of his that gives me unalloyed pleasure'.[3] We do not, to be fair, know the full context of this statement, which is certainly at odds with his estimates elsewhere; but perhaps time and circumstance had covered over the more (to Tolkien) painful parts of the work. It is true that Lewis's *OHEL* is a very fine and readable book, which bears revisiting more than do most comparable things.

Lewis had also begun his Narnia stories for children, and read parts to Tolkien; Tolkien detested them. He deplored their eclecticism (Father Christmas appears alongside the fauns and satyrs of Greek myth, talking animals, and children straight from E. Nesbit) bound together only by Lewis's own taste, and what was to him the evident haste and carelessness of the writing. Tolkien said, to a former pupil who had also seen the stories, 'It really won't do, you know!' Ironically, it can surely be contended that, in many ways, *The Hobbit* was equally eclectic in its sources (Eddas, William Morris, Dr Dolittle, *The Marvellous Land of Snergs*); but perhaps Tolkien may be allowed to have integrated them better, and also Tolkien's taste was more homogeneous than Lewis's. Nevertheless, Lewis published the Narnia stories, finely illustrated by Pauline Baynes, with great success. The contrast with Tolkien's own slow and laborious methods of composition was surely a painful one. Lewis was undoubtedly disappointed and hurt by Tolkien's reaction; he had, after all, been unfailingly supportive of Tolkien's writing and scrupulously constructive in his criticism of it. To be faced, in his turn, with flat condemnation impatient of any mitigation or suggested improvement was surely hard. Lewis was, moreover, himself diffident about the quality of the Narnia stories, and might have abandoned them outright had he not been encouraged to persevere by Tolkien's former pupil Roger Lancelyn Green – the very man to whom Tolkien had been so forthright about his own views of Narnia.

Lewis seems to have read some of *The Lion, the Witch, and the Wardrobe* to Tolkien, perhaps in company with others, early in 1949. Five of the Narnia books were written in a burst between the summer of 1948 and March 1951; he began *The Magician's Nephew* thereafter, but ran into difficulties and put it aside for a year or more. He then, early in 1953, wrote *The Last Battle*, before returning to *The Magician's Nephew* later that year. It is the most personal of the books – Digory Kirke is an almost exact figure of Lewis in age and setting, from the time when Lewis's mother, like Digory's, was dying of cancer. Digory brings back a golden apple from the Garden of the Hesperides and effects her miraculous cure. There is something almost inexpressibly painful and touching about this; a middle-aged man reaches back to heal, at least in fiction, the overwhelming grief of his childhood, when 'all settled happiness ... disappeared from my life'[4]. Tolkien of all people would surely have recognized this; but probably by this time he had made his feelings about Narnia so clear that Lewis did not bother to show the story to him. Tolkien had however recommended Lewis approach Pauline Baynes to illustrate the books; her pictures are, for many readers, as memorable as the text. The Narnia books were published, one a year, between 1950 and 1956. Lewis had also begun to write his autobiography, *Surprised by Joy*, in 1948; it was finished seven years later. It is a fine and evocative book, although hardly an exhaustively honest one; indeed, its elisions and partialities are such that one who knew Lewis well, his doctor Robert Havard, in a letter to another of Lewis's friends renamed it 'Suppressed by Jack'.[5] A recent biographer has argued, though, that the driving force of these suppressions – notably about Janie Moore, his wartime service and his father's death – was not dishonesty so much as pain.[6] This may well be partly true in the last instance, and mainly in the second; in the first case, however, it looks like special pleading.

Lewis's academic career, however, was not prospering at Oxford.

In 1948, two years after he missed out on the Merton chair, the same had happened with the newly created Goldsmith's Chair of English Literature, which, although Lewis was considered, went instead to Lord David Cecil. In early 1951, Lewis stood for the Professorship of Poetry, which uniquely amongst Oxford chairs is directly elected by graduates of the University. After vigorous campaigning on both sides, Lewis lost narrowly to his near-namesake, the Anglo-Irish Communist poet Cecil Day Lewis. Part of this might have been a hangover from an unfortunate episode a dozen years before, when Lewis had masterminded the election to the same chair of his friend Adam Fox, Magdalen's Dean of Divinity (chaplain), who was an amateur poet but otherwise little qualified for the position, against a pair of distinguished literary critics who had also been put up for the post. Fox, so the story goes, had remarked dismissively on one of the other candidates at breakfast at Magdalen, saying, 'they might as well elect me!'; to which Lewis answered, 'Well, we will.' This sort of thing, in Oxford, tends to be long remembered and (in some quarters) resented. Tolkien had, in a letter of June 1938 to Stanley Unwin, applauded Fox's election as one of 'our literary club of *practising poets*'.[7] Over time, his views changed; in 1973, he voted against John Wain, who was elected, on the grounds that 'It is high time the chair came back to what it was originally intended for, scholars interested in poetry, but not practising poets, who are not in general very good lecturers on the subject.'[8] As well as being disappointed at Fox's tenure, Tolkien is also on record as attending at least one lecture by Robert Graves, Professor of Poetry in 1961–5, 'the most ludicrously bad lecture I have ever heard'.[9]

The Thursday evening meetings of the Inklings seem to have come to an end at this time; in his diary for 27 October 1949, Warnie Lewis recorded 'No one turned up.' Various theories have been advanced to explain this: as the group had grown and changed over the years, its original focus (on reading out works in progress) had been diluted, particularly under pressure from the corrosive criticism of Hugo Dyson; Charles Williams's death had removed another prop, whilst the general amelioration of social life as the austerities of wartime gradually receded may have been another factor. Newer members had as we have seen been introduced, and the old intimacy receded. Tensions between Tolkien and Lewis could not have helped, although Lewis remained a strong advocate of *The Lord of the Rings*. Morning sessions over beer carried on for some years, though; but these were necessarily confined to general conversation, and reading works aloud was precluded. This meant, in effect, that the Inklings was no longer a practical 'writers' group' so much as a collection of like-minded friends who met for talk. This had an inevitable effect on Tolkien's writing. Reading his work aloud to an (at least in theory) sympathetic audience had been an important part of his self-confidence as a writer, and also a reassurance as to the quality of his work. Without these things, he was increasingly liable not merely to self-doubt (this seems an inevitable if thankfully intermittent part of writing anything) but also to self-doubt that became debilitating.

III – But who would publish?

The Lord of the Rings had been written in response to Stanley Unwin's request for a sequel, which Unwin had hoped might appear within a year or two of *The Hobbit,* and be of comparable size and tone. Now, twelve years later, it was actually finished, and looked very different from what Unwin had expected, Tolkien needed to get it published. It took five years for this to happen.

Late in 1949, Unwin finally published *Farmer Giles of Ham.* After agreeing to ask Pauline Baynes to act as illustrator, Unwin had sent her a typescript of the book, which got lost in the post, or was mispacked, but at any rate disappeared for a month. In the interim, he sent her another copy, which she read and enjoyed; she then set to work. She sent a large number of illustrations to Unwin that March; Unwin forwarded them to Tolkien, who was delighted. The text was in proof by April, but Tolkien was bothered by conferences and examination setting, and took a month to return the text with corrections. By mid-June details of illustrations and dust-jacket were agreed; Tolkien sent back corrected proofs in July. In mid-September, Unwin sent Tolkien an advance copy and his £25 publication fee. *Farmer Giles* appeared in bookshops on 20 October.

The book sold only slowly, and Tolkien was not convinced of Unwin's enthusiasm for his work, still less for the now-finished *Lord of the Rings.* Increasingly, Tolkien wanted *The Silmarillion* published at the same time; only thus, he reckoned, could the mass of allusions within the text to his legendarium be made sense of.

It was against this background of unhappiness with Unwin that Fr Gervase Mathew had introduced Tolkien to Milton Waldman, a Catholic who worked as an adviser to the publisher Collins. Late in 1949, Waldman was given the completed *Lord of the Rings* to read. In the new year, he told Tolkien he wanted to publish both *The Lord of the Rings* and *The Silmarillion* if Tolkien had no 'moral or legal' commitment to Unwin. Collins were quietly eager to obtain the rights to *The Hobbit*; Waldman baited his hook by telling Tolkien that, since Collins were stationers and printers as well as publishers, they had access to larger supplies of now heavily rationed paper than did Unwin, and so might more calmly entertain publishing an unusually long book.

Late in February 1950, Tolkien asked Stanley Unwin to publish both books, *The Silmarillion* and *The Lord of the Rings* together; Unwin told him it would be difficult and expensive, but not impossible. At the start of April, he sent Tolkien a copy of a report written by his son, Rayner, who had seen *The Lord of the Rings* but not *The Silmarillion*. Rayner recommended incorporating anything essential from *The Silmarillion* into *The Lord of the Rings*, if necessary by cutting material from the latter; or, if Tolkien would not entertain this, publishing *The Lord of the Rings* and, 'after having a second look at it', 'dropping' *The Silmarillion*. Tolkien was furious, and was baffled that Unwin had thought showing him Rayner's letter might be helpful. He insisted Unwin answer his flat question: would he publish *The Lord of the Rings* and *The Silmarillion* together, both uncut? Not unnaturally (since he had never seen a completed typescript of the latter – in fact, one did not then exist) Unwin refused, as Tolkien must have known he would, in a letter dated 17 April 1950. Tolkien then approached Milton Waldman, who invited him to London to discuss publication. Waldman bluntly told him *The Lord of the Rings* was too long. Nevertheless, Tolkien still meant to publish both works together.

In May 1950, there was another disruption, when Tolkien, Edith and Priscilla moved again, from Manor Road to a bigger college house in Holywell Street.

IV – *The Silmarillion* renewed

If Tolkien was to hope to publish *The Silmarillion*, it needed to be set in order and, for the most part, largely revised, both in light of how his mythology had developed since the previous draft, and also to make sure it was congruent with *The Lord of the Rings*. His earlier revisions in 1937 had not covered the whole text, and had been abandoned late in 1937 when, as Tolkien understood it, the book had been rejected by Unwin. Typically, Tolkien did not begin by completing the earlier revision, but started again at the beginning of the work, and reached roughly the same point as he had in 1937 before, some time in 1951, again laying the work aside. He also revised the two sets of *Annals* (of Beleriand and of Valinor), now renamed the *Annals of Aman* and the *Grey Annals*. At the same time, he began to rewrite the three Great Tales of the legendarium on ampler scale, from which, he planned, the latter parts of the eventual *Silmarillion* would derive.

For the story of Beren and Lúthien, he had already started, in 1949 or so, to rewrite the old *Lay of Leithian*; the rewritten text forms no more than one-sixth of the original four thousand lines of rhyming couplets; and even that, we should remember, had not completed the story. At the same time, he began a prose version of the same tale; it did not proceed very far. In 1951, he started an extended prose saga of *The Fall of Gondolin*; sadly, he took the story only as far as Tuor's arrival at the hidden city, and never wrote the planned account of its fall. John Garth has pointed out that this text specifies Tuor's age when he begins his quest: twenty-three, the exact age Tolkien was when he joined the Army in 1915.[10]

He also began a long and ambitious prose version of the Túrin story, the *Narn i Chîn Húrin* ('Tale of the Children of Húrin'). The *Narn* drew heavily on the alliterative verse *Lay* of the 1920s and 1930s; indeed, the *Narn* itself (Tolkien feigned) was a translation of a text (by a Mannish poet, Dírhaval) composed in an Elvish verse mode (*Minlamad thent/ estent*) designed to be spoken, not sung, and whose notional form, it has been plausibly argued, is supposed to be an Elvish alliterative line. The prose *Narn* as we have it, then, would be rather like Tolkien's prose translation of *Beowulf*.[11] The *Narn*, too, was set aside incomplete. All three of the long versions of the Great Tales, then, were stalled in their revision; this meant that, in effect, the last third or so of the *Silmarillion* text was also stalled, since Tolkien intended to derive it from the longer Tales.

There is also mention of a fourth Great Tale, of Eärendil the Wanderer; this seems to have been merely projected rather than actually written down even in draft (the same, as we saw, had been true of the cognate text in the *Book of Lost Tales*).[12]

The revisions and new compositions of this time, written in the immediate aftermath of *The Lord of the Rings*, show Tolkien at the top of his literary game: vigorous, eloquent, fertile of imagination and prolific in human sympathy.

He had also begun a revision of his creation narrative, *Ainulindalë*, perhaps as early as 1946; certainly at that time he had experimented with a wholly new concept, incorporating not the naïve 'flat world' of his original but a cosmologically more accurate 'round world'. In the event, however, he stayed with the 'flat world' version, although incorporating much of the newer material from the 'round world' text. Unusually for Tolkien, he had shown both variants to Katharine Farrer, who much preferred the 'flat world' original. It may not be wholly fanciful to see in this hesitation over what had hitherto been a wholly uncontroverted part of the legendarium a hint of the doubts over fundamentals of his work as it had grown up that would, in coming years, increasingly paralyse Tolkien's invention. At this juncture, however, he was still confident enough in his capacity to produce a series of fine manuscript versions of the renewed *Ainulindalë*; although these, inevitably, later became the vehicle for disfiguring revisions and interpolations.

A fascinating text from (probably) the early 1950s is *Dangweth Pengoloð* ('The Answers of Pengoloð'), presented as answers given by Pengoloð to specifically linguistic questions posed by Ælfwine: why, if the elves are immortal and changeless, do their languages show change and variation? It stands, in effect, as a manifesto of 'art language' – the Noldor (later Ñoldor, or Ngoldor) are presented as a race of philologists, and change in Elvish (or at least in Quenya) as conscious and patterned, illustrating Elvish linguistic taste as much, or more, than the familiar forms of historical change seen in human languages.[13] This trope of the Noldor as philologists was taken up again in the late text *The Shibboleth of Fëanor*.[14]

The major substantive changes to the Silmarillion text, however, were not simple authorial perfectionism or 'niggling': they necessarily followed on the enormous expansion of the history and geography of the legendarium consequent on the incorporation of the *Lord of the Rings* into the context of the Elvish tongues. This meant that the in some ways naïve geography of *The Hobbit*, as modified and enlarged in its sequel, now had to supersede whatever notions Tolkien had previously had for the 'eastern extension' of the lands beyond Beleriand. When *The Hobbit*'s map was drawn, Tolkien had taken no especial care to integrate it with existing concepts of the legendarium; these emerged in *The Hobbit* only incidentally during its writing as, at first, mere 'colour and texture'. Now, however, this was by default a map of the world of his legendary. Most importantly, since *The Lord of the Rings* map shows the state of affairs after the destruction of Beleriand, and does not correspond to historical European geography, it was no longer possible simply to equate the island of Britain with one of the fragments of fallen Beleriand. At a stroke, this severed the strongest surviving link between the legendarium and English legend: the old equations between the places of legend and the towns of Tolkien's youth could no longer stand. If Ælfwine and his voyage were to be retained as framework for the stories, they would need to be given a new and wholly different context. These problems were all of a piece with questions of the plausibility of 'flat-world' mythology, and the post-Númenórean disjuncture of straight road and bent road to Elvenhome. Tolkien experimented with schemes attributing the 'erroneous' (i.e. 'flat world') cosmologies to human as opposed to Elvish traditions, and this led to further questioning of his established narrative framework for the Silmarillion stories. If some Númenórean influence or transmission was required to explain the very shape of the stories, they could no longer simply be told to Ælfwine by the Eressëan elves, but would have to represent (perhaps) traditions of Gondor.

These were tricky but resolvable questions of textual transmission, matters of the sort that Tolkien in his professional life was well able to explain; coming up with a plausible vehicle for the tales' transmission was not of itself an impossible difficulty. The issue of 'round world' versus 'flat world' was of a wholly different order. There were essentially two possible solutions: one, which is implicit behind *The Lord of the Rings,* has a previously flat world made round after the Downfall of Númenor. This leaves unresolved wider cosmological questions: was the original world a small bounded universe, that subsequently was changed to be the vast field of stars and galaxies known to modern science? This sort of uncomfortable question led Tolkien to posit his second alternative: that the world had been round from the beginning, and was known by the elves to be so (otherwise, they would be very poor observers and would have had to have been misled by the Valar), but their traditions had become garbled and confused when passed through generations of men, and thus the flat world was devised. This was unsatisfactory on various grounds; but, all else aside, it was clearly and immediately fatal to what had become the cardinal myth of the legendarium, that of the Light of the Two Trees, as preserved unstained only in the Silmarils, which stood before and superior to the lesser lights of sun and moon, which were mere fruits of the Two Trees. If the world was round from the beginning, amidst a cosmos of stars and a solar system like the one known to modern science, none of this could stand, and the whole fabric of the legendary would unravel. We have seen Tolkien dissuaded by Katharine Farrer from making such a radical shift; but throughout the 1950s, he searched for a way out of this dilemma.

One effect of these uncertainties was to loosen the attribution of these texts to what we might call the Ælfwine–Pengolodh tradition, and thus further dissolve the old connexion between the legendarium and England. Nevertheless, Ælfwine was still supposed the translator of the *Narn*, and had made his version in Eressea, although the *Narn* itself was attributed to a Mannish poet, Dírhaval. Here there seems to be no supposition of an intermediate Númenórean phase in the transmission of the text, which was reckoned one of the major parts of the Silmarillion complex. Clearly Tolkien at this time was hesitating between different frameworks to account for the existence of the Silmarillion texts; he does not seem to have made any final decision.

A completed Silmarillion, at this time, would have consisted of the *Quenta, Ainulindalë*, four 'Great Tales' (*Beren and Lúthien, The Children of Húrin, The Fall of Gondolin* and *Eärendil the Wanderer*), and two tales from the Second Age: *The Downfall of Númenor* and *The Rings of Power*. The two sets of *Annals* may have been intended for the final compilation, but this is not clear.[15]

Early in 1951, *The Hobbit* was again reprinted. Tolkien was surprised to find that, alongside the trivial corrections he had made to the previous reprint of 1947, the new fifth chapter, which he had sent speculatively, appeared without further ado. The story of the earlier book was now, in its published form, more congruent with its impending sequel; but, paradoxically, the publication of that sequel now looked less likely than it had done three years earlier.

Chapter 12 – Philology at Bay

I – Lit and lang, again

We now come to a slightly complicated episode. According to Humphrey Carpenter, in 1951, the perennial dispute over the details of the Oxford English syllabus came to one of its periodic crises. The new holders of the professorial chairs were, unlike Tolkien and Lewis, keen for the academic study of Victorian literature to be restored to the syllabus, inevitably at the expense of philological concerns. In Carpenter's account, Tolkien was appointed to the committee to consider this. The other members, says Carpenter, were the two new professors, David Cecil and F.P. Wilson, Helen Gardner and Humphry House. Gardner was a Fellow of St Hilda's with decided interests in post-medieval literature; she published a book on T.S. Eliot in 1949, and one on Donne in 1952. House was a Fellow of Wadham, engaged since 1949 on a complete edition of the letters of Charles Dickens. Neither Dickens nor Eliot, of course, might be studied by undergraduates except, for the former, as an optional subject. Tolkien was persuaded to support the majority view, and to recommend that the syllabus he and Lewis had fought hard for should be replaced. Lewis was appalled, and at once badgered Tolkien to change his mind; so when the new syllabus came to a general vote of the Faculty Board, Tolkien sided with Lewis in opposing it. It passed, despite their opposition.[1]

The problem is that the archives of the English Faculty do not seem to bear out this version of events, which Carpenter probably got from someone present who may have conflated events from several different efforts at syllabus reform. There was certainly discussion of the syllabus at faculty meetings in early 1951, very probably with a view to making it less philological and more 'literary', but no decisive change was made, nor (and this is the important point) was a committee set up to consider one.[2] In fact, the story seems to relate actually to a meeting that happened in 1954, three years later. It seems probable, though, that the 1951 discussions led, eventually, to the committee of 1954; and that even in 1951, the prognosis for philology was not good.[3] Five years earlier, the National Union of Students had passed a resolution calling for the abolition of compulsory philology for undergraduates; they were supported by an article from Hector Chadwick, grand old man of Anglo-Saxon studies at Cambridge (he was seventy-six when the article appeared, and died the following year), arguing that philology should be reserved for postgraduate work.[4]

Some Oxford undergraduates, at least, shared this dislike of philology: 'All Old English and nearly all Middle English works produced hatred and weariness in nearly everybody who studied them. The former carried the redoubled impediment of having Tolkien, incoherent and often inaudible, lecturing on it.' Thus Kingsley Amis;[5] his great cohort Philip Larkin was equally dismissive. Old English verse, he declared, was 'ape's bumfodder': 'I can just about stand learning the filthy lingo it's written in. What gets me down is being expected to *admire* the bloody stuff.'[6] Amis and Larkin may not have been wholly representative, but in this particular they were probably not unusual.

Professional matters, then, were not going wholly Tolkien's way; nor, it seemed, were his literary efforts. Negotiations with Collins over *The Lord of the Rings* first stalled, then petered out entirely; Waldman was often away (he lived much of the year in Italy), and his colleagues were not sympathetic to Tolkien's work. In late 1951, Tolkien wrote a long letter to Waldman explaining the two works and their interrelations, in the hope of persuading him to get Collins to act; but it was not successful.[7] Apart from anything else, the price of paper rose sharply in 1951: the outbreak of the Korean War the previous year had led to global shortages in many commodities and consequent price rises. Tolkien, however, would not settle for an abridgement; which looked like meaning no book at all.

That June, Tolkien finally gathered together all his papers relating to the much-delayed Clarendon Chaucer, and handed them to the OUP for them to be passed to a younger or more leisured man to finish; in the event, nothing was done with them. Sisam advised that nothing should be done before Tolkien retired to avoid embarrassing him, and thereafter no one with the required competences had the necessary leisure for the job. The book was never finished or published. The very considerable time and effort Tolkien had put into it came, then, to nothing; it had served only as a perduring roadblock to his further collaboration with the University Press throughout his whole time as an Oxford professor.

II – Return to Unwin

In November 1951, Rayner Unwin wrote to Tolkien, and asked him about *The Lord of the Rings* and *The Silmarillion*; Tolkien didn't reply, and Rayner wrote again in June 1952. In answer to this second letter, after shamefacedly mentioning the first, Tolkien asked if Unwin was still interested in the book: 'Can anything be done ... to unlock gates I slammed myself?'[8] Rayner Unwin was given *The Lord of the Rings* to read, and advised his father that it should be published, even at a loss. In November 1952, Stanley Unwin offered to publish the book, on a profit-sharing basis (which meant that Tolkien received no royalties until the publisher's costs were covered, but thereafter a half-share of the profits: if the book sold well, he would benefit much more than under a normal royalty agreement). Tolkien accepted.

On 30 March 1953, Tolkien and Edith moved from Holywell Street to Sandfield Road in Headington, two miles from the city centre. This was for two main reasons: increasing city centre traffic had made the house too noisy; and Edith's growing ill-health required her to move to a higher and drier climate (central Oxford is notoriously damp and miasmic). Headington-on-the-Hill, by the road to London, was the nearest residential high ground to the University. Their children were all now away, John as curate in a sprawling urban parish in Sparkhill, Birmingham. He was there until 1957, when he became Chaplain at the University College of North Staffordshire (now Keele University) and to two Catholic grammar schools, as well as parish priest at Knutton. In 1966, he was moved again, and, aged almost fifty, became parish priest in Stoke-on-Trent; in 1987, aged seventy, he was moved to the smaller rural parish of Eynsham until his retirement in 1994. Michael was teaching at the Oratory School (he later moved to Ampleforth, then to Stonyhurst); Christopher, now done with his B.Litt., was making his way as a junior lecturer in Old and Middle English and Icelandic (he was appointed University Lecturer in these subjects in the mid-1950s); Priscilla had taken her degree and was working in Bristol as a secretary.

Their new house was closer to the Lewis establishment, The Kilns, a couple of miles to the south-east; there is no particular evidence that

Lewis and Tolkien met any more frequently, however. R.E. 'Humphrey' Havard was also now a nearish neighbour, and attended the same church as Tolkien, usually sitting next to him (he was often on his own) and sometimes driving him home.[9] In May 1953, the Lewis brothers visited Havard's house one evening, and found Tolkien there. The four men drank burgundy and talked about translation, particularly Ronald Knox's Bible, which was then only a few years old (the New Testament appeared in 1945, the Old on 1950). It had been made from the Latin Vulgate, as had for centuries been mandated for Catholics, and aimed to replace the old and frequently incomprehensible Douay-Rheims-Challoner version. Unfortunately, it was quickly overtaken by history, since even before it was finished a papal encyclical (*Divino afflante spiritu* of 1943) had both permitted and encouraged translation from the original languages. According to Warnie Lewis's diary, Tolkien was dismissive of Knox's work: 'Ronnie, he said, had written so much parody and pastiche that he had lost what little ear for prose he had ever had.'[10] We might tenuously argue that the use of the familiar 'Ronnie' argues for some acquaintance between Tolkien and Knox; but the familiarity could just as easily be Warnie Lewis's, or simply in popular use around Oxford. Tolkien's verdict on Knox's Bible may seem harsh, although even a sympathetic reader of his Old Testament must admit that it is, for long stretches, idiosyncratic to the point of, almost, unreadability (the Wisdom books in particular use systematic inversion of normal sentence order with such persistence that they read, to a modern, as if written by Yoda). It might seem odd to attribute this to Knox's bravura stylistic virtuosity, shown off to such effect in the (to my mind) wholly marvellous *Let Dons Delight*, written in 1939 immediately before he began his Bible work, but it is arguable that Knox's own native style had become so etiolated as to be irrecoverable; and that the self-described 'timeless English' he adopted for his Bible is itself just another stylistic hat, an attenuated late Victorian fustian that reads, now, awkwardly at best. There are certainly passages, particularly in the Pauline letters, where Knox's native clarity of expression and light felicity of phrase are remarkable; but they are wrapped about in great swathes of enervated thee-and-thou-ing that only highlight the basic artificiality of Knox's project. Tolkien's own approach to Englishing the Bible would appear later in the decade.

In October 1953, Tolkien's alliterative poem, 'The Homecoming of Beorhtnoth', begun at least twenty years previously as a 'sequel' to the Old English *Battle of Maldon*, was finally published in *Essays and Studies*;[11]

even with the addition of a prose commentary, it was one of the more unusual scholarly journal articles of that (or any) year. It is an implicit criticism of the view of *Maldon* taken by E.V. Gordon in his edition, namely that it celebrates the heroism of Beorhtnoth's retainers, and the 'northern theory of courage' in general. Tolkien felt, rather, that the poet was critical of the consequences of Beorhtnoth's rashness (*ofermod*) in inviting battle when he need not, at the price of his own life and that of his men. 'Northern courage', or at least the version of it imbibed from (Tolkien claimed) the old poets, might intoxicate a man and throw his judgement badly awry. It is perhaps worth noting that although Tolkien's reading of *Maldon* as critical of Beorhtnoth has been very influential, and has largely supplanted E.V. Gordon's interpretation of it as a 'straight' praise poem, Tom Shippey believes Tolkien is mistaken.[12]

III – Slow death by committee

In March 1954, Tolkien had been appointed to a committee considering proposed changes to the English syllabus, specifically making the optional paper on nineteenth-century literature compulsory for any taking Course III.[13] It is not clear what it was to replace, but the probability is that it was either the Old or Middle English paper. The committee decided to recommend the change; when it was presented to the Faculty Board on 18 May, however, it was rejected. This is almost certainly the source of Carpenter's phantom 1951 committee and proposal, so it was presumably on this occasion that Lewis, scenting the beginnings of an anti-philological movement, rallied his colleagues, and Tolkien, to defeat the change.

Although the motion was defeated, it was clearly only a matter of time (and a few retirements) before it passed; the mood of the younger faculty was less philological, and more literary, than it had been before the war. Lewis seems to have been more exercised than Tolkien about this; we may tentatively place here the subsequent chance meeting with Roger Lancelyn Green at which Lewis exclaimed, 'Even Tolkien didn't understand what it means! He at least should have supported me!'[14]

This, in some ways, marks the start of what Tom Shippey has called 'the long defeat' of academic philology; over the following half-century, even at Oxford, university English faculties gradually stripped the syllabuses of their historical elements, which became, at best, options taken by a diminishing few, where they were not suppressed altogether, and replaced by fashionable (and intellectually negligible) alternatives (literary theory, post-colonial this or that, and such things). Shippey comments:

> I would myself put it this way: Tolkien was the most talented philologist of his generation, but like other talented philologists, he did not bother to establish the security of his profession in educational institutions, as a result of which it is now all but dead – not defeated in argument, but bypassed and allowed to wither on the vine.[15]

This development was some years in the future, of course; but the signs were already there. We may wonder, incidentally, what Shippey supposes Tolkien and his philological allies might have done, practically, to 'establish the security' of their avocation; Shippey himself reckons that, despite his efforts to the contrary, Tolkien never managed to heal the breach between linguistic and literary study of texts.[16] Most Oxford undergraduates, then as later, saw Old English as a pointless chore of cribs and cramming, and never passed to truly literary appreciation of the texts. They were only too happy to skimp on the hard study required so as to pass to less challenging, or more immediately rewarding, topics; and in this a good and growing proportion of the faculty were happy to encourage them. If Tolkien had been a better lecturer, or a more prolific and less niggling writer, he might have been able to make *Beowulf* (say) come alive (by, for example, finishing and publishing his translation) and so lure struggling undergraduates through the dense thickets of grammar and syntax to the grand philological landscape he saw so well but somehow never managed to convey except to a minority of his audience. As it was, philology and philologists were diminishing year by year; and without a continually refreshed majority of advocates, the more difficult elements of the English syllabus, at Oxford and elsewhere, would sooner or later be dropped, regretfully or otherwise.

In the immediate term, however, there were younger philologists of talent and achievement, many – perhaps most – of them Tolkien's sometime pupils, usually for the B.Litt. Gabriel Turville-Petre, Christopher's sometime supervisor, was scion of grand if slightly raffish Leicestershire recusant gentry; he had been Reader in Old Icelandic since 1941 (although war service postponed his taking up the post until 1946), and published a series of important books: *The Heroic Age of Scandinavia* in 1951, in 1953 the highly regarded *Origins of Icelandic Literature*, in the preface to which he thanks Tolkien for 'many useful suggestions', and in 1964 *Myth and Religion of the North*. That year, aged forty-five, he was given the title Professor of Old Icelandic. A year his senior was Alistair Campbell, since 1949 University Lecturer in Middle English and engaged on what, in 1959, was published as his monumental and definitive *Old English Grammar* (Tolkien is thanked in his acknowledgements; he had been one of the examiners of Campbell's B.Litt. thesis). The New Zealander Norman Davis, five years younger than Turville-Petre, taught at Oxford from 1947 to 1949, when he was appointed to a chair in Glasgow.

If younger allies were still to be found, Tolkien was soon to lose his oldest and closest. At the start of 1954, the University of Cambridge decided to create a new professorship in Medieval and Renaissance English, hitherto covered only inadequately by another professor whose expertise was in more recent writing. The deadline for applications was the end of April 1954. Lewis had just published his *OHEL* volume, and was without question the leading candidate for the job, which might fairly be said to have been tailor-made for him. He had been almost thirty years in Oxford as a tutorial fellow, and was utterly weary of teaching undergraduates; he had, moreover, been passed over for three separate Oxford professorships in quick succession.

Nevertheless, Lewis did not apply; he felt tied to Oxford by his domestic arrangements: although his 'adopted mother' Janie Moore had died in the January 1951 influenza epidemic, his brother Warren, who was by now a solid alcoholic, and their old gardener were both very dependent on him. Instead, he encouraged G.V. Smithers, a philologist then teaching at UCL, to apply, even though, unknown to Lewis, the statutes of the chair required a literary-critical rather than philological approach to the subject. When the electors, who included Tolkien and Lewis's old tutor F.P. Wilson, met in early May, they resolved unanimously to offer the chair to Lewis in any case. He declined, citing 'domestic necessities', his having told another candidate (Smithers) he was not applying, and, last, his own loss of energy due to age (Lewis was fifty-six, but considered he came 'of a stock that grows early old'[17]). The chairman of the electors offered to postpone the decision until June to give Lewis time to consider, but Lewis was firm in his refusal. The electors accordingly approached their second choice, Helen Gardner of St Hilda's. In the meantime, however, Tolkien went to see Lewis, and managed to persuade him his objections were groundless: Smithers was ineligible for the job, and Lewis could fairly discharge its responsibilities in a four-day week, which would allow him to keep up his Oxford household with its miscellaneous personnel. Tolkien spoke to Warnie Lewis and secured his support for the move. He was also convinced that a change of air would do much to renew Lewis's energy and enthusiasm. Tolkien's conversation with Lewis about this took place on 17 May, the day before the faculty meeting at which the syllabus changes were rejected. The meeting could well have settled Lewis's disenchantment with the Oxford English School. On consideration, Lewis concluded that, if he stayed in Cambridge only during the week, his complicated domestic arrangements could cope without him. He wrote to the chairman signalling his tentative interest, if (what he was not wholly convinced of) Tolkien had not overstated the case. The chairman replied that he would be happy to discuss the business, if their second choice (Helen Gardner) declined. She heard rumours that Lewis was again interested, and chose to withdraw and take up a readership at Oxford instead. Lewis was accordingly elected to the Cambridge chair from October 1954, although (to tie up loose ends) he took up his duties only from the following 1 January. He left Oxford, then, after almost thirty years, and a series of disappointments over jobs. Walter Hooper remembers him claiming Oxford tried, belatedly, to keep him by offering him a chair immediately after the Cambridge election; no evidence for this survives. Certainly Lewis was approached in 1957 when Wilson retired from his Merton chair, the chair that Lewis had missed out on in 1946, and perhaps this is what lies behind Hooper's story; but this was too little, too late: Lewis had concluded Oxford wanted none of him, and was happy in his new job.[18]

Warnie marked his brother's election with a drinking spree, which led to another stay in a nursing home and postponement of their summer holiday to Ireland.

Although Lewis still lived in Oxford at the weekends, this meant that he saw less of Tolkien, although their days of very close friendship had been over for a decade. There was also, as we shall see, a woman.

For the moment, though, Lewis was strongly encouraging of Tolkien's efforts to get *The Lord of the Rings* into print.

Chapter 13 – 'My heart, to be shot at'

I – 'The long-delayed appearance'

Between July 1953 and mid-1955, Tolkien was busy with proofs of *The Lord of the Rings*, which (he had conceded, reluctantly) should be published serially, in three volumes, although it was not in any sense a 'trilogy' as normally understood. The first volume, *The Fellowship of the Ring*, was published on 29 July 1954, and the second, *The Two Towers*, on 11 November that same year. There was then a delay of almost a year before the final volume was published, as Tolkien scrambled to complete the Appendices which, in the absence of the full *Silmarillion,* he saw as the irreducible minimum of additional information needed to make the book comprehensible. It seems that, at about this time, he started *Tal-Elmar,* a story of the interaction between Númenor and 'Wild Men' in the Dark Years of the Second Age; presumably it arose in the course of his work on what became Appendix B. It did not proceed beyond its first chapter.[1] Inevitably, he produced more material than there was space for in the Appendices, and a good deal had to be dropped. It included a reworking of *The Hobbit*, eventually published (in *Unfinished Tales*) as *The Quest of Erebor,* and other material collected in volume 12 of *The History of Middle Earth*. Some of the texts in that volume show signs of furious compression and recasting, rewriting material against time when elements of it were still inchoate or shifting: 'the situation was indeed afflicting';[2] Tolkien also abandoned a promised index. Finally, on 20 October 1955, the last volume, *The Return of the King,* was published. The following day, Tolkien gave the first of a series of annual lectures on 'English and Welsh'; he mentioned 'the long-delayed appearance of a large "work" … which contains, in the way of presentation that I find most natural, much of what I personally have received from the study of things Celtic'.[3]

Tolkien was apprehensive: 'I have exposed my heart to be shot at.'[4] Despite Tolkien's apprehension, and his publisher's caution, *The Lord of the Rings* was a success from the start; when cheap American editions of it appeared in the mid-1960s, his fame became global.

Unwin initially printed 3,000 copies of the first volume and 3,250 of the second, and a further 1,500 and 1,000 copies of each which were sent to America to be bound and issued by Houghton Mifflin; these initial impressions sold out in six weeks, so for the third volume, the run was increased to 7,000 copies with 5,000 unbound for the American market.

II – Bafflement and praise

In the manner of publishers, Unwin had sent proof copies of the first volume to several well-disposed writers, and had elicited from them remarks, excerpts of which were used as 'blurb' on the inside of the dust-jacket. Richard Hughes, Naomi Mitchison and C.S. Lewis were all fulsome in praise, citing Spenser, Malory, Ariosto, and claiming Tolkien had outdone them all. Lewis followed this with a review in *Time and Tide* on 14 August, in which he stated, 'Nothing quite like it was ever done before.'

Most of the initial review notices were, in fact, baffled. Alfred Duggan, Lord Curzon's half-Brazilian stepson, reformed drunk, pedestrian historical novelist and friend to Evelyn Waugh, was given *The Fellowship of the Ring* to review, anonymously, by the *TLS*; he praised its 'sound prose and rare imagination' but thought its moral framework simplistic and unexamined, and its plot unbalanced; his, or anyway the *TLS*'s, opinion improved as succeeding volumes appeared. There was much dismissive reference to schoolboy literature amongst the more self-consciously literary reviewers. The American *littérateur* Edmund Wilson, writing in the left-wing (and anti-Catholic) magazine *The Nation*, attributed any success the book ('these long-winded volumes of what looks to this reviewer like balderdash') might enjoy to the 'life-long appetite ... for juvenile trash' he thought especially characteristic of the British public. Otherwise, he wrote, 'Dr. Tolkien has little skill at narrative and no instinct for literary form.'[5]

Some of Tolkien's colleagues at Oxford were privately, or not so privately, suspicious that he had written *The Lord of the Rings* in time that would have been better spent on proper scholarship. C.L. Wrenn, who was a fellow Catholic, and had been a family friend as well as a professional colleague since the 1930s, held Tolkien in the highest regard as a scholar (according to one of his pupils, Wrenn reckoned him the only man of genius in the English School[6]). He was correspondingly shocked by *The Lord of the Rings*, 'the fall of a philological into "Trivial literature"'[7]. Other scholars agreed: Ida Gordon, widow of his sometime Leeds colleague E.V. Gordon and herself a considerable philologist, wrote, 'I have very little interest in the Tolkien of *The Lord of the Rings*. In my opinion that side of him robbed us of a very fine medieval scholar.'[8] This was not an isolated view; when I was an undergraduate at Oxford in the late 1980s, my tutor – a humane and diligent scholar of Old and Middle English, a published poet in Welsh and English, and a Christian – told me it was a tremendous shame Tolkien had spent so much time writing fairy stories rather than making proper editions of Middle English texts. The Scots academic and novelist J.I.M. Stewart's five-book sequence *A Staircase in Surrey* features a 'Professor Timbermill', author of *The Magic Quest*: 'A notable scholar, it seems. Unchallenged in his field. But he ran off the rails somehow, and produced a long mad book – a kind of apocalyptic romance.'[9] Stewart was an English don at Oxford from 1949 onwards, and this may be taken as an accurate pastiche of contemporary Oxford gossip about Tolkien. In a letter of 1956, Tolkien said, 'anyway the cry is "now we know how you have been wasting your time for 20 years". So the screw is on for many things of a more professional kind long overdue. Alas! I like them both, but have only one man's time.'[10]

III – The fruits of research?

It is indisputably true that Tolkien was intellectually capable of writing a big and important book on English philology, and never did so; and that the vast intellectual efforts and energies expended on his legendarium must in part be to blame. Naturally, his academic contemporaries and colleagues noticed.

It is notable, for instance, that he was never elected Fellow of the British Academy (FBA), unlike C.S. Lewis (elected in 1955, in the afterglow of *OHEL*), or (say) Craigie, W.P. Ker, Henry Bradley, Joseph Wright, Chambers, Sisam, Dorothy Whitelock, F.P. Wilson even (not to mention great panjandrums like Stenton and Mortimer Wheeler). Lewis had given the Academy's Shakespeare Lecture in 1942; soon afterwards, he wrote to one of the Anglican nuns at Wantage, 'The British Academy made a v. stupid audience compared with your young ladies! They were all the sort of people whom one often sees getting out of taxis and going into big doorways and wonders who on earth they are – all those beards and double chins and fur collars and lorgnettes. Now I know.'[11] Whilst election to that august body is doubtless governed by coteries and dilections which the uninitiated can hardly suspect, it represents, in some sense, the verdict of Tolkien's academic peers, and a verdict of, if not quite failure, then certainly disappointed promise. FBAs have typically produced at least one great book, or 'work', or have one in the offing; no one could detect Tolkien doing this.

It would of course be wrong to suppose that Tolkien alone was responsible, by neglect, for the decline of philology as an academic subject; although one could argue that, had he devoted the energies spent on *The Lord of the Rings* to writing, say, a great study of English medieval language and literature, he might have done something to arrest or slow that decline. But one suspects that the tide of academic fashion, in English departments at least, was running strongly away from the sort of close, textually rigorous, historically based work Tolkien thought essential, and any efforts by one man could not have been permanently effective. On another level, though, exactly the reverse is true: outside the narrow compass of university English faculties, Tolkien's success has been remarkable and seems likely to be enduring (he is repeatedly, and by a long chalk, voted the 'best author' in any number of popular polls). What marks him off from his hordes of imitators is, precisely, philology: the fact that his imaginary world is deeply rooted in language, in names and words with their own inner consistency, meaning and resonance, which have in fact arguably given rise to that world, is in the best and broadest sense a philological one, and is (I would suggest) the key to his success.

It may be worth expanding on this point. It was Tolkien's contention, and corresponds (I maintain) with the experience of his readers, that one of the most characteristic and compelling features of his books is their ability to evoke a palpable sense of untold stories and unexplored vistas, of landscapes glimpsed at the edges of other foregrounded pictures, that are at once suggestive, enticing and unbreachably distant: we desire to go there (to hear the story), and at the same time know it is, for now, unbearably beyond our reach – like the luminous countries glimpsed through windows in fifteenth-century Italian paintings. The means Tolkien uses to achieve this effect are, most usually, names: unglossed but resonant, with a felt (because real) internal consistency and meaning. This is the fruit of the linguistic background of his tales; the languages, he insisted, presupposed a world they described, and so by devising the one he necessarily created the other. This is exactly the function that technical philology had for Tolkien and for scholars like him: words and phrases implied a reality, a world inhabited by their speakers and best described by these very words.

Whilst philology was defeated in the academy, then, outside, amongst people who read books for enjoyment, it has won a stupendous victory, although, since philology is not now a familiar scholarly discipline, probably most of Tolkien's readers are unaware of it.[12] This does mean, of course, that his achievement can probably not now ever be reproduced: there are no more philologists like him, or at least none being produced by today's universities.

His personal academic achievement is perhaps another matter; whilst it is doubtless true that all but the very best-regulated academic careers (and perhaps even them) are almost necessarily filled with uncompleted projects, Tolkien's case was an extreme one, although not without parallel. The problem for his colleagues, I have no doubt, is not that he did not finish all the academic work he started (most dons are self-aware enough to know that, in this respect, their own houses are at least partly glass-built), nor even that his hobby was to write fairy tales on a preposterously grand scale, but that he chose, and was able, to finish the second, but not the first; and that his failure to complete (or even properly begin) any large-scale academic work was arguably due precisely to the time and effort he had expended on *The Lord of the Rings*. Tolkien would have been as aware of this as any man alive; it may give us some idea of the courage he showed in finishing and publishing the book, and also of the value he set on it, knowing, as he must have done, that for many even of his friends and allies it would be an end to his academic credibility. There were other factors, too, of course: he was much burdened by teaching and administration, by piece-work persistently taken on to supplement an inadequate salary (inadequate for a father of children, at any rate) and by his own tendency to self-doubt and to distraction. But he had early in his professional career given clear proof he was capable of hard and concentrated work, and of finishing complex work against the odds (his *Middle English Vocabulary* done for Sisam's anthology is no negligible piece of work); in middle life, he deployed the same capacity primarily in the service of his imaginative writing. This was on one level a choice, of faërie over scholarship; on another level, being the man he was, he could not have done otherwise.

Failure to be elected to the British Academy was perhaps mildly compensated by his election, in 1957, as a Fellow of the Royal Society of Literature, a distinction, as he remarked, rarely accorded to scholars from the 'language' side.

Another compensation, it might be thought, was financial: the royalties from *The Lord of the Rings* were considerable. The punitive tax regime of post-war Britain, however, meant that, until he retired at least, the bulk of Tolkien's literary earnings were confiscated by the Inland Revenue. He was unlikely, now, ever again to be poor, but he was not exactly rich.

IV – Next, the *Jerusalem Bible*?

Tolkien contemplated at least one direct sequel to *The Lord of the Rings*. In the late 1950s, he began *The New Shadow*, a story of Gondor a hundred years after the Downfall of the Ring; it was abandoned after a single short chapter. Tolkien was understandably depressed at he thought of writing a story which would take as its theme the resurrection of human wickedness (devil-worship, 'orc cults' and the like) after its apparent ending and amidst the external trappings of a 'golden age'. Resolution of such a tale would, he reckoned, be little more than a 'thriller', and thus comparatively uninteresting to write.[13] There were various abortive proposals for film adaptations of *The Lord of the Rings*; Tolkien spent some time and effort on these in the decade or so after publication.[14]

In 1956, preparation began of the *Jerusalem Bible*, an English version of the great monument of French Biblical scholarship, the *Bible de Jérusalem*. The general editor of the English version, Fr Alexander Jones of Upholland seminary, assembled a mixed bag of scholars, writers and his own friends and relations (including his young nephew, Fr (later Sir) Anthony Kenny) to produce the text. He approached Tolkien, who agreed to help. Tolkien produced a complete draft of the book of Jonah, although it is unclear how closely the published text reflects his work; he may also have drafted some other texts, but in a more fragmentary form (possibly Job, although the published text is Anthony Kenny's). Draft texts from original translators were passed to a 'literary editor' for polish; the literary editor for the Old Testament was the novelist, translator and popular historian Alan Neame (the New Testament was given to the Benedictine aesthete Sylvester Houédard).[15] Neame certainly tinkered extensively with Tolkien's draft, with mixed results. In the early 2000s, the original publisher of the *Jerusalem Bible,* Darton, Longman and Todd, mooted an edition of Tolkien's translation as originally drafted; at a late stage, though, copyright issues prevented its appearing.

In the event, pressure of work meant Tolkien was unable to do as much as he, or Jones, had supposed; at one stage Jones seems to have hoped Tolkien would agree, after his retirement in 1959, to act as literary editor for the whole project, but that scheme came to nothing.

V – Breach with Lewis

There had been growing distance between Tolkien and Lewis since, at least, 1940, when Charles Williams had arrived in Oxford and almost overnight took over Tolkien's former place as primary focus for Lewis's enthusiasms. As we have seen, even after Williams's death, professional matters, not uninfluenced by religious difference, introduced tension between Tolkien and Lewis, and in 1954 Lewis left Oxford altogether. The gradual decay of friendship is one thing; a positive breach is another, and that came with Lewis's unexpected marriage.

Lewis's marriage is probably best known now through the sentimentalized version of it offered by the 1993 film *Shadowlands*; it is not a wholly accurate picture.[16] Joy Gresham (née Davidman) had come to England first in August 1952, ostensibly to visit a (woman) penfriend and to finish a book on the Ten Commandments (it appeared, dedicated to Lewis, in 1954, as *Smoke on the Mountain*; an English edition, with a preface by Lewis, followed in 1955, and sold twice as many copies as the American one). She left her two sons with her husband; a female cousin of hers went to stay with him to help out.

Born in New York in 1915 to non-practising Jewish parents, Joy Davidman had become an atheist and communist; her husband had fought for the Spanish Republic. Around 1946, worn down by her husband's drinking and affairs, she had experienced a sudden conversion to Christianity; she soon discovered Lewis's apologetic works, and became an ardent fan and, from January 1950, a correspondent. There is some evidence that the real aim of her visit to England was to meet Lewis and, if possible, insert herself into his affections. She went twice to Oxford and each time met Lewis for lunch; he was careful they should not be alone. Early in December, she met Lewis for lunch again, but this time in London and alone. This led to an invitation to spend Christmas 1952 at The Kilns, now a bachelor establishment (Mrs Moore, remember, had died in 1951) and increasingly on the squalid side of shabby. She loved it, or said she did. In the meantime her husband wrote to tell her he had in her absence, and hardly unexpectedly, begun an affair with her cousin, and wanted a divorce. After telling Lewis about her husband's letter, she returned to America at the start of January 1953.

Joy's husband divorced her for desertion, and in November 1953 she returned to England, this time, to her husband's dismay, bringing her sons. Her visitor's visa did not allow her to work, so her means of support are unclear; it seems very likely that Lewis volunteered to cover her rent and her sons' school fees. It is possible that part of her motive was fear that her Communist past would, in the years of the House Un-American Activities Committee, catch up with her and make it impossible for her to live from writing in America (she had been a member of the American Communist Party between 1938 and her conversion to Christianity). This at least may be what she told Lewis; her position in England on a visitor's visa was not, of course, much different, with one exception: Lewis. He found himself cast in the unlikely role of, as one of his biographers has put it, 'an American divorcée's sugar daddy'.[17]

She found a rented house in London, in Belsize Park, and a prep school for her boys. They all visited Lewis and his brother in December 1953. Warnie, together with other observers, was convinced she had set her cap at Lewis: 'it was obvious what was going to happen'.[18]

These were years of change for Lewis; Mrs Moore had gone, and he was about to leave Oxford for Cambridge, to live there four nights each week during term: all the old routines were disarranged. Even the Tuesday morning Inklings was moved to Monday, so that Lewis could attend before, refreshed by beer, taking the train to Cambridge.

VI – A very odd marriage

Early in 1956, the Home Office declined to renew Joy Davidman's visa, which had only ever been a temporary visitor's one. Suggestions that she was to be deported as an ex-Communist are apparently unfounded, although she may have hinted to Lewis that this lay behind the non-renewal of her visa. By now, her sons were at a prep school near Woking (the fees paid by Lewis) and she was living in a house in Headington (the rent, again, paid by Lewis), within walking distance of Lewis's house. Joy and her sons moved there in the summer of 1955; the boys were sent to Dane Court as boarders, where Douglas (the younger), at least, was intensely unhappy. Given Lewis's own miserable experience as a boarder, it is perhaps surprising that he acquiesced in this; perhaps he was not asked.

Lewis agreed to a civil marriage to allow her to stay in the country; it would also allow her to take paid work, which her previous visa had not, and so (perhaps) remove from Lewis some of the financial burden, which he had assumed, of supporting her and her children. The civil marriage took place on 23 April 1956. Here was a practical test of Lewis's vigorously asserted claim, made in *Christian Behaviour* against Tolkien's vehement objection, that civil marriage and Christian marriage were two plain different things, and should not by Christians be confused.[19] Nevertheless, the civil marriage had given Joy and her sons various legal rights relative to her husband, which she now was at pains to assert. One was the right to cohabitation.

Lewis and Joy continued to live apart; she complained that their being constantly together, often until late in the evening, was causing scandal. Lewis conceded that she and her boys should come to live at The Kilns. She seems to have determined that the house would come to her and her boys after Lewis's death, and forcibly told Mrs Moore's daughter Maureen this; in fact, as Maureen (and Lewis) well knew, the house had been in Mrs Moore's name, and the Lewis brothers had only a life interest in it: after their death, it was to be Maureen's. Joy Davidman was a bossy and pushful woman, who clearly saw her civil marriage to Lewis as a meal ticket (McGrath calls her simply 'mercenary'[20]). Nevertheless Lewis obviously valued her advice and enjoyed her company; during this time and under her influence, he began what is arguably his best novel, *Till We Have Faces* (it is dedicated to her). We may infer that Lewis's affections were at this point unengaged from the fact that, when in July he was invited to bring a guest to a Buckingham Palace garden party, he asked not Joy, his legal wife, but his friend the poet Ruth Pitter (she couldn't come).

In October 1956, however, before Joy and her boys could move in at The Kilns, she was diagnosed with incurable cancer, and Lewis discovered he was in love with her. Those who reckon such things significant may note that Lewis's mother had died of cancer when she was forty-six; in 1956 Joy Davidman was forty-one. They were married by an Anglican priest (one of Lewis's former pupils, whom Lewis rather bounced into performing the rite) on 21 March 1957, although the Bishop of Oxford had refused them leave to marry as Joy was divorced. She was also, in the eyes of the law, already married to Lewis after the civil ceremony, and thus, since the Church of England recognized any legal marriage as a valid one, in the eyes of the Church also. Lewis may be forgiven a certain confusion in sacramental theology under the circumstances: Joy was reliably said to be dying, and fast. Soon afterwards, however, her cancer went into remission.

Remarriage of divorcés was something the Church of England was at that time particular about; although the issue is complicated by the fact that Joy's husband was himself divorced when they married. Had she been a Catholic, it is likely she would have been considered free to marry, although this would have depended on the determined status of William Gresham's first marriage, which might not have been a valid one. But according to an Anglican understanding, as we have seen, any legal marriage (such as hers had been) was a valid one. The Bishop of Oxford concerned was Harry Carpenter, whose son Humphrey was to become Tolkien's biographer.

Tolkien did not find out about Lewis's marriage until eight months after the event, when he read a notice of it in *The Times*; this appeared on Christmas Eve of 1956, and was prompted by wild rumours of Lewis marrying one person or another. It was no more than a belated admission of the civil ceremony; no public notice of the religious service ever appeared.

Tolkien could not approve of marriage to a divorced woman, and was suspicious both of her motives and of Lewis's gullibility: 'Lewis has always been taken in by someone. First, it was Mrs Moore, then Charles Williams, and then Joy Davidman';[21] but mostly he was hurt to have been kept wholly in the dark. He may have taken a certain bitter pleasure in this practical sequel (he might even say, confirmation) of his carefully argued, and wholly ignored, demolition of Lewis's views on marriage.

He did not wholly stop seeing Lewis; at the start of September 1958, Joy took her children away on holiday, and left Lewis alone. He was taken out to dinner by Havard, Tolkien and George Sayer. Whilst the dinner, according to Sayer, was 'uproarious', Tolkien was concerned about his old friend:

Tolkien was gloomy about the terrible strains and anxieties Jack was suffering: Warren's drunkenness, two rather difficult boys, and 'a strange marriage' to 'a sick and domineering woman'. It turned out that what worried him most was that she was a divorcée. He did not accept my argument that she could not have been divorced, since, as a Christian, she had never been married. However, the reappearance of Jack [who had been absent paying the bill] forestalled a discussion of this question.[22]

This meeting was exceptional. Their intimacy was now decidedly past; apart from anything else, Lewis was in Cambridge four nights each week. Tolkien may have sometimes come into central Oxford for the Monday morning pub sessions if he was not already there on University business, although his house in Headington was much further from the Eagle and Child than he had been before. But the other breaches between them were deeper than physical distance, and less easily remedied.

Part IV – Last Years

'ragged I walk. To myself I talk;
for still they speak not, men that I meet.'[1]

Chapter 14 – Silmarillion and Scholarship?

I – Chairless in Oxford

In 1959, Tolkien retired, aged sixty-seven. His last few years as a professor were not hugely productive: he lectured, set and marked exams, supervised theses and went to Ireland several times as an examiner. He also worked on a transcript of *Ancrene Wisse*. He was on sabbatical leave for two terms in 1958 (Hilary and Trinity Terms), with the aim of finishing various projects before retiring; in the event, some of this time was spent looking after Edith, who was ill, and dealing with proposals for film versions of his books. In 1959, he was ill with appendicitis and spent much of the first half of the year recovering; he retired in June.

He gave a valedictory lecture, melancholy and waspish in part, compounded of regret, nostalgia and a barely concealed frustration at the state of his subject; but all done with wit and courtesy.[2] The Oxford English School was a very different beast from the one he had joined in 1913, and rejoined in 1925; the changes were not, in some part, those he would have preferred, and more of the same were clear on the horizon. At any rate, he was now free of the burdens of office as well as its emoluments. *The Lord of the Rings* was an established success; his public was eager for more; he now had, presumably, leisure. What, now, was to prevent him from finishing *The Silmarillion*, his long-prepared legendarium?

In the event, he published nothing else on the matter of Middle Earth during his lifetime.

II – Delays and frustrations

To understand why, we need to look at the state of the work by the late

259

1950s. Little had been done to most of the material since the 1937 *Quenta Silmarillion* had been left incomplete when Tolkien began serious work on the *Hobbit* sequel that year. We saw Tolkien begin revising some parts of *The Silmarillion* in the early 1950s, when he had hoped Collins would publish it alongside *The Lord of the Rings*, but a deal of his effort at that time went into writing extended versions of the three Great Tales, all abandoned unfinished, rather than the main narrative *Silmarillion* proper (which, he had decided, could be done only after the narratives of the Great Tales were fixed). He had, also, taken up some of the old texts when preparing the Appendices published with *The Return of the King*, and had (inevitably) introduced some changes of detail; but the great bulk of the Silmarillion stories were in a state of sometimes great confusion, with in some cases multiple partly revised versions in existence, and in others (such as the famous, and central, *Fall of Gondolin*) nothing completed later than the original version from the 1917 *Book of Lost Tales*. At every turn, his efforts at reducing this mass of text to order met with knotty problems of consistency, of nomenclature, of (in some cases) philosophical and theological uncertainty. Resolving these questions was at least as likely to lead to his beginning a wholly new text, whether story or discursive essay, as to connected revision of the existing material. Even had his time been otherwise uninterrupted and tranquil, untangling all this would have been a stiff task for a man approaching his eighth decade. And of course, Tolkien's life, like anyone else's, never contained only the problems and tasks of his choosing. Interruptions came thick and fast.

One problem was a series of physical dislocations. When Tolkien retired as Professor of English Language, he also had to give up his rooms as Fellow of Merton. This meant finding room to house the thousands of books and other material he had kept there. Some of his library was dispersed;[3] the remainder ended up in the garage attached to his house in Headington.

Then there was the unavoidable human condition. Edith had been in poor health for years; Tolkien, too, had been often ill, and both were now old.

There were other books, long-promised and long overdue, to be finished: his translations of three Middle English poems (*Sir Gawain and the Green Knight*, *Sir Orfeo* and *Pearl*), made some years before, had been promised to Unwin; but they needed introductions and some commentary, and these were never completed. He had also a diplomatic edition of *Ancrene Wisse*, a thirteenth-century guide for anchoresses (enclosed women solitaries), first promised to the EETS as early as 1935. After a quarter of a century of sporadic work, and several abortive attempts to pass the job to other, younger scholars, he finally sent in a text in late 1958; a printers' strike meant that the proofs were not sent back to him until the summer of 1960, when he was in the thick of *The Silmarillion*. That work had to be put to one side, and the threads of the Middle English taken up again so an introduction (written by another hand) could be revised, his own preface written, and a number of inadvertent mistakes corrected and unapproved changes reversed. He wrote to Rayner Unwin,

> I am in fact utterly stuck – lost in a bottomless bog ... The crimes of omission that I committed in order to complete the 'L. of the R.' are being avenged.[4]

The principal neglected project was his long-promised edition of the *Ancrene Wisse*. It eventually and after much labour and frustration appeared in 1962, in time for Tolkien's seventieth birthday. It was greeted respectfully, but was clearly not the definitive word on the text that Tolkien's colleagues and pupils knew he was capable of giving.[5]

Tolkien's seventieth birthday was marked by a *Festschrift*, *English and Medieval Studies Presented to J.R.R. Tolkien*, published by Allen & Unwin. Charles Wrenn and Norman Davis assembled twenty-two 'former pupils, friends and colleagues' to contribute articles. They included Lewis, who wrote on 'The Anthropological Approach', Simonne d'Ardenne, Nevill Coghill and Alistair Campbell; there was also an ode to Tolkien by W.H. Auden (Auden had heard Tolkien lecture as an undergraduate, had become a fan of *The Lord of the Rings* when it was published and later struck up a friendship with Tolkien, mostly by letter).[6]

In the Michaelmas Term of 1962 and the following 1963 Hilary Term, Tolkien came out of retirement to cover for C.L. Wrenn, his successor in the Chair of Anglo-Saxon, who was in America on leave (and was himself soon to retire).

The effects of all this on his work on *The Silmarillion* cannot be measured simply in terms of time expended; anyone who has ever worked on a complex intellectual project knows that, after it has been put aside for some time, it cannot be resumed without considerable mental effort re-familiarizing oneself with the problems involved. These are the customary perils of the scholarly life, of course; but this does not make them any less real in any given case.

Another problem for Tolkien was the lack of an audience. The role C.S. Lewis played in encouraging and accompanying the gestation of *The Lord of the Rings* can hardly be overstated; Tolkien, as we have seen, saw clearly that without him it would never have been finished. Now, however, Tolkien had been estranged from Lewis for some years, and he had found no one able to take his place, as audience, sympathetic critic, general encourager. Tolkien essayed various schemes to enlist one or another of his American fans to help in the preparation of *The Silmarillion*, but none worked out as he hoped. Probably his closest literary confidant was his son Christopher, whom he had for some years determined was his imagined audience; but Christopher, for all his sympathy and his knowledge of northern literature, did not command the same authority as Lewis did as a critic, nor the same breadth of reading, nor (crucially) the same effectiveness as cajoler, persuader and general literary midwife.

Lewis's life, meanwhile, had continued on what, to Tolkien, was its strange path. The matter of Lewis's marriage had made a barrier between him and Tolkien that now was hardly ever crossed. After two years of remission, Joy's cancer eventually returned. One of Edith Tolkien's occasional stays at the Acland Nursing Home in north Oxford coincided with one of Joy Lewis's visits there for treatment; the two women met, discovered each other's identity and became friendly. Their respective husbands bumped into each other whilst visiting; this was the only time on record that Tolkien met Joy.[7] In July 1960 she died. The following year, Lewis published, anonymously, *A Grief Observed*, one of the most honest accounts of bereavement ever written. He was now responsible for Joy's two sons, neither of whom was an easy child. Their father, William Gresham, once came to visit, but was otherwise little involved; in September 1962, with his sight failing, and after being diagnosed with cancer, he killed himself with sleeping pills.

Warnie's drinking was no better, and, as is the way of these things, tended to get worse at times coincident with other unrelated crises. Deprived thus for long stretches of Warnie's secretarial help, Lewis was run ragged. His health was now bad; kidney and prostate and bladder all began to fail him.

Still he and Tolkien were no longer close. In some ways, of course, as Robert Havard remarked, 'the surprising thing ... is that they became such close friends, rather than that differences appeared and separated them'.[8] Yet despite their (to him inexplicable) personal estrangement,

Lewis still promoted Tolkien's work. In 1961, he nominated Tolkien for the Nobel Prize for Literature; Tolkien was rejected, on the grounds that he did not tell stories well enough. The Prize that year went, instead, to a Bosnian folklorist.

Perhaps all this miscellaneous distraction does something to balance the impression inattentive readers of Humphrey Carpenter's biography may have, that Tolkien spent the next fourteen years doing crossword puzzles and doodling elvishly on newspapers. Like any of us, of course, Tolkien sometimes wasted time, and newspapers and crosswords were one of his relaxations (another was interminable and complex games of Patience); but the main reasons for delay were those I have described: interruptions, dislocations, ill-health and old age.

III – Revisions and late-written works

We saw that the 1951 revision to the Silmarillion had encompassed only those parts of the text that did not derive from the three Great Tales, of Turin, Tuor, and Beren and Lúthien. Completing these narratives to his satisfaction was the necessary precursor to producing a final text of *The Silmarillion*.

Charles Noad has compiled a scheme of what, he reckons, a completed *Silmarillion* from this period might have comprised: first, as always, the *Quenta* proper; then *Ainulindalë*; then, newly split off from the *Quenta*, its chapter on the Valar, now considered a separate work and titled *Valaquenta*; then the four Great Tales, and the two tales of the Second Age, *Akallabêth* and *The Rings of Power*; last, five appended works on miscellaneous matters – *The Tale of Years* (in place of both sets of *Annals*, now abandoned and used as quarries for the later *Quenta*); *Laws and Customs of the Eldar*; *Dangweth Pengolodh* (or *Pengoloð*); *Athrabeth Finrod ah Andreth*; *Quendi and Eldar*.[9] Three of the last five items were recent compositions addressing controverted points.

Work on the Great Tales themselves was at best sporadic. In the years 1958–60, Tolkien turned again to the *Narn i Chîn Húrin*, which was within striking distance of being finished. It never reached a fully satisfactory form, however; and meanwhile, in 1958–9, he began another subsidiary text, to take up the unresolved elements of the *Narn* and round out the long and involved tragic history of Túrin; it seems to have been meant as a supplement to the *Narn* rather than part of *The Silmarillion* proper. The resulting text was titled *The Wanderings of Húrin*, and is the last true narrative addition Tolkien made to his account of the Elder Days.

From this period date various shorter ancillary works that sought to clarify particular issues now problematic or inconsistent in the light of the material already published. These are (from 1958) *The Laws and Customs among the Eldar* and *The Converse of Manwë and Eru*; (from 1959) *The Reincarnation of Elves*; *Athrabeth*; *Concerning Galadriel and Celeborn*.[10] As we have seen, several of these texts seem to have been meant, or were incorporated as, appendices to the projected *Silmarillion*: *Laws and Customs* deals with marriage, death, reincarnation and remarriage, *Converse* with reincarnation (as, obviously, does *Reincarnation*); the *Athrabeth* is a debate between Finrod and a mortal woman about death (it also contains the barest hint of a natural theology of the Incarnation); whilst *Quendi and Eldar* examines the elves' names for themselves in an extended philological treatment, and also includes an Elvish myth of their Awakening. The sheer multitudinousness of the questions to be addressed and problems to be resolved, all of which needed to be wholly consistent, must have seemed, often, overwhelming.

The question of transmission and framework was still unresolved. Ælfwine was still named as translator of the *Quenta*, and of the *Laws and Customs*, and was explicitly addressed in the *Dangweth*; but the *Akallabêth* was now attributed to no less a figure than Elendil, founder of the Númenórean kingdoms in Middle Earth.[11]

At this time, Tolkien tentatively introduced a device that might, he hoped, rescue his legendarium from the flat-world–round-world dilemma we noted above. This was the 'Dome of Varda', a great mist-wrought barrier set above the world and inscribed on its inside with facsimiles of the constellated stars; this was to hide the world from Melkor in the time of its fashioning, and thus preserve the appearance of a naïve flat-world cosmology whilst retaining a round-world one in fact. It also hid Valinor from the light of the Sun, now supposed of primæval making but, after assault by Melkor, giving only fierce and tainted light; the Two Trees were endowed with the last of the holy light of the One, which the Sun had borne before it was ravished, and were set in Valinor to light it alone. After the destruction of the Trees, the Dome was removed, and the light of the Sun was over all. This was at best a cumbersome account, and one that exists only as roughly drafted, and in several incompatible variants; but it is telling that the latest manuscripts of the *Quenta* omit the chapter on the making of the sun and moon from the last fruit and blossom of the Trees. The scale and implications of these changes, however, were such that, even had they been less tentative, they could not quickly have been implemented.[12]

I have said little about Tolkien's work on his invented languages, mostly because with some few exceptions little detailed material has been published that was written later than the 1920s; it remains true, however, that throughout his life the linguistic core of his legendarium was constantly evolving, and was the subject of persistent revision, discussion, elaboration and general tinkering, which often generated or reacted from the narrative growth of his various tales. Tolkien clearly spent unquantifiable time and effort on this – the extant linguistic manuscripts run, apparently, to three thousand pages; we should not see this as a distraction exactly, since it remains true that Tolkien's imagination was intimately bound up with linguistic speculation, but it must to some extent have meant a dispersal of effort.

Perhaps some of this miscellaneous writing was 'displacement activity', tasks Tolkien undertook to occupy himself because he was unable to engage properly with the main problem at hand: how to make *The Silmarillion* work. Its component tales were all written in a high style, without the mediation provided in his published works by hobbits; there was, for the contemporary reader, no obvious 'way in'. On one visit, Rayner Unwin was shown 'serried ranks of box files' which contained the Silmarillion tales, 'like beads without a string'.[13] This, perhaps, is the essence of the problem: Tolkien could not find a string on which to thread the beads he had so lovingly crafted. For many years, as we have seen, Tolkien had tried out variations on the device of an Anglo-Saxon seafarer as a 'framing device' for the stories, and a means of accounting for their transmission; he could not wholly abandon the connexion between England, the Lúthien or Luthany of his earliest stories, with ruined Beleriand, or Eressëa the gull-haunted, but the simple device of a lost sailor no longer seemed adequate (although we should remember that the *Dangweth Pengoloð* was represented as answers to Ælfwine). Increasingly, he felt that the nature of the texts (particularly their apparent confusion regarding cosmology, and the fates of elves and men, a confusion he decided was incompatible with his now very elevated notion of elvish wisdom and knowledge, derived as it was from the Valar) required an intermediate stage of Mannish transmission, via Númenor and Gondor. This of course would most probably sever completely the direct link between England and the elves; unless, as Tolkien may have intended, the Númenórean tales were preserved in Tol Eressëa by the elves and seen by Ælfwine there. But this introduced a level of redundancy that was hardly satisfactory.

Latterly, he considered presenting the Silmarillion texts as tales 'translated from the Elvish' by Bilbo Baggins. Hobbits, perhaps, were now to be the means these texts were passed to the tenth-century Englishman Ælfwine.[14] But these resolutions themselves raised further questions, and he could settle on no satisfying answer to the conundrum; this in itself tended to make work on the central texts slow and difficult.

From this time, also, comes the unfinished *Aldarion and Erendis* (which Tolkien seems to have called *The Mariner's Wife*, or *The Shadow of the Shadow*), the only surviving tale of Númenor before its Downfall; it is a sympathetically drawn account of an unhappy marriage. Erendis's mother tells her, 'A woman must share her husband's love with his work and the fire of his spirit, or make him a thing not loveable.'[15]

To it was prefixed, perhaps several years later, *A Description of the Island of Númenor*; this, and presumably also the story itself, was described as based on material preserved in Gondor. *The Line of Elros*, a Númenórean king-list, is undated but very likely comes from the same period, between 1960, when the story was first drafted, and 1965, when a final typescript of it was made.[16]

Tolkien himself recognized his long-standing tendency to be distracted into new projects:

> When I was supposed to be studying Latin and Greek, I studied Welsh and English. When I was supposed to be concentrating on English, I took up Finnish. I have always been incapable of doing the job in hand.[17]

This is, surely, an overstatement of the case: 'the job in hand' was never wholly neglected; but we may recognize, here, a late and melancholy self-excoriation for what Lewis had years before called Tolkien's 'dilatory and unmethodical' nature.

Chapter 15 – Unfinished Tales

I – Endings and renewals

In 1960, in another distraction, Tolkien started a wholesale rewriting of *The Hobbit*; he had grown to regret the tone of much of the book, particularly the intrusive narrator, and decided to recast the story to make it stylistically more like *The Lord of the Rings*, and to resolve some other niggling problems. After a few chapters, however, he got tangled in an unavailing attempt to make sense of the phases of the moon in the book, and put it aside.

The year 1962 saw the publication of *The Adventures of Tom Bombadil*, collecting mostly older verse. The impulse to collect and publish them came from Tolkien's aunt Jane Neave, now ninety, who the year before had asked him to put together 'a small book with Tom Bombadil at the heart of it'. The book appeared some months before her death in 1963.

Most of Tolkien's poems were frequently rewritten and adapted to new contexts; they were, in this, not of course unlike much of his other work, although their shorter compass and more readily defined form meant that, for the shorter pieces in any event, he was much more likely to produce finished versions. Most of the poems in this collection had been published before, in some form or other; they were now reworked and given the character of marginalia from the notional archetype of *The Lord of the Rings*, the Red Book of Westmarch, although the preface refers to 'the High-elvish and Númenorean legends of Eärendil', alluding to Tolkien's now (it seems) settled purpose to give his legendarium this 'mixed' character, transmitted (in part) through Rivendell.[1] Charles Noad notes that 'The Hoard' begins, 'when the moon was new and the sun young', which assumes their creation in recorded history as in the older creation.[2] The broadly comic aim of most of the pieces has probably masked the serious intent of some of them, particularly the last two, 'Sea-Bell' and 'The Last Ship'; although not new, they were for this version given a newly elegiac cast.[3] Tolkien felt that at some level his contact with faërie, with the sources of his inspiration, was now fading or uncertain. Allen & Unwin wrote to C.S. Lewis asking for a 'puff' quotation for the book; Lewis, in answer, wrote directly to Tolkien, although he did not know his current Oxford address and addressed his letter to Merton to be forwarded. He thought Unwin did not realize how much he, Lewis, was disliked, and that approval from him might actually damage sales; also,

> The public – little dreaming how much you dislike my work, bless you! – regard us as a sort of firm and wd. only laugh at what wd. seem to them mutual back-scratching.

Lewis ended, 'I wish we cd. ever meet.'[4] Christopher had been encouraging his father for years to go and see Lewis; now, at last, Tolkien gave in. He and Christopher went to The Kilns in the depths of the cold winter of 1962–3. But the visit was not a success; the two men had, now, little to say to one another.

Lewis had been ill with kidney and prostate problems for some time, and that July almost died of a heart attack. He was briefly in a coma, and then spent a week confused as a result of septicaemia. Tolkien visited him in hospital, and then, in September, he and his eldest son John drove to The Kilns. They talked about the '*Morte d'Arthur*, and whether trees died'.[5] Lewis had resigned his job in Cambridge; by mid-November, his kidneys were failing. Death came suddenly, but hardly unexpectedly.

On 22 November 1963, C.S. Lewis died. He was only sixty-five. Tolkien wrote to his daughter, 'this feels like an axe-blow near the roots'.[6] The following year, Lewis's posthumous work *Letters to Malcolm: Mainly on Prayer* appeared. Tolkien was appalled by it ('a distressing and in parts horrifying work'[7]); he began an essay discussing Lewis's religious views, which (Tolkien was increasingly convinced) had been dominated by the Protestantism, or better anti-Catholicism, of his Ulster childhood. The essay was called 'The Ulsterior Motive'. It has never been published.

Tolkien had been asked, presumably some years earlier, to write Lewis's obituary for *The Times*; he had refused. In January 1964, the Royal Society of Literature asked him if he would write an obituary for their journal; he again refused, this time giving a reason: 'I feel his loss so deeply that I have since his death refused to write or speak about him.'[8]

II – American copyrights and other diversions

The collection *Tree and Leaf* appeared in 1964; this reprinted, for the first time since 1945, *Leaf by Niggle*, alongside the expanded text of the lecture *On Fairy Stories*. American copyright law required that a new edition of *The Hobbit* be produced; Tolkien was unable to find his 1960 revision notes, and so made only a small number of less radical changes, although along comparable lines. It appeared as the 'third edition' in 1966.

Christopher Tolkien had been elected Fellow of New College in 1963, aged thirty-eight; the following year, 1964, he and his wife separated. This was a grief to Tolkien.[9]

In 1964 Donald Wollheim, science fiction writer and editor at the American paperback science fiction publisher Ace Books, asked Tolkien for rights to publish *The Lord of the Rings* in paperback and (he claimed) was brusquely rebuffed; Tolkien, Wollheim said, deplored the thought of his book appearing in 'so degenerate a form' as a paperback.[10] Wollheim was both annoyed and obstinate, and identified what he considered was a flaw in the copyright status of the existing American (hardback) edition of the book. He argued that since Houghton Mifflin's edition of *The Lord of the Rings* was in fact merely a binding of pages printed in England by Unwin, the text itself was not printed in America and was thus not covered by American copyright law.[11] Ace quickly produced a cheap paperback edition, which sold at 75¢ a volume besides Houghton Mifflin's $5-a-volume hardback. It appeared in 1965, and sold briskly.

Between July and September 1965, Tolkien sent a series of revisions to his American publisher, Houghton Mifflin, to the end of establishing a secure copyright on their edition under even the loosest interpretation of American copyright law. These revisions might have been mere perfunctory removal of typographical mistakes and the other inevitable elisions that arise in any large book during the process of publishing; Tolkien, however, characteristically took this opportunity to make some more substantive changes. All of this was, of course, further distraction from work on *The Silmarillion*.

One major addition was the 'Note on the Shire Records' appended to the Prologue; here, the volumes of 'Translations from the Elvish' given by Bilbo to Frodo (three volumes in the revision, merely 'some books' in the earlier text) are implicitly declared to be *The Silmarillion*, made from 'all the sources available ... in Rivendell, both living and written'.[12]

This was in line with Tolkien's now-favoured source for his legendarium (since at Rivendell were kept the surviving records of the Númenórean North Kingdom), although it was not wholly satisfactory, since the 'living sources' could presumably have disposed of any supposed misunderstandings in the 'Mannish' recensions of (for instance) the creation myth. Tolkien may have intended to add a rider, as described in an undated note (probably from the late 1950s or early 1960s): 'A note should say that the Wise of Númenor recorded that the making of the stars was not so, nor of Sun and Moon',[13] although one wonders why in that case the legends themselves were not emended, except (perhaps) by presumed reverence for older records, notionally on the part of the Númenórean sages but in fact by Tolkien himself. There is a further question, within the internal consistency of the legendary itself, as to the supposed time when these 'mixed' Númenórean myths were written down, since at no point within the history of the legendarium were the Houses of Men not in contact with High Elves who knew the 'true' cosmogony. Doubtless Tolkien could have improvised a plausible explanation, but it would inevitably have partaken to some degree in the nature of special pleading. In any event, however, the Anglo-Saxon link to Eriol Wæfre/Ælfwine now looked tenuous in the extreme.

Six months after the Ace edition, Ballantine, another publisher of paperback science fiction, brought out an authorized paperback, incorporating Tolkien's revisions, which were enough to establish its copyright status.[14] The price of their book included a royalty to Tolkien, however; it sold at 95¢ per volume, 20¢ more than the Ace pirate edition.

It was at this juncture that Tolkien's scrupulous courtesy to his fans paid dividends. He had answered numerous written queries by hand, often at some length; amongst the fans who received such letters was the young Gene Wolfe, who got one dated 7 November 1966 giving a brief but courteous answer giving the (English) etymologies of the words *orc* and *warg*.[15] Tolkien now added to all such replies a brief request to make the irregular nature of the Ace edition known, and to buy instead the Ballantine text, which in addition was printed with a message from Tolkien on its back cover asking readers to buy it rather than any 'unauthorized' edition. The various Tolkien societies were also enlisted to help. Within six months of publication, Ballantine had sold over a million copies, Ace no more than a hundred thousand. Ace came to an out-of-court settlement, paid Tolkien a lump sum of $9,000 in lieu of royalties (reckoned as a rough 4 per cent on copies sold) and undertook not to reprint the book. Naturally, the controversy only helped sales. The next British edition, brought out by Unwin in 1966, incorporated the changes made to the Ballantine text, and became the 'second edition' of the text. Further revisions, which Tolkien had submitted too late for the 1965 American paperback, were also incorporated into the next Unwin printing of 1967. This text of the book was current for the next twenty years.[16]

In the strange heady days of the mid- to late 1960s, *The Lord of the Rings* became what is usually called a cult classic, first in America but then afterwards in Britain also (the first British paperback, a single volume with severely abridged appendices, was produced in 1968 at thirty shillings, or £1 10s.). A full British paperback text, in three volumes with appendices, became available only in 1974.

A BBC documentary of 1968 gives a good sample of the sort of soft-minded nonsense that often accompanied this enthusiasm, in the minds of some at least of its readers.[17] Tolkien Societies sprang up across the world: the Tolkien Society of America was founded in February 1965, and a British analogue followed four years later: the author found himself famous. This was (surely) a source of pleasure and satisfaction (the book's success was, Tolkien reflected, 'as if the horns of hope had been heard again'[18]), as well as of money, which for the first time in Tolkien's life was not a constant worry; but also of further distractions. Tolkien had no full-time secretary, and an increasing volume of fan-letters, many of which requested, and got, sometimes long handwritten answers. Whilst this exercise, which was in origin perhaps one of simple courtesy, was often useful in bringing to light problems that needed to be clarified, the resulting tangents along which Tolkien was frequently led did not make it easier for him to concentrate on *The Silmarillion*.

III – 'His way now led back to bereavement'

In the summer of 1966, Clyde Kilby, an American fan who was curator of the Tolkien and Lewis manuscripts at Wheaton College, Illinois, spent three months in Oxford helping Tolkien sort through the manuscripts of *The Silmarillion*.[19] Kilby was struck by the sheer quantity and variety of the unpublished material:

> One can imagine the perplexity of a writer with so many ideas and so many incomplete or unperfected writings on hand and with the

realization of so little time left. He was then seventy-four.

Two things immediately impressed me. One was that *The Silmarillion* would never be completed. The other was the size of my own task.[20]

In the event, whilst the visit doubtless helped to introduce a little more order to Tolkien's papers, it was only a small start on a large problem, and was soon overtaken by further sources of entropy.

The short tale *Smith of Wootton Major* appeared in 1967; it is another minor work (it in fact began as an introduction, never finished, to a volume of George MacDonald), but one which again expresses Tolkien's sadness at what he saw as his exile from faërie, the elvish springs of his creativity. Unusually, Tolkien simply shows us Smith's wanderings, or some of them, in faërie, as a series of pictures, all unexplained. Verlyn Flieger has commented:

Wandering in a myth he does not understand, Smith ... witnesses a whole world to which he does not have the key; nor, in consequence, does the reader.[21]

Some elements of the story may perhaps be deciphered: the birch that shelters Smith from the wind that hunts him is, probably, philology, as it was in Tolkien's Old English and Gothic 'syllabus' poems of the early 1920s; Tolkien sometimes named the birch as his 'totem tree'. It shelters Smith from the wind, but in sheltering him, it is not unscathed:

When at last the Wind passed he rose and saw that the birch was naked. It was stripped of every leaf, and it wept, and tears fell from its branches like rain. He set his hand upon its white bark, saying: 'Blessed be the birch! What can I do to make amends or give thanks?' He felt the answer of the tree pass up from his hand: 'Nothing', it said. 'Go away! The Wind is hunting you. You do not belong here. Go away and never return!'

As he climbed back out of that dale he felt the tears of the birch trickle down his face and they were bitter on his lips.[22]

Tolkien, we might translate, had been sheltered and favoured by philology, but by his trespassing into faërie had drawn the 'world's wind' onto it, to its lasting harm. Certainly the standing of philology as a school of learning was, in 1967, immeasurably lower than it had been in Tolkien's youth. He could not, perhaps, wholly absolve himself from blame. But this is not to make *Smith* a narrow allegory of academic politics; it is, above all, a lament for the inevitable transience of mortal dealings with the Perilous Realm. The sorrow that arises from this is an inescapable accompaniment to the freight that any mortal carries back with him across the border with faërie.

Increasingly, Tolkien saw his writing as something given to him rather than invented by him; he had always tended to view creative work in this way (indeed, it is not unusual amongst writers – both C.S. Lewis and Robert Graves, to name no others, say something very similar), but as he grew older, and the strong impact of his work on others' lives and imaginations was shown to him (as it was, most days, in his still-innumerable fan letters), his sense of this developed. There is a curious anecdote in a late letter, referring (probably) to an incident from this time. Tolkien was visited by a man who reckoned various (unspecified) old pictures were apt illustrations of *The Lord of the Rings*. He showed Tolkien some reproductions; Tolkien had never seen them before. The man was silent, and stared at him.

> Suddenly he said: 'Of course you don't suppose, do you, that you wrote all that book yourself?' ... I have never since been able to suppose so. An alarming conclusion for an old philologist to draw concerning his private amusement.[23]

With a heightened sense of 'mission', if you like, went also and inevitably a sense of unworthiness, of incapacity; and also, what was worse, that the gift might be withdrawn – might already, indeed, have been withdrawn, leaving him, like Smith, cold and cut off from what had hitherto nourished him.

In September and October of 1967 Tolkien was ill with a viral infection, which needed daily visits from his doctor over a month and left him 'an emaciated wreck'; he was laid up for another two months to recover.[24] His eldest son, Fr John Tolkien, came to stay with his parents to recover, as he had several times before, from nervous exhaustion. The following January, Edith's health failed owing, in great part, to the strain of looking after them both.

IV – Bournemouth

For some years Tolkien and Edith had taken holidays in Bournemouth, usually staying at the Miramar Hotel on the sea-front. This provided the sort of agreeable, unstuffy (and unbookish) society in which Edith flourished. She became very attached to their visits; in 1968, Tolkien decided they should move there permanently, to make some belated recompense to her for the years of her loneliness amongst his friends and occupations in Oxford. They rather impulsively bought a bungalow a short distance from the hotel, and began, once more, to pack up and move house.

In mid-June, before they had moved from their Oxford house, Tolkien fell downstairs and broke his leg badly; he spent the next month in hospital, and never went back to Sandfield Road. The contents of his study were packed and moved in his absence. The disruption to his books and papers was considerable; although not as much was actually lost as Tolkien feared, nevertheless this chaos, added to the shock of the injury, interrupted him when, at last, he had begun to make some progress with his writing. His wife was too frail properly to supervise the movers, and Tolkien's boxed books and papers were piled indiscriminately in the garage. When he left hospital, he and Edith spent another month living in the Miramar whilst their house was made ready. His leg was another month in plaster, and he was unable to walk without crutches or a stick for the rest of the year. His library and papers remained in chaos for months.

In June 1969, the film, stage and merchandising rights to *The Lord of the Rings* and *The Hobbit* were sold to United Artists for $250,000, some £100,000 at the then exchange rate. The terms of the sale did not give Tolkien or his heirs much control over any subsequent film or other product; this was, perhaps, in line with his previous declaration to Rayner Unwin that the rights must produce 'cash or kudos' – either complete artistic veto or, in compensation, a very substantial fee. We may wonder whether the money they actually brought was, even in 1969 terms, in fact very substantial; it has been suggested that the expenses of the move to Bournemouth, and the unexpectedly extended hotel stays caused by Tolkien's fall, left him with a pressing need for ready cash; or, alternatively, that he sought by this sale to secure a lump sum with which to offset likely inheritance tax on his estate. Without inspection of his financial accounts for the period in question, it is impossible to know if either of these explanations is correct, but it seems possible that one of them, or even both in combination, is close to the truth.[25]

Edith was happy to be in Bournemouth, and regained something of the vivacity she had possessed as a young woman; Tolkien, although he took pleasure in his wife's happiness, felt isolated, cut off from the society of his intellectual peers. Friends visited occasionally, but it was not like living in Oxford. For all his adult life, he had been what used to be called a clubbable man, much given to talk with male cronies and belonging to various societies and clubs whose meetings were often enriched by dinners. Oxford is much given to this sort of association, partly as an excuse for good food and company, partly to cater for the myriad shared interests that dons nurture, partly to allow the ceremonious mock-solemnity that collegiate life permits so well. All of this now came to an end; Tolkien had no car, and travel to Oxford was hardly straightforward.

Slowly, after his papers had finally been set in order, he began to write. As in 1958–60, however, rather than undertaking further on *The Silmarillion* proper, he wrote a number of speculative treatises addressing particular questions from the legendarium; usually these began as philological investigations (sometimes in answer to readers' letters, and often into names that, as the languages had subsequently evolved, were now anomalous but were 'fixed' by their appearance in *The Lord of the Rings*) but soon developed into philosophical, theological or simple narrative directions. Many of these texts survive only in more or less illegible manuscripts. Datable texts from this time, that have been published, include *The Shibboleth of Fëanor* (1968), *The Disaster of the Gladden Fields* (1969), *The Battles of the Fords of Isen* (1969 or later), 'Nomenclature', published as *The Rivers and Beacon-hills of Gondor* (July 1969), *Cirion and Eorl* (summer 1969) and *Part of the Legend of Amroth and Nimrodel* (1969 or later).[26] This burst of creativity (Tolkien, remember, was now seventy-seven) was interrupted by illness in July. He resumed work in October 1969, and wrote a short text, *Of Dwarves and Men*. It contains much previously unrecorded material about the early history and relations of dwarves. It also, whilst discussing the (what he had come to consider mistaken) use of Norse dwarf-names in what purported to be the facsimile inscriptions in *The Lord of the Rings*, betrays a fundamental uncertainty in Tolkien's mind. If already published material was both fixed and radically inconsistent with itself, how could his legendarium ever achieve final form? Amidst the still-fecund narrative invention is an air of grave self-doubt.

A fascinating text from this time is *The Shibboleth of Fëanor*, an explanation for what had become an anomalous variation in Quenya between /þ/ and /s/. Tolkien's ingenious account locates this in a conscious decision by Fëanor, the Noldorin arch-maker who here also appears as arch-philologist, betrayed by pride. Indeed, Fëanor is almost a shadow-self for Tolkien, the maker and philologist seduced by pride in his creations.

At the start of 1970, he complained to his son Michael that progress on *The Silmarillion* was slow, mostly confined to co-ordinating details of nomenclature, and constantly interrupted: Edith's health was poor, he was feeling his own age, and there was a constant press of 'business' and chores.[27] He had no permanent secretary or domestic help. At the start of 1971, he made some revision and expansions to what became the *Silmarillion* chapter 'Of Maeglin'. This seems to have been intended by Tolkien as a later chapter for the extended, if radically incomplete, tale *Tuor and the Fall of Gondolin*.

In July he wrote to Roger Lancelyn Green, and in a discussion of the 'immortal lands' remarked that the tales of his legendarium were now to be explained as predominantly 'Mannish' in origin, but influenced by Sindar and other elves who had never seen Valinor;[28] this was perhaps now necessary to explain what he saw as their anomalous cosmogony, but raised a whole series of other questions about the transmission, if this were so, of the purely 'Valinorean' element of the stories (the doings of the Noldor before their Exile, for instance). Why should these have become contaminated with a whole framework of erroneous cosmology? And if there were contamination in the cosmological framework, why not in the narrative matter also? One problem might be removed, but only at the cost of raising another. The reader may feel that Tolkien was overly exercised about a phantom consistency that could never have been fully achieved, and (moreover) did not matter, since the power and coherence of the tales was hardly affected by it; but whilst this is certainly true of (to use Tolkien's own metaphor) the 'beads' of the necklace, he was, I suggest, not wrong to think that the 'string', their framework, was of critical importance for the reception of the stories: how we read something is not wholly determined but is surely profoundly affected by its explicit or implicit status. Many readers have felt the absence of such a framework in the posthumously published *Silmarillion*; in its absence, many simply do not know how to situate the book within their previous experience not just of reading in general, but even of reading Tolkien's other works. In his essay *On Fairy Stories* Tolkien had noted Andrew Lang's observation, that for children "'Is it true" is the great question'; but he had added, in a footnote, that in his own experience this was not the most important one, which was, instead, 'Was he good? Was he wicked?'[29] In old age, Tolkien seems to have found that the first question kept tripping him up in his efforts to organize his various answers to the second.

He did little for the rest of the year, and in October was ill again.

V – Oxford at last

On 29 November 1971, after ten days' illness, Edith Tolkien died. She fell ill on the 19th with an inflamed gall-bladder, and hung on for a week to what her husband reckoned 'the brink of recovery' before suffering a relapse.[30] Tolkien was bereft; 'she was (and knew she was) my Lúthien. But the story has gone crooked, and I am left, and *I* cannot plead before the inexorable Mandos.'[31] He was not sure he could write again. Certainly, he did not want to stay in Bournemouth. He began to cast about for a house in Oxford; he stayed with his daughter Priscilla, who still lived there (although he spent Christmas with his eldest son John).

Early in the new year, he visited Christopher Wiseman, who now lived in Milford-on-Sea, some sixteen miles or so east of Bournemouth (where, if we remember, Fr Augustine Emery had also lived in retirement). Wiseman was also recently widowed, but also (and more recently) remarried. Tolkien walked in their garden with Wiseman, his wife and her daughter, but, although Tolkien said much, the Great Twin Brethren said little to each other directly, or of any great moment: certainly nothing of bereavement.[32]

In the 1972 New Year's Honours, Tolkien was appointed CBE; later that month, Christopher, still a Fellow of New College, wrote unprompted to the Warden of Merton asking about college rooms for his father; the governing body there unanimously voted Tolkien should be made a residential fellow. In the meantime, he went to stay with Christopher and his family in their house in West Hanney, a Berkshire village a dozen miles south-west of Oxford. In mid-March, Tolkien moved to a flat in Merton Street, with a college scout (servant) and his wife to look after him. At the end of March, he went to Buckingham Palace to receive his CBE. He planned to resume writing, and publish *The Silmarillion* in instalments. Tolkien sometimes observed that he came of long-lived stock, and might have many years left (his Suffield grandfather, remember, had lived to ninety-seven). On 3 June, he was awarded an honorary D.Litt.;

the University Orator's speech, composed and given (in Latin) by his old friend Colin Hardie, hoped he would yet 'produce from his store Silmarillion and scholarship'[33]. Later that month, his rooms were burgled and his CBE medal, together with some of Edith's jewellery, was stolen. His papers remained in storage for some time; he wrote nothing, it seems, until that November. Thereafter he produced some brief discussions of particular points, often (as before) provoked by questions in readers' letters: on elvish reincarnation, wizards and minor characters from the legendarium.

He was ill again at the start of 1973, with persistent and severe indigestion; his doctor banned wine and rich food. He wrote little or nothing other than letters; at the end of May he finally wrote to Wiseman, suggesting they meet again. He signed himself 'JRRT. TCBS.'[34]

That summer, he wrote to a friend, 'over and above all the afflictions and obstacles I have endured since *The Lord of the Rings* came out, I have lost confidence'.[35] That year, he made a few notes in August, nothing more.

On 28 August, he was driven to Bournemouth to stay with friends. He planned to spend a few days at the Miramar from 4 September, and to visit Christopher Wiseman. During the night of 30 August, after attending a birthday party, he was taken ill; a hospital diagnosed a bleeding gastric ulcer. Two of his children were abroad, but John and Priscilla came to Bournemouth at once. He seemed to be getting better; but the next day, 1 September, he developed a chest infection.

In the early hours of the following morning, Sunday, 2 September 1973, John Ronald Reuel Tolkien died. He was eighty-one years old.

Part V – Niggle's Parish

'At any minute it is what we are and are doing, not what we plan to be and do that counts.'[1]

Chapter 16 – Posthumous Publications

Tolkien's will named his third son Christopher as his literary executor. His immediate task was to see what could be done with his father's papers. Could the long-promised *Silmarillion* ever be published?

The Silmarillion

Tolkien had perhaps hoped to finish *The Silmarillion* in time for the Queen's Silver Jubilee in 1977; he still thought of it as dedicated 'to England, to my country'. In 1975 Christopher Tolkien resigned his fellowship at New College to devote himself full-time to his father's estate. With the help of Guy Gavriel Kay (a Canadian law student, later himself a noted writer of quasi-historical fantasy fiction) he compiled the published *Silmarillion*. He was under considerable pressure from readers, his publisher and his own sense of duty as his father's literary executor to produce a readable text quickly; inevitably, he made a number of editorial decisions that, with hindsight and given leisure, he might have made otherwise. But the nature of the component texts would hardly admit of any other procedure. As we have seen, any continuous narrative was perforce a patchwork of texts from wildly varying dates and (sometimes) in distinct styles. Absolute consistency was neither sought nor achieved. The book was published in 1977.

Unfinished Tales

Three years later, another volume, *Unfinished Tales*, appeared; it collected fourteen long texts, in various stages of incompleteness, dealing with a range of subjects across the legendarium. These included the texts of the last, longer versions of two of the three Great Tales, *Tuor and his Coming to Gondolin* (originally meant to be a full retelling of the fall of the city, the first since 1917) and substantial fragments of the *Tale of the Children of Húrin* (otherwise known as *Narn i Chîn Húrin*).

The History of Middle Earth

Christopher Tolkien now began the enormous task of preparing and publishing the various component texts that underlay the 1977 *Silmarillion*. The result, embracing also the drafts of *The Lord of the Rings*, some technical treatises on the Elvish languages and various miscellaneous works (such as two unfinished 'time travel' novels, *The Lost Road* and *The Notion Club Papers*), was published in twelve volumes between 1983 and 1996, under the overarching title of *The History of Middle Earth*. This, taken together with his earlier work on *The Silmarillion* and *Unfinished Tales*, is a very considerable work of textual scholarship, collating large numbers of manuscript and typescript texts, held in various different places (some of Tolkien's manuscripts were sold by him in his lifetime to American university collections; the remainder are in the Bodleian Library in Oxford). Tolkien and his readers have been fortunate in his literary executor, who combines an exhaustive knowledge of the material, expertise in his father's academic interests and training in the delicate and rigorous art of editing texts (his major academic publication was an edition of the Norse *King Heidrek's Saga*). It has been said that 'one man's imaginative genius has had the benefit of two lifetimes' work'.[2]

The Children of Húrin

In April 2007, Christopher Tolkien published an edition of a complete text of this, a prose version of one of the three Great Tales; fragments had appeared previously, but this is as near as we are likely to come to an achieved text.

Academic texts

The primary text here is the volume titled *The Monsters and the Critics*, which collects seven 'essays' by Tolkien (in fact, all but one were originally public lectures) on academic subjects. It includes the famous *Beowulf* lecture, his Andrew Lang lecture *On Fairy Stories* and two texts (*English and Welsh* and *A Secret Vice*) giving extensive personal reflexion on Tolkien's own linguistic taste, and on his 'private languages'. None of the pieces is overly technical, indeed Tolkien's written style (as opposed to his spoken delivery, which was reportedly terrible) is beguiling. For anyone interested in the intellectual sources of Tolkien's fiction, or indeed in the language and literature of the old north, this is the best place to start.

The Monsters and the Critics appeared in 1983. It was not in fact the first of his academic works to be posthumously published. The previous year saw a small edition of a book called *The Old English Exodus* – Tolkien's edition of the poem, with translation and commentary reconstructed from his notes. This probably represents in some form the material that Tolkien mentioned to the OUP in the 1930s as a possible future edition.[3] The published text met with a mixed reaction from current scholars of Old English, and has never been reprinted (and is accordingly both rare and expensive). It is probable that a comparable edition and commentary exist for the Old English poem *Elene*, which Tolkien had also tentatively proposed for publication.

In January 1983, another of his former pupils edited *Finn and Hengest*, which gives texts of Tolkien's lectures on a much-disputed passage from *Beowulf* and a parallel, fragmentary poem known as the Finnesburg Fragment; as with *Exodus*, Tolkien had also prepared editions of the texts; unlike *Exodus*, this book is still in print. Tolkien first lectured on this subject in 1928, and did so regularly during the 1930s. Unlike his *Beowulf* lecture, his theory here has (sadly) had almost no influence on subsequent criticism of the text; probably most fans of *The Lord of the Rings* coming to this book will find it baffling. For a patient reader with an interest in northern antiquity, however (and this sort of reader is more likely to be found amongst Tolkien fans than elsewhere), it is a luminous text; the fact, moreover, that Tolkien begins his exegesis of these poems with a long annotated glossary of names is additional confirmation, if any were needed, of the way his mind worked: first names, then the stories enfolded in and around the names.

There are extensive lecture notes amongst the Tolkien papers held in the Bodleian Library; brief extracts from them feature in *The Keys of Middle-Earth* by Lee and Solopova. None has yet been published *in extenso*, and it is unclear whether the condition of the texts (often in rapid and elliptical pencil) would often permit this.

The one exception is the earlier texts that underlay the famous 'Beowulf: The Monsters and the Critics' lecture; these appear, edited and copiously annotated by Michael Drout, in *Beowulf and the Critics*; they represent Tolkien's lecture series 'Beowulf: General Criticism' given several times in the early 1930s.

The expanded text of the lecture *On Fairy Stories* was given in a number of different versions; the various longer and shorter texts of this, and Tolkien's original drafts, have been edited in an attractive volume by Verlyn Flieger and Douglas A. Anderson.

Christopher Tolkien has also given us an edition of the Völsung and Gudrún poems from the early 1930s (*The Legend of Sigurd and Gudrún*, May 2009); it also includes a text of an introductory lecture on the *Elder Edda*.

Tolkien made two translations of *Beowulf*, a complete one in prose, and a partial one (600 lines) in alliterative verse. These were begun when Tolkien was at Leeds, and worked on during the 1930s. The manuscripts are in the Bodleian Library; Christopher Tolkien's edition of the prose translation, with a generous commentary drawn from his father's lectures, finally appeared in May 2014.

Tolkien's translation of three Middle English poems (*Sir Gawain and the Green Knight, Pearl and Sir Orfeo*) into modern English verse was published in 1975. His unfinished Arthurian epic, *The Fall of Arthur*, appeared in May 2013.

Linguistic writings

In the early 1990s, Christopher Tolkien entrusted the great bulk of his father's purely linguistic manuscripts (those dealing, that is, with his invented languages) to a group of American scholars. The materials amount to roughly 3,000 manuscript and typescript pages. Some of the material has subsequently been published, in the journals *Vinyar Tengwar* and *Parma Eldalamberon*; sadly, whilst all issues of the first of these are still available to buy, early issues of the latter (which include, at time of writing, the text of the early 'Gnomish Lexicon') remain out of print. There seems little good reason for this, given the ready availability of print-to-order publishing.

Still unpublished

A volume of Tolkien's *Letters* appeared in 1981; it is a fascinating volume, containing some 350 letters; many of them have been heavily abridged, however, and they represent only a fraction of the surviving letters (which number at least 1,500, with undiscovered texts still coming to light). The letters are the only part of Tolkien's extensive private papers ever to be published. These exist in substantial quantities, some in the Bodleian Library, others still in the family's keeping; they are not available for general consultation. There are, as far as I know, no immediate plans for any of them to be published.

A biographer will obviously be disappointed that these materials have not yet been released; but those who have charge of such things can presumably reckon possible hurt to the sensibilities of the living better than we who have never seen them.

There are numerous shorter poems by Tolkien scattered over six decades of miscellaneous periodical publications; some were collected in The *Adventures of Tom Bombadil*, but many have never been republished, or even, in the case of some of his earlier poems, published at all. It would be a service for someone to collect all of these in a single volume, including such things as the *Songs for the Philologists* and *Doworst*.

Chapter 17 – A Cinematic Afterlife

As was mentioned above, Tolkien sold the film rights to *The Hobbit* and *The Lord of the Rings* in 1969. This was not his first encounter with this world, however; in 1957, he was approached by a consortium of American filmmakers (Forrest J. Ackermann, Morton Grady Zimmerman and Al Brodax) who wished to turn *The Lord of the Rings* into an animated feature, and had prepared a script and some proposed artwork. Tolkien thought the art promising, but the script dreadful; he was prepared to compromise, however, if the fee was large enough. The details of this and all subsequent negotiations were left to Allen & Unwin. The filmmakers were given a six-month option, to run from the time when Tolkien submitted comments on their script. He sent in some detailed (and corrosive) comments in June 1958, asking for a thorough rewrite or, failing that, a very large fee indeed. Presumably they were disinclined to offer either; they let the option lapse.[1]

Next was a proposal for a feature-length animated *Hobbit*, to be made by William L. Snyder's Rembrandt Films (Snyder had won an Oscar in 1960 for best animated short film; he also made some *Tom and Jerry* cartoons). An agreement was concluded in April 1962, but questions were raised about the American copyright status of the text, and Snyder ended up producing only a token version (a twelve-minute montage of stills) with no more than a tangential relation to the book.[2]

In the late 1960s, the Beatles were keen to make a version of *The Lord of the Rings*, with the four of them playing Gollum, Frodo, Sam and Gandalf. Tolkien, who detested the group as a whole, and the bumptious John Lennon in particular, was furiously opposed; they did not secure the rights.

After some years of preliminary negotiation, then, the film rights were sold initially to United Artists. The following year, the company asked the director John Boorman (then best known for the Lee Marvin *noir Point Blank; Deliverance, Zardoz* and *Excalibur* were all in the future) to make a film; Boorman and a screenwriter produced a script for a two-and-a-half-hour version, heavily spiced with the sex and drugs references tediously inevitable, it seems, at that time (pipeweed is a narcotic, mush-rooms invariably hallucinogens, Galadriel a sexualized matriarch who seduces Frodo, and so boringly on). New management at United Artists sensibly dropped the project. Six years later, the rights were sold to the Saul Zaentz company, and assigned to their wholly owned subsidiary Tolkien Enterprises; they commissioned Ralph Bakshi, then well known for his animated films, to make *The Lord of the Rings*. In 1978, he released the first part of a projected two-part animated film, which combined rotoscoped live action with animated characters. It was not a success, and the second part was never made. Almost twenty years later, nothing further had been done before the New Zealand filmmaker Peter Jackson (then best known, to this writer at least, as director of the vastly enter-taining man-eating aliens splatter-film *Bad Taste*) acquired the rights, via the Warner Brothers affiliate New Line Cinema.

After an inevitably protracted development and production process, the resulting three films were released, one a year, between 2001 and 2003. Taken together, the three films are a cinematic monster, running to nine hours in all for theatrical release; a subsequent 'special extended' edition occupies a full twelve hours. Others have ably discussed the various changes and compromises introduced into the screenplays as against the book's narrative, some inevitable and in their place effective, others bizarre or distasteful; it is perhaps enough to say that although many reckon the film versions great masterpieces, this is not a universal view. I shall not particularize my own reactions here; enough to say that, aside from the first of the films, which I enjoyed well enough, I am not a fan.

At the same time, Tolkien Enterprises licensed a bewildering variety of additional merchandise to coincide with the films' release and borrowing their images of Tolkien's characters and world: computer games, board games, miniature figures in a variety of sizes and materials, books and guides and goblets and chess sets, Lego, ringtones, watches and a panoply of other nick-nacks and gewgaws. The Zaentz corporation, and New Line Cinema, did very well out of it all; it is unclear how much of the money made its way back to the Tolkien Estate, but the always healthy sales of the books (in, inevitably, film tie-in editions) rose dramatically.

A decade later, and with this now being for the younger generation the defining visual character of Tolkien's work (and maybe, for some, also its narrative character), Jackson has now turned to *The Hobbit*. Thus far, this project is, I reckon, much more promising. *The Hobbit* is simpler in narrative structure, and, suitably garnished with additional dwarven material culled from Appendix A III of *The Lord of the Rings*, offers a strong and visually very promising tale of loyalty and revenge, with a subsidiary development of the hero (from unpromising domesticity to morally competent agent) of a type familiar to screenwriters and thus audiences. It is a children's tale, and can readily admit (indeed, it already to some extent contains) the sort of cartoonish divertissement (comic trolls, squabbling rock-giants, pompous and hubristic goblin-kings) that would, and did, sit uncomfortably in the grand narrative of *The Lord of the Rings*. Even Jackson's regrettable tendency to play dwarves for laughs has some support in the original tale. The second film has much more narrative amplification than the first, some (Dol Guldur) good, some (Laketown) indifferent, some plain bad: the barrel-escape from the Elvenking's halls has become a rollercoaster platform fight in the now familiar vein of computer-game cinematography; whilst an inserted elven-dwarven love triangle is simply ridiculous. Rivendell, in the earlier films, was memorably described as apparently furnished with garden-centre statuary, hardly a convincing version of the last hold of the Noldor, the supreme makers of Middle Earth; their distant Silvan and Sindarin cousins in Mirkwood are perhaps better served, although Jackson's Thranduil is distressingly reminiscent of Caligula as he might have been played by David Bowie in his cross-dressing phase. All in all, though, it is not as bad as it might be; and the dragon is splendid. However it concludes, though, it will not really be *The Hobbit* we (but perhaps no one henceforth) grew up with. But this should not surprise anyone, I think.

Epilogue

"'At any rate, I shall get this one picture done, my real picture, before I have to go on that wretched journey,' he used to say.'[1]

What are we to make of Tolkien's achievement? In one sense, like Niggle, he died with his great picture unfinished – the Silmarillion texts were never set in order, never fully achieved, and were published in a form that, although superficially finished, is in fact radically disparate and incomplete. Perhaps, if Tolkien had been more focussed and disciplined, less 'dilatory and unmethodical', less susceptible to despondency, inertia and sloth, he might have been able to finish the legendarium to his own satisfaction, or something approaching it. Perhaps; certainly, other men have laboured under difficulties and calls on their time as great as or greater than his, and have finished their 'life's work' in a way that Tolkien never did. But if he had done so, he would have been a different man; the same sources that gave rise to his characteristic type of magnificent and heroic melancholy also yielded self-doubt and depression; the perfectionist who brought his prose style to such a pitch of achievement was also, for this very reason, liable to abandon in weary disgust writings that were good, but not so good that bringing them to that perfection was not an insupportable burden; or whose delight in intricate structure and close-woven narrative could, in a moment, become enmeshment in confused strands whose entanglement was irresolvable.

All of these things are true; and yet, what is remarkable, *The Lord of the Rings* was finished and published. Aside from the incalculable delight it has brought to generations of readers, it has also unsealed a whole vast area of the human imagination (Niggle's Parish, if you like, of which we are all now to some extent free). None of the myriad popular forms in which high or low fantasy is now found would have happened without

289

Tolkien; the same impulse that languished for decades in obscure pulp magazines is now definitively 'mainstream literature', if not, still, wholly respectable. But Tolkien's legacy is not primarily his hordes of imitators, good, bad, indifferent; it is the enduring way he has given us of escape from a prison-house of the mind into the clearer, stronger reality he saw and embodied in words: it is his books, which convey, still, the perilous air of faërie into hearts ready, albeit unknown, to receive it and be awoken.

> Whether or not this tale have a moral it is not for me to say. The King (who told it me) said that it had, and quoted a scrap of Latin, for he had been at Oxford in his youth before he fell heir to his kingdom. One may hear tunes from the Rime, said he, in the thick of a storm on the scarp of a rough hill, in the soft June weather, or in the sunset silence of a winter's night. But let none, he added, pray to have the full music: for it will make him who hears it a footsore traveller in the ways o' the world and a masterless man till death.[2]

Appendix – Tolkien the Catholic

Religion took a central role in Tolkien's life; he is often seen now, too, as a specifically Catholic writer, and his writings are sometimes interpreted in ways that may appear fanciful (and not just to non-Catholics). It is worth looking at this question in a little more depth, and under two aspects.

1 – Life

Tolkien was throughout his life a faithful Mass-goer, and a man who took prayer seriously. Some writers have seized on statements from various letters and asserted that Tolkien was throughout his life, at least in aspiration, a daily Mass-goer.[1] The main evidence for this usually cited is a letter written to his son Michael in 1963. This can hardly be solid evidence for his practice of decades earlier; in fact, he explicitly says there that he neglected his religion 'especially at Leeds, and at 22 Northmoor Road',[2] which would cover the years 1920–30. We might note, also, the anecdote cited in Chapter 10.III above in which Tolkien declared he was so depressed he had not been to Mass for a fortnight. These evidences, and others, are hardly reconcilable with an invariable habit of daily Mass-going. Certainly, this was his practice as a schoolboy, and probably became so again at various times in his life, particularly as he grew older; but my sense is of a man who was much afflicted by (self-perceived) laziness or inertia ('wickedness and sloth', in the same 1963 letter), and affronted by the shortcomings of the clergy and his fellow Catholics, all of which he cannily names as a cloak for temptations to unbelief. This is a dynamic many of us will find all too plausible and familiar. It remains true that his eucharistic piety was intense, and continuing.

As Stratford Caldecott has pointed out, Tolkien's 'spirituality was one of gratitude and praise', in which man gives voice to the otherwise mute rejoicing of all creation.[3] Tolkien counselled one of his sons to learn prayers of praise by heart: he recommended, what he himself found helpful, the Glory Be, the *Gloria*, Psalms 112 and 116, the *Magnificat*, the Litany of Loreto and the prayer *Sub tuum praesidium*. Tolkien himself usually said his prayers in Latin, although this was simple habit rather than any sense of obligation. He did compose Quenya versions of five prayers – the Our Father, Hail Mary, Glory Be, *Sub tuum praesidium* and the Litany of Loreto – but there is no suggestion he used these devotionally.[4] He also suggested learning the Canon of the Mass by heart, so that it could be recited privately if circumstances prevented one getting to Mass.[5] If this seems a daunting regimen, we should remember that as a boy he had served Fr Francis Morgan's Mass daily, and was doubtless saturated with the rhythms of the Latin liturgy.

He had a great devotion to the Blessed Sacrament, although reluctance to make his confession (which he had been brought up to think an essential preliminary) sometimes meant he abstained from Communion for a time.

Primarily, religion consisted for him of the sacraments and private prayer; he did not, like C.S. Lewis, feel under a duty to engage in public evangelism or intellectual justification of belief. He was not wholly uninvolved in the wider life of the Church, however; he had as we have seen links with the convent at Cherwell Edge, run by the nuns of the Society of the Holy Child Jesus. In 1944 he was a founder member, and Vice-President, of the Oxford Circle of the Catenians, an association of Catholic professional men. On the whole, though, corporate religion (apart from Sunday Mass) did not play an obviously great part in Tolkien's religious life; but this was not unusual amongst Catholics of his time.

He was in favour of ecumenical initiatives with other Christian bodies, but the liturgical changes of the mid- to late 1960s were not to his taste. One of his grandsons remembers him determinedly making the responses in Latin at an English-language Mass; but although the aesthetic of the reformed Rite was not his, and we may guess he disliked the style of the English translation,[6] he made no fuss about the validity of the Rite. He remained an obedient son of the Church: 'There is nowhere else to go! … there is nothing to do but to pray … the virtue of loyalty … indeed only becomes a virtue when one is under pressure to desert.'[7] Tellingly, his name does not appear amongst those who signed the petition to Pope Paul VI that secured the so-called 'Agatha Christie indult' (granted to Cardinal Heenan on, ironically enough, 5 November 1971) permitting *ad hoc* celebration of the unreformed Rite of Mass in England and Wales, although it seems very likely he was approached.[8]

He did not, in fact, have any fundamental objections to vernacular liturgy; indeed, in the last months of his life, Tolkien vigorously expressed the opinion that the greatest disaster in history was the lapse of the Goths into Arianism, at the very point when their language, which had already been used for a version of the Bible, might have been after the Byzantine (and Cyrillic) practice used in the liturgy. This would have given a strong exemplar for dignified worship in the Germanic tongues, and thus a Catholicism that would have become native to the peoples later most affected by the Protestant Reformation (he had made a similar point in a letter of 1965). He illustrated this point by reciting the Our Father in Gothic in 'splendidly sonorous tones'.[9] He was also fond of citing the Old English version of the prologue to John's Gospel, to show that English could move naturally amongst abstract concepts at a time, he said, when French was merely 'a vulgar Norman *patois*'.[10]

II – Work

The second aspect of Tolkien's Catholicism is its presence in his writings. In some ways, this presence is so structural, so basic to his imagination, that analysis of it risks (as he said of the author of *Beowulf*) pushing over the tower to see where he got his building material.

In one strong sense, Tolkien is not a professedly Catholic writer in the consciously assertive tradition of Belloc or Chesterton, and he seems deliberately to have avoided identifying himself in this way; in one of his *Beowulf* lectures, he dismisses an erroneous opinion (that he believed, as it happens wrongly, was Chesterton's) as 'Bellocian prejudice'.[11] Efforts to recruit him posthumously as a member of such an 'English Catholic tradition' should be resisted; Tolkien reckoned unthinking advocacy of lazily assumed religious prejudice in the intellectual sphere wholly pernicious, and of no service to the Faith (in a letter of 1945, he complains about a 'sentimentalist' in the *Catholic Herald* who asserted that a wholly fanciful etymology should be adopted because it was 'in keeping with Catholic tradition'[12]).

There is no organized religion in Tolkien's Middle Earth, apart from a few Númenórean ceremonies, and obviously wicked worship (with human sacrifice) of the diabolus Morgoth. His characters, overwhelmingly, are what would be conventionally thought of as virtuous pagans, although they move in a world where a creator God is acknowledged if not worshipped or prayed to. Nevertheless, Tolkien insisted to a friend, the convert and Jesuit Robert Murray, that *The Lord of the Rings* was 'a fundamentally religious and Catholic work'.[13] It is interesting to note some superficial connexions;[14] but too much should not be made of them. Many were entirely adventitious developments, not essential elements of the story; easy parallels between his story and Christianity (Frodo as a 'type' of Christ, for example) were things Tolkien himself always resisted, although they are still found amongst some of his commentators. Joseph Pearce, for example, is a serial offender in this regard: '*The Lord of the Rings* is a sublimely mystical Passion Play. The carrying of the Ring – the emblem of Sin – is the Carrying of the Cross. The mythological quest is a veritable Via Dolorosa.'[15] These may, in Tolkien's terms, be legitimate *applications* of the story, but to suggest they are its whole meaning, that the book is in fact a 'Passion Play' calquing the story of salvation, is to reduce it to a facile allegory, which (surely) he would have disapproved of, as denying the validity of the story itself. Our own tales are not simply types of Christ's, but are first of all themselves.

Insofar as any of these parallels are valid, it is only because the moral pattern of Christianity (with regard, say, to suffering and its value) is a universally valid one and thus holds for his characters as much as for anyone else. The story, he strongly insisted, is just that: a story, not an allegory of the Christian life.

George Sayer remembers Tolkien commenting on this:

> He would sometimes pull a bunch of American letters or reviews towards him and say, 'You know, they're now telling me that ...' and then he would say some of the things they'd told him about *The Lord of the Rings*. He'd say, 'You know, I never thought of that. I thought I was writing it as pure story'. He gradually came to believe some of the things that, well, you were telling him.[16]

We should not place too much stress on the last sentence. What Tolkien 'came to believe' were what he would call 'applicabilities', parallels and tropes that might be discerned precisely because they were deployed unconsciously rather than with design. If Tolkien wrote a Christian story, it is because all stories are Christian stories.

What makes Tolkien a specifically Christian writer, and his books specifically Christian books, is his absolute conviction of the power and validity, under God, of our capacity to tell stories. This is a bold and not uncontroversial claim.

The short story *Leaf by Niggle* is illuminating here. Niggle is a painter, working on a great canvas of a Tree, which is perpetually ramifying and taking over more of his life. He is also constantly interrupted; the last of these interruptions prevents him finishing the picture before he dies. After passage through Purgatory, and reconciliation with his bothersome neighbour, he finds his Tree, finished and alive, set in a landscape on the approaches to the Mountains, which are God's country, heaven. This puts in fictional form an insight Tolkien expressed forcibly to C.S. Lewis, and later put into his poem 'Mythopoeia': that our stories, particularly as they approach that high style we call 'myth', necessarily and inevitably express something of God's truth, precisely because this is what human beings do. He does not mean that stories must be allegories, in which characters and events 'stand for' particular moral or spiritual truths (in fact, he disliked this type of story); rather, any well-told tale will convey some elements of God's truth not normally or otherwise expressible. In his lecture *On Fairy Stories*, Tolkien elaborated his theory, which he called 'sub-creation': art exists, story exists, because human beings as images of God the Creator, are by nature makers. God may even choose, *Leaf by Niggle* suggests, to give a measure of primary reality (the 'Secret Fire') to these products of our secondary art:

> [the Christian] may now, perhaps, fairly dare to guess that in Fantasy
> he may actually assist in the effoliation and multiple enrichment of
> creation. All tales may come true …[17]

His concern was, however, that our stories should, properly to exercise our sub-creative faculty, not be morally or theologically inconsistent with what we know as the primary world; we have seen the lengths to which he went to devise an acceptable model of Elvish reincarnation, although (arguably) the simple fact could have stood as a given of his secondary universe.[18]

There is an unspoken question here, of course: does this 'effoliation and multiple enrichment' apply to all imaginative writing, or only to that done in an explicitly Christian context and with deliberate purpose? What about consciously anti-Christian stories? Does it also apply to them? Tolkien never addressed these specific objections, but I think it reasonable to suppose he would not have thought his theory disproved by them. This is, in fact, only to transfer a basic question of theodicy into the sphere of storytelling, and the answer would (surely) be analogous. If God's providence can encompass deliberate human evil, and (in some incalculable but real way) not just nullify it but turn it to positive good, then surely the same must be true on the (in one sense less acute) level of human storytelling. The sub-creative faculty can doubtless be turned to an evil or immoral end, but its native virtue, which is one of making, will in some fashion, and under God's mercy, assert itself. If being – existence, things, stuff, creation – is of itself good, although it can be perverted to partial ends, then the making or effoliation of it, such as storytelling is, must also be good in itself, despite (it may be) our deliberate efforts to the contrary. This is mysterious (in the technical theological sense, as well as the usual meaning of the word) but no more so than any other question of why evil exists and how a good and loving God is able not merely to tolerate it but also to incorporate it in his plan so as in some fashion to make that plan greater. We may believe this or not; it has however been the usual understanding of Christian theology since it first became articulate; and Tolkien, as we see from his own creation stories, certainly assented to it.

This doctrine of storytelling, which we might call one of implied Christian content, may be contrasted with the explicit allegorizing many claim to prefer, and indeed to detect in Tolkien's major fiction. The problem with allegory, for Tolkien as for others of similar temper, is that (as we have noted) it tends to reduce all stories to versions of a single story – characters, places, meetings within the tale, all become counters equivalent to elements in one overarching narrative of which all other stories are simply pale analogues: our tales are no more than bad versions of a Platonic archetype of human nature, or some aspect of it. Tolkien complained in his lecture On Fairy Stories of the reductive nature of 'comparative folklore'; tales can only be made 'versions' of one another by abstracting them from the particular elements that make them distinctive.[19] This tends both to undervalue the very elements characteristic to any given tale, and to devalue particular instances of created or sub-created reality.

If Tolkien disagreed with C.S. Lewis about allegory (of which Lewis was preternaturally fond), he also, in On Fairy Stories, gives clear signs he knew what later emerged as the central thesis of Lewis's Surprised by

Joy, and may be his most original contribution to Christian apologetics: 'joy' itself, an indescribable desire awoken by particular encounters (very often literary), and pointing always beyond itself to what, Lewis eventually determined, is a signpost to God. Tolkien writes, first, of fairy stories 'If they awakened *desire*, satisfying it while often whetting it unbearably, they succeeded'; then, speaking of the particular emotion evoked by what he called the *eucatastrophe*, the unexpected happy ending, he says:

> It does not deny the existence of *dyscatastrophe*, of sorrow and failure: the possibility of these is necessary to the joy of deliverance; it denies (in the face of much evidence, if you will) universal final defeat and in so far is *evangelium*, giving a fleeting glimpse of Joy, Joy beyond the walls of the world, poignant as grief.[20]

Two things are notable here; first, that Tolkien characteristically sees 'Joy' in the context of the northern theory of courage, of the prospect of 'universal final defeat'; second, that although this lecture (in its developed form at least) precedes Lewis's *Surprised by Joy* by a good dozen years, we should be shy of claiming Tolkien as somehow the source of Lewis's theory: Lewis had made various attempts to describe and explain this crucial element in his religious experience before this time, notably in the preface to the 1943 edition of *The Pilgrim's Regress*, his 'allegorical apology for Christianity, Reason and Romanticism', written at much the same time as Tolkien expanded the lecture and presumably therefore much in the air of the Inklings' discussions that year. He had also begun an account of it in 1930, formalizing hints in his diaries of the previous decade, and an abortive verse account two years later, before, in September of 1932, writing *The Pilgrim's Regress*, which implies the later theory even if it does not, exactly, state it.[21] Lewis's 'Joy', rather, had (like Tolkien's 'sub-creation') become part of the common stock of ideas alive in their circle.

Recent writers on what we might call Tolkien's religious aesthetic (Verlyn Flieger, Stratford Caldecott) have given prominence to his use of light as a fundamental symbol of God's presence, and its purity or tainting as a sign of the working-out of his providential purposes in accord with, or in despite of, created wills. The light of the Trees is qualitatively different from the later lights of sun and moon, holier, more life-giving; its memory stays with the Eldar and in some sense transfigures them, whilst its enduring presence in the Silmarils, in Eärendel's star and latterly in Galadriel's glass, is both physical reminder of hope and, in several instances, an operative instance of it. By making its wearer invisible, the Ring makes him untouchable by light, and thus cut off from the presence of God, confined to the blind realm of the Fallen One.[22] Stratford Caldecott remarks,

> original sin ... also resulted in a kind of invisibility, as Adam hid from the Lord in the forest of Eden: 'But the Lord God called to the man, and said to him, "Where are you?"'[23]

As was mentioned earlier, Tolkien's constant theme was 'death: inevitable death'. The 'message' of *Leaf by Niggle*, inasmuch as it can be reduced to a single item, is that death is not the end of sub-creation, but a way to the fulfilment of it, to the achieving of what we had long ago despaired of ever finishing, let alone of bringing to the very perfection that, in vision, had inspired us: to its incorporation into the loving plan of God.

This is one of Tolkien's approaches to the problem; the other is through the elves: they are above all makers, of song, story, works of hand and mind, freed from the limits imposed by a human life-span and gifted with skill beyond human measure. They are arch-sub-creators who are yet bounded by the world in a way men are not. The Silmarils are the great embodiment of elvish art; but they are also the cause of their maker's ruin, and that of his whole people, who are caught by selfish love of what has been made, rather than joy in the making and giving. An image of God-given beauty can, too easily, become an idol; the elven dilemma is our own writ large.

There is, then, at the heart of Tolkien's work a conviction that what we say, and in particular the tales we tell, expresses as well as anything else we do the image we bear of the Creator God, the gift granted our first parents, not wholly lost by them in the Fall and now redeemed – both rescued from debility and made new and greater – by the Incarnation. Even death, which Tolkien once named as his greatest theme, is now not wholly a defeat, but a means despite itself of greater victory, beyond hope or expectation.

He also gives a profound, if unfashionable, reflexion on the nature of evil, and the temporary and provisional nature of our victories over it in this life, whether small and private victories over vice or great national triumphs over a tyrant or oppressor. In one sense, the northern theory of courage was true: defeat, in this world, was inevitable, and all our hopes and schemes and efforts would fail. But this was still the proper side to fight on, and courage in its service was the only proper attitude. Tom Shippey puts it thus: 'dying undaunted is no defeat; furthermore … this was true before the Christian myth that came to explain why'[24]. The Christian revelation does not abolish 'northern courage'; rather it fulfils and redeems it, because it adds that, beyond the end of all things in defeat and fire, there is a new life, and a redeemed world, healed from its hurts and new-made according to its Creator's mind, only this time further enriched and made beautiful by the works of his children. This is the whole burden, in one sense, of *The Silmarillion*, from its creation story to its prophecy of the End. Tolkien's elves are bound to the circles of the world, and endure whilst it does, tending and making as they live, enfolded in and in some way giving voice to its joys and sorrows; but man's fate lies beyond the world, in the good counsels of the One.

References

Chapter 1 - Early Years

1. *HME*, 9.233.
2. See Max Mechow, *Deutsche Familiennamen prussischer Herkunft*, Dieburg, Tolkemita, 1994.
3. *Letters*, pp. 428–9.
4. Cf. *Letters*, p. 73.
5. 'Reuel', 'friend of God', is from the Hebrew scriptures, where (in Exodus 2:18 and Numbers 10:29) it is an alternative name for Moses' father-in-law, elsewhere called Jethro (modern criticism detects here the conflation of two separate traditions), and, in the extended form Raguel, of Tobias's father-in-law in the book of Tobit, and also the name of several otherwise unattested Israelites.
6. *HME* 5.37.
7. *Letters*, pp. 68, 213.
8. Carpenter prints an example of it in *Biography*, p. 36.
9. *OFS*, p. 188.
10. Atherton, *There and Back Again*, p. 40.
11. See *OFS*, pp. 107–8.
12. The Barry buildings were demolished in 1936, allegedly as a fire risk, and the school moved to its current site, an undistinguished complex in Edgbaston. Part of an upper corridor of the Barry building was moved brick by brick, and re-erected to act as school chapel.
13. Slim had in fact been brought up as a Catholic, and was at the Oratorian school, St Philip's, between 1903 and 1908, when he went to King Edward's; Tolkien was briefly at St Philip's in 1902–3, but for the rest of his schooldays (1900–11) was at King Edward's, whilst Slim left King Edward's within a year of arriving to work as a schoolmaster.
14. She was a schoolteacher in Birmingham between 1892 and 1905. See Morton, *Tolkien's Bag End*, p. 28.
15. Carpenter, *Biography*, p. 31.
16. *Letters*, p. 416 (to Michael Tolkien, 24 January 1972).
17. *Letters*, p. 354 (to Michael Tolkien, 9–10 January 1965).
18. The school was based there until 1922, when it moved to Caversham outside Reading.
19. *Letters*, pp. 416–17 (to Michael Tolkien, 24 January 1972).
20. See *OFS*, p. 108.
21. So, at least, suggest Flieger and Anderson in their edition of *OFS* (pp. 56, 108); although we should also note in the same volume (p. 234) that Tolkien said his boyhood reading of fairy tales finished when he was eight. It is possible he was mistaken about dates, as he often was; or, although this would be a rather forced reading of the text, that he meant he stopped reading new stories, as opposed to rereading old ones.
22. *Letters*, p. 395 (to Michael Tolkien, 1967/8).
23. See Fox-Davies, *Armorial Families*, vol. 2, p. 1629, and 'Francis Vincent Reade', *Oratory Parish Magazine* (early 2007), pp. 2–3 (No. 1 of the series 'Fathers of the Birmingham Oratory'). H&S 2, p. 814, says he was born c.1895; Fox-Davies states 1874, which is much more probable.

24. See Garth, pp. 22–4, and H&S 2, pp. 952–3.

25. In 1908, as part of the Haldane reforms of the Army after the Boer War, where there had been a shortage of trained officers, Army Order 160 incorporated existing school cadet corps across the country into a national Officer Training Corps (OTC). The aim was to give basic military training (drill, musketry, map-reading, fieldwork) to boys who might then go on to commissions in the regular or territorial forces. Successful cadets were given a certificate by their OTC that would gain them preferential consideration for commissioned rank. The King Edward's School cadet corps may not have formally become an OTC until 1910; see H&S 2, p. 952.

26. Wiseman's father held this position in 1912; from 1914, he was also President of the National Free Church Council. In 1932, various separate Methodist bodies joined together in the Methodist Union; Wiseman senior was its second President.

27. *Letters*, p. 395 (to Michael Tolkien, 1967/8).

28. See H&S 1, p. 9. Hammond and Scull date the purchase to 1903, on uncertain grounds.

29. See the catalogue to the Bodleian Library's Tolkien centenary exhibition (Priestman, *J.R.R. Tolkien, Life and Legend*, p. 16), and Atherton, *There and Back Again*, p. 183.

30. See *Letters*, p. 212.

31. It might possibly have been, instead, Sweet's *First Steps in Anglo-Saxon*. For a useful discussion of Tolkien's first encounter with philology, see chapter 13 of Atherton's *There and Back Again* (pp. 183–203).

32. *Letters*, p. 343 (to the Rev. Denis Tyndall, 9 January 1964).

33. See the lecture 'English and Welsh' in *M&C*, pp. 190–1.

34. There is a very extensive literature on the Modernist crisis, most of it partisan from one side or another. There is a useful summary of 'Modernist' positions and partial attempt at justifying the Church's actions, in Aidan Nichols, *Criticising the Critics* (Oxford, Family Publications, 2010), chapter 1, the best short account of the phenomenon as a whole remains Alec Vidler, *A Variety of Catholic Modernists* (London, Cambridge University Press, 1970), although Vidler, as a liberal Anglican, obviously brings his own preconceptions to the account.

35. *Letters*, p. 395 (to Michael Tolkien, 1967/8).

36. See H&S 2, p.1012, and corrigenda to it at http://www.hammondandscull.com/addenda.html.

37. See Duriez, *J.R.R. Tolkien: The Making of a Legend*, pp. 33, 222.

38. His private diaries have never been published, and are not available for public consultation; however Humphrey Carpenter, Tolkien's official biographer, drew on them for his biography.

39. See *Letters*, pp. 356–8, which include a facsimile of the inscription.

40. £60 in 1910 apparently equates to about £6,000 today.

41. *Letters*, p. 52 (to Michael Tolkien, 6–8 March 1941).

42. I have no idea whether this is still true, although it would be a tearing shame if it were not; I was certainly made to read him (aloud) as a schoolboy in the early 1980s, and in hindsight see this as a wholly profitable experience for which I remain profoundly grateful.

43. See the 1919 collection *Pastiches et mélanges*.

44. Cited in the article by John Garth in *TEnc*, p. 220.

45. These are all taken from 'Sister Songs'; see *The Poems of Francis Thompson* (London, Hollis and Carter, 1946), pp. 23–60.

46. See Carpenter, *Biography*, pp. 73–4. The comment was first made by the poet and critic Arthur Symons about the novelist George Meredith's verse. This Symons should not be confused with the biographer A.J.A. Symons (*The Quest for Corvo*), brother to the crime writer Julian Symons, nor any of them with the historian and homosexual proselytizer John Addington (J.A.) Symonds. All are roughly contemporary, which does not help.

47. See H&S 2, p. 815.

48. See *HME* 10.157–8, where Tolkien explicitly acknowledges the link.

49. Quoted in Carpenter, *Biography*, p. 47.

50. Quoted in Carpenter, *Biography*, pp. 47–8.

51. In 1917, two girls in Yorkshire, one sixteen and one nine, took five photographs that were made famous by Conan Doyle in a magazine article; half a century later, they confessed to having faked them, but claimed to have been too intimidated by the weight of adult interest (particularly from theosophists and spiritualists of one stripe or another) to admit the fraud at the time.

52. 'The Cottage of Lost Play'. See Chapter 3.V below.

53. All of these are conveniently included in the volume *Time and the Gods* (London, Gollancz, 2000) in the excellent Gollancz Fantasy Masterworks series.

54. *The Watcher by the Threshold*, in the portmanteau edition *Four Tales* (Edinburgh, William Blackwood, 1936), p. 240.

55. Likewise in *Four Tales*, pp. 622–32, esp. pp. 627–30.

56. H&S 1, p. 26.

57. Compare, at a slightly later date, the lyrical nostalgia of Cyril Connolly's *Enemies of Promise*; or the account of Ronald Knox's Etonian career in Evelyn Waugh's biography.

58. For Jane Neave, see Andrew H. Morton and John Hayes's careful and illuminating *Tolkien's Gedling 1914* (Studley, Brewin Books, 2008).

59. The only evidence for this visit is a drawing Tolkien did of *St Andrews from Kinkell Brae*; see H&S 1, p. 20.

60. *Letters*, p. 393 (to Michael Tolkien, 1967–8).

61. See Chapter 8.IV below.

62. See Carpenter, *Biography*, p. 51, and Zimmermann, Manfred, 'The Origin of Gandalf and Josef Madlener' in *Mythlore*, 34 (1983), pp. 22, 24.

Chapter 2 – University and Edith

1   The exception was the elder Payton brother, Wilfrid, who went up to Cambridge in the autumn of 1911.

2   Tolkien's obituary in *The Times*, drafted by C.S. Lewis, and reprinted in Salu and Farrell (eds), *J.R.R. Tolkien, Scholar and Storyteller*, pp. 11–15.

3   It was eventually annexed to his legendarium, and, titled *The Horns of Ylmir*, is printed (in a version made in 1917) in *HME* 4.213–18. Hammond and Scull (H&S 1, p. 54) are inclined to place this visit to St Andrews in the summer, rather than at Easter; but after April, Jane Neave was living on the farm in Nottinghamshire she had bought with the Brooke-Smiths, not at St Andrews at all, and it seems reasonable to suppose he went there to see her. The 1912 Easter vacation ran from 16 March to 28 April; Tolkien was in Birmingham for the annual King Edward's Open Debate on 2 April, but April is otherwise unoccupied. Easter fell that year on 7 April.

4   The poem remains unpublished. See H&S 1, pp. 25, 776, where, however, it is placed, following a manuscript note, in June or July 1911; but this must be a mistake by Tolkien, since the Newdigate is open only to undergraduate members of the University, and he did not matriculate until that October.

5   The play was called *The Bloodhound, the Chef, and the Suffragette*; it has, needless to say, never been published. See Carpenter, *Biography*, p. 59.

6   Quoted in Tolkien, *The Tolkien Family Album*, p. 34.

7   See *OFS*, p. 41.

8   Shippey, *Road*, p. 24.

9   Revision by D.Q. Adams in the 1997 *Encyclopedia of Indo-European Culture* (London, Routledge, 1997), p. 501. There is a further, radically different attempt, published in 2007 (see: www.kortlandt. nl) by the Dutch scholar Frederik Kortlandt: 'ʕʷeuis ʔkeuskʷeʕʷeuis iosmi ʕuelʔn neʔst ʔekuns ʔe ‹dērkt, tom ‹gʷrʕeum uogom ugentm, tom m›geʕm borom, tom dgmenm ʔoʔku brentm. ʔe ueukʷt ʕʷeuis ʔkumus: kʷntske ʔmoi kērt ʕnerm ui›denti ʔekuns ʕ›gentm. ʔe ueukʷnt ʔkeus: kludi ʕʷuei, kʷntske nsmi kērt ui›dntsu: ʕnēr potis ʕʷuiom ʕulʔenm subi gʷormom uestrom kʷrneuti, ʕʷuimus kʷe ʕuelʔn neʔsti. To›d kekluus ʕʷeuis ʕe›grom ʔe bēu›gd.'

10   More ambitious efforts, too, have been made to recover the nature and characteristic themes and vocabulary of proto-Indo-European folktales; see Calvert Watkins's fascinating *How to Kill a Dragon: Aspects of Indo-European Poetics* (Oxford, OUP, 1995), or the comprehensive and eclectic *Indo-European Poetry and Myth* of M.L. West (Oxford, OUP, 2007), which culminates in a reconstructed 'Elegy on an Indo-European Hero', done in modern English.

11   There is, indeed, still much research done into this topic; see, for example, J.P. Mallory and D.Q. Adams (eds), *The Oxford Introduction to Proto-Indo-European and the Proto-Indo-European World* (Oxford, OUP, 2006).

12 *Letters*, p. 214 (to W.H. Auden, 7 June 1955); Tolkien first borrowed Eliot's *Finnish Grammar* on 25 November 1911.

13 Kirby's version appeared first in 1907. Tolkien, as we saw, wrote a verse pastiche of Kirby called 'The New Lemminkäinen'; Hammond and Scull call it a parody, but I suspect it to be closer in intention to his earlier Macaulay pastiche, *The Battle of the Eastern Field*.

14 Essay on the *Kalevala*, quoted in H&S 1, p. 29.

15 *Letters*, p. 214 (to W.H. Auden, 7 June 1955); see the journal *Parma Eldalamberon*, 12 (1998), pp. iv, x–xi, and Garth, p. 17.

16 See Garth, p. 24.

17 See H&S 1, p. 39.

18 His resignation was dated 28 February, when he was in the midst of Honour Moderations, although this may be purely an administrative quirk. It seems most likely that Tolkien resigned because he could not afford the time, and perhaps also the expense, of membership; it is also coincidentally the case that in 1913 King Edward's Horse was transferred from the Volunteer Forces to the Special Reserve, a distinct social downgrading (the Special Reserve was the successor of the old militia, and functioned as home training units for (largely) working-class men, whereas the Volunteers, and especially the mounted Yeomanry, were both middle class and expected to function as active service units during wartime). They remained a cavalry regiment, though, and as such saw service in France and Italy. They were disbanded in 1924.

19 C.S. Lewis's diaries, quoted in McGrath, *C.S.Lewis: A Life*, p. 99.

20 Ker, *The Dark Ages*, pp. 104–5.

21 *The Dark Ages* was published first in 1904, as part of a series 'Periods of European Literature' published by Blackwood; Tolkien certainly read it at some stage, for he quotes extensively from it in lectures given in the early 1930s (see Chapter 7 below).

22 He published, in 1892, a scientific *Grammar of the Dialect of Windhill in the West Riding of Yorkshire*, on his mother dialect.

23 Shippey in particular cites *Lear* and *Macbeth*; according to Hammond and Scull (H&S 1, p. 40), the Oxford syllabus at this time prescribed *Love's Labours Lost*, the two *Henry IVs*, *Hamlet* and *Antony and Cleopatra*. We may however assume Tolkien brought a good working knowledge of much Shakespeare from his schooldays.

24 Carpenter, *Biography*, pp. 67–8.

25 Carpenter, *Biography*, pp. 67–8.

26 See Carpenter, *Biography*, p. 54, and H&S 1, p. 46. This incident cannot be located more precisely than the academic year 1913–14, if Smith was indeed the 'Geoffrey' whom Tolkien names as his cohort in the business.

27 John Garth (Garth, p. 33) has suggested he deputed Smith to write to the others, but this remains unproven. See H&S 2, p. 778. At any rate they were told of the engagement by letter.

28 *M&C*, p. 192.

29 Some of these are reproduced in Hammond and Scull's *J.R.R. Tolkien: Artist & Illustrator*. They are curious and occasionally striking, if technically unremarkable.

Chapter 3 – War

1 Sir John (he was knighted in 1914) inherited his father's business as a building contractor, and was a local worthy; he was also educated at King Edward's. His military experience, as far as I can determine, was entirely in the voluntary reserves rather than the Regular Army.

2 For the history of the farm, of Jane Neave's time there and of Tolkien's 1914 visit, see Morton and Hayes, *Tolkien's Gedling 1914*.

3 Tolkien used this term himself in a number of letters written between 1951 and 1955; it is used historically to describe collections of saints' lives, but seems to have become accepted shorthand amongst writers on Tolkien, so I have adopted it for convenience.

4 See, here, *Letters*, p. 231 (to 'Mr Thompson', 14 January 1956).

5 The Magnificat antiphon for Evening Prayer (Vespers) on 21 December. The English is from the current Breviary; the Latin text is *O Oriens, splendor lucis æternæ et sol iustitiæ: veni, et illumine*

sedentes in tenebris et umbra mortis. Oriens would seem to be the rising sun rather than the morning star, and this would be supported by the occurrence of *sol iustitiæ* later in the antiphon. On the other hand, the scriptural source is from the canticle of Zechariah in Luke's Gospel, which in its second part is addressed to John the Baptist.

6 One of the tenth-century *Blickling Homilies* refers to John the Baptist as *se niwa éorendel*; see *Letters*, p. 385.

7 Ker, *The Dark Ages*, p. 66.

8 *Letters*, p. 144 (to Milton Waldman, late 1951).

9 See Garth, p. 48.

10 Carpenter, *Biography*, p. 72.

11 Two years later, C.S. Lewis was to suffer much anxious fear of being conscripted into the ranks (although as an Irishman he was exempt) or being morally bullied into enlisting, before he too discovered the Oxford OTC as a route to a commission: see McGrath, *C.S. Lewis: A Life*, pp. 43–7.

12 See Carpenter, *Biography*, p. 75, *HME* 2.2613 and Garth, p. 53.

13 See *HME* 2.269–70, where part of one late text is given.

14 See H&S 2, pp. 106–7.

15 He worked on *The Story of Kullervo* for at least two years, but it was never finished. It runs to twenty-one foolscap pages, and covers about three-quarters of the projected narrative. It was published in the journal *Tolkien Studies* for 2010 (vol.7, pp. 211–78). There is an abstract in H&S 2, pp. 445–6; see also H&S 1, p. 55.

16 For these letters and their content, see H&S 1, pp. 56–7.

17 See Garth, p. 100.

18 Smith's then unit was training in Oxford, and he was billeted at Magdalen College.

19 This early text, which Tolkien came to call *Qenyaqetsa*, was published in *Parma Eldalamberon*, 12 (1998); it was also used to compile the nominal appendices to *HME* 1 and *HME* 2.

20 See H&S 1, pp. 58–9.

21 *HME* 1.136.

22 See here Garth, pp. 95–100.

23 Garth, p. 98.

24 It was sent to France as part of the 25th Division in September 1915.

25 These included 'The Princess Ní', another short imagistic poem about a fairy, written on 9 July. It was published in 1924.

26 The earliest text of the poem is in Carpenter, *Biography*, pp. 76–7; a later revision (perhaps as late as 1924) is in *HME* 2.271–2.

27 It was published in 1920, and again (with very light revisions) in 1923; it was further revised in 1940, but not then republished. The original and the 1940 texts are in *HME* 2.273–7.

28 'Kortirion among the Trees', 1915 version, lines 80–2; in *HME* 1.34.

29 Garth, p. 76.

30 'Narqelion' was written between November 1915 and March 1916; four lines from it are given in Carpenter, *Biography*, pp. 75–6, the complete text in *Mythlore*, 15 (1988), pp. 47–52, and *Vinyar Tengwar*, 6 (July 1989), pp. 12–13.

31 The vestigial proto-mythology of early 1916 is well summarized by John Garth: see Garth, pp. 125–9.

32 Various texts of it, with commentary, are printed in *HME* 2.295–300.

33 Rob Gilson, 30 June 1916: quoted in Garth, p. 151.

34 Late interview, quoted in Garth, p. 138.

35 It appeared in a collection of *Leeds University Verse* published in 1924; it is reprinted in Garth, p. 145.

36 See *Letters*, p. 78.

37 *Letters*, p. 10 (to Geoffrey Smith, 12 August 1916).

38 H&S 1, p. 88.

39 H&S 1, p. 89.

40 Edmund Blunden, 'Thiepval Wood' (written in September 1916).

41 Carpenter, *Biography*, p. 84.

42 Presumably named after Staufen-im-Breisgau in the Black Forest, where, legend has it, Dr Faustus sold his soul to the devil; many German trench systems were given this sort of name, perhaps initially by troops from the area named.

43 It is reproduced in the catalogue of the centenary exhibition, Priestman (ed.), *J.R.R. Tolkien, Life and Legend*, p. 32.

44 The following March, the ship that had carried Tolkien was torpedoed by a German submarine and sank with the loss of all its crew; the sick and wounded, fortunately, had already been disembarked.

45 Francis Thompson, 'The Mistress of Vision' (*The Poems of Francis Thompson*, pp. 283–9).

46 Quoted in Carpenter, *Biography*, p. 86.

47 There is an extant manuscript of *The Fall of Gondolin* (actually titled *Tuor and the Exiles of Gondolin*, but invariably referred to by Tolkien under the familiar name) in Edith's handwriting; it seems to date from 1919 or early 1920, however, rather than from this period (see *HME* 2.146–7).

48 See Garth, p. 186.

49 *Letters*, p. 78 (to Christopher Tolkien, 6 May 1944).

50 See *HME* 2.290–2, and Garth, p. 226.

51 *HME* 2.323.

52 *HME* 2.290.

53 *HME* 2.304.

54 *HME* 1.31. Two versions of the poem, titled 'You and Me and the Cottage of Lost Play', are given in *HME* 1.28–31. Christopher Tolkien points out that it includes a clear reference to Francis Thompson's mawkish poem 'Daisy'.

55 Dale Nelson (*TEnc*, p. 375) lists only three direct references (in a letter of 1972, an interview, and the poem 'The Mewlips' of, originally, 1927), all to stories from the 1912 collection *The Book of Wonder*.

56 There is an account of these two earliest lexicons in *HME* 1.246ff. They have been published in the journal *Parma Eldalamberon*, 11 (1995) and 12 (1998, revised 2011).

57 See *HME* 1.99.

58 *HME* 2.70.

59 These casualty figures are from Garth's essay 'Tolkien, Exeter College, and the Great War' published online at http://www.johngarth.co.uk/php/tolkien_exeter_great_war.php. In absolute terms, of 771 Exonians who served in the armed forces in the Great War, 141 were killed: fully two and a half years' worth of undergraduate intake, or 18 per cent – one in five – of those who fought. See also Garth, pp. 249–50.

60 There is an interesting anecdote in the (highly literate) spy-thriller *Tomorrow's Ghost* by Anthony Price: 'But he [Tolkien] was fascinated by trenches, certainly ... I can remember meeting him in the High once – at Oxford. He was standing in the rain watching workmen digging a trench in the road, absolutely transfixed by them ...' (Grafton edition, 1990, p. 44). This may be fictional, or may not: Price has lived in Oxford for much of his life, and (after Merton between 1949 and 1952, during Tolkien's time as a professorial fellow there) worked as a journalist on various Oxford papers, ending as editor of *The Oxford Times*. *Tomorrow's Ghost* was first published in 1979, and probably written the year before, as it refers to *The Silmarillion*, and Carpenter's biography, as 'just out'.

61 *Letters*, p. 46 (to Michael Tolkien, 6 October 1940).

Chapter 4 – The Young Scholar

1 See the obituary in *Interpreters*, pp. 172–91.

2 The *OED* was at the time Tolkien worked for it usually known as the *New English Dictionary* or *NED*, although the more familiar title had appeared on its covers since 1895.

3 See Gilliver, Marshall and Weiner, *The Ring of Words*, for a good account of his time at the *OED*.

4 *A Spring Harvest*, published by Erskine Macdonald, London. R.W. Reynolds had arranged for it to be considered by Sidgwick and Jackson, but they were no more interested in Smith's verse than they had been in Tolkien's. Eight of the poems are printed in an appendix to Mark Atherton's *There and Back Again*; a new edition is being prepared by the American Tolkienist Douglas A. Anderson. Tolkien also inherited some of Smith's books of Celtic scholarship.

5 See Garth, pp. 250–1.

6 A New Zealander of Scots descent, Rutherford was the (in 1919 newly appointed) Director of the Cavendish Laboratory and a pioneer of nuclear physics. He devised his model of atomic structure (nucleus and orbiting electrons) in 1911, and it has been universally adopted. He was the first to 'split

the atom' in 1917; in 1920 he discovered the proton, and he was at the time Wiseman worked with him hypothesizing the existence of the neutron (it was demonstrated by one of his pupils in 1932). He is reckoned the 'father of nuclear physics'; his pupils were central to the wartime Manhattan Project (Rutherford himself died suddenly in 1937, aged only sixty-six, of a strangulated hernia).

7   For Sisam, no experience was it seems ever wholly wasted: in an article published in 1925, his knowl-edge of the pig meat market contributed one of the grounds for arguing an Elizabethan printing of an Old English law code was not genuine but a sixteenth-century fake – see his *Studies in the History of Old English Literature*, pp. 240–1.

8   See *HME* 1 and 2, ad loc.

9   The order of the Tales in the published text in *HME* 1 and 2 reflects that of the later *Silmarillion*, not that of composition.

10 *HME* 2.242.

11 *HME* 2.278–334, 'The History of Eriol or Ælfwine'.

12 *HME* 2.287–8.

13 *Modern Language Review*, 14 (1919), pp. 202–5.

14 The *Letter of Alexander* is reckoned to derive, in some part, from the lost *Indica* of the fifth-century BC Greek doctor Ctesias of Cnidos, physician at the Persian royal court, who also wrote a history of Persia; both works survive only in fragments. An Indian legend would not necessarily feel alien; the mythological as well as etymological connexions between India and Europe had been thoroughly and convincingly established in the nineteenth century. The great popular advocate of India and Indian material as archetypally explanatory was Max Müller, whose conclusions Tolkien distrusted; but he had probably read him with attention (see *OFS*, pp. 41, 74).

15 Cockayne, Oswald, *Narratiunculae Anglice Conscriptae* (London, I.R. Smith, 1861), pp. 51ff; W.M. Baskervill, 'The Anglo-Saxon Version of the *Epistola Alexandri ad Aristotelem*', *Anglia*, 4 (1881), pp. 139–67.

16 *Modern Language Review*, 14 (1919), pp. 203, 204.

17 It may well be, also, that a relevant passage either appeared in a volume of extracts illustrative of dialectical phonology, or had been privately extracted by Sisam for teaching purposes, since he noted that the unexpected 'Mercian' form *triow* (instead of the usual 'west-Saxonized' *treow*) is found fifteen times in the text, all in this passage (see Sisam, 'The Compilation of the Beowulf Manuscript' in *Studies in the History of Old English Literature*, p. 93, first published in that collection in 1953). He, or another, may well have lighted on the trees for philological reasons, which would have interested Tolkien also, and which served to bring the content of the text to Tolkien's attention.

18 *OFS*, p. 68.

19 Steele's 1894 children's book, *The Story of Alexander*, pp. 158–70, esp. p. 165; see H&S 2, p. 174. It is a finely illustrated and bound volume that would surely have appealed to the same side of the young Tolkien that later relished Morris's tales.

20 See *Interpreters*, p.108.

21 Quoted in *Interpreters*, p. 182.

22 *Letters*, p. 56.

23 See H&S 1, p. 109.

24 Printed in *Parma Eldalamberon*, 15 (2004), pp.31–40.

25 *HME* 2.321.

26 See *Letters*, p. 56.

27 Shippey, *Author*, p. xii; his italics.

28 Tolkien's diary for January 1922, quoted in Carpenter, *Biography*, p. 104.

29 'The Song of Right and Wrong', first published in the January 1913 *New Witness*, contains the famous stanza, 'Tea, although an Oriental, / Is a gentleman at least; / Cocoa is a cad and coward, / Cocoa is a vulgar beast, / Cocoa is a dull, disloyal, / Lying, crawling cad and clown, / And may very well be grateful / To the fool that takes him down.' This was universally taken, probably fairly, as an attack on the *Daily News*, a Liberal paper Chesterton had written much for in the past but had fallen out with over the Marconi scandal; it was owned by George Cadbury, the cocoa magnate, and was widely known as 'the Cocoa Press'.

30 They, and two other poems, are printed by Shippey in an appendix to *Road*. The original mimeo-graphed booklet was only ever produced for private circulation amongst Leeds students (presumably as song-books for Viking Club meetings). In 1935 or 1936, one of them, A.H. (Hugh) Smith, by

then teaching at UCL and a stalwart of place-name studies (he later succeeded Chambers as Quain Professor), had his students print a selection of the songs as an exercise in book production – Smith had obtained a working hand-press for the College. This small booklet was titled *Songs for the Philologists*; Smith quickly realized he had not asked either Tolkien or Gordon for permission to publish their work, and so most of the copies printed were withdrawn from distribution, and were later lost in a fire. Tolkien later commented that, in any case, the texts were in many places badly garbled in reproduction.

31 Shippey, *Road*, p. 402; he translates, 'The oak will fall into the fire, losing joy and leaf and life. The birch shall keep its glory long, shine in splendour over the bright plain' (*Road*, p. 403).

32 See, here, Shippey, *Road*, esp. pp. 316–17.

33 Bodley 34 contains five texts: lives of SS Catherine of Alexandria, Juliana of Nicomedia, and Margaret of Antioch; the admonitory *Hali Meiðhad*; and a treatise on the soul, its friends and enemies, *Sawles Warde* (translated from a Latin original sometimes attributed to Anselm). The *Ancrene Riwle*, a handbook for anchoresses which exists in multiple manuscripts and several versions, is another product of the same school or author; there are also six short devotional pieces, usually called the 'Wooing Group' (after the first of them, *Þe Wohunge of Ure Lauerd*), addressed to a similar audience and in the same literary dialect.

34 Quoted Carpenter, *Biography*, p. 106.

35 'The Nameless Land' was published in 1927, in an anthology done to benefit a children's hospital, and never reprinted, although later revised and attributed to Ælfwine; texts are in *HME* 5.98–104.

36 Jason Fisher, 'Tolkien and Source Criticism', in Fisher (ed.), *Tolkien and the Study of his Sources*, p. 40.

37 Kingsley Amis, introduction to *The Faber Popular Reciter* (London, Faber & Faber, 1978), pp. 17–18.

38 It was published in *Parma Eldalamberon*, 14 (2003), pp. 35–86, edited by Carl Hostetter and Bill Welden, under the title 'Early Qenya Grammar'.

39 These early Noldorin texts are collected in *Parma Eldalamberon*, 13 (2001).

40 See H&S 1, p. 124.

41 The 1923 review appeared in January 1925; that for 1924, which ran to thirty pages, in March 1926; and that for 1925, fully thirty-five pages, in February 1927.

42 *Review of English Studies*, 1, no. 1 (January 1925), pp. 4–23, reprinted as a pamphlet by Sidgwick and Jackson that same year. I cite references from the reprint.

43 Chambers, 'Recent Research', p. 20.

44 Chambers, 'Recent Research', p. 13.

45 *Review of English Studies*, 1, no. 3 (July 1925), pp. 331–6.

46 Drout, Michael D.C. (ed.), *Beowulf and the Critics by J.R.R. Tolkien*, revised second edition (Tempe, AZ, ACMRS, 2011), p. 68.

47 See Shippey's article 'Scholars of Medieval Literature, Influence of', in *TEnc*, pp. 594–8, esp. pp. 596–7.

48 Chambers, *Widsith*, pp. 1–2.

49 Garth, p. 229.

50 Although, oddly enough, Cambridge University Press reprinted the unrevised (1898) edition of Wyatt in 1914 also (that, at least, is the date in my copy).

51 Chambers published an expanded edition in 1932; in 1959, a third edition was issued with a supplement by C.L. Wrenn, incorporating more recent scholarship.

52 *M&C*, p. 12. 'Heroic Age' in Chambers's title was a reference to Hector Chadwick's 1912 book *The Heroic Age*, which examines a conspectus of 'heroic' verse from across Europe, from Homer to medieval Serbian epic.

53 *The Library* (Transactions of the Bibliographical Society), 4th series, 5, no. 4 (March 1925), pp. 293–321.

54 Shippey, *Author*, p. 62.

55 *Letters*, p. 20 (to C.A. Furth of Allen & Unwin, 31 August 1937).

56 For more on Chambers, see the obituary for the British Academy, reprinted in *Interpreters*, pp. 221–33.

57 Bradley had died in 1923, so the reference was presumably one provided when Tolkien applied to Leeds.

58 Mawer had considered applying for the chair himself. Tolkien probably knew him through the

English Place-Name Society, which Mawer had founded in 1923 and which Tolkien had joined at its inception; Tolkien's student Hugh Smith (the one who eventually printed *Songs for the Philologists*) had done a doctoral thesis on Yorkshire place-names, and Mawer had perhaps been involved, most likely as an external examiner.

59 Quoted in H&S 2, p. 349.

60 In 1916 Sisam had published a short but important article on the *Beowulf* manuscript (reprinted in *Studies in the History of Old English Literature*, pp. 61–4, immediately before a later piece expanding on the question), and in 1923 both an edition of a previously unpublished Old English translation of one of St Boniface's letters (reprinted in *Studies in the History of Old English Literature*, pp. 199–224) and a long review article exposing some reputed Old English law codes as sixteenth-century pastiche; in 1925, he followed up the latter piece with a conclusive rebuttal of objections to it (collected in *Studies in the History of Old English Literature*, pp. 232–58).

61 *Letters*, p. 13.

62 Francis Fortescue 'Sligger' Urquhart was elected Fellow of Balliol in 1896, and was the first Catholic don since the sixteenth century. By 1925, however, Catholic dons were less unusual: both the Jesus Professor of Celtic, John Fraser, and the Regius Professor of Civil Law, Francis de Zulueta, were Catholic: the latter stood godfather to Priscilla Tolkien.

63 Quoted in *TMed*, p. 16.

64 Reprinted in *M&C*, p. 238.

65 The Leeds professorship had brought £800 a year. The £1,000 seems to have been a concession to new circumstances; as we saw, Craigie had been told to make do with £600 a year, and the chair had been omitted from a salary review in 1920 on the grounds that Craigie also enjoyed a salary from the *OED*; he not unnaturally thought this reasoning bogus, and it seems to have soured his relations with the English Faculty (particularly with Joseph Wright, to whose influence he attributed the decision) and led in part to his eventual resignation. See the British Academy obituary of Craigie, reprinted in *Interpreters*, pp. 173–91, esp. pp. 181–2.

66 He had in fact been an external examiner for Oxford Final Schools since 1923, presumably for similar reasons.

Chapter 5 – Oxford and Storytelling

1 Ker, *The Dark Ages*, p. 141 (on the Venerable Bede).

2 We are more than usually reliant on secondary sources for this period of Tolkien's life; his published *Letters* contain nothing between 1925, the year of his election to the Chair of Anglo-Saxon, and 1937, when *The Hobbit* was in proof. There is some useful material in H&S 1, drawn from (amongst other places) the OUP correspondence archive.

3 Derek Brewer in Como (ed.), *C.S. Lewis at the Breakfast Table*, p. 51. This is borne out by such versions of Tolkien's textual lectures as have been published.

4 See Carpenter, *Biography*, p. 135; Shippey (*Author*, p. 270) reckons Carpenter's figure of thirty-six lectures a mistake for thirty-five, being five sets of seven. H&S 2, p. 722 supports Carpenter's figure.

5 See H&S 2, p. 722.

6 He may not actually have received the notes until 1928: see H&S 1, p. 144, but also H&S 2, p. 154.

7 See, here, H&S 2, pp. 735–8.

8 See *OFS*, p. 47.

9 See Noad in *TLeg*, pp. 39–40, and *HME* 2.278–334, esp. pp. 304–10.

10 Garth, p. 280.

11 George Sayer, however, claims the nickname was a reflexion of Lewis's physique – since leaving the Army he had filled out, and was 'heavy but not tall'. There is of course no reason why both explanations should not be simultaneously true. See Sayer, *Jack*, p. 100. McGrath, rather implausibly, tries to make it a pun on the Army issue Lewis Light Machine Gun; this, however, was universally known not as a 'Light Lewis' but as a 'Lewis gun' without further qualifier. See McGrath, *C.S. Lewis: A Life*, p. 98.

12 Quoted in Carpenter, *The Inklings*, pp. 22–3.

13 C.S. Lewis, *Surprised by Joy: the Shape of My Early Life* (London, Collins, 2012), p. 22.

14   Letter to Miss Bodle, 25 March 1954; quoted in Wilson, *C.S. Lewis*, p. 114.

15   Quotations from Albert Lewis's diary are taken from McGrath, *C.S. Lewis: A Life*, pp. 85–6.

16   C.S. Lewis, *Surprised by Joy: the Shape of My Early Life* (London, Collins, 2012), p. 231.

17   Tolkien may have met the term first in a footnote to the introduction to Dasent's *Popular Tales from the Norse*, if he read it as a boy.

18   A distant connexion, it would seem, of his later namesake, the atheistical evolutionist.

19   See the essay by Robert Scoble reprinted in *Raven: The Turbulent World of Baron Corvo*, pp. 274–307.

20   Coghill and Lewis had been undergraduate contemporaries; it is not impossible, however, that Lewis was invited via the Magdalen Senior Common Room, of which a good proportion of the Coalbiters were members (Onions, McFarlane and from 1928 George Gordon).

21   Tolkien, *Letters*, p. 362 (to Dick Plotz, 12 September 1965).

22   See the Appendix, 'Tolkien the Catholic', below.

23   See McGrath, *C.S. Lewis: A Life*, pp. 131–46, esp. pp. 141–6.

24   One might think this a little *bien trouvé*, and more likely (perhaps) to be a pun on, or local pronunciation of, 'poop'; in fact, in its original context (Wilson, *C.S. Lewis*, p. 9), taken from the oral testimony of Christopher Tolkien, the 'popes' are implied to be particles of mud in puddles. As repeated by McGrath (*C.S. Lewis: A Life*, p. 4), they are reassigned to mean 'stool'; McGrath is like Lewis an Ulsterman, and so may be drawing on local knowledge, or additional sources he does not mention.

25   C.S. Lewis, *Surprised by Joy: the Shape of My Early Life* (London, Collins, 2012), p. 252.

26   Lewis, *Collected Letters*, vol. 2, p. 96 (to Arthur Greeves, 4 February 1933).

27   The stages of composition have been painstakingly catalogued and analysed by John D. Rateliff in his careful and illuminating two-volume edition of *The History of the Hobbit* manuscripts.

28   There were certainly elements in the story that approached the status of private joke: Bag End, for instance, was the name of an Elizabethan manor house and farm owned by Tolkien's aunt Jane Neave between 1922 and 1931. It is almost certain that Tolkien visited her there. See Morton, *Tolkien's Bag End*.

29   'AW & HM', p. 106; quoted in Shippey, *Road*, p. 46. The theme was expanded on by R.W. Chambers in his 1932 study, *On The Continuity of English Prose from Alfred to More*, first published as an introduction to the EETS edition of Harpsfield's *Life of More*. Chambers quotes this same paragraph from Tolkien's article on p. xcv, and is at pains to approve Tolkien's approach; although one may wonder what Tolkien made of a passage on p. xcvii, which claims 'that the cult of the "Rule" is not a fad of the modern grammarian. It is not a conspiracy between those strange yoke-fellows, the philological pedant and the papistical mystic, but a fact of English history with which every serious student must reckon.' A comparable argument for the continuity of English verse, although without such fierce philological evidence, had been made by Sir Israel Gollancz in a 1921 pamphlet, *The Middle Ages in the Lineage of English Poetry*.

30   Tom Shippey suggests that the very success of Tolkien's article in fact impeded Middle English dialectology for a generation; if the 'AB text' scribes were as fearsomely good, and philologically sensitive, as Tolkien plausibly argued they were, other scribes by comparison seemed bunglers, unworthy of close attention and certainly unreliable as evidence for the development of English dialects. In fact, Shippey (following others) has argued, scribes 'translating' texts into their own dialect provide good dialectal evidence even if theirs is not the same language as the original writer's, and that language itself philologically less 'pure' than the renowned 'AB' standard. See Shippey, 'Tolkien's Academic Reputation Now', in *Roots and Branches*, pp. 208–9.

31   This syllabus was broadly unchanged for the remainder of Tolkien's professional life; after his retirement, it was re-organized, with Courses II and II being folded into each other and renamed Course I, and the old Course I, confusingly enough, becoming Course II. This later Course II was the Final Honour School that I read as an undergraduate.

Chapter 6 – Delays and Frustrations

1   Or perhaps 1928: see Chapter 5.I above. In either case, Gordon had sat on the work for a good time.

2   Sisam presumably contrasted this laboriousness with his own brisk approach to Chaucerian

editions: he produced workable student texts of the *Clerk's Tale* and the *Nun's Priest's Tale* in 1925 and 1927 respectively.

3   These dates are from Alan Bliss's introduction to *Finn and Hengest*, pp. v–vi, modified by H&S 1, pp. 145 (Trinity Term 1928), 153 (Trinity 1930), 163 (Trinity 1932), 174 (Trinity 1934), 178 (Michaelmas 1935), 203 (Michaelmas 1937). He was scheduled to lecture on the Freswael again in Michaelmas 1939, but the lecture list for that term was cancelled (H&S 1, pp. 790–1).

4   Peter Lucas, in *Notes and Queries*, 30, no. 3 (June 1983), p. 243 (reviewing the posthumous edition of Tolkien's *Exodus*); see H&S 2, p. 682.

5   For these abortive proposals to the OUP, see H&S 1, pp. 165–6, and H&S 2, pp. 681–2; and, on emendation, Sisam's essay 'The Authority of Old English Poetical Manuscripts', first published in the *Review of English Studies*, 22 (1946), pp. 257ff, and reprinted in his *Studies in the History of Old English Literature*, pp. 29–44.

6   Several of Tolkien's pupils lodged there over the years; the convent and attached hostel were taken over by Linacre College in 1977.

7   *Postmaster* (the Merton College magazine) (January 1976), p. 11; quoted in H&S 2, p. 202. A corrected text of *Seinte Iuliene* was published by the EETS in 1961.

8   Quoted in H&S 1, p. 185.

9   See Anderson in *TMed*, p. 22; he notes that Gordon's review declared, 'there is probably no other edition of a Middle English text with so many new contributions and discoveries in it'.

10   The article appeared in *Medium Aevum* 1 (December 1932), pp. 183–96; and *Medium Aevum* 3 (June 1934), pp. 95–111.

11   Tolkien's son Christopher published editions of several of the *Canterbury Tales* in the 1950s and 1960s (the *Pardoner's Tale* in 1958, the *Nun's Priest's Tale* in 1959, the *Man of Law's Tale* in 1969); we may wonder whether, although his primary collaborator was Nevill Coghill, he found anything of use in his father's still unpublished edition.

12   On Chambers's death, the manuscript passed to a friend and colleague at UCL, who in turn on her retirement gave it to one of his students, who by then was teaching at Monash University; and thus the manuscript made its way to Australia. Parts of it appeared in the *Monash Review* for July 1975. A manuscript of a revised version was given by Tolkien to an Oxford colleague in 1953.

13   The excavation is described in Mortimer Wheeler's autobiography, *Still Digging*, pp. 95–8, and in Jacquetta Hawkes's *Mortimer Wheeler: Adventurer in Archaeology*, pp. 144–9.

14   See H&S 2, p. 163.

15   See Chapter 12.II below.

16   They were eventually published, with commentary by Christopher Tolkien, in 2009.

17   954 lines in all. It was finally published in May 2013.

18   See Christopher Tolkien's introduction and commentary to *The Fall of Arthur*, esp. the essay 'The Unwritten Poem and its Relation to *The Silmarillion*' (pp. 125–68).

19   Written in May 1924.

20   It is printed in *HME* 4.76–218.

21   Noad in *TLeg*, p. 42.

22   Noad in *TLeg*, p. 44.

23   See *HME* 4.235–61.

24   *Letters*, p. 421 (to Christopher Tolkien, 11 July 1972).

25   Carpenter, *Inklings*, p. 32.

26   Quoted in Carpenter, *Biography*, p. 148, and *Inklings*, p. 32 (whence the date).

27   Lewis, *Collected Letters*, vol. 2, p. 297 (24 November 1939); quoted in Kilby, *Tolkien and the Silmarillion*, p. 33.

28   Much of this is to a degree speculative whilst Tolkien's private papers remain unpublished and off limits to research; but I have tried to introduce nothing that is not justified by such material as has been made public.

29   Lewis, *Collected Letters*, vol. 1, p. 969 (to Arthur Greeves, 22 September 1931); also *They Stand Together: The Letters of C.S. Lewis to Arthur Greeves (1914–1963)*, Walter Hooper (ed.), London, Collins, 1979, p. 421. 'Macfarlane' is presumably K.B. (Kenneth Bruce) McFarlane, history tutor at Magdalen 1927–66, an authority on fifteenth-century England and a notably private man; we met him briefly above as one of the Coalbiters.

30   Warren Lewis's diary for 4 December 1933, quoted in Carpenter, *Inklings*, p. 55.

31   *Letters*, p. 416 (to Michael Tolkien, 24 January 1972).

32   Certainly between 1933 and 1938, probably towards the early end of the range; if Robert Havard's memory is accurate, by 1935 at the latest.

33   The original Inklings was founded by Edward Tangye Lean, an undergraduate at University College, at some point during his undergraduate career (1929–33). He probably met Lewis, who had also been an undergraduate at University College, through another college club. Lewis and Tolkien had been enlisted by Lean as 'senior members' of the original Inklings; neither was ever Lean's tutor. Lean's elder brother was the film director (Sir) David Lean.

34   'Professor J.R.R. Tolkien: A Personal Memoir', *Mythlore*, 17, no. 2 (Winter 1990), p. 61; quoted in H&S 2, p. 361.

35   See my review of Duriez and Porter's *The Inklings Handbook* in *The Tablet* (5 January 2002).

36   See Havard in Como (ed.), *C.S. Lewis at the Breakfast Table*, p. 216.

Chapter 7 – A Wilderness of Dragons: *Beowulf* and *The Hobbit*

1   It was originally published as a pamphlet, on 1 July 1937, by the OUP, then definitively reprinted in the *Proceedings of the British Academy* for 1936, which appeared on 30 December 1937; it has often been reprinted since.

2   In the Michaelmas Terms of 1933, 1934 and 1936; in 1935, its place was taken by lectures on the text of the poem (see H&S 1, *ad loc*, and Drout, Michael D.C. (ed.), *Beowulf and the Critics by J.R.R. Tolkien*, revised second edition (Tempe, AZ, ACMRS, 2011), passim. The 1933 series was revised, probably for the 1934 series; these represent, respectively, the 'A' (original) and 'B' (revised) texts printed by Drout.

3   Most of them (Jusserand, Strong, Shane Leslie) are now rightly forgotten; see Drout, Michael D.C. (ed.), *Beowulf and the Critics by J.R.R. Tolkien*, revised second edition (Tempe, AZ, ACMRS, 2011) for details.

4   Chambers, *Beowulf: An Introduction*, end of Chapter 3 (p. 128 in the 3rd edition of 1959). Frederick Klaeber had made a comparable point, if less eloquently, in a 1911-12 article, 'Die christlichen Elemente im *Beowulf*' that appeared over two issues of the journal *Anglia* (Vol. 35, pp. 111–36, 249–70, 453–82; Vol. 36, pp. 169–99).

5   Lewis, *Collected Letters*, vol. 1, p. 909 (to Arthur Greeves, 22 June 1930). We should note, however, that in the very next sentence Lewis admits, 'My pen has run away with me on this subject', so the detail of the passage may reflect Lewis's amplification of the idea rather than Tolkien's original expression of it; but we can be confident that Tolkien insisted on the importance of a *physical* connexion between man and place.

6   Ker, *The Dark Ages* (1955 edition), p. 58.

7   See Shippey's *Roots and Branches*, particularly the essay 'Tolkien's Academic Reputation Now' (pp. 203–12).

8   After the death of their lord fighting a Viking army, the retainers of Beorhtnoth (or Byrhtnoth) of Essex fall in a last stand around his body; one of them exclaims, 'Hige sceal þe heordra heorte þe cenra / Mod sceal þe mara þe ure mægen lytlað' (lines 312–13), roughly 'Mind shall be the harder, heart the bolder, spirit prouder as our strength dwindles.' Tolkien's own verse translation is included in 'The Homecoming of Beorhtnoth'; see *TL* (2001 edition), p. 141.

9   Carpenter, *Biography*, p. 104.

10   Anderson (*TMed*, p. 21) argues that the existence of a fragment of the text on the back of a manuscript copy of 'Bilbo's Song at Rivendell' means that *Beorhtnoth* 'seems to predate Gordon's edition by some years'; but I do not see that the evidence as cited (in *HME* 7.106–7) requires this conclusion, and it is wholly possible that the draft dates from the early 1940s.

11   Carpenter, *Biography*, p. 105. As an instance of this, we may note that, in the same year as his Maldon came out, Gordon also published a translation of a then-standard work, *Scandinavian Archaeology*, a long and technically complex text. See Anderson in *TMed*, p. 19. That September, Tolkien sent Gordon one of his new-minted author's copies of *The Hobbit*.

12   For the 'wager', its background and its consequences, see Rateliff's fine essay in *TLeg*, pp. 199–218.

13   We might suspect a looser parallel with Ronald Knox's *Let Dons Delight*, a virtuoso stylistic exercise

tracking themes of exile and return through snapshots of an Oxford common room at fifty-year intervals; but this cannot stand if we look at the strict chronology of publication – *Let Dons Delight* appeared in 1939. It is not of course impossible Tolkien had had personal communication from Knox or one of his friends of the theme of his book in advance of its appearance in print, but the influence if any could only have been slight.

14 *HME* 5.41. See Glyer and Long in Fisher (ed.), *Tolkien and the Study of his Sources*, pp. 197–8.
15 See Noad in *TLeg*, p. 46, and *HME* 5.18.
16 See Chambers's *Widsith*, a book that Tolkien certainly knew and read closely, pp. 117–21.
17 Chambers, *Widsith*, p. 124.
18 *HME* 5.98.
19 The superior of the convent, Revd Mother St Teresa Gale, was one of these early readers.
20 She worked on an (unfinished) B.Litt., on the vocabulary of the Corpus manuscript of the *Ancrene Wisse*, between 1933 and 1936, supervised by Tolkien; she also helped him with a transcription of the manuscript for his projected edition. In 1938, she was elected Fellow in English at the Society of Oxford Home-Students, later St Anne's College.
21 It is also possible that Griffiths merely told Dagnall about the book, and she subsequently borrowed it from Tolkien directly, perhaps when visiting him in connexion with a proposed revision of the old Clark Hall translation of *Beowulf*, which Unwin wanted him to do (but which he declined, eventually providing a brief preface). Elaine Griffiths began a revision, but abandoned it; one was eventually completed by C.L. Wrenn, and published in 1940.
22 See *Letters*, p. 20.
23 *HME* 6.7.
24 The 1937 *Quenta Silmarillion* is in *HME* 5.199–338.
25 See Noad in *TLeg*, esp. pp. 47–50.
26 The genealogies are described, but not given in full, in *HME* 5.403–4; *The Tale of Years* is unpublished: a later version is given in *HME* 11.342–56. *The Tale of Battles* is apparently wholly unknown, apart from the reference in the 1937 *Quenta* preamble (*HME* 5.202).
27 For the preamble, see *HME* 5.203.
28 According to Rayner Unwin, *TLeg*, p. 3.
29 Carpenter, *Biography*, p. 183.
30 Letter to Stanley Unwin, 16 December 1937; quoted in H&S 1, p. 208.
31 *Letters*, p. 346 (to Christopher Bretherton, 16 July 1964). See also the account in *HME* 3.364–7.

Chapter 8 – In the Background, War

1 Letter to Stanley Unwin, 31 July 1947, in *Letters*, p. 122.
2 Paul Edmund Thomas, in *TLeg*, p. 177.
3 This date was Tolkien's own for the writing of *Leaf by Niggle*; Hammond and Scull, however, date it to April 1942 (on the basis of a postcard seen on eBay – see H&S 2, p. 495), which would coincide with a hiatus in the composition of *The Lord of the Rings*.
4 Dawson had been a part-time lecturer at the University College of the South West of England (later Exeter University) between 1924 and 1933. He was a Catholic convert, three years older than Tolkien; like Tolkien, he had made a wartime marriage, although ill-health kept him from the army. Unlike Tolkien, he had a modest private income, which allowed him to study and write without needing a university job. *Progress & Religion* was first published in 1929, when Dawson was forty; Tolkien seems to have read it in a paperback reprint of 1938 (see *OFS*, p. 104). Dawson's only full-time academic job was a chair at Harvard awarded him when he was sixty-nine. There is no evidence he and Tolkien ever met (although Dawson knew Robert Havard, Tolkien's doctor, so it is possible) or that Tolkien read any of his other books. Dawson was involved with the *Dublin Review* between 1940 and 1956, and in 1945 Tolkien published a short story in it; but this seems to have been at the instance of its then editor, T.S. Gregory, rather than Dawson. Claims (made for example by Bradley J. Birzer, *Tolkien's Sanctifying Myth: Understanding Middle-earth* (Wilmington, DE, ISI Books, 2002), p. 136) that Dawson is a major influence on Tolkien's thought may be thus a touch exaggerated.
5 See *OFS*, esp. pp. 192, 203.

6   These are printed in *OFS*. The lecture was first called 'Fairy Stories'; it became *On Fairy-Stories* only in revision.

7   The original report of this episode (in *The Daily Telegraph* for 16 September 2009) claimed that the assessors had marked Tolkien as 'keen' to do the work; this is almost certainly a misunderstanding of a note on how to pronounce his name (as, 'Tolkien ("-keen")') rather than a comment on his disposition.

8   Cf. Robert Havard as quoted in Duriez and Porter, *The Inklings Handbook*, p. 118.

9   It is printed by Carpenter, *The Inklings*, pp. 123–6.

10   Lewis, *Collected Letters*, vol. 2, p. 273 (to W.H. Lewis, 10 September 1939).

11   See *Letters*, p. 55 (to Michael Tolkien, 9 June 1941).

12   Letter to Arthur Greeves of December 1940, quoted in Hooper, *C.S. Lewis: A Companion and Guide*, p. 32.

13   It is possible he was evacuated via Dunkirk in late May, or (along with tens of thousands of other line-of-service troops) via Cherbourg or St Nazaire in mid-June. Both were highly dangerous affairs; the liner *Lancastria*, for example, was sunk by bombers off St Nazaire on 17 June with the loss of considerably over 3,000 lives.

14   Sayer, *Jack*, pp. 161–2.

15   See H&S 1, p. 236.

16   Tolkien's preface is reprinted as the essay 'On Translating *Beowulf*' in *M&C*, pp. 49–71.

17   See *Letters*, pp. 48–54 (to Michael Tolkien, 6–8 March 1941).

18   See the lectures reproduced at www.michaeltolkien.com.

19   He transferred to the RAF at the end of 1941; rear-gunners were not usually commissioned officers, so he may not have carried over an Army commission, if indeed he ever received one.

20   *Letters*, p. 41 (to Stanley Unwin, 13 October 1938).

21   Carpenter, *Biography*, p. 151.

22   *Letters*, pp. 55–6 (to Michael Tolkien, 9 June 1941).

23   *Letters*, p. 65 (to Christopher Tolkien, 9 December 1943).

24   See *Letters*, p. 393.

25   *Letters*, p. 76 (to Christopher Tolkien, 30 April 1944).

26   Lewis, *Collected Letters*, vol. 2, p. 631 (to Charles A. Brady, 6 December 1944).

27   See *Letters*, p. 342.

28   See note 3 on previous page, discussing Hammond and Scull's proposed dating for the story.

29   Each of course was later revised: the *Grammatik* over eighteen years from the time Grimm was thirty-seven; the *Mythologie* twice, when he was fifty-nine and sixty-nine; the revised *Geschichte* appeared posthumously in 1868.

30   *TL*, p. 93. Glyer and Long compare this to his declaration, in a newspaper interview given a quarter of a century later, that 'Most of the time I'm fighting against the natural inertia of the lazy human being' (in Fisher (ed.), *Tolkien and the Study of his Sources*, p. 205).

31   See the Appendix for a more developed discussion of this question.

32   Quoted in Sisam's British Academy obituary (by Neil Ker), reprinted in *Interpreters*, pp. 331–48; cf. p. 345.

33   See the obituary of Napier (also by Ker) in *Interpreters*, pp. 91–116, esp. pp. 113–16.

34   Chambers, *Beowulf*, p .68.

35   *Letters*, p. 58.

36   See *Letters*, pp. 59–62. The relevant section is now pp. 104–14 of *Mere Christianity* (London, Collins, 2012); the passage Tolkien specially objected to is on p. 112. A draft of Tolkien's letter was found in the pages of his copy of *Christian Behaviour*.

37   See Chapter 8.II above.

38   Duriez and Porter, *The Inklings Handbook*, p. 13; Tolkien's lecture would have been on either *Beowulf* or Old English texts: see H&S 1, p. 262. The incident is dated to 11 November, which was a Thursday; Tolkien lectured on those two subjects back to back between 10 a.m. and midday.

39   *Letters*, p. 68 (to Christopher Tolkien, 30 March 1944).

40   *Letters*, p. 91 (to Christopher Tolkien, 12 August 1944).

41   Tolkien mistakenly thought it had appeared in the *Oxford Magazine*; Lewis often placed poems in the latter journal. See Lewis's *Poems* (London, HarperCollins, 1994), pp. 79, 156. Most accounts of the incident suppose Lewis's lampoon recent; but in fact it had appeared five years before, in May 1939.

42 See *Letters*, pp. 95–6 (to Christopher Tolkien, 6 October 1944).

43 H&S 1, p. 311.

44 *Letters*, p. 105 (to Christopher Tolkien, 18 December 1944).

45 See the note on *Letters*, p. 440.

46 Lewis, *Collected Letters*, vol. 3, pp. 5–6 (to Sr Penelope CSMV); also in W.H. Lewis (ed.), *Letters of C.S. Lewis* (London, Geoffrey Bles, 1966), p. 222 (this is the original heavily edited volume produced by Lewis's brother Warnie).

47 *M&C*, p. 238.

48 See *Letters*, pp. 112–14 (to Stanley Unwin, 18 March 1945).

49 See Flieger and Anderson's introduction to *OFS*.

50 *The Four Loves* (London, Collins, 2012), p. 74.

51 Eddison's books (*The Worm Ouroboros* of 1922, and the 'Zimiamvia Trilogy' (*Mistress of Mistresses* of 1935, *A Fish Dinner in Memison* of 1941, and the posthumously published *Mezentian Gate* of 1958), are sometimes reckoned comparable to *The Lord of the Rings*, in extent and genre at least; but there is no 'influence' from one to the other.

52 See *Letters*, pp. 49–50.

53 See *Letters*, p. 83.

Chapter 9 – Peace, Not Rest

1 In fact it was never finished by Tolkien; Mlle d'Ardenne finally published an edition of it in 1981, jointly with the philologist Eric Dobson (whose D.Phil. thesis Tolkien had examined). The concrete results of the 1945–6 Tolkien–d'Ardenne collaboration were two short articles: "'Iþþlen' in *Sawles Warde*', *English Studies*, 28, no. 6 (December 1947), pp. 168–70, and, in response to an article by the Swedish scholar Ragnar Furuskog (who had bothered Tolkien during the war with requests for photographs of manuscripts), 'MS Bodley 34: A Re-Collation of a Collation', *Studia Philologica*, 20, nos. 1–2 (1947–8), pp. 65–72. They had projected an edition of the whole manuscript Bodley 34; Simonne d'Ardenne published a transcript, rather than an edition, of the whole text in 1977.

2 He seems to have been meditating the story as early as mid-December 1944; see *Letters*, p. 105.

3 See Caldecott, *The Power of the Ring*, p. 29. The text also included a poem on St Brendan's last voyage; this was later published as a separate work, titled *Imram* (in *Time and Tide* for 3 December 1955; this version is reprinted in *HME* 9.296–9). Tolkien also carried over the 'King Sheave' verses from the legendary opening of *Beowulf* first included in *The Lost Road*.

4 *HME* 9.227.

5 *Letters*, p. 55 (to Michael Tolkien, 9 June 1941).

6 Caldecott, *The Power of the Ring*, p. 30.

7 Caldecott, *The Power of the Ring*, p. 30.

8 See Rateliff's fine article in *TLeg*, esp. pp. 212–13.

9 From the unprinted portion of a letter to Stanley Unwin of 21 July 1946 (extracts from which are in *Letters*, no. 105 (pp. 117–18), quoted in H&S 1, p. 299.

10 For 14 April 1946. The review was of E.K. Chambers's volume of the *Oxford History of English Literature* (*OHEL*), *English Literature at the Close of the Middle Ages*, under the bland (and presumably editorial) title 'Research v. Literature'.

11 Sayer, *Jack*, p. 199. Heathcote William Garrod was a classicist and veteran Fellow of Merton (he was twenty years older than Lewis, and was first elected Fellow when Victoria was Queen) who had also published on Keats; Darbishire had just retired as Principal of Somerville, and was an authority on Wordsworth and Milton; Cyril Hackett Wilkinson, Vice-Provost of Worcester, was another literary scholar of an older generation (he was born in 1888) with interests in the seventeenth century (Lovelace). Lewis had had dealings with him as an examiner for the School Certificate, and refers to him approvingly (see Lewis's *Collected Letters*, vol. 2, pp. 304, 323–4); either the regard was not mutual, or Wilkinson's personal views on Lewis did not colour his estimate of him as a scholar.

12 Carpenter, *The Inklings*, p. 205.

13 See Dundas-Grant's charming, if factually imprecise, memoir in Como (ed.), *C.S. Lewis at the Breakfast Table*, esp. pp. 230–1. He describes Lewis's attendance at 'our meetings' as briefly

interrupted by his wife's death; but this happened in 1960, by which time the Inklings as generally conceived had dissolved. Clearly Lewis maintained the habit of morning beer with cronies some years after its literary function had expired. This may suggest a proper caution about much of the anecdotal evidence from this circle.

14 His essay in Como (ed.), *C.S. Lewis at the Breakfast Table* (pp. 68–76) is a good illustration of this: glib, witty, chock-full of blandly dismissive (and plain wrong) aphorisms ('his novels, which I take it are simply bad – he developed in later years a telltale interest in science fiction, which is usually a reliable sign of imaginative bankruptcy'), it is nevertheless admiring, of Lewis's literary talent if of little else.

15 *Letters*, p. 119.

16 See Austin Farrer's sermon 'On Being an Anglican', preached in 1960 and published posthumously in 1973; it is reprinted in *The Truth Seeking Heart* (Norwich, SCM-Canterbury Press, 2006), pp. 143–7; the quoted passage is on p. 145.

17 See Wilson, *C.S. Lewis*, p. 217. One of Wilson's informants was Christopher Tolkien, who was presumably present, so the story may be allowed to be truthful.

Chapter 10 – Hyde and Jekyll

1 *Letters*, p. 124 (to Sir Stanley Unwin, 21 September 1947).

2 In a letter to Unwin in July, Tolkien had mentioned revision of Chapter 5 of *The Hobbit* as the easiest way to fix the incompatibilities (primarily, the way Gollum, in the earlier text, apparently planned to give the Ring to Bilbo as a prize in the riddle-game); see *Letters*, p. 122.

3 Its site at Caversham Park had been requisitioned as a BBC listening station in 1942, and was retained as such after the war.

4 *Letters*, p. 131 (to Hugh Brogan, 31 October 1948).

5 *Letters*, pp. 321–2 (to Jane Neave, 8/9 September 1962).

6 Tolkien acted as external examiner for the Irish National University in seven of the ten years from 1949 (1949–51, 1954, 1956, 1958–9).

7 The dedicatory elements in the foreword were removed in the book's second edition; they can be found in *HME* 12.19, 25–6.

8 See Carpenter, *Biography*, p. 130.

9 Rayner Unwin, *George Allen & Unwin: A Remembrancer* (Ludlow, privately printed for the author by Merlin Unwin Books, 1999), pp. 114–15, quoted in H&S 2, pp. 361–2.

10 Sayer, *Jack*, p. 151.

11 It was published in the British Academy's *Proceedings* for 1953, although, unusually, it does not seem to have been given as a lecture.

12 Sisam, *The Structure of Beowulf*, pp. 20–2.

13 Sisam, *The Structure of Beowulf*, p. 1, footnote 1.

14 See H&S 1, p. 287; the last efforts to get Tolkien to abridge his Chaucer notes had been made, via George Gordon, in 1936.

Chapter 11 – Finished, at Last

1 Shippey's books and Fisher (ed.), *Tolkien and the Study of his Sources* can be recommended here.

2 *Letters*, p. 145 (to Milton Waldman, c.1951).

3 Undated letter (from 1963 or later) to George Sayer, quoted in Sayer, *Jack*, p. 197.

4 C.S. Lewis, *Surprised by Joy: the Shape of My Early Life* (London, Collins, 2012), p. 22.

5 See Sayer, *Jack*, p. 198. Sayer there advances the theory that Lewis wrote *Surprised by Joy* as a therapeutic 'deck-clearing' exercise before turning to the Narnia books; the relative chronology of these texts, however, makes this impossible. The Narnia books were mostly written by early 1951; the autobiography was not finished until four years after that. The one definite exception is *The Magician's Nephew*, which was unfinished at least as late as 1953, and (as we have seen) is the most personal

of the stories. Perhaps the most we can say is that the writing of *Surprised by Joy* was contemporary with the Narnia books, and that they represent two parallel encounters with the wellsprings of Lewis's imagination.

6   See McGrath, *C.S. Lewis: A Life*, p. 124.
7   *Letters*, p. 36.
8   Quoted in H&S 2, p. 1084.
9   *Letters*, p. 353 (to Michael Tolkien, 9–10 January 1965). This was one of the lectures later collected in *Poetic Craft and Principle* (London, Cassell, 1967).
10 Garth, p. 216; *UT*, p. 20.
11 See the careful article by Wynne and Hostetter in *TLeg*, pp. 113–39, esp. pp. 120–30; and *HME* 11.311–15.
12 See Chapter 4.I above.
13 The *Dangweth* is in *HME* 12.395–402.
14 See Chapter 15.IV below.
15 For more detail, see Noad in *TLeg*, pp. 50ff.

Chapter 12 – Philology at Bay

1   For details, see Carpenter, *Inklings*, pp. 229–30.
2   See H&S 1, pp. 372–3 (entries for 26 January, 12 February, 9 March).
3   Hammond and Scull note two other Faculty Board meetings, in June and October 1952 (H&S 1, pp. 385, 391), at which Humphry House and Helen Gardner proposed changes to the 'Prelim', but secured only a minor and wholly insignificant substitution of one Old English text for another.
4   See Chadwick's obituary in *Interpreters*, esp. p. 213. He had made a similar point in a small book, *The Study of Anglo-Saxon*, which appeared in 1941.
5   Kingsley Amis, *Memoirs* (London, Hutchinson, 1991), p. 52.
6   Quoted in Z. Leader, *The Life of Kingsley Amis* (London, Jonathan Cape, 2006), p. 123.
7   It is no. 131 in *Letters* (pp. 143–61).
8   *Letters*, p. 163 (to Rayner Unwin, 22 June 1952).
9   In fact, Mass for Catholics in Headington was celebrated in a hall in Jack Straw's Lane until 1960, when the church of St Anthony of Padua was built in Headley Way; neither site was more than a mile from Tolkien's house.
10 Warnie Lewis, *Brothers and Friends*, p. 242; quoted in H&S 1, p. 399.
11 New series, 6 (October 1953), pp. 1–18.
12 See Shippey, *Roots and Branches*, pp. 206 and 323–39.
13 Tolkien's colleagues on the committee were Humphry House, David Cecil, F.P. Wilson and (as chairman) J.N. Bryson of Balliol, an authority on Pre-Raphaelites but also a competent Anglo-Saxonist.
14 Quoted in Green and Hooper, *C.S. Lewis: A Biography*, p. 339. For details of the supposed 1951 meeting and its origin here, see H&S 1, pp. 432, 795–6.
15 Shippey, 'Tolkien's Academic Reputation Now', in *Roots and Branches*, p. 211.
16 See Shippey's essay 'Fighting the Long Defeat: Philology in Tolkien's Life and Fiction' in *Roots and Branches*, pp. 139–56.
17 Lewis to the Master of Magdalene, 12 May 1954; quoted in Green and Hooper, *C.S. Lewis: A Biography*, p. 341.
18 For details of the Cambridge election, see Green and Hooper, *C.S. Lewis: A Biography*, pp. 340–5, and Wilson, *C.S. Lewis*, pp. 245–6.

Chapter 13 – 'My heart, to be shot at'

1   Printed in *HME* 12.422–37.
2   *HME* 12.178.

3   'English and Welsh', reprinted in *M&C*, p. 162.

4   *Letters*, p. 172.

5   Edmund Wilson, 'Oo, Those Awful Orcs', *The Nation* (14 April 1956), pp. 312–14.

6   Peter Milward, quoted in H&S 2, p. 1124.

7   See *Letters*, p. 238 (from 1956). There may be an unconscious reminiscence of one of W.P. Ker's observations on *Beowulf*: 'With a plot like *Beowulf* it might seem that there was danger of a lapse from the more serious kind of heroic composition into a more trivial kind' (*Epic and Romance*, chapter II.vi, p. 167).

8   Letter to John D. Rateliff (editor of the manuscripts of *The Hobbit*), quoted by Douglas Anderson in *TMed*, p. 24.

9   From Stewart's *A Memorial Service*, the third book in the sequence, published in 1976; quoted in Shippey, *Author*, p. 271.

10   *Letters*, p. 238.

11   *Collected Letters*, vol. 2, p. 520 (to Sister Penelope CSMV, 11 May 1942).

12   For more on this theme, see Shippey, *Road*, pp. 379–87.

13   The extant chapter is printed in *HME* 12.410–18.

14   See Chapter 17 below.

15   Neame was a prolific writer in the early 1950s; as well as writing a full-length study of Ezra Pound (*The Pisan Cantos: An Approach*) he had work published in, amongst other places, the Pound-inspired *Agenda* and Diana Mosley's magazine *The European*. He later published a rather good book on Lourdes (*The Happening at Lourdes*, 1967) and another on the Holy Maid of Kent (1971), as well as a novel (*Maud Noakes, Guerilla*, 1965). He was later engaged in the early stages of the revision that produced the *New Jerusalem Bible*.

16   The following section draws on various sources, in particular the careful account in McGrath, *C.S. Lewis: A Life*, pp. 320–41.

17   Alan Jacobs, *The Narnian* (San Francisco, HarperSanFrancisco, 2005), p. 275; quoted in McGrath, *C.S. Lewis: A Life*, p. 331.

18   Warnie Lewis's diary, quoted in Wilson, *C.S. Lewis*, p. 255.

19   See, as above, *Letters*, pp. 59–62; although that is avowedly a draft, and there is no absolute evidence that it was ever finished and sent. Nevertheless, it is very difficult to believe that Tolkien did not bring his objections to Lewis's notice in some form, even if not precisely in this one.

20   McGrath, *C.S. Lewis: A Life*, p. 333.

21   Undated conversation with Walter Hooper, quoted in Green and Hooper, *C.S. Lewis: A Biography*, p. 217.

22   Sayer, *Jack*, p. 229.

Chapter 14 – Silmarillion and Scholarship?

1   'The Sea-Bell', in *ATB*, p. 60.

2   It is included in *M&C*, and also in Salu and Farrell (eds), *J.R.R. Tolkien, Scholar and Storyteller*, pp. 16–32: the texts differ slightly, that in *M&C* incorporating changes that may have been made after it was delivered. Amongst the poems Tolkien alluded to in the lecture was Macaulay's *Horatius*.

3   This partial dispersal was the source of most of the books signed by Tolkien that still appear in sales catalogues.

4   *Letters*, p. 301 (to Rayner Unwin, 31 July 1960).

5   A number of later scholars (Geoffrey Shepherd, Eric Dobson and especially Bella Millett) have to some extent completed the task that Tolkien outlined, although in the course of their work his (and Chambers's) theories on the supposed continuity of English prose have largely been abandoned.

6   Lewis's article was reprinted in *Selected Literary Essays*, ed. Walter Hooper (Cambridge, Cambridge University Press, 1969), pp. 301–11. The *Festschrift* was reissued as a print-to-order book in 2011.

7   Green and Hooper, *C.S. Lewis: A Biography*, p. 398.

8   Quoted in Duriez and Porter, *The Inklings Handbook*, p. 119.

9   See Noad in *TLeg*, pp. 66–7.

10 A number of these have been published in *HME. Laws and Customs* is in *HME* 10.207–53; 'Converse' is in 10.361–2; *Reincarnation* is summarized in 10.363–6. *Athrabeth*, with additional authorial notes and commentary, is in 10.303–60. *Quendi and Eldar* is in 11.359–424. *Galadriel and Celeborn* is in *UT*, pp. 233–40.

11 See *The Line of Elros* in *UT*, p. 224. *The Notion Club Papers* probably alluded to the same idea, in noting, 'Elendil has a book which he has written' (*HME* 9.279).

12 See the texts and commentary in *HME* 10.375–90.

13 Rayner Unwin in *TLeg*, p. 4.

14 For the persistence of Ælfwine, see Flieger in *TLeg*, pp. 183–98.

15 *UT*, p. 183.

16 Selections from all these Númenórean fragments are included in *UT*.

17 From a newspaper interview (with the *Daily Telegraph* magazine) published in March 1968, quoted by Glyer and Long in Fisher (ed.), *Tolkien and the Study of his Sources*, p. 198.

Chapter 15 – Unfinished Tales

1   *ATB*, p. 8.

2   See Noad in *TLeg*, p. 61.

3   This collection does not exhaust Tolkien's short verse; occasional fugitive pieces appeared in various periodicals throughout his life; a third Tom Bombadil poem, for instance, 'Once upon a Time', was included in a children's anthology published in 1965. It has not been republished. See H&S 2, p. 689.

4   Quoted in Wilson, *C.S. Lewis*, p. 294.

5   John Tolkien, quoted in Green and Hooper, *C.S. Lewis*, p. 430.

6   *Letters*, p. 341 (26 November 1963).

7   *Letters*, p. 352 (to David Kolb SJ, 11 November 1964).

8   Quoted in H&S 1, p. 615.

9   *Letters*, p. 354 (to Michael Tolkien, 9–10 January 1965). Christopher Tolkien is not mentioned in the published part of this letter, but the inference seems a reasonable one. In September 1967, after divorcing his wife, he married Baillie Klass (who, as Baillie Knapheis, had briefly acted as his father's secretary).

10 We have only Wollheim's daughter's authority for this description (in an interview given to *LOCUS* magazine in June 2006), and may wonder whether the story has been improved by time and in the telling; but it would not be an implausible response by Tolkien to a request that, perhaps, was made abruptly and ill timed.

11 This is to simplify the matter very slightly: in fact the first 1,500 copies of any imported text could be protected by an interim copyright against the appearance of an American-printed text; but Houghton Mifflin soon exceeded this quota on the first two volumes, and outran it from the start on the third. For details of the whole Ace Books affair and the nature of American copyright law at the time, see the full discussion in H&S 2, pp. 1–7.

12 *LOTR*, Prologue (p. 15).

13 *HME* 10.374.

14 Ballantine was founded in 1952 and from the start had published simultaneous paperback editions of books that Houghton Mifflin issued in hardback; they also published original science fiction in paperback.

15 It appears in Wolfe's essay 'The Best Introduction to the Mountains', available online (www. thenightland.co.uk/MYWEB/wolfemountains.html) but not, I think, in book form, although it was printed in the magazine *Interzone* in December 2001. It was offered to the editor of the (uneven) 2001 anthology *Meditations on Middle Earth* (essays on Tolkien by writers of science fiction and fantasy), who turned it down.

16 Details of subsequent editions, and the textual vagaries they exhibit, can be found in *The Lord of the Rings: A Reader's Companion* by the indefatigable and compendious Hammond and Scull, esp. pp. xl–xlv, and, in outline, in Hammond's 'Note on the Text' prefixed (in successive forms) to editions published since 1994.

17 *Tolkien in Oxford*. It can be seen online (www.bbc.co.uk/archive/writers/12237/.shtml); some good

footage of Tolkien himself is intercut with preposterous interviews with undergraduates in a very irritating directorial style.

18   *Letters*, p. 413 (to Carole Batten-Phelps, autumn 1971).
19   Tolkien sold the manuscripts of *The Hobbit*, *Farmer Giles of Ham* and *The Lord of the Rings*, together with the unpublished *Mr Bliss*, to Wheaton in May 1957 for £1,500.
20   Kilby, *Tolkien and the Silmarillion*, p. 20.
21   Flieger in *TLeg*, p. 196. See also Flieger's edition of *SWM* (Extended edition, London, HarperCollins, 2005).
22   *SWM*, p. 32.
23   *Letters*, p. 413 (to Carole Batten-Phelps, autumn 1971).
24   Unpublished letter to Clyde Kilby, December 1967; quoted in H&S 2, p. 364.
25   See *TEnc*, pp. 417–18.
26   All, apart from *The Shibboleth* (*HME* 12.331–66), are in *UT* in whole or in part.
27   *Letters*, p. 404 (1 January 1970).
28   *Letters*, p. 411 (17 July 1971).
29   *OFS*, p. 53 and footnote 1.
30   *Letters*, p. 415.
31   *Letters*, p. 420 (to Christopher Tolkien, 11 July 1972).
32   See Garth, p. 283.
33   Carpenter, *Biography*, p. 255.
34   *Letters*, p. 429.
35   *Letters*, p. 431 (to Lord Halsbury, 4 August 1973).

Chapter 16 – Posthumous Publications

1   Letter to Michael Tolkien, 6 October 1940, in *Letters*, p. 46.
2   Rayner Unwin in *TLeg*, p. 6.
3   See Chapter 6.I above.

Chapter 17 – A Cinematic Afterlife

1   See Carpenter, *Biography*, p. 226, and H&S 2, pp. 16–20.
2   The curious may find it on YouTube. It is very bad.

Epilogue

1   *Leaf by Niggle*, in *TL* (2001 edition) p. 95.
2   John Buchan, 'The Rime of True Thomas', in *The Moon Endureth* (in *Four Tales*, pp. 631–2).

Appendix – Tolkien the Catholic

1   Stratford Caldecott, for instance: see p. 86 of *The Power of the Ring*.
2   *Letters*, p. 340.
3   Caldecott, *The Power of the Ring*, pp. 90–1.
4   Their various versions appeared in *Vinyar Tengwar* 43 (January 2002) pp. 4–38 and 44 (June 2002), pp. 5–20.
5   *Letters*, p. 66 (to Christopher Tolkien, 8 January 1944).
6   The full ICEL translation of the 1969 *Missale Romanum* was not adopted in England and Wales until 1973; from 1970, however, a composite translation was in use, combining the ICEL Ordinary

of the Mass with Propers translated by the English National Liturgical Commission, which are of significantly higher literary quality (and accuracy) than either of the later ICEL versions (1973, 2010) subsequently adopted; before this composite Missal (known as the 'Gordon Wheeler Missal' after the Commission's chairman) was adopted, however, various quasi-official English translations of very uneven quality were in use. ICEL, for those who may not know, is the International Commission on English in the Liturgy, the body responsible for providing English versions of Catholic liturgical texts to a number of different Bishops' Conferences.

7   *Letters*, p. 393 (to Michael Tolkien, 1967/8).

8   For those interested in liturgical history, it should be noted that the indult gave permission for the celebration of Mass with the modifications introduced in 1965 and 1967 (principally, the dropping of certain duplicated prayers and with scripture readings normatively in the vernacular) and not according to the Roman Missal of 1962, which has subsequently become the touchstone of Tridentinist praxis. That text owes its vogue to its adoption by the (eventually) schismatic Society of St Pius X of Archbishop Marcel Lefebvre; it was later officially sanctioned (without mention of the 1965 and 1967 modifications) by the 'universal indult' *Quattuor abhinc annos* of 1984, and subsequently by other magisterial texts culminating in the remarkable *Summorum pontificum* of 2007, which effectively rewrote history by declaring by papal fiat that the 1962 Missal was 'never abrogated', although the invariable practice of the Church, and the assumption of numerous documents issued in the immediate aftermath of the introduction of the reformed Missal, is that any subsequent edition of the Roman Missal automatically replaces its predecessor, which is thus *de facto* abrogated. Austin Farrer's papal fact factory is clearly still functioning. But this digression has probably strained the patience of my readers, and so should end.

9   Robert Murray SJ, 'A Tribute to Tolkien', *The Tablet* (15 September 1973); quoted in H&S 2, p. 467. See also *Letters*, p. 357 (to Zillah Sherring, 20 July 1965).

10   Anthony Curtis, 'Remembering Tolkien and Lewis', *British Book News* (June 1977), p. 429, quoted in H&S 2, p. 464. Curtis was an RAF cadet during the war, whom Tolkien taught for one of the short courses described in Chapter 8.III above.

11   See Drout, Michael D.C. (ed.), *Beowulf and the Critics by J.R.R. Tolkien*, revised second edition (Tempe, AZ, ACMRS, 2011), p. 125.

12   *Letters*, p. 112 (to Christopher Tolkien, 11 February 1945).

13   *Letters*, p. 172 (2 December 1953). Murray's grandfather was the great Sir James Murray, founder of the *OED*.

14   Notably, the destruction of the Ring, and the power of Sauron, on 25 March, a date on which thereafter 'the New Year will always now begin'; it is also, of course, the feast of the Annunciation, which marks the coming of Christ into the womb of Mary, and thus the beginning of defeat of death and sin, and was until the eighteenth century the start of the calendar year. We could also instance the Elvish invocations of Elbereth (Varda) as analogous to Marian devotion.

15   Foreword to Bradley J. Birzer, *Tolkien's Sanctifying Myth: Understanding Middle-earth* (Wilmington DE, ISI Books, 2002), p. xiii.

16   Quoted in H&S 2, p. 838.

17   *OFS*, Epilogue (p. 79); also in *M&C*, p. 156, and *TL*, p. 73.

18   See the essay *The Reincarnation of Elves*, written in 1959–60 and printed in part in *HME* 10.363–6.

19   *OFS*, pp. 38–9.

20   *OFS*, pp. 55, 75; also in *M&C*, pp. 134, 153, and *TL*, pp. 41, 69.

21   For details, see Hooper, *C.S. Lewis: A Companion and Guide*, pp. 181–2. Earliest of all is a poem, 'Joy', from 1924: it is printed in the 'Miscellany of Additional Poems' in the 1994 edition of Lewis's *Poems* (London, HarperCollins) (it does not appear in other editions).

22   See Caldecott, *The Power of the Ring*, p. 82.

23   Caldecott, *The Power of the Ring*, p. 83.

24   Shippey, *Road* (3rd edition), p. 244.

Further Reading and Bibliography

Further reading

To help the reader who is interested to navigate further the crowded waters of Tolkieniana, these are some of the books I have personally found most useful and informative. There is now a thriving academic field of Tolkien Studies, with the regular appurtenances of conferences, volumes of collected papers and learned journals. As with most fields of academic study, a good deal of this is sad stuff, and I confess I have not been so diligent in my special walk as duly to read all that has been printed on this man and his work. But I have read a good deal of it, and some of it has both enriched my understanding of Tolkien and, if it were possible, increased my enjoyment of his work.

The first place to start is of course with Tolkien's own writings, readily available (for the most part) in numerous cheap editions; collectors and the curious will find in Hammond and Anderson a comprehensive bibliography.

The best source for his life remains Humphrey Carpenter's authorized biography; Carpenter is the only writer ever to have had access to all of Tolkien's private papers, and this alone gives his book enduring value, although obviously it does not cover most of the posthumously published work in full. It is usefully supplemented by Carpenter's later book *The Inklings*, which is especially good on C.S. Lewis. More recently, John Garth's *Tolkien and the Great War* gives invaluable detail on Tolkien's early life and writing. Anyone seeking additional detail should consult the magisterial and very comprehensive *J.R.R. Tolkien: A Companion and Guide* by Christina Scull and Wayne Hammond. Relations between Tolkien and C.S. Lewis are well covered by a number of complementary biographies of the latter: Green and Hooper, A.N. Wilson and most recently Alister McGrath are all worth reading, as is the idiosyncratic but illuminating *Jack* by George Sayer. The old collection *C.S. Lewis at the Breakfast Table* (edited by James T. Como and reissued in 2005 as *Remembering C.S. Lewis*) is a modest gold-mine of personal accounts.

The best work on Tolkien's academic background and its fundamental influence on, and importance to, his writing is Tom Shippey's *The Road to Middle-Earth* (first published in 1982, revised for its second edition in 1992, and again for its third – much expanded – edition of 2005), supplemented by the same author's later collection, *Roots and Branches*. Also useful are *The Ring of Words: Tolkien and the Oxford English Dictionary* by three of the *OED*'s current editors, Peter Gilliver, Jeremy Marshall and Edmund Weiner, and *Tolkien the Medievalist* (edited by Jane Chance). The collection *Tolkien's Legendarium* is uneven, but contains some valuable work; Charles Noad's essay 'On the Construction of the Silmarillion' is fundamental.

For literary criticism of Tolkien, the best place to start is again with Tom Shippey, *J.R.R. Tolkien: Author of the Century*. For the theological undercurrents in Tolkien, see Stratford Caldecott's *Secret Fire*, now in its revised American edition, *The Power of the Ring*. Copies of Clyde Kilby's *Tolkien and the Silmarillion* can still be found second-hand; it is an interesting if slight book.

There are hundreds of other books – big and small, good and bad – on Tolkien and his writings; some of them are listed in the works named above. The journal *Tolkien Studies* has been published annually since 2004; it is a useful source of often more academically substantial Tolkien criticism.

It is perhaps worth saying something further about my use of sources. For those who want to know the mature Tolkien – discursive, forcible, unexpected, eloquent – his published *Letters* are invaluable. Copyright law means that my quotations from them here are exiguous and give little idea of the enjoyment to be had from reading them *in extenso*. From the earlier part of his life – before, in fact, the publication of *The Hobbit*, when he was forty-five – there is very little in the public domain. The published volume of *Letters* contains just over 350 items, but of these only a bare dozen date from before *The Hobbit* was published; and it contains nothing at all from the first dozen years of his tenure as Professor of Anglo-Saxon at Oxford, which from an academic point of view are perhaps the most interesting of his career. The editors had a great profusion of material to select from, and reckoned, probably rightly, that most readers were primarily interested in the genesis of Tolkien's published work rather than his campaign for syllabus reform, or his abortive negotiations with the OUP. But this does throw us back on inference and speculation more than we might wish. Extensive letters between Tolkien and his fiancée-then-wife exist, but are not accessible; nor is the diary he kept between 1919 and 1933 and again between 1964 and his death (see Carpenter, *Biography*, p. 277). So we must rely, to a great extent, on what can be inferred from the external facts of his life; our best insight into his inner life comes, in fact, from what we know – and it is fairly large – about his intellectual interests and academic focus.

Bibliography

This, as I have said, has no pretensions to being a complete bibliography of books and articles on Tolkien; I have merely collected references to the material I have used or cited in my text. This should make it easier for those who are interested in such things to follow up what I have said, or see whence I have drawn and from whom. I have omitted works by Tolkien himself.

Adams, D.Q. and Mallory, J.P. (eds), *The Encyclopedia of Indo-European Culture*. London, Routledge, 1997.

Amis, Kingsley, *Memoirs*. London, Hutchinson, 1991.

Atherton, Mark, *There and Back Again: J.R.R. Tolkien and the Origins of The Hobbit*. London, I.B. Tauris, 2012.

Barfield, Owen, *Poetic Diction: A Study in Meaning*. London, Faber & Gwyer, 1928; Middletown CT, Wesleyan University Press, 1973.

Birzer, Bradley J., *Tolkien's Sanctifying Myth: Understanding Middle-earth*. Wilmington, DE, ISI Books, 2002.

Buchan, John (Lord Tweedsmuir), *Four Tales*. Edinburgh, William Blackwood & Sons, 1936; frequently reprinted.

Caldecott, Stratford, *The Power of the Ring*. New York, Crossroad, 2012.

Campbell, Alistair, *Old English Grammar*. Oxford, OUP, 1959.

Carpenter, Humphrey, *J.R.R. Tolkien: A Biography*. London, George Allen & Unwin, 1977.

—— *The Inklings*. London, George Allen & Unwin, 1978.

Chambers, R.W., *Widsith: A Study in Old English Heroic Poetry*. London, Cambridge University Press, 1912; reprinted 2010.

—— *Beowulf: An Introduction.* London, Cambridge University Press, 1921; 2nd edition, 1932; 3rd edition, with Supplement by C.L. Wrenn, 1959.

—— 'Recent Research upon the *"Ancren Riwle"*', *Review of English Studies*, 1, no. 1 (January 1925), pp. 4–23; reprinted London, Sidgwick and Jackson [1925].

—— *On the Continuity of English Prose from Alfred to More and his School.* London, OUP for the EETS, 1932.

Chance, Jane (ed.), *Tolkien the Medievalist.* New York and London, Routledge, 2003.

Cockayne, Oswald, *Narratiunculae Anglice Conscriptae.* London, I.R. Smith, 1861.

Como, James T. (ed.), *C.S. Lewis at the Breakfast Table.* London, Wm Collins, 1980.

Dawson, Christopher, *Progress & Religion: An Historical Inquiry.* London, Sheed & Ward, 1929; Washington, DC, CUA Press, 2001.

Drout, Michael D.C. (ed.), *J.R.R. Tolkien Encyclopedia: Scholarship and Critical Assessment.* New York and London, Routledge, 2007.

Dunsany, Lord, *Time and the Gods.* London, Victor Gollancz, 2000.

Duriez, Colin, *J.R.R. Tolkien: The Making of a Legend.* Oxford, Lion Hudson, 2012.

—— and Porter, David, *The Inklings Handbook.* London, Azure, 2001.

Fisher, Jason (ed.), *Tolkien and the Study of his Sources.* Jefferson, NC, McFarland & Company, 2011.

Flieger, Verlyn, and Hostetter, Carl F., *Tolkien's Legendarium: Essays on The History of Middle-earth.* Westport, CT, Greenwood Press, 2000.

Fox-Davies, Arthur Charles, *Armorial Families: A Directory of Gentlemen of Coat-Armour* (7th edition). London, Hurst & Blackett, 1929.

Garth, John, *Tolkien and the Great War.* London, HarperCollins, 2003.

Gilliver, Peter, Marshall, Jeremy, and Weiner, Edmund, *The Ring of Words: Tolkien and the Oxford English Dictionary.* Oxford, OUP, 2006.

Green, Roger Lancelyn, and Hooper, Walter, *C.S. Lewis: A Biography* (rev. and expanded edition). London, HarperCollins, 2002.

Hammond, Wayne, and Anderson, Douglas A., *J.R.R. Tolkien: A Descriptive Bibliography.* New Castle, DE, Oak Knoll Press, 1993.

Hammond, Wayne G., and Scull, Christina, *J.R.R. Tolkien: Artist & Illustrator.* London, HarperCollins, 1995.

—— *The Lord of the Rings: A Reader's Companion.* London, HarperCollins, 2005.

—— *J.R.R. Tolkien: A Companion and Guide*, 2 vols. London, HarperCollins, 2006.

Hawkes, Jacquetta, *Mortimer Wheeler: Adventurer in Archaeology.* London, Weidenfeld & Nicolson, 1982; Abacus, 1984.

Hooper, Walter, *C.S. Lewis: A Companion and Guide.* London, HarperCollins, 1996.

Ker, W.P., *Epic and Romance: Essays on Medieval Literature.* New York, Dover, 1957 (reprints rev. edition of 1908; 1st edition 1896).

—— *The Dark Ages.* Edinburgh, William Blackwood & Sons, 1904; reprinted Edinburgh and London, Thomas Nelson, 1955.

Kilby, Clyde, *Tolkien and the Silmarillion.* Berkhamsted, Lion, 1977.

Lapidge, Michael (ed.), *Interpreters of Early Medieval Britain*. Oxford, OUP for The British Academy, 2002.

Lee, Stuart D., and Solopova, Elizabeth, *The Keys of Middle-Earth*. Basingstoke, Palgrave Macmillan, 2005.

Lewis, C.S., *Collected Letters*, ed. Walter Hooper, 3 vols. London, HarperCollins, 2000–6.

—— *Poems*. London, HarperCollins, 1994.

—— *Surprised by Joy: the Shape of My Early Life*. London, Collins, 2012.

Loades, Ann and MacSwain, Robert, *The Truth Seeking Heart*. Norwich, SCM Canterbury Press, 2006.

McGrath, Alister, *C.S. Lewis: A Life*. London, Hodder & Stoughton, 2013.

Morton, Andrew H., *Tolkien's Bag End*. Studley, Brewin Books, 2009.

—— and Hayes, John, *Tolkien's Gedling 1914*. Studley, Brewin Books, 2008.

Price, Anthony, *Tomorrow's Ghost*. London, Victor Gollancz, 1979; Grafton Books, 1990.

Priestman, Judith (ed.), *J.R.R. Tolkien, Life and Legend: An Exhibition to Commemorate the Centenary of the Birth of J.R.R. Tolkien*. Oxford, Bodleian Library, 1992.

Rateliff, John D., *The History of the Hobbit*, 2 vols. London, HarperCollins, 2007.

Salu, Mary, and Farrell, Robert T. (eds), *J.R.R. Tolkien, Scholar and Storyteller: Essays in Memoriam*. New York and London, Cornell University Press, 1979.

Sayer, George, *Jack: C.S. Lewis and His Times*. London, Macmillan, 1988.

Scoble, Robert, *Raven: The Turbulent World of Baron Corvo*. London, Strange Attractor Press, 2013.

Seymour-Smith, Martin, *Robert Graves: His Life and Work*. London, Collins, 1987.

Shippey, Tom, *J.R.R. Tolkien: Author of the Century*. London, HarperCollins, 2000.

—— *The Road to Middle-Earth* (3rd edition). London, HarperCollins, 2005.

—— *Roots and Branches: Selected Papers on Tolkien*. Zollikofen, Walking Tree Publishers, 2007.

Sisam, Kenneth, *Studies in the History of Old English Literature*. Oxford, OUP, 1953.

—— *The Structure of Beowulf*. Oxford, OUP, 1965.

Stanley, E.G. (ed.), *British Academy Papers on Anglo-Saxon England*. Oxford, OUP for The British Academy, 1990.

Steele, Robert, *The Story of Alexander*. London, David Nutt, 1894.

Thompson, Francis, *The Poems of Francis Thompson*. London, Hollis & Carter, 1946.

Tolkien, John and Priscilla, *The Tolkien Family Album*. London, HarperCollins, 1992.

Turville-Petre, Gabriel, *The Heroic Age of Scandinavia*. London, Hutchinson, 1951.

—— *Origins of Icelandic Literature*. Oxford, OUP, 1953.

Unwin, Rayner, *George Allen & Unwin: A Remembrancer*. Ludlow, Privately printed for the author by Merlin Unwin Books, 1999.

Walsh, Jill Paton, *Hengest's Tale*. London, Macmillan, 1966; Penguin Books, 1971.

Watkins, Calvert, *How to Kill a Dragon: Aspects of Indo-European Poetics*. Oxford, OUP, 1995.

West, M.L., *Indo-European Poetry and Myth.* Oxford, OUP, 2007.

Wheeler, R.E.M., *Still Digging.* London, Michael Joseph, 1955.

Wilson, A.N., *C.S. Lewis: A Biography.* London, Wm Collins, 1990.

Wilson, R.M., *The Lost Literature of Medieval England.* London, Methuen, 1952; rev. edition 1970.

Wolfe, Gene, 'The Best Introduction to the Mountains', *Interzone*, vol. 174 (December 2001), pp. 49–51; available online at www.thenightland.co.uk/MYWEB/wolfe-mountains.html.

Index

A

'AB language': *see* languages, historical: Middle English
Abercrombie, Lascelles, 117, 127
Ace Books, 269–71
Acland Nursing Home, 262
Alfred, King, 124
Amigo, Archbishop Peter, 34
Amis, Sir Kingsley, 121, 239
  Faber Popular Reciter, 121
Ampleforth, 240
Ancrene Riwle, 148, 153
Ancrene Wisse: *see Ancrene Riwle*
Anderson, Douglas A., 284
Anglo-Saxon (language): *see* languages, historical: Old English
Animalic: *see* languages, invented
Ardenne, Simonne d', 156–7, 207, 209, 211, 221, 261
Asquith, Herbert, 71
Auden, Wystan Hugh, 261

B

Bakshi, Ralph, 287
Ballantine Books, 270–71
Bank of Africa, 20
Barfield, Owen, 141, 165, 166, 185, 211, 222
  Poetic Diction, 185
Barnsley, Sir John, 76
Barnsley, T.K., 40, 52, 76, 102
Barrie, J.M., 43
  Peter Pan, 43
Barrowclough, Sidney, 40, 102
Battenberg, Prince Louis of, 76
Battle of Maldon, The, 170–71, 241–2
Baynes, Pauline, 228, 229, 230, 232
Beatles, The, 286

Beauval, 95
Belloc, Hilaire, 293
Bennett, J.A.W., 217, 226
Beowulf, 60, 67, 98, 119, 120, 149, 154, 168–70, 174, 190, 199–200, 206, 226, 228, 234, 243, 282, 283, 293
Bible de Jérusalem, 251
Birmingham, 12, 20, 23, 28–30, 35, 79, 88, 95, 99, 240
Birmingham Oratory: *see* Oratory, Birmingham
Bishop, Edmund, 68, 116, 128, 196
  Liturgica Historica, 196
Bjarkamál, 199
Blackwell, Basil, 129, 130, 200, 202, 204, 207
Blackwood, Algernon, 186
Bletchley Park, 185
Bloemfontein, 20–22
Bodleian Library, 32, 62, 94, 282, 283, 284, 285
Bodley Head, 176
Boer War,
  First, 21
  Second, 23, 46, 73
Boorman, John, 287
Bosnia-Herzegovina, 75
Bosworth, Joseph, 62, 63
Bourne, Francis Cardinal, 34, 160
Bournemouth, 70, 274–5, 277, 278
Bouzincourt, 90–91, 93
Bowie, David, 289
Bradley, Henry, 65, 104, 107–8, 127, 248
Bratt, Edith Mary: *see* Tolkien, Edith Mary
Bratt, Frances, 35
Braunholtz, Gustav, 142
Brett-Smith, H.F.B., 152, 158, 206
British Academy, 168, 226, 248–9, 251
Brittany, 70
Brooks-Smith family, 47–8

Brown, Peter, 196
   Augustine, 196
Bryson, John, 143
Buchan, John (Lord Tweedsmuir), 41, 44–5, 72
   The Moon Endureth, 45
   The Path of the King, 173
   The Watcher by the Threshold, 45–6

C

Caldecott, Stratford, 9, 212–13, 291–2, 297–8
Cambridge, 25, 56, 63, 80, 105, 128–9, 152, 244–5, 253, 256, 268
Campbell, Alistair, 244, 261
   Old English Grammar, 244
Campbell, Roy, 204–5
   'Flowering Rifle', 204
Cape Town, 21, 113
Capel, Mgr Thomas, 27–8
Carpenter, Bishop Harry, 254–5
Carpenter, Humphrey, 48–9, 133–4, 164, 179, 225, 238, 242, 255, 263
Catenians, 292
Catholic Herald, 293
Catholic University College, Kensington, 27–8
Catholicism, 23, 26, 53, 55, 164, 216–18, 219, 291–9 *passim*
Cecil, Lord David, 166–7, 215, 216, 231, 238
Chadwick, Hector, 128–9, 152, 239
   The Heroic Age, 129
Chamberlain, Joseph, 30, 73
Chamberlain, Neville, 185
Chambers, Raymond Wilson, 66, 124, 125–6, 127, 128, 153, 158, 168–9, 174–5, 176, 196, 198, 199, 226, 229, 248
   'Beowulf and the Heroic Age', 126
   Beowulf: An Introduction, 126, 196, 199
   'The Lost Literature of Medieval England', 126
   'Recent research upon the Ancren Riwle', 124
   Widsith, 125–6, 129, 154, 169, 196, 199
Cheltenham, 36, 54–5, 97, 100–101
Cherwell Edge, 175, 292
Chesterton, G.K., 115, 185, 293
   The Coloured Lands, 185
Child, Francis James, 115
Childe, Wilfred, 113, 118, 123, 205
   Dream English, 113
Classics: *see* Literae Humaniores
Coalbiters, 142–3
Coghill, Nevill, 143, 152, 166, 261
Coldstream Guards, 44, 102

Collins (publisher), 232–3, 239
Corvo, Baron: *see* Rolfe, Frederick
Cosman, Milein, 220, 222–3
Craigie, Sir William, 73, 74, 79, 104, 109, 127, 226, 248
   Dictionary of American English on Historical Principles, 127
   Dictionary of the Older Scots Tongue, 127
Crankshaw, Edward, 178–80
Crist, 77, 78
Crockett, S.R., 41
Cullis, Colin, 79, 102
Curzon, George Nathaniel, Marquess Curzon of Kedleston, 247

D

Dagnall, Susan, 175–6, 179
Dane Court, 253–4
Darbishire, Helen, 215
Darton, Longman and Todd, 251–2
Dasent, Sir George Webbe, 24, 184
   Popular Tales from the Norse, 24, 184
Davidman, Joy: *see* Lewis, Joy
Davin, D.M., 226
Davis, Norman, 124, 130, 156, 244, 261
Dawkins, R.M., 142–3
Dawson, Christopher, 184–5
   Progress and Religion, 184
Day Lewis, Cecil, 231
Dent, J.M., 176
'Deor', 98
Deutsches Wörterbuch, 59–60
Dickens, Charles, 238
Downside, 223
Doyle, Sir Arthur Conan, 41, 43
Dragon School, 216
Drout, Michael, 284
Dublin Review, 207
Duggan, Alfred, 247
Dundas-Grant, James, 218
Dunne, J.W., 213–14
   An Experiment with Time, 214
Dunsany, Edward Plunkett 18th Baron (Lord Dunsany), 41, 44, 99
Dyson, H.V.D. 'Hugo', 144, 152, 164–5, 166, 194, 209–10, 211, 220, 231

E

Eagle and Child (public house), 165, 204, 256
Earle, John, 63
Early English Text Society (E.E.T.S.), 207, 261

Eddison, E.R., 208
Edgbaston Waterworks, 30
Elder Edda, 177, 284
Elene, 154, 283
Eliot, T.S., 238
Emery, Fr Augustine, 88, 110, 277
English and Medieval Studies presented to J.R.R. Tolkien, 261
Essays Presented to Charles Williams, 222
Essays and Studies, 148, 241
Étaples, 89, 90
Everett, Dorothy, 152, 209
Exeter Book, 77
Exeter College: *see* Oxford
Exodus, 154–5

F

Fairford, 211
Farrer, Austin, 219
Farrer, Katherine, 219, 235, 236–7
Faulkner, Mr and Mrs, 35
Fiedler, Hermann, 128
Finnish (language): *see* languages, historical
First World War, 73–103 *passim*
  Passchendaele (Third Ypres), Battle of, 100, 102
  Somme, Battle of the, 12, 88, 90–95
Fisher, St John, 229
Fleet Air Arm, 208, 214
Flieger, Verlyn, 272, 284, 297
Fox, Rev. Adam, 166, 231
Foyles, 200, 202
Franz Ferdinand, Archduke, 75
Fraser, John, 142

G

Gardner, Helen, 156, 238, 244–5
Garrod, H.W., 215
Garth, John, 126, 139, 234
Gedling, Nottinghamshire, 47, 77
George Allen & Unwin, 176, 193, 201, 213, 221, 232–3, 247, 260, 268, 269, 271, 286
Gilson, Cary, 30, 39
Gilson, Robert Quilter, 39–40, 52, 74, 80–81, 84, 85, 90, 91, 92, 100, 102
Golden Dawn, Hermetic Order of the, 186–7
Goldsmith's Professorship of English Literature, 231
Gordon, Eric Valentine, 113, 116, 118, 121, 124, 153, 156, 168, 170–71, 207, 220, 226, 242, 248
  Introduction to Old Norse, 171

Gordon, George, 112–13, 114, 117, 121–7 *passim*, 134, 135, 140, 143, 153, 176, 198
Gordon, Ida, 171, 207, 220, 248
Gothic (language): *see* languages, historical; *see also* Wright, Joseph
Gough, General Sir Hubert, 90, 93, 95
Government Code and Cipher School (G.C.C.S.), 185–6
Graves, Robert, 83, 86, 231, 273
  Fairies and Fusiliers, 86
Great Haywood, 88, 89, 95, 97, 98
Greek (language): *see* languages, historical
Green, Roger Lancelyn, 229–30, 242, 276
Greeves, Arthur, 141, 164–5
Gresham, David, 252–4, 255, 262
Gresham, Douglas, 252–4, 255, 262
Gresham, Joy: *see* Lewis, Joy
Gresham, William, 252–3, 255, 262
Grettis Saga, 199
Griffiths, Elaine, 175
Grimm, Jacob, 59–60, 78, 125, 128, 138, 196
  Deutsche Grammatik, 59, 196
  Deutsche Mythologie, 59, 196
  Geschichte der deutschen Sprache, 196
  Kinder- und Hausmärchen (*Grimms' Fairy Tales*), 59, 185
Grimm, Wilhelm, 59, 78
Grove, Jennie, 55, 88, 100, 101, 102, 104, 111
Grundtvig, Nicolai, 199–200
Gryphon, 119

H

Haggard, Sir Henry Rider, 41, 97
  She, 97
Haig, Field Marshal Sir Douglas (Earl Haig), 95
Hali Meiðhad, 124, 148
Hardie, Colin, 216–17, 278
Hardie, Frank, 216
Harrogate, 99–100
Havard, Robert 'Humphrey', 166–7, 193, 211, 216, 225, 230, 241, 255, 262
Headington-on-the-Hill, 240–41, 253, 256, 260
Heenan, John Carmel Cardinal, 293
Hessian Trench, 94
Hitler, Adolf, 193, 194
Holywell Street, 233, 240
Home Guard, 189
Hooper, Walter, 245
Houédard, Dom Sylvester, 251
Houghton Mifflin, 247, 269
House, Humphrey, 238
Housman, A.E., 125

Hughes, Richard, 247
Hull, 100–102
Humber Garrison, 99

I

Indian Civil Service, 62
Inklings, The, 165–7, 194–5, 205–6, 211, 216–18, 220, 224, 231–2, 253
Irish (language): *see* languages, historical
Irish National University, 224

J

Jackson, Peter, 287–8
Jerusalem Bible, 251–2
Jessop, Mr and Mrs, 54–5
Jeyes Fluid, 20
Johnson, Samuel, 195
Jones, Fr Alexander, 251–2
Jones, Gwyn, 199, 211

K

Kalevala, 49, 60, 80, 84, 120, 206
Katherine Group, 148–9, 156–7
Kay, Guy Gavriel, 281
Keller, Hans, 220
Kenny, Sir Anthony, 251
Ker, William Paton, 65–6, 78, 125, 127, 128, 169, 170, 196, 248
    The Dark Ages, 65–6, 78
    Epic & Romance, 65, 66
Kilby, Clyde, 271–2
Kilns, The, 145, 240–41, 252–3, 254, 268
King Edward's Horse (King's Oversea Dominions Regiment), 52, 60–61
King Edward's School, Birmingham (K.E.S.), 25–7, 32–4, 37–40, 46–7, 52, 74, 89, 215
Kitchener, Field Marshal Horatio Herbert, Earl Kitchener of Khartoum, 76, 86, 90
Klaeber, Frederick, 169, 206
Knox, Dilwyn, 185
Knox, Mgr Ronald Arbuthnott, 160–61, 185, 217, 241
    The Holy Bible (translation), 241
    Let Dons Delight, 241
Korean War, 239

L

Lady Margaret Hall: *see* Oxford
Lancashire Fusiliers, 84, 88, 90, 93, 94, 100, 101
Lang, Andrew, 24, 41, 184, 276–7

Red Fairy Book, 24–5, 160
languages, historical
    Finnish, 50, 60, 80–81, 266
    French, 31, 114
    German, 31, 114
    Gothic, 31–2, 37–8, 50, 81, 114–15
    Greek, 30–31, 37, 50, 114, 266
    Irish, 224
    Latin, 30–31, 37, 114, 266
    Middle English, 114, 123, 148–9, 156–7, 209, 239, 248; 'AB language', 148–9
    Old English, 33, 37, 50, 114–15, 149, 157, 199–200, 209, 239, 242–3, 248, 266
    Old French, 114
    Old High German, 114
    Old Norse (Old Icelandic), 68, 114–15
    Polish, 203
    Spanish, 31
    Welsh, 30, 40, 50, 74, 100, 114, 248
languages, invented, general, 265
    Animalic, 24, 50
    Gautisk, 60
    Goldogrin, 100, 121
    Naffarin, 31, 37, 60
    Nevbosh, 24
    Noldorin, 121
    Qenya, 60, 81, 82–3, 86–7, 100, 121, 235
    Sindarin, 100
Larkin, Philip, 239
Leeds, 122–3, 291
Leeds University Verse 1914–24, 118
Leeds, University of, 110–18 *passim*, 130
Lennon, John, 286
Lewis, Albert, 141–2, 144–5, 230
Lewis, Clive Staples ('Jack'), 83, 139–42, 143–5, 147, 152, 156, 158, 164–7, 169, 172–4, 187–8, 193–4, 197–222 *passim*, 228–32, 238, 240–56 *passim*, 261–3, 266, 268, 273, 292, 295, 296–7
    The Allegory of Love, 172, 187
    The Dark Tower, 213–14
    English Literature in the Sixteenth Century (O.H.E.L.), 228–9, 244, 248
    The Four Loves, 208
    The Great Divorce, 195, 203, 213
    A Grief Observed, 262
    That Hideous Strength, 173, 188, 198
    Language and Human Nature, 206
    The Last Battle, 230
    Letters to Malcolm, 268
    The Lion, the Witch, and the Wardrobe, 230
    The Magician's Nephew, 230
    Mere Christianity, 202, 254
    'Narnia' books, 229–30

Out of the Silent Planet, 172–4, 176
Perelandra, 173, 195
The Pilgrim's Regress, 172, 176
The Problem of Pain, 193, 195
The Screwtape Letters, 195
Surprised by Joy, 230, 297
Till We Have Faces, 254
Lewis, Flora (née Hamilton), 140, 230, 254
Lewis, Joy (née Davidman, sometime Gresham), 245, 252–6, 262
   Smoke on the Mountain, 252
Lewis, Sinclair, 147
   Babbitt, 147
Lewis, Major Warren Hamilton ("Warnie"), 141, 145, 165, 166, 189, 203, 204, 211, 217, 220, 221, 222, 231, 240–41, 244–5, 253, 254, 255, 262
   The Splendid Century, 222
Lindsay, David, 172
   Voyage to Arcturus, 172
Literae Humaniores (Classics), 38, 50, 134
Lloyd George, David (Earl Lloyd-George), 71
Lloyds Bank, 20
Longfellow, Henry Wadsworth, 60, 206
   Hiawatha, 60, 206
Lönnrot, Elias, 60
Lovecraft, H.P., 99, 159
Lydney Park, 158–60
Lyme Regis, 30, 34, 165, 173

M

Mabinogion, The, 74
McCallum, R.B., 217
Macaulay, Thomas Babington (Lord Macaulay), 31, 38–9, 44, 120–21
   Lays of Ancient Rome, 38–9, 44
MacDonald, George, 41, 272
McFarlane, Bruce, 143, 165
McGrath, Alister, 144, 254
Machen, Arthur, 159, 186
   The Great God Pan, 159
Macmillan, Hugh, 184
Madlener, Josef, 48–9
Manning, Henry Edward Cardinal, 27
Manor Road, 219, 233
Masefield, John, 157
Mathew, Archbishop David, 217
Mathew, Fr Gervase, 217
Mawer, Allen, 127
Merton College: *see* Oxford
Merton Professorship of English Language and Literature, 63, 109, 112, 128, 206, 208–9, 260

Merton Professorship of English Literature, 109, 117, 152, 206, 215, 231, 245
Merton Street, 277
Microcosm, 118
Middle English: *see* languages, historical
Milford-on-Sea, 110, 277
Minden, Battle of, 93, 100
Miramar Hotel, 275, 278
Mitchison, Naomi, 247
Moore, Jane ('Janie'), 140–41, 145, 230, 244, 252–3, 254, 255
Moore, Maureen (Lady Dunbar of Hempriggs), 145, 254
Moorman, F.W., 110, 117
More, St Thomas, 198, 229
Morgan, Fr Francis (JRRT's guardian), 26–30, 33–8, 51, 55, 69, 74, 79, 87, 101, 165, 173, 292
Morris, William, 24, 41, 74, 92, 96–7, 99, 108, 113, 118, 143, 174, 177, 229
   The Earthly Paradise, 92, 97
   Icelandic Journals, 177
Müllenhoff, Karl, 169
Müller, Max, 56–7, 63, 67
Murray, Gilbert, 184
Murray, Fr Robert, 294

N

Naffarin: *see* languages, invented
Napier, Arthur, 63, 64–5, 66, 68, 73, 74, 79, 104, 109, 128, 198, 226
Nation, The, 247
National Union of Students, 239
Neame, Alan, 251
Neave, Edwin, 47
Neave, Jane (née Suffield; J.R.R.T.'s aunt), 20, 26, 47–9, 53, 77, 267
New College: *see* Oxford
New Line Cinema, 287
Newdigate Prize, 54, 92
Noad, Charles, 263, 267
Nobel Prize for Literature, 263
Noldorin: *see* languages, invented
Northern Venture, A, 118
Northmoor Road
   no. 20: 130, 189, 194, 214, 219
   no. 22: 130, 291

O

Old English: *see* languages, historical
Olrik, Axel, 199
Onions, C.T., 116, 128, 136, 143, 209

Orange Free State, 21–2

Oratory, Birmingham, 26, 28–30, 79, 87

Oratory School (Edgbaston, then Caversham, later Woodcote), 27, 165, 191, 192, 216, 222–3, 240

Oxford, 12–13, 50–54, 87, 98, 102–3, 104, 193, 275, 277–8 and *passim*
    English Dictionary, 65, 69, 73, 104–5, 109, 127, 209, 226
    English School, 61–9, 108–9, 133–7, 215, 222, 238–9, 245, 259
    Latin Dictionary, 226
    University: Blackfriars, 217; Corpus Christi, 73, 216; Exeter College, 38, 74, 79, 80, 81, 102, 113, 143, 190; Lady Margaret Hall, 226; Magdalen College, 112, 113, 139, 143, 152, 166, 198, 209, 216, 217, 231; Merton College, 68, 112, 143, 206, 209–10, 219, 220, 221–2, 260, 268, 277; New College, 218, 269, 277, 281; Oxford Society of Home-Students, 156; Pembroke College, 161, 206, 209, 217; St Anne's College, 156; St Hilda's College, 209, 238, 244; Trinity College, 160, 191–2; Wadham College, 128–9, 238
    University Press, 67, 68, 116, 186, 187, 198, 210, 225, 226, 239–40

Oxford Blackfriars: *see* Oxford

Oxford English Monographs, 155–6

Oxford High School for Girls, 192

Oxford History of English Literature (O.H.E.L.), 155, 215, 244

Oxford Magazine, 149, 162, 206

Oxfordshire and Buckinghamshire Light Infantry, 79

P

Paris, 69–70

Parma Eldalamberon, 284

Passchendaele (Third Ypres), Battle of: *see* First World War

Paul VI, Pope, 293

Payton, R.S., 40, 76, 102

Payton, W.H., 40, 102

Pearce, Joseph, 294

Pearl, 119, 171, 200

Pembroke College: *see* Oxford

Perrott's Folly, 30

philology
    definition, 57–60, 111–12
    at Oxford, 50, 53, 61–9, 108–9, 238–9, 242–4

Piers Plowman, 158

Pirie-Gordon, Harry, 143

Pitter, Ruth, 254

Pius XI, Pope, 229

Plummer, Charles, 128–9

Pope, Alexander, 206

Powell, J. Enoch, 25

Powicke, F.M., 209

Princip, Gavrilo, 75

Professorship of Medieval and Renaissance Literature (Cambridge), 244–5

Professorship of Poetry, 231

Q

Quain Professorship of English Language and Literature, 65, 125, 127

R

Raleigh, Sir Walter, 64–5, 79, 109, 112, 152

Ransome, Arthur, 176

Rateliff, John, 172, 213

Rawlinson, Richard, 62–3

Rawlinson and Bosworth Professorship of Anglo-Saxon, 62–3, 104, 109, 127–30, 133–4, 148, 206–7, 214, 218, 261

Reade, Fr Vincent, 29, 77, 89

Rednal, 26, 28, 30, 85

Regina Trench (*Staufen Riegel*/Stuff Trench), 94

Review of English Studies, 124

Reynolds, R.W., 33, 50, 86, 139

Rhys, Sir John, 74

Rice-Oxley, Leonard, 152

Ridley, M.R., 152

Rolfe, Frederick, 143

Roos, 100, 101

Royal Air Force, 191–3, 194, 208

Royal Artillery, 191

Royal Society of Literature, 251, 268

Royal Warwickshire Regiment, 76, 89

Royal Welch Fusiliers, 86

Russell, Bertrand (3rd Earl Russell), 176

Rutherford, Sir Ernest, 105

S

Sackville-West, Vita, 205

St Aloysius' (church), 161, 215

St Andrew's, University of, 47–8, 55, 184

St Anne's College: *see* Oxford

St Gregory and St Augustine (church), 161

St Hilda's College: *see* Oxford

St Philip's (Birmingham Oratory grammar school), 26, 28–9

Salu, Mary, 209
Sandfield Road, 240, 274
Sarehole, 23, 26
Sassoon, Siegfried, 86
Saul Zaentz Company, 287
Saxo Grammaticus, 199
Saxony, 19, 93–4
Sayer, George, 145, 189, 215, 225, 255–6, 284
Schleicher, August, 58
  Schleicher's Fable, 58–9, 199
Schwaben Redoubt, 93–4
Seafarer, The, 171
Second World War, 185–94 *passim*
  Battle of Britain, 191–2
  Battle of France, 189
  Fall of Singapore, 194
  sinking of *Prince of Wales* and *Repulse*, 194
Seven Years' War, 93–4
Shaw, George Bernard, 63, 64
Shippey, T.A. (Tom), 53, 68, 111–12, 114, 125,
  126, 153, 170, 196, 242–3, 299
Sidmouth, 191
Sime, Sidney, 44, 99
Sir Gawain and the Green Knight, 116, 119, 121,
  122, 124, 128, 149, 260
Sir Orfeo, 201
Sisam, Celia, 198
Sisam, Kenneth, 13, 68–9, 73, 74, 79, 105, 107–8,
  110, 113, 116, 121–2, 123, 124–5, 127–30, 134,
  153–5, 198, 209–10, 225–6, 239, 248
  Fourteenth Century Verse and Prose, 105,
    116, 128, 201
  The Structure of Beowulf, 226
  *Studies in the History of Old English
    Literature*, 226
Skeat, Walter, 122
Slim, Field Marshal William Viscount, 25
Smith, A.H., 118
Smith, David Nichol, 64, 152, 155, 156, 209, 215
Smith, Geoffrey Bache, 40, 52, 73, 74, 80–86
  passim, 89, 90–97 *passim*, 100, 102, 104
  'The Burial of Socrates', 92
  A Spring Harvest, 105
Smithers, G.V., 244–5
Snyder, William, 286
Society of the Holy Child Jesus, 175, 292
Society of Oxford Home-Students: *see* Oxford
Somme, Battle of the: *see* First World War
South Africa, 19, 20–23, 47, 89, 113, 192, 194,
  203, 204–5, 208, 224
Stapeldon Society, 53, 69, 74
Staufen Riegel: *see* Regina Trench
Steele, Robert, 108

Stenton, Sir Frank, 128–9, 196, 209, 248
  Anglo-Saxon England, 196, 209
Stevens, C.E., 217
Stewart, J.I.M., 248
  A Staircase in Surrey, 248
Steyn, Mark, 26
Stonyhurst College, 68–70, 191, 214, 221
Strong, Sir Archibald, 126
Stuff Trench: *see* Regina Trench
Sudetenland, 185
Suffield, Beatrice (J.R.R.T.'s aunt), 29, 34–5
Suffield, (Emily) Jane: *see* Neave, Jane
Suffield, John (J.R.R.T.'s maternal grandfather),
  20, 118, 277
Suffield, Mabel: *see* Tolkien, Mabel
Suffolk Regiment, 84, 100
Sunday Times, The, 214
Superb, HMS, 214
Sweet, Henry, 63–4, 107, 206
  Anglo-Saxon Primer, 33, 107
  Anglo-Saxon Reader, 64, 67, 68
Switzerland, 47–8, 197

T

'T.C.B.S.' ('Tea Club, Barrovian Society'),
  39–40, 52, 80–81, 84, 87, 88, 92, 96, 102, 103,
  104, 278
Ten Brink, Bernhard, 169
Tennyson, Alfred Lord, 206
Thiepval, 91, 92–3
Thompson, Francis, 41–4, 99
  'Daisy', 43–4
  'The Mistress of Vision', 44
  'Sister Songs', 41–2, 43
'Timbermill, Professor', 248
Time and Tide, 247
Times, The, 268
Times Literary Supplement (T.L.S.), 117–18, 247
Tolkien, Arthur (J.R.R.T.'s father), 20–22, 162,
  212–13
Tolkien, Christopher (J.R.R.T.'s third son),
  99, 130, 173, 175, 177, 183, 192–3, 194, 201–8
  passim, 214, 216, 222, 223, 240, 243, 262, 268,
  269, 277, 281, 284
  Heiðreks Saga, 223, 282
  History of Middle Earth, 183, 246, 282
Tolkien, Edith Mary (née Bratt; J.R.R.T.'s wife),
  35–6, 43, 54–6, 61, 70, 74, 75, 77, 81, 84, 87–9,
  90, 95, 98–101, 104, 110–18 *passim*, 122–3, 130,
  163–4, 190, 193–4, 214, 219, 221, 225, 226, 233,
  234, 259–60, 262, 273–8 *passim*
Tolkien Enterprises, 287

Tolkien Estate, 287

Tolkien, Hilary (J.R.R.T.'s brother), 22, 26, 34–5, 47, 76, 79, 87, 88, 89, 104, 118

Tolkien, John (J.R.R.T.'s grandfather), 20

Tolkien, Fr John Francis (J.R.R.T.'s eldest son), 100, 111, 130, 146, 190–91, 214, 240, 268, 273, 277, 278

Tolkien, John Ronald Reuel: academic reputation, 247–51; Air Raid Warden, 189, 194; ancestry, 19, 188; appointed CBE, 277; born, 22; breach with C.S. Lewis, 252–6; death of Edith, 277; elected Merton Professor, 208–9; elected Professor of Anglo-Saxon at Oxford, 127–30; engaged to be married, 54–6; falls in love, 35–7; health problems, 224–5; *Jerusalem Bible*, 251–2; last illness and death, 278; married, 87–8; moves to Bournemouth, 274–5; *OED*, 104–5; publishes *Lord of the Rings*, 246–7; retires, 259; returns to Oxford, 277; schooldays, 25, 30–34, 37–40; Second World War, 185–94; syllabus reform, 149–52, 238–9, 242–3, 245; teaches at Leeds University, 110–18; teaching at Oxford, 133–7; university, 50–54; war service, 88–95, 99–103;

    shorter poems: 'The Adventures of Tom Bombadil', 162, 201; 'As Two Fair Trees', 81; 'Bagme Bloma', 115, 273; 'Before Jerusalem Richard Makes an End of Speech', 53–4; 'The Bidding of the Minstrel', 80; 'The Cat and the Fiddle', 118–19; 'The City of the Gods', 118; 'A Closed Letter to … Charles Williams', 188, 202; 'Companions of the Rose', 100; 'Consolatrix Afflictorum', 93; 'Copernicus and Ptolemy', 84; 'Dark', 81; 'The Dragon's Visit', 162; 'A Dream of Coming Home', 118–19, 190; Éadig Béo Þu', 115, 273; 'Enigmata Saxonica Nuper Inventa Duo', 118–19; 'Errantry', 162; 'Ferrum et Sanguis: 1914', 81; 'The Flight of the Noldoli', 119; 'The Forest Walker', 92; 'G.B.S.', 96–7; 'Goblin Feet', 85; 'The Grimness of the Sea', 53; 'Habannan Beneath the Stars', 89; 'The Happy Mariners', 85, 118; 'Iumonna Gold Galdre Bewunden' ('The Hoard'), 119, 162, 267; 'King Sheave', 174–5; 'Knocking at the Door' ('The Mewlips'), 162; 'Kôr: In a City Lost and Dead', 81; 'Kortirion among the Trees', 85, 86; 'The Last Ship', 268; 'The Lay of Éarendel', 119; 'The Lonely Harebell', 97; 'The Lonely Isle',

89, 98, 118; 'Looney' ('The Sea-Bell'), 162, 268; 'The Man in the Moon Came Down Too Soon', 118–19; 'A Memory of July in England', 90; 'The Mermaid's Flute', 80; 'The Nameless Land', 119, 162; 'Narqelion', 86; 'The New Lemminkäinen', 49; 'Outside', 81, 86; 'Princess Ní', 86, 118; 'The Ruined Enchanter', 110; 'Sea-Song of an Elder Day', 42, 86; 'The Shores of Faery (Ielfalandes Strand)', 84, 86; 'A Song of Aryador', 85, 86; 'The Song of Eriol', 96–7; 'A Thatch of Poppies', 92; 'The Town of Dreams and the City of Present Sorrow', 87, 96; 'The Trumpets of Faerie', 85, 86; 'The Voyage of Earendel the Evening Star', 77, 109; 'The Wanderer's Allegiance', 98; 'Wood-sunshine', 43; 'You and Me and the Cottage of Lost Play', 86, 98–9

works:

    The Adventures of Tom Bombadil, 266, 285
    Ælfwine of England, 138
    Ainulindalë, 163, 178, 234–5, 237, 263
    Akallabêth (The Downfall of Númenor), 237, 263–4
    Aldarion and Erendis, 266
    Ambarkanta, 163, 174, 178
    Ancrene Wisse (edition), 207, 259, 260–61
    'Ancrene Wisse and Hali Meiðhad', 148
    Annals of Aman, 234, 237, 263
    Annals of Beleriand, 163, 177–8, 234
    Annals of Valinor, 163, 177–8, 234
    Athrabeth Finrod ah Andreth, 263–4
    The Battles of the Fords of Isen, 275
    Beowulf (translation), 154–5, 284
    Beowulf and the Critics, 168, 283–4
    'Beowulf: the Monsters and the Critics', 168–70, 283
    The Book of Ishness, 74, 119
    Book of Lost Tales, 96–9, 100, 105–6, 110, 113, 118–19, 138–9, 163, 174, 234, 260
    'Chaucer as Philologist', 157
    Cirion and Eorl, 275
    'Clarendon Chaucer' (*Selections from Chaucer's Poetry and Prose*), 116, 121–2, 123, 124–5, 128, 134, 153–8 *passim*, 198, 207, 226, 239–40
    Concerning Galadriel and Celeborn, 264
    The Converse of Manwë and Eru, 264
    Dangweth Pengoloð, 235, 263–5
    Description of the Island of Númenor, 266
    A Descriptive Grammar of the Qenya Language, 121
    'The Devil's Coach-Horses', 124

The Disaster of the Gladden Fields, 275
Of Dwarves and Men, 275
'English and Welsh', 246, 283
'Fairy Stories', 184, 201
The Fall of Arthur, 23, 161–2, 175, 187, 284
The Fall of Gondolin, 96, 97, 105, 109, 234, 237, 260, 276, 282
The Fall of Númenor, 192
Farmer Giles of Ham, 146, 178, 190, 201, 218, 220, 222–3, 228, 232
The Father Christmas Letters, 146
Finn and Hengest, 170, 199, 283
Grey Annals, 234, 237, 263
The Hobbit, 12–13, 20, 146–8, 159–60, 175–85 passim, 190, 193, 195, 200–201, 202, 213, 214, 215, 219, 221, 227–8, 232, 235, 237, 267, 269, 274, 286, 288
'The Homecoming of Beorhtnoth', 170, 199, 241–2
Language and Human Nature, 206
Laws and Customs of the Eldar, 263–4
'Lay of Aotrou and Itroun', 211
Lay of the Children of Húrin, 119, 137, 139, 178
Lay of the Fall of Gondolin, 119
Lay of Leithian, 137–8, 139, 144, 161, 178, 179, 234
Leaf by Niggle, 184, 196–7, 201–2, 207, 269, 295, 298
Letters, 284–5
Lhammas, 177–8
The Line of Elros, 266
The Lord of the Rings, 12–13, 15, 91, 102, 159–60, 166, 179–80, 183–7 passim, 190, 192–6, 200–201, 203–6, 207, 212–28 passim, 231, 232–7, 239, 240, 245, 246–51, 259–60, 262, 266–78 passim, 282, 283, 286–8, 289, 294
The Lost Road, 22, 172–9 passim, 199, 211–14
A Middle English Vocabulary, 105, 116, 123, 250
Mr Bliss, 146, 178
The Monsters and the Critics, 282–3
'Mythopoeia', 144, 295
Narn i Chin Húrin, 234, 237, 263, 282
Nauglafring, 105, 106
New Lay of Gudrún, 161, 199, 284
New Lay of the Völsungs, 161, 199, 284
The New Shadow, 251
'Noldorin Dictionary', 121
'Noldorin Grammar', 121
Notion Club Papers, 23, 212–14, 216, 287

The Old English Exodus, 283
On Fairy-Stories, 201–2, 208, 222, 276–7, 282, 284, 295, 296–7
'The Oxford English School', 149–50
Part of the Legend of Amroth and Nimrodel, 275
Pearl (translation), 200, 202, 204, 207, 284
Quendi and Eldar, 263–4
Quenta Noldorinwa, 162–3, 174, 177
Quenta Silmarillion, 177–8, 237, 260, 263–5
The Quest of Erebor, 246
The Reincarnation of Elves, 264
The Rings of Power, 237, 263
Rivers and Beacon-hills of Gondor ('Nomenclature'), 275
Roverandom, 146
'A Secret Vice', 283
Seinte Katerine (edition), 207, 211, 221
Sellic Spell, 199–200, 218
The Shibboleth of Fëanor, 235, 275–6
'Si Qente Feanor', 110
'Sigelwara Land', 157
The Silmarillion, 28, 139, 162–3, 177–80, 184, 212, 219, 227, 232–7, 240, 246, 259–82 passim, 289, 299
Sir Gawain and the Green Knight (edition), 116, 121–2, 124, 128, 171
Sir Gawain and the Green Knight (translation), 284
Sir Orfeo (translation), 201, 284
'A Sketch of the Mythology', 138–9, 162
Smith of Wootton Major, 272–3
'Some Contributions to Middle-English Lexicography', 124
Songs for the Philologists, 115, 285
Tal-Elmar, 246
The Tale of Battles, 178
The Tale of Tinúviel, 100–101, 105
The Tale of Years, 178, 263
'On Translating Beowulf', 190
Tree and Leaf, 269
The Trumpets of Faerie, 86, 88, 96, 172
Turambar and the Foalókë, 101, 105
'The Ulsterior Motive', 268
Unfinished Tales, 281–2
Valaquenta, 263
'Valedictory Lecture', 259
Visio Petri Aratoris de Doworst, 158, 206, 285
The Wanderings of Húrin, 263–4
Tolkien, Mabel (née Suffield; J.R.R.T.'s mother), 20–24, 26–7, 37

Tolkien, Michael (J.R.R.T.'s second son), 110, 113, 130, 146, 173, 191–2, 212, 216, 240, 276, 291
Tolkien, Michael John (J.R.R.T.'s grandson), 191
Tolkien, Priscilla (J.R.R.T.'s daughter), 24, 130, 146, 190, 192, 194, 201, 204, 219, 220, 225, 226, 233, 240, 277, 278
Tolkien Society, 271
Tolkien Society of America, 271
trench fever, 12, 95, 140
Trought, Vincent, 32, 39–40, 52–3, 102
Turville-Petre, Gabriel, 223, 243–4
    The Heroic Age of Scandinavia, 243
    Myth and Religion of the North, 244
    Origins of Icelandic Literature, 243–4

U

Underhill, Evelyn, 186
United Artists, 274, 286–7
University College London, 65, 125, 127, 169, 198, 244
Unwin, Rayner, 126, 207, 220, 221, 225, 233, 240, 261, 265, 274
Unwin, Sir Stanley, 175, 178–9, 190, 201, 207, 214, 219, 220, 231–3, 240

V

Venerable English College, Rome, 190–91
Verdun, 90
Vinaver, Eugène, 129–30
Vinyar Tengwar, 284
Vyne, The, 159–60

W

Wade-Gery, Henry, 84, 92, 97, 129
Wain, John, 218, 231
Waldman, Milton, 232–3, 239
Walsh, Jill Paton, 154
    Hengest's Tale, 154
Wanderer, The, 171
Wanley, Humphrey, 128
Ward, Arthur ('Sax Rohmer'), 186
Ward, Maisie, 185
Warner Brothers, 287
Warrilow, Alfred, 35

Warwick, 55, 70, 74, 75, 77, 84, 87, 97, 98, 102
Waugh, Evelyn, 247
Wells, Joseph, 128–9
Welsh (language): *see* languages, historical
Welsh Review, 199, 211
Weston-super-Mare, 190
Wheaton College, Illinois, 271
Wheeler, Sir R.E. Mortimer, 158–60, 248
Whitelock, Dorothy, 209, 248
Widsith, 125, 138
Wilkinson, C.H., 215
Williams, Charles, 166, 172, 186–8, 195, 202–3, 204, 208, 211, 216, 220, 222, 231, 252, 255
    All Hallows' Eve, 195
    The Place of the Lion, 172
    The Region of the Summer Stars, 195
Wilson, A.N., 143
Wilson, Edmund, 247
Wilson, F.P., 156, 215, 238, 244–5, 248
Wiseman, Christopher, 31, 38–9, 52, 56, 74, 80–81, 85, 86, 95, 100, 102, 104, 277–8
Wiseman, Frederick Luke, 31
Wolfe, Gene, 270
Wollheim, Donald, 269
Wrenn, C.L., 152, 158, 161, 166–7, 209, 214, 216, 218, 247–8, 261
Wright, Joseph, 31, 53, 56, 60–61, 67, 76, 109, 113, 125, 127, 129, 142, 152, 248
    English Dialect Dictionary, 67
    A Primer of the Gothic Language, 31–2, 53
Wyatt, A.J., 126
Wyld, Henry Cecil Kennedy, 109, 128–9, 136, 206–7
    'Experiments in translating *Beowulf*', 206
    Gothique, 206
Wyllie, James, 226

Y

Year's Work in English Studies (YWES), 117–18, 123
Yoda, 241
Yorkshire Poetry, 118

Z

Zupitza, Julius, 63